SwiftUI Cookbook

Discover solutions and best practices to tackle the most common problems while building SwiftUI apps

Giordano Scalzo

Edgar Nzokwe

BIRMINGHAM—MUMBAI

SwiftUI Cookbook

Commissioning Editor: Ashwin Nair
Acquisition Editor: Rohit Rajkumar
Senior Editor: Sofi Rogers
Content Development Editor: Mrudgandha Kulkarni
Technical Editor: Deepesh Patel
Copy Editor: Safis Editing
Project Coordinator: Kinjal Bari
Proofreader: Safis Editing
Indexer: Pratik Shirodkar
Production Designer: Roshan Kawale

Production reference: 1161020

Published by Packt Publishing Ltd.
Livery Place
35 Livery Street
Birmingham
B3 2PB, UK.

ISBN 978-1-83898-186-0

www.packt.com

It wasn't easy to write a book during a global pandemic, but in the end, it gave me a reason to concentrate and have solace from the bad news.

I want to thank my better half Valentina, who lovingly supports me in everything I do: without you, none of this would have been possible.

Thanks to my bright future, Mattia and Luca, for giving me lots of smiles and hugs when I needed them.

Finally, thanks to Mrudgandha Kulkarni and the rest of the Packt team for the help, suggestions, and encouragement.

- Giordano Scalzo

To my wife Mabelle and children Neil, Zoe.

- Edgar Nzokwe

`Packt.com`

Subscribe to our online digital library for full access to over 7,000 books and videos, as well as industry leading tools to help you plan your personal development and advance your career. For more information, please visit our website.

Why subscribe?

- Spend less time learning and more time coding with practical eBooks and Videos from over 4,000 industry professionals

- Improve your learning with Skill Plans built especially for you

- Get a free eBook or video every month

- Fully searchable for easy access to vital information

- Copy and paste, print, and bookmark content

Did you know that Packt offers eBook versions of every book published, with PDF and ePub files available? You can upgrade to the eBook version at `packt.com` and as a print book customer, you are entitled to a discount on the eBook copy. Get in touch with us at `customercare@packtpub.com` for more details.

At `www.packt.com`, you can also read a collection of free technical articles, sign up for a range of free newsletters, and receive exclusive discounts and offers on Packt books and eBooks.

Contributors

About the authors

Giordano Scalzo is a developer with 20 years of programming experience, since the days of the ZX Spectrum. He has worked in Swift, Objective-C, C/C++, Java, .Net, Ruby, Python, and in a ton of other languages that he has forgotten the names of. After years of backend development, over the past 5 years Giordano has developed extensively for iOS, releasing more than 20 apps—apps that he wrote for clients, enterprise applications, or on his own. Currently, he is a contractor in London, where he delivers code for iOS through his company, Effective Code Ltd, with the objective being quality and reliability.

Edgar Nzokwe is a software engineer at Booz Allen and an adjunct computer science instructor at Howard Community College in Maryland. He has more than 5 years of experience in the field of software engineering and has spent most of that time building web and mobile applications. His areas of expertise include SwiftUI, UIKit, and Kotlin. Edgar is dedicated to advancing the knowledge base of SwiftUI because he believes it will significantly improve UI and cross-platform app development time.

About the reviewer

Danny Bolella has over a decade of software engineering experience working in the energy, financial, and medical device industries. His work spans full-stack, report tooling, automation/scripting, and mobile app development (both iOS and Android, with several apps having been published). His true passion, however, has been working with Swift for over half his career. In his own time, Danny regularly publishes technical articles, works on open source projects, and produces his own third-party libraries. To Danny, they offer opportunities to share his passions with other developers in the hope that they, too, will be inspired to build great things. Danny also enjoys reading, listening to music, and volunteering with College Ministry.

Danny thanks his wife and son, who are his absolute world. They are the loves of his life and a daily inspiration to always do more and do great things. He also thanks his parents, who have always believed in him and allowed him to pursue his passions. Special thanks to all the mentors, teachers, colleagues, and friends who have supported him. Lastly, thanks to God for continuing to guide his steps in love.

Packt is searching for authors like you

If you're interested in becoming an author for Packt, please visit `authors.packtpub.com` and apply today. We have worked with thousands of developers and tech professionals, just like you, to help them share their insight with the global tech community. You can make a general application, apply for a specific hot topic that we are recruiting an author for, or submit your own idea.

Table of Contents

Preface

1

Using the Basic SwiftUI Views and Controls

Technical requirements	18
How to lay out components	18
Getting ready	18
How to do it...	19
How it works...	22
Dealing with text	23
Getting ready	23
How to do it...	23
How it works...	26
There's more...	27
See also	27
Using images	27
Getting ready	27
How to do it...	27
How it works...	31
See also	34
Adding buttons and navigating with them	34
Getting ready	34
How to do it...	35
How it works...	38
See also	39

Beyond buttons – how to use advanced pickers	39
Getting ready	39
How to do it...	40
How it works...	42
How to apply groups of styles using ViewModifiers	44
Getting ready	44
How to do it...	44
How it works...	46
See also	46
Separating presentation from content with ViewBuilder	46
Getting ready	46
How to do it...	46
How it works...	48
See also	48
Simple graphics using SF Symbols	49
Getting ready	49
How to do it...	49
How it works...	50
See also	51

The best of both worlds – integrating UIKit into SwiftUI 51

Getting ready 51
How to do it... 51
How it works... 53
See also 54

Adding SwiftUI to an existing app 54

Getting ready 54
How to do it... 55
How it works... 58

More views and controls (iOS 14+) 59

Getting ready 59
How to do it... 59
How it works... 63

2

Going Beyond the Single Component with Lists and Scroll Views

Technical requirements 68
Using scroll views 68

Getting ready 69
How to do it... 69
How it works... 71
See also 72

Creating a list of static items 72

Getting ready 72
How to do it... 72
How it works... 74

Using custom rows in a list 75

Getting ready 75
How to do it... 75
How it works... 79

Adding rows to a list 80

Getting ready 80
How to do it... 80
How it works... 82

Deleting rows from a list 83

Getting ready 83
How to do it... 83
How it works... 85

There's more... 86

Editing a list 86

Getting ready 86
How to do it... 86
How it works... 87
There's more... 88

Moving rows in a list 88

Getting ready 88
How to do it... 88
How it works... 91

Adding sections to a list 92

Getting ready 92
How to do it... 92
How it works... 94

Using LazyHStack and LazyVStack (iOS 14+) 95

Getting ready 95
How to do it... 96
How it works... 98
There's more... 99

Using LazyHGrid and
LazyVGrid (iOS 14+)   99
Getting ready   100
How to do it...   100
How it works...   103

Using ScrollViewReader
(iOS 14+)   103
Getting ready   104
How to do it...   104
How it works...   107

Using expanding lists (iOS 14+)   108
Getting ready   108
How to do it...   109
How it works...   111
There's more...   112
See also   113

Using disclosure groups to hide
and show content (iOS 14+)   113
Getting ready   113
How to do it...   113
How it works...   116

3
Viewing while Building with SwiftUI Preview

Technical requirements   118
Previewing the layout in dark
mode   118
Getting ready   118
How to do it...   118
How it works...   120

Previewing the layout at
different dynamic type sizes   121
Getting ready   121
How to do it...   121
How it works...   127
See also   127

Previewing the layout in
a navigation view   127
Getting ready   128
How to do it...   128
How it works...   131

Previewing the layout on
different devices   131
Getting ready   131
How to do it...   131
How it works...   134

Using previews in UIKit   134
Getting ready   135
How to do it...   135
How it works...   140

Using mock data for previews   140
Getting ready   140
How to do it...   141
How it works...   144

4

Creating New Components and Grouping Views in Container Views

Technical requirements	**148**	There's more	156
Showing and hiding sections in forms	**148**	**Navigating between multiple views with TabView**	**157**
Getting ready	148	Getting ready	158
How to do it...	148	How to do it	158
How it works...	151	How it works	163
There's more	152	There's more	164
Disabling/enabling items in a form	**152**	**Using gestures with TabView**	**164**
Getting ready	153	Getting ready	165
How to do it...	153	How to do it	165
How it works	156	How it works	167

5

Presenting Extra Information to the User

Technical requirements	**170**	How to do it	178
Presenting alerts	**170**	How it works	181
Getting ready	170	**Presenting ActionSheet views**	**182**
How to do it	170	Getting ready	182
How it works	173	How to do it	182
See also	173	How it works	185
Adding actions to alert buttons	**173**	**Showing a sheet modally**	**186**
Getting ready	173	Getting ready	186
How to do it	174	How to do it	186
How it works	176	How it works	189
See also	177	See also	190
Presenting multiple alerts	**177**	**Creating a context menu**	**190**
Getting ready	177	Getting ready	191
		How to do it	191

How it works 192
See also 192

Implementing a popover 193

Getting ready 193
How to do it 193
How it works 195
See also 196

6

Drawing with SwiftUI

Technical requirements 198
Using SwiftUI's built-in shapes 198
Getting ready 198
How to do it... 198
How it works 200

Creating a dashed border in SwiftUI 201
Getting ready 202
How to do it... 202
How it works 203

Drawing a custom shape 204
Getting ready 204
How to do it... 205
How it works 206

Drawing a curved custom shape 207
Getting ready 207
How to do it... 207
How it works 210

Using UIBezierPath with SwiftUI 210
Getting ready 211
How to do it... 211
How it works 213
There's more 213

Implementing a progress ring 213
Getting ready 213
How to do it... 214

How it works 217

Implementing a Tic-Tac-Toe game in SwiftUI 218
Getting ready 218
How to do it... 218
How it works 223
There's more 224

Rendering a gradient view in SwiftUI 224
Getting ready 224
How to do it... 224
How it works 228
There's more 229

Rendering a border with a gradient 229
Getting ready 229
How to do it... 229
How it works 233

Filling a border with an image 234
Getting ready 234
How to do it... 234
How it works 235

Building a bar chart 236
Getting ready 236
How to do it... 236
How it works 240
There's more 241

Building a pie chart 241
Getting ready 241

How to do it... 241
How it works 250

7

Animating with SwiftUI

Technical requirements 254
Creating basic animations 254
Getting ready 255
How to do it... 255
How it works... 259
There's more... 260
See also 260

Transforming shapes 260
Getting ready 261
How to do it... 261
How it works... 263

Creating a banner with a spring animation 264
Getting ready 265
How to do it... 265
How it works... 267

Applying a delay to a view modifier animation to create a sequence of animations 268
Getting ready 268
How to do it... 268
How it works... 270

Applying a delay to a withAnimation function to create a sequence of animations 271
Getting ready 271
How to do it... 271
How it works... 274

Applying multiple animations to a view 275
Getting ready 275
How to do it... 275
How it works... 277

Creating custom view transitions 277
Getting ready 278
How to do it... 278
How it works... 282
There's more... 282

Creating a hero view transition with .matchedGeometryEffect 282
Getting ready 283
How to do it... 284
How it works... 290

Creating an animated pressable button 291
Getting ready 292
How to do it... 292
How it works... 295

Lottie animations in SwiftUI 295
Getting ready 296
How to do it... 298
How it works... 301

Implementing a stretchable header in SwiftUI 302
Getting ready 302
How to do it... 302
How it works... 306

Creating floating hearts in
SwiftUI   306
Getting ready   306
How to do it...   309
How it works...   315
See also   317

How to implement a swipeable
stack of cards in SwiftUI   317
Getting ready   318
How to do it...   318
How it works...   324

8

Driving SwiftUI with Data

Technical requirements   327
Using @State to drive
Views behavior   327
Getting ready   327
How to do it...   327
How it works...   330
See also   331

Using @Binding to pass
a state variable to child Views   331
Getting ready   331
How to do it...   331
How it works...   337

Implementing a CoreLocation
wrapper as @ObservedObject   337
Getting ready   338
How to do it...   339
How it works...   343

Sharing state objects with
multiple views using
@EnvironmentObject   344
Getting ready   344
How to do it...   345
How it works...   352
See also   352

9

Driving SwiftUI with Combine

Technical requirements   355
Introducing Combine in a
SwiftUI project   355
Getting ready   355
How to do it...   356
How it works...   364
See also   367

Managing the memory in
Combine to build a timer app   368
Getting ready   368
How to do it...   368
How it works...   372

Validating a form using
Combine   374

Getting ready 374

How to do it... 375

How it works... 384

There's more... 384

Fetching remote data using Combine and visualizing it in SwiftUI 385

Getting ready 385

How to do it... 386

How it works... 394

There's more... 396

Debugging an app based on Combine 397

Getting ready 397

How to do it... 397

How it works... 402

There's more... 402

Unit testing an app based on Combine 403

Getting ready 403

How to do it... 404

How it works... 411

10

Handling Authentication and Firebase with SwiftUI

Technical requirements 415

Implementing SwiftUI Sign in with Apple 415

Getting ready 416

How to do it... 416

How it works... 421

Implementing UIKit Sign in with Apple to be used in SwiftUI 423

Getting ready 423

How to do it... 424

How it works... 430

Integrating Firebase into a SwiftUI project 431

Getting ready 431

How to do it... 432

How it works... 442

There's more... 443

Using Firebase to sign in using Google 443

Getting ready 443

How to do it... 443

How it works... 455

Implementing a distributed Notes app with Firebase and SwiftUI 455

Getting ready 456

How to do it... 456

How it works... 468

There's more... 470

11

Handling Core Data in SwiftUI

Technical requirements 472

Integrating Core Data with

SwiftUI 472

Getting ready 473

How to do it...   474
How it works...   477

**Showing Core Data objects
with @FetchRequest**   **478**
Getting ready   478
How to do it...   479
How it works...   483

**Adding Core Data objects
to a SwiftUI view**   **484**
Getting ready   484
How to do it...   485

How it works...   491

**Filtering Core Data
requests using a predicate**   **491**
Getting ready   492
How to do it...   492
How it works...   499

**Deleting Core Data objects
from a SwiftUI view**   **500**
Getting ready   500
How to do it...   500
How it works...   506

12
Cross-Platform SwiftUI

Technical requirements   **508**
Creating an iOS app in SwiftUI **508**
Getting ready   508
How to do it   508
How it works   517

**Creating the macOS version
of the iOS app**   **518**
Getting ready   518

How to do it   519
How it works   529

**Creating the watchOS
version of the iOS app**   **530**
Getting ready   530
How to do it   531
How it works   539

13
SwiftUI Tips and Tricks

Technical requirements   **542**
Snapshot testing SwiftUI views **542**
Getting ready   543
How to do it...   545
How it works...   550

**Unit testing SwiftUI with
ViewInspector**   **552**
Getting ready   552
How to do it   554

How it works   559

**Implementing a multilanguage
app with localized strings in
SwiftUI**   **560**
Getting ready   561
How to do it   563
How it works   568

Showing a PDF in SwiftUI   **569**

Getting ready 569

How to do it 570

How it works 572

There's more 573

Embedding a MapView in SwiftUI 573

Getting ready 573

How to do it 573

How it works 577

Embedding a UIKit MapView in SwiftUI 578

Getting ready 579

How to do it 579

How it works 584

Implementing SwiftUI views using Playground 584

Getting ready 584

How to do it 584

How it works 587

Using custom fonts in SwiftUI 587

Getting ready 587

How to do it 588

How it works 590

Implementing asynchronous images in SwiftUI 591

Getting ready 591

How to do it 591

How it works 595

There's more 596

Other Books You May Enjoy

Index

Preface

SwiftUI, introduced during Apple's 2019 **Worldwide Developer Conference (WWDC)** 2019, provides an innovative and simple way to build user interfaces across all Apple platforms. SwiftUI code is easy to read and write because it uses Swift's declarative programming syntax.

This book covers the foundations of SwiftUI, as well as the new features of SwiftUI 2.0 introduced in iOS 14. A few recipes are addressed to make some new SwiftUI 2.0 components retrocompatible with iOS 13, such as the Map View or the Sign in with Apple View.

By the end of this book, you'll have simple, direct solutions to common problems found in building SwiftUI apps, and you'll know how to build visually compelling apps using SwiftUI 2.0 and iOS 14.

Who this book is for

This book is for mobile developers who want to learn SwiftUI as well as experienced iOS developers transitioning from UIKit to SwiftUI. The book assumes knowledge of the Swift programming language. Although knowledge of object-oriented design and data structures will be useful, it is not necessary.

What this book covers

Chapter 1, Using the Basic SwiftUI Views and Controls, explains how to implement various SwiftUI layout components, such as HStack, VStack, ZStack, LazyHStack, LazyVStack, LazyHGrid, LazyVGrid, and other layout components. It also covers how to capture various user gestures and how to use form fields. This chapter covers the basic building blocks for creating SwiftUI apps.

Chapter 2, Going Beyond the Single Component with List and Scroll Views, explains how to implement Lists, ScrollViews, and Expanding views. Learn to improve the load time of large data by using Lazy Grids and Lazy Stacks.

Chapter 3, Viewing while Building with SwiftUI Preview, explains how to unleash the power and capabilities of SwiftUI previews to speed up UI development time.

Chapter 4, Creating New Components and Grouping Views in Container Views, explains how to group views, use container views, and implement architectural views such as NavigationView and TabView.

Chapter 5, Presenting Extra Information to the User, provides various ways of presenting extra information to the user, such as alerts, modals, context menus, and popovers.

Chapter 6, Drawing with SwiftUI, explains how to implement drawings in SwiftUI by using built-in shapes, and drawing custom paths and polygons, using UIBezierPath and CGPath.

Chapter 7, Animating with SwiftUI, explains how to implement basic animations, spring animations, and implicit and delayed animations, as well as how to combine transitions, create custom transitions, and create asymmetric transitions.

Chapter 8, Driving SwiftUI with Data, explains how to use the SwiftUI binding mechanism to populate and change views when the bounded data changes.

Chapter 9, Driving SwiftUI with Combine, explains how to integrate Combine to drive the changes of the SwiftUI views. You'll explore how to validate forms, fetch data asynchronously from the network, and test Combine-based apps.

Chapter 10, Handling Authentication and Firebase with SwiftUI, explains how to implement authentication in your app and store user information.

Chapter 11, Handling Core Data in SwiftUI, explains how to implement persistence using SwiftUI and Core Data, saving, deleting, and modifying objects in a Core Data local database.

Chapter 12, Cross-Platform SwiftUI, explains how to create a cross-platform SwiftUI app that works on iOS, macOS, and watchOS.

Chapter 13, SwiftUI Tips and Tricks, covers several SwiftUI tips and tricks that will help you solve a number of common problems, such as testing the views, integrating a MapKit view, and using custom fonts.

To get the most out of this book

You will need an Xcode 12 and iOS 14 installed in your Mac, if possible. All code examples have been tested using iOS 14. However, they should work with future version releases, too:

Software/hardware covered in the book	OS requirements
Xcode 12	macOS
CocoaPods 1.10	macOS

If you are using the digital version of this book, we advise you to type the code yourself or access the code via the GitHub repository (link available in the next section). Doing so will help you avoid any potential errors related to the copying and pasting of code.

Download the example code files

You can download the example code files for this book from your account at www.packt.com. If you purchased this book elsewhere, you can visit www.packtpub.com/support and register to have the files emailed directly to you.

You can download the code files by following these steps:

1. Log in or register at www.packt.com.
2. Select the **Support** tab.
3. Click on **Code Downloads**.
4. Enter the name of the book in the **Search** box and follow the onscreen instructions.

Once the file is downloaded, please make sure that you unzip or extract the folder using the latest version of:

- WinRAR/7-Zip for Windows
- Zipeg/iZip/UnRarX for Mac
- 7-Zip/PeaZip for Linux

The code bundle for the book is also hosted on GitHub at https://github.com/PacktPublishing/SwiftUI-Cookbook. In case there's an update to the code, it will be updated on the existing GitHub repository.

We also have other code bundles from our rich catalog of books and videos available at https://github.com/PacktPublishing/. Check them out!

Conventions used

There are a number of text conventions used throughout this book.

`Code in text`: Indicates code words in text, database table names, folder names, filenames, file extensions, pathnames, dummy URLs, user input, and Twitter handles. Here is an example: "Let's create a SwiftUI app called `FetchContactsApp`."

A block of code is set as follows:

```
guard managedObjectContext.hasChanges else { return }
do {
    try managedObjectContext.save()
} catch {
    print(error)
}
```

When we wish to draw your attention to a particular part of a code block, the relevant lines or items are set in bold:

```
Image(item.image)
    //...
    .shadow(radius: 5)
    .matchedGeometryEffect(id: item.image,
                           in: animation)
```

Bold: Indicates a new term, an important word, or words that you see on screen. For example, words in menus or dialog boxes appear in the text like this. Here is an example: "Select **Swift file** and then click **Next**."

> **Tips or important notes**
> Appear like this.

Get in touch

Feedback from our readers is always welcome.

General feedback: If you have questions about any aspect of this book, mention the book title in the subject of your message and email us at customercare@packtpub.com.

Errata: Although we have taken every care to ensure the accuracy of our content, mistakes do happen. If you have found a mistake in this book, we would be grateful if you would report this to us. Please visit www.packtpub.com/support/errata, selecting your book, clicking on the Errata Submission Form link, and entering the details.

Piracy: If you come across any illegal copies of our works in any form on the internet, we would be grateful if you would provide us with the location address or website name. Please contact us at copyright@packt.com with a link to the material.

If you are interested in becoming an author: If there is a topic that you have expertise in, and you are interested in either writing or contributing to a book, please visit authors.packtpub.com.

Reviews

Please leave a review. Once you have read and used this book, why not leave a review on the site that you purchased it from? Potential readers can then see and use your unbiased opinion to make purchase decisions, we at Packt can understand what you think about our products, and our authors can see your feedback on their book. Thank you!

For more information about Packt, please visit packt.com.

1
Using the Basic SwiftUI Views and Controls

In this chapter, we'll learn about SwiftUI's innovative way of building user interfaces across all platforms. SwiftUI does not use UIKit concepts such as Auto Layout. It has a completely new layout system designed to make it easy to write applications that work across Apple platforms.

We'll also learn about views and controls, SwiftUI's visual building blocks for app interfaces. We will look at how to use text, images, buttons, navigation, and much more.

By the end of the chapter, you'll be able to combine various views and components to create crisp and beautiful user interfaces.

In this chapter, we will cover the following recipes:

- How to lay out components
- Dealing with text
- Using images
- Adding buttons and navigating with them

- Beyond buttons – how to use advanced pickers
- How to apply groups of styles using ViewModifiers
- Separating presentation from content with `ViewBuilder`
- Simple graphics using SF Symbols
- The best of both worlds – integrating UIKit into SwiftUI
- Adding SwiftUI to an existing app
- More views and controls (iOS 14+)

Technical requirements

The code in this chapter is based on Xcode 12 with iOS 13 as a minimum iOS target.

You can find the code in the book's GitHub repository at `https://github.com/PacktPublishing/SwiftUI-Cookbook/tree/master/Chapter01%20-%20Using%20the%20basic%20SwiftUI%20Views%20and%20Controls`

How to lay out components

SwiftUI uses three basic layout components – `VStack`, `HStack`, and `ZStack`. `VStack` is a view that arranges its children in a vertical line, `HStack` arranges its children in a horizontal line, and `ZStack` arranges its children by aligning them with the vertical and horizontal axes.

We will also take a look at how spacers and dividers can be used for layout.

Getting ready

Let's start by creating a new SwiftUI project with Xcode, calling it `TheStacks`. Use the following steps:

1. Start the Xcode program.
2. Click on **Create a new Xcode project** from the left pane.
3. Leave the default selected application, **Single View App**. Click **Next**.
4. In the project options menu, make sure **SwiftUI** is selected instead of storyboard.
5. Enter the product name, `TheStacks`.
6. Select the folder location to store the project and click **Create**.

How to do it...

1. Replace Text in ContentView with a vertical stack containing three elements:

```
struct ContentView: View {
    var body: some View {
VStack{
    Text("VStack Item 1")
    Text("VStack Item 2")
    Text("VStack Item 3")
    }.background(Color.blue)
  }
}
```

This renders like the following in the canvas preview:

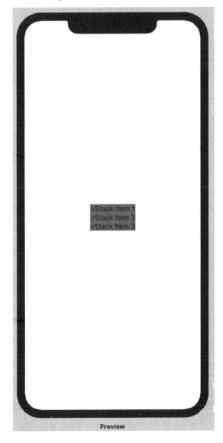

Figure 1.1 – VStack with three items

2. Add a `Spacer` and a `Divider` between items 2 and 3:

```
Spacer()
Divider()
```

This renders the following preview:

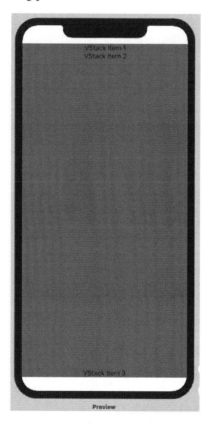

Figure 1.2 – VStack, HStack, and ZStack

3. Add the following `HStack` and `ZStack` to the bottom of the `VStack`:

```
HStack{
    Text("Item 1")
    Text("HStack Item 2")
    Divider().background(Color.black)
    Spacer()
    Text("HStack Item 3")
}.background(Color.red)
```

```
ZStack{
            Text("ZStack Item 1")
            .padding()
            .background(Color.green)
            .opacity(0.8)
            Spacer()
    Text("ZStack Item 2")
    .padding()
        .background(Color.green)
        .offset(x: 80, y: -400)
    }
```

This renders the following preview:

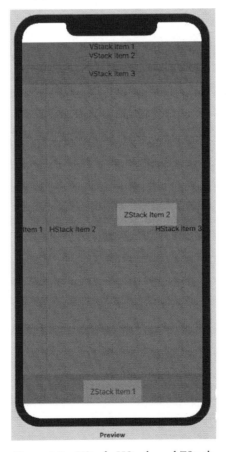

Figure 1.3 – VStack, HStack, and ZStack

That concludes our recipe on using stacks. Going forward, we'll make extensive use of VStacks and HStacks to position elements in our views.

How it works...

The SwiftUI stack layout process consists of three steps:

- The parent proposes the size for the child.

- The child chooses its size.

- The parent places the child in the parent's coordinate space.

Following the preceding steps, the initial text view on a new project gets placed at the center of the screen. Adding a divider causes the stack view to extend and use the full width of the screen.

Stacks also define a layout process for items added to the stack:

- The stack figures out its internal spacing and subtracts it from the size proposed by its parent view.

- The stack then divides the remaining space into equal parts, processes the size of its least flexible view, and divides the remaining unclaimed space by the unallocated space, and then repeats *step 2*.

- The stack then aligns its content and chooses its own size to exactly enclose its children.

A `VStack` adds items in a vertical way, with new views added from top to bottom. Adding the `Spacer()` forces the view to use the maximum amount of vertical space. Adding a `Divider()` draws a line that uses the maximum horizontal space allowed. By default, the divider line does not have a color. To set the divider color, we add the `.background(Color.black)` modifier. Items such as `background(Color.black)`, `.padding()`, and `.offsets(...)` are called `ViewModifiers`, or just modifiers. Modifiers can be applied to views or other modifiers, producing a different version of the original value.

The `HStack` also works in a similar manner. However, since items are added to an `HStack` in a horizontal manner, the `Spacer()` causes the `HStack` to fill the available horizontal space, while the `Divider()` draws a vertical line to separate items in the `HStack`. The `Divider()` thus causes the `HStack` to fill the maximum vertical space available.

The `ZStack` overlays its content on top of existing items. It uses the `.offsets()` modifier to position items along the *X* and *Y* axes.

Dealing with text

The SwiftUI text struct is a view that displays one or more lines of read-only text. Text structs come with a number of standard modifiers to format text. In this section, we will create a project that applies modifiers to 10 different texts.

We will also implement `TextField`, which is used to display an editable text interface. We will also look at `SecureField`. `SecureField` is almost identical to `TextField`, but masks its content for privacy.

Getting ready

Create a new SwiftUI project named `FormattedText`.

How to do it...

1. Enclose the text in the `body` view with a `VStack`:

```
struct ContentView: View {
    var body: some View {
        VStack{
            Text("Hello World")
        }
    }
}
```

2. Add the `.fontWeight(.medium)` modifier to the text and observe the weight change in the canvas preview:

```
Text("Hello World")
.fontWeight(.medium)
```

3. Add two state variables to `ContentView`, `password` and `someText`. These variables will store the user input placed in `SecureField` and `TextField`, respectively:

```
struct ContentView: View {
@State var password = ""
@State var someText = ""
var body: someView {
    ...
}
```

4. Add `SecureField` and a `Text` view to display the value entered in `TextField`:

```
SecureField("Enter a password", text: $password)
    .padding()
Text("password entered: \(password)")
    .italic()
```

5. Add `TextField` and a `Text` view to display the value entered in `TextField`:

```
TextField("Enter some text", text: $someText)
    .padding()
Text("\(someText)")
    .font(.largeTitle)
    .underline()
```

6. Now, let's add some other texts and modifiers to the list:

```
Text("\(someText)")
    .font(.largeTitle)
    .underline()
Text("Changing text color and make it bold")
    .foregroundColor(Color.blue)
    .bold()
Text("Use kerning to change space between
    lines of text")
    .kerning(7)
Text("Changing baseline offset")
    .baselineOffset(100)
Text("Strikethrough")
    .strikethrough()


Text("This is a multiline text implemented
    in swiftUI. The trailing modifier was
    added to the text. This text also
    implements multiple modifiers")
    .background(Color.yellow)
    .multilineTextAlignment(.trailing)
    .lineSpacing(10)
```

The resulting preview should look as follows:

Figure 1.4 – FormattedText preview

7. Run the code in a simulator or click the play button next to the preview. Enter some text in the SecureField and TextField.

Text entered in the SecureField will be masked, while text in the TextField will be in clear text.

How it works...

Text views have a number of modifiers for font, spacing, and other formatting requirements. When in doubt, type . after the text view and choose from the list of possible options that will appear. This is shown in the following example:

```
14        Text("Hello World").
15    M              Text baselineOffset(baselineOffset: CGFloat)
16    M            Text bold()
17    M           Text font(font: Font?)
18
19    M          Text fontWeight(weight: Font.Weight?)
20    M          Text foregroundColor(color: Color?)
21    M        Text italic()
22    M        Text kerning(kerning: CGFloat)
23           Text self
24
     Sets the baseline offset for the text.
25
26            .strikethrough()
27        Text("Underline")
28            .underline()
29        Text("Italisized text")
30            .italic()
```

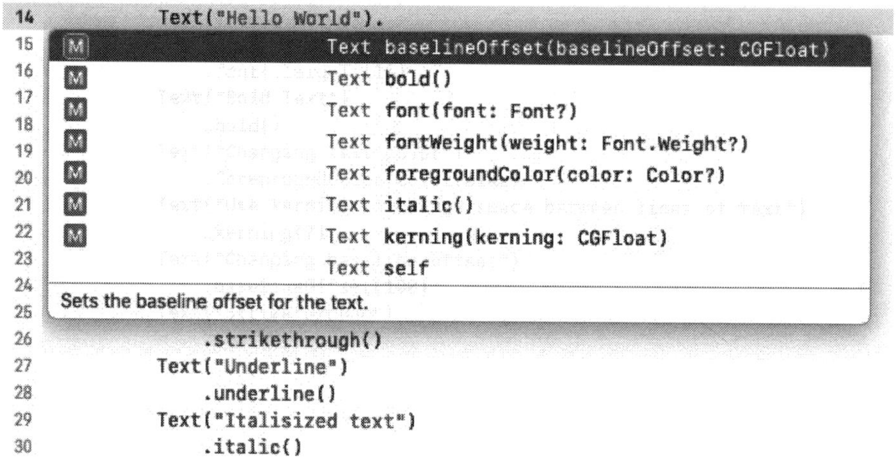

Figure 1.5 – Using Xcode autocomplete to view formatting options

Unlike regular text views, `TextFields` and `SecureFields` require state variables to store the value entered by the user. State variables are declared using the keyword @ `State`. Values entered by the user are stored using the process of binding, where the state variable is bound to the `SecureField` or `TextField` input parameter. The $ symbol is used to bind a state variable to the field. Using the $ symbol ensures that the state variable's value is changed to correspond to the value entered by the user, as shown in the following example:

```
TextField("Enter some text", text: $someText)
```

Binding also notifies other views of state changes and causes the views to be redrawn on state change.

The content of bound state variables is displayed without using the $ symbol because no binding is required when displaying content, as shown in the following code:

```
Text("\(someText)")
```

There's more...

Try adding an eleventh element to the `VStack`. You will get an error, because SwiftUI views can hold a maximum of 10 elements. To add an eleventh element, you would have to enclose the first 10 elements in a `Group` view. Groups are required because the SwiftUI view building system has various code designed to allow the addition of views 1 through 10 but not beyond. A `Group` view can be used as shown in the following code:

```
Group {
    Text("Item 1")
    ...
    Text("Item 10")
}
Text("Item 11")
```

Items in a `Group` are considered as one view. The preceding code thus allows us to display 11 items as two views, the `Group` view, and the `Text` view at the bottom.

See also

Apple documentation regarding SwiftUI Text view: `https://developer.apple.com/documentation/swiftui/text`

Using images

In this recipe, we will learn how to add an image to a view, use an already existing UIImage, put an image in a frame, and use modifiers to present beautiful images. The images in this section were obtained from `https://unsplash.com/`. Special thanks to *jf-brou*, *Kieran White,* and *Camilo Fierro*.

Getting ready

Create a new SwiftUI project named `ImageApp`.

How to do it...

1. Replace the initial `Text` view with a `Vstack`.

2. Download the project images from the GitHub link at `https://github.com/PacktPublishing/SwiftUI-Cookbook/tree/master/Chapter01%20-%20Using%20the%20basic%20SwiftUI%20Views%20and%20Controls/03%20-%20Using%20Images`

3. Drag and drop the downloaded images for this recipe into the project's `Assets.xcassets` folder, as shown in the following screenshot:

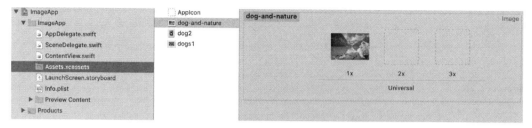

Figure 1.6 – Assets.xcassets folder in Xcode

4. Add an `Image` view to `VStack`:

```
Image("dogs1")
```

Observe the result in the canvas preview.

5. Add a `.resizable()` modifier to the image and allow SwiftUI to adjust the image such that it fits the screen space available:

```
Image("dogs1")
        .resizable()
```

6. The `.resizable()` modifier causes the full image to fit on the screen, but the proportions are distorted. That can be fixed by adding the `.aspectRatio(contentMode: .fit)` modifier:

```
Image("dogs1")
          .resizable()
          .aspectRatio(contentMode: .fit)
```

7. Add the `dog-and-nature` image to `VStack`:

```
Image("dog-and-nature")
        .resizable()
        .aspectRatio(contentMode: .fit)
        .frame(width:300, height:200)
        .clipShape(Circle())
        .overlay(Circle().stroke(Color.blue, lineWidth: 6))
        .shadow(radius: 10)
```

8. To use a `UIImage` class as input for images, create a function, `getImageFromUIImage(image: String)`, that accepts an image name and returns a `UIImage`:

```
func getImageFromUIImage(image:String) -> UIImage {
    guard let img = UIImage(named: image) else {
        fatalError("Unable to load image")
    }
    return img
}
```

9. Use `getImageFromUIImage(image: String)` to display a `UIImage` within the `VStack`. The resulting code should look as follows:

```
struct ContentView: View {
    var body: some View {
        VStack{
            Image("dogs1")
            .resizable()
            .aspectRatio(contentMode: .fit)
            Image("dog-and-nature")
                .resizable()
                .aspectRatio(contentMode: .fit)
                .frame(width:300, height:200)
                .clipShape(Circle())
                .overlay(Circle().stroke(Color.blue,
                    lineWidth: 6))
            .shadow(radius: 10)
            Image(uiImage: getImageFromUIImage(image:
                "dog2"))
            .resizable()
            .frame(width: 200, height: 200)
            .aspectRatio(contentMode: .fit)


        }
    }
}
func getImageFromUIImage(image:String) -> UIImage {
```

```
    guard let img = UIImage(named: image) else {
        fatalError("Unable to load image")
    }
    return img
}
```

The completed application should look as follows:

Figure 1.7 – ImageApp preview

How it works...

Adding the `Image` view to SwiftUI displays the image in its original proportions. The image might be too small or too big for the device's display. For example, without any modifiers, the `dog-and-nature` image fills up the full iPhone 11 Pro Max screen:

Figure 1.8 – Dog-and-nature image without the resizable modifier

To allow an image to shrink or enlarge to fit the device screen size, add the `.resizable()` modifier to the image.

Adding the `.resizable()` modifier causes the image to fit within its view, but it may be distorted due to changes in proportion:

Figure 1.9 – Image with resizable modifier

To address the issue, add the `.aspectRatio(contentMode: .fit)` modifier to the image:

Figure 1.10 – Image with AspectRatio set

To specify the width and height of an image, add the `.frame(width, height)` modifier to the view and set the `width` and `height`:

```
.frame(width: 200, height: 200)
```

Images can be clipped to specific shapes. The `.clipShape(Circle())` modifier changes the image shape to a circle:

Figure 1.11 – Image with the clipShape(Circle()) modifier

The `.overlay(Circle().stroke(Color.blue, lineWidth: 6))` and `.shadow(radius: 10)` modifiers were used to draw a blue line around the image circle and add a shadow to the circle:

Figure 1.12 – Stroke and shadow applied to image

> **Important note**
>
> The order in which the modifiers are added matters. Adding the `.frame()` modifier before the `.resizable ()` modifier may lead to different results, or cause an error.

See also

Apple documentation regarding SwiftUI images: `https://developer.apple.com/documentation/swiftui/image`

Adding buttons and navigating with them

In this recipe, we will learn how to use various buttons available in SwiftUI. We will use a `Button` view to trigger the change of a count when clicked, implement a `navigationView` to move between various SwiftUI views, and an `EditButton` to remove items from a list. We will also briefly discuss the `MenuButton` and `PasteButton`, only available in macOS.

Getting ready

Create a new SwiftUI project named `ButtonsApp`.

How to do it...

1. Add a new SwiftUI `View` file called `ButtonView` to the project: **File | New | File**, or press the shortcut keys: ⌘ + N.

2. Select **SwiftUI View** from the **User Interface templates**.

3. In the **Save As** field of the pop-up menu, enter the filename `ButtonView`.

4. Repeat *step 1* and enter the filename `EditButtonView`.

5. Repeat *step 1* and enter the filename `PasteButtonView`.

6. Repeat *step 1* and enter the filename `MenuButtonView`.

7. Open the `ContentView.swift` file and create a `NavigationView` to navigate between the SwiftUI views we added to the project:

```
NavigationView {
            VStack{
                NavigationLink(destination: ButtonView()){
                    Text("Buttons")
                }


                NavigationLink(destination:
                            EditButtonView()) {
                    Text("EditButtons")
                        .padding()
                }
                NavigationLink(destination:
                            MenuButtonView()) {
                    Text("MenuButtons")
                        .padding()
                }
                NavigationLink(destination:
                            PasteButtonView()) {
                    Text("PasteButtons")
                        .padding()
                }
                NavigationLink(destination:
                    Text("Very long text that should
                        not be displayed in a single
                        line because it is not good design")
```

```
                    .padding()
                    .navigationBarTitle(Text("Detail"))
        ) {
                Text("details about text")
                    .padding()
        }

        }.navigationBarTitle(Text("Main View"),
            displayMode: .inline)
```

Upon completion, the `ContentView` preview should look like the following screenshot:

Figure 1.13 – ButtonsApp ContentView

8. Open the `EditButtonView.swift` file in the project navigator and add the following code that implements an `EditButton`:

```
@State private var animals = ["Cats", "Dogs", "Goats"]
var body: some View {
    NavigationView{
        List{
            ForEach(animals, id: \.self){ animal in
                Text(animal)
            }.onDelete(perform: removeAnimal)
        }
        .navigationBarItems(trailing:EditButton())
        .navigationBarTitle(Text("EditButtonView"),
            displayMode: .inline)
    }
}
func removeAnimal(at offsets: IndexSet){
    animals.remove(atOffsets: offsets)
}
```

9. Open the `MenuButtonView.swift` file and add the code for `MenuButtons`:

```
var body: some View {
    Text("MenuButtons are currently available on
        MacOS currently")
        .padding()
        .navigationBarTitle("MenuButtons",
            displayMode: .inline)
    /*
    MenuButton("country +") {
        Button("USA") { print("Selected USA") }
            .background(Color.accentColor)
        Button("India") { print("Selected India") }
    }
    */
}
```

10. Open the `PasteButtonView.swift` file and implement the text regarding PasteButtons:

```
@State var text  = String()
var body: some View {
    VStack{
        Text("PasteButton controls how you paste in
            macOS but is not available in iOS. For more
            information, check the \"See also\" section
            of this recipe")
        .padding()
    }.navigationBarTitle("PasteButton", displayMode:
        .inline)
}
```

Go back to `ContentView` and run the code in the canvas preview or simulator and play around with it to see what the results look like.

How it works...

A `NavigationLink` has to be placed in a `NavigationView` prior to being used. It takes two parameters – `destination` and `label`. The `destination` parameter represents the view that would be displayed when the label is clicked, while the `label` parameter represents the text to be displayed within `NavigationLink`.

`NavigationLink` buttons can be used to move from one SwiftUI view file to another, for example, moving from `ContentView` to `EditButtonView`. It can also be used to display text details without creating a SwiftUI view file, such as in the last `NavigationLink`, where a click just presents a long piece of text with more information. This is made possible because the text struct conforms to the view protocol

The `.navigationBarTitle(Text("Main View"), displayMode: .inline)` modifier adds a title to `ContentViewPage`. The first argument passed to the modifier represents the title to be displayed, and the `displayMode` argument controls the style for displaying the navigation bar.

The `.navigationBarTitle()` modifier was also added to `EditButtonView` and other views. Since these views do not contain `NavigationView` structs, the titles would not be displayed when viewing the page directly from the preview, but would show up when running the code and navigating from `ContentView.swift` to the view provided in `NavigationLink`.

The `EditButton` view is used in conjunction with `List` views to make lists editable. We will go over Lists and Scroll Views in *Chapter 2, Going Beyond the Single Component with List and Scroll Views*, but `EditButtonView` provides a peek into how to create an editable list.

As of April 2020, `MenuButtons` and `PasteButtons` are only available on macOS. This recipe provides some sample code for menu buttons. Refer to the *See also* section of this recipe for code on how the `PasteButton` is implemented.

See also

The code for implementing `PasteButtons` can be found here: `https://gist.github.com/sturdysturge/79c73600cfb683663c1d70f5c0778020#file-swiftuidocumentationpastebutton-swift`

More information regarding `NavigationLink` buttons can be found here: `https://developer.apple.com/documentation/swiftui/navigationlink`

Beyond buttons – how to use advanced pickers

In this recipe, we will learn how to implement the pickers, namely, `Picker`, `Toggle`, `Slider`, `Stepper`, and `DatePickers`. **Pickers** are typically used to prompt the user to select from a set of mutually exclusive values; **Toggles** are used to switch between on/off states; and **Sliders** are used to select a value from a bounded linear range of values. Like Sliders, **Steppers** also provide the user interface for selecting from a range of values. However, Steppers use a + and – sign to allow the users to increment the desired value by a certain amount. Finally, **DatePickers** are used to select dates.

Getting ready

Create a new SwiftUI project named `PickersApp`.

How to do it...

1. In `ContentView.swift`, create `@State` variables to hold the values selected from `Pickers` and other controls. Place the variables between the `ContentView` struct and the body:

```
@State var choice = 0
@State var showText = false
@State var transitModes = ["Bike", "Car", "Bus"]
@State var sliderVal: Float = 0
@State var stepVal = 0
@State var gameTime = Date()
```

2. Create a `Form` view within the body view of the `ContentView` struct. Add a `Section` view and a `Picker` to the form:

```
Form{
    Section{
        Picker(selection: $choice, label:Text("Transit
            Mode")){
            ForEach( 0 ..< transitModes.count) { index in
                Text("\(self.transitModes[index])")
            }
        }.pickerStyle(SegmentedPickerStyle())
        Text("Current choice: \
            (transitModes[choice])")
    }
}
```

3. Now, add a `Section` view and a `Toggle` view:

```
Section{
    Toggle(isOn: $showText){
        Text("Show Text")
    }
    if showText {
        Text("The Text toggle is on")
    }
}
```

4. Add a `Section` view and a `Slider` view:

```
Section{
    Slider(value: $sliderVal, in: 0...10,
        step: 0.001)
    Text("Slider current value \(sliderVal,
        specifier: "%.1f")")
}
```

5. Add a `Section` view and a `Stepper` view:

```
Section {
    Stepper("Stepper", value: $stepVal, in:
        0...5)
    Text("Stepper current value \(stepVal)")
}
```

6. Add a `Section` view and a `DatePicker` view:

```
Section {
    DatePicker("Please select a date",
        selection: $gameTime)
}
```

7. Add a `Section` view and a slightly modified `DatePicker` view that only accepts future dates:

```
Section {
    DatePicker("Please select a date",
        selection: $gameTime, in: Date()...)
}
```

The result should be a beautiful form, as seen in the following diagram:

Figure 1.14 – SwiftUI form with pickers

How it works...

Form views group controls used for data entry and Section creates hierarchical view content. Enclosing Section views, our Form creates the gray area between each picker.

To use SwiftUI pickers, we first need to declare @State variables to store the values from the pickers.

Pickers are used for selecting from a set of mutually exclusive values. In the following example, Picker is used to select a transit mode from an array of strings called TransitModes:

```
Picker(selection: $choice, label:Text("Transit Mode")){
    ForEach( 0 ..< transitModes.count) { index in
        Text("\(self.transitModes[index])")
```

```
        }
    }.pickerStyle(SegmentedPickerStyle())
```

As shown in the example, a `Picker` view takes two parameters, a state variable that holds the value selected, and a label. The state variable should be of the same type as the range of values to select from. In this case, the `ForEach` loop iterates through the `transitModes` array indices. The value selected would be an `Int` within the range of transit mode indices. The transit mode located in the selected index can then be displayed using `Text("\(self.transitModes[index])")`.

`Toggles` are controls that switch between on and off states. The state variable for holding the toggle selection should be of the `Bool` type. The section with the `Toggle` view also contains some text. The current value of the toggle `@State` property stores the current value of the Toggle and can be used to show or hide the view as necessary.

Creating a `Slider` requires three arguments:

- **Value**: The `@State` variable to bind the user input to
- **In**: The range of the `Slider`
- **Step**: By how much the `Slider` should change when the user moves it

In the sample code, our slider moves can hold values between 0 and 10, with a step of 0.001.

`Steppers` take three arguments too, the first being a string representing the label of the `Stepper`. The two other arguments, `value` and `in`, hold the `@State` variable that binds the user input and the range of the `Stepper`, respectively.

Two applications of `DatePickers` are demonstrated in this recipe. The first from the top shows one whose first argument is the label of `DatePicker`, and the second argument, selection, holds the state variable that binds the user input. Such a `DatePicker` would allow the user to pick any date. In the second version of `DatePicker`, the last contains a third parameter, `in`, representing the date range. The date range here only allows future dates to be selected.

> **Important note**
>
> The `@State` variables should be of the same type as the data to be stored. For example, the `gameTime` state variable is of the `Date` type.
>
> Picker styles change based on its ancestor. The default appearance of a picker may be different when placed within a form or list instead of a `VStack` or some other view. Styles can be overridden using the `.pickerStyle(..)` modifier.

How to apply groups of styles using ViewModifiers

SwiftUI comes with built-in modifiers such as `background()` and `fontWeight()`, among others. SwiftUI also gives programmers the ability to create their own custom modifiers to do something specific. Custom modifiers allow the programmer to combine multiple existing modifiers into a single modifier.

In this section, we will create a custom modifier that adds rounded corners and a background to a `Text` view.

Getting ready

Create a new SwiftUI project named `ViewModifiersApp`.

How to do it...

1. Change the `Text` in `ContentView` to `"Perfect"`:

```
Text("Perfect")
```

2. In the `ContentView.swift` file, create a struct that conforms to the `ViewModifier` protocol, accepts parameter of the `Color` type, and applies styles to the body:

```
struct BackgroundStyle: ViewModifier {
    var bgColor: Color
    func body(content: Content) -> some View{
        content
            .frame(width:UIScreen.main.bounds.width * 0.3)
            .foregroundColor(Color.black)
            .padding()
            .background(bgColor)
            .cornerRadius(CGFloat(20))
    }
}
```

3. Add the custom style to the text using the `modifier()` modifier:

```
Text("Perfect").modifier(BackgroundStyle(bgColor: .blue))
```

4. To apply styles without using the `modifier()` modifier, create an extension to the `View` protocol:

```
extension View {
    func backgroundStyle(color: Color) -> some View{
        self.modifier(BackgroundStyle(bgColor: color))
    }
}
```

5. Remove the modifier on the `Text` view and add your custom style using the `backgroundStyle()` modifier you just created:

```
Text("Perfect")
        .backgroundStyle(color: Color.red)
```

The result should be as follows:

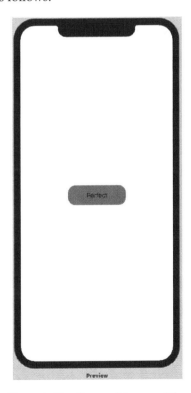

Figure 1.15 – Custom View modifier

This concludes the section on View modifiers. View modifiers promote clean coding and reduce repetition.

How it works...

A `ViewModifier` modifies a view, thereby producing a different version of the original value. To apply `ViewModifier`, we first create a view that conforms to the `ViewModifier` protocol. In this example, we created the `BackgroundStyle` modifier.

The `bgColor` variable in `BackgroundStyle` means it would accept a color as a parameter and use it to change the style of the view.

The body function within the view gets the current body of the caller. Styles applied to the content parameter will be applied to the caller's view.

To make custom modifiers easier to use, we create an extension of `View` and add a function that calls our custom modifier. The `backgroundStyle(color: Color)` function in our `View` extension allows us to apply the custom modifier to the view using `.backgroundStyle(color:Color)` instead of `.modifier(BackgroundStyle(bgColor: Color))`.

See also

Apple documentation on view modifiers: `https://developer.apple.com/documentation/swiftui/viewmodifier`

Separating presentation from content with ViewBuilder

`ViewBuilder` is a custom parameter attribute that constructs views from closures. `ViewBuilder` can be used to create custom views that can be used across the application with minimal or no code duplication. We will create a SwiftUI view, `BlueCircle.swift`, for declaring the `ViewBuilder` and implement the custom `ViewBuilder`. The `ContentView.swift` file will be used to implement the custom view.

Getting ready

Create a new SwiftUI project named `ViewBuildersApp`.

How to do it...

1. Open the **ViewBuildersApp** and add a new **SwiftUI** view to the project from the menu: **File | New | File**.

2. Select the **SwiftUI** view from the menu.

3. Click **Next**.

4. Name the file `BlueCircle` and click **Create**.

5. Delete the `BlueCircle_Previews`: struct from the file (delete all five lines of code).

6. Add `BlueCircle ViewModifier` to the file:

```
struct BlueCircle<Content: View>: View {
    let content: Content
    init(@ViewBuilder content: () -> Content) {
        self.content = content()
    }
    var body: some View {
        HStack {
            content
            Spacer()
            Circle()
                .fill(Color.blue)
                .frame(width:20, height:30)
        }.padding()
    }
}
```

7. Open the `ContentView.swift` file and implement `BlueCircle ViewModifier`:

```
VStack {
    BlueCircle {
        Text("some text here")
        Rectangle()
            .fill(Color.red)
            .frame(width: 40, height: 40)
    }
    BlueCircle {
        Text("Another example")
    }
}
```

The result should look like the following screenshot:

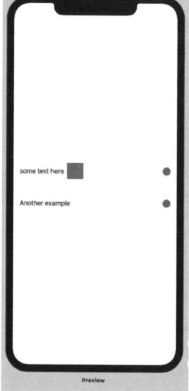

Figure 1.16 – ViewModifiers preview

How it works...

`ViewBuilder` structs create view templates that can be used without the need to duplicate code.

`ViewBuilder` is a struct that implements the `View` protocol and therefore should have a body variable within it.

Once created and initialized, the UI logic added within `ViewBuilder` would be displayed each time the custom view is used. The location of the `Content` constant determines where items added to the custom view would be displayed.

See also

Apple documentation on `ViewBuilder`: https://developer.apple.com/documentation/swiftui/viewbuilder

Simple graphics using SF Symbols

The **San Francisco Symbols** (also known as **SF Symbols**) provide a set of over 1,500 consistent and highly configurable symbols.

To browse through the list or look at symbol names, you can download the SF Symbols app from `https://developer.apple.com/design/downloads/SF-Symbols.dmg`.

In this recipe, we will create a project that uses various SF Symbols and applies different styles to them.

Getting ready

Create a new SwiftUI project named `SFSybmolsApp`.

How to do it...

Using SF Symbols is very similar to using images.

1. Open the `ContentView.swift` file and delete the default `Text` view.

2. Add a `VStack` and an `HStack` to the `ContentView` body and implement various SF symbols:

```
VStack {
    HStack{
        Image(systemName: "c.circle.fill")
        Image(systemName: "o.circle.fill")
        Image(systemName: "o.circle.fill")
        Image(systemName: "k.circle.fill")
        Image(systemName: "b.circle.fill")
        Image(systemName: "o.circle.fill")
        Image(systemName: "o.circle.fill")
        Image(systemName: "k.circle.fill")
    }.foregroundColor(.blue)
        .font(.title)
        .padding()
    HStack{
        Image(systemName: "clock")
            .foregroundColor(Color.purple)
            .font(.largeTitle)
```

```
Image(systemName: "wifi")
    .foregroundColor(Color.red)
    .font(.largeTitle)
        }
    }
```

The resulting preview should appear as shown in the following diagram:

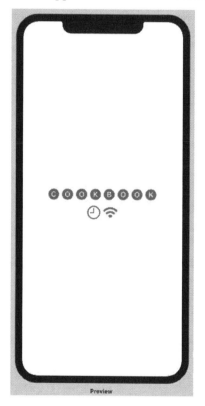

Figure 1.17 – SF symbols in action

How it works...

SF Symbols are displayed using the `Image` view and a `systemName` parameter. Most modifiers used on `Image` and `Text` views can then be applied to SF Symbols. In this example, fonts, frame, and background modifiers were applied to the images.

See also

Apple documentation on SF Symbols:

```
https://developer.apple.com/design/human-interface-guidelines/
sf-symbols/overview/
```

The best of both worlds – integrating UIKit into SwiftUI

SwiftUI was announced at WWDC 2019 and is only available on iOS 13 devices or later. Due to its relative newness, SwiftUI lacks broad API coverage compared to UIKit. For example, as of April 2020, `UICollectionViews`, `UITextView`, UIKit APIs for displaying grids, and multiline texts are not available in SwiftUI. There is therefore a need to implement certain UIKit APIs in SwiftUI.

This recipe goes over the required process for integrating UIKit into SwiftUI. We will create a project that wraps instances of `UIActivityIndicatorView` to display an indicator in SwiftUI.

Getting ready

Open Xcode and create a SwiftUI project named `UIKitToSwiftUI`.

How to do it...

UIKit views are displayed in SwiftUI by using the representable protocol. Follow these steps to implement `UIActivityIndicatorView` in SwiftUI.

1. Within the Xcode menu, click **File | New | File** and select **SwiftUI view**. Name the view `ActivityIndicator`.

2. Import `UIKit` into `ActivityIndicator`.

3. Modify the code to make `ActivityIndicator` use the representable protocol:

```swift
struct ActivityIndicator: UIViewRepresentable {
    var animating: Bool

    func makeUIView(context: Context) ->
        UIActivityIndicatorView {
        return UIActivityIndicatorView()
    }

    func updateUIView(_ activityIndicator:
        UIActivityIndicatorView, context: Context) {
        if animating {
            activityIndicator.startAnimating()
        } else {
            activityIndicator.stopAnimating()
        }
    }
}
```

4. Open the `ContentView.swift` file and add the following code to apply `ActivityIndicator`. Also add a toggle control to turn the indicator on or off.

```swift
struct ContentView: View {
    @State var animate = true
    var body: some View {
        VStack{
            ActivityIndicator(animating:  animate)
            HStack{
                Toggle(isOn: $animate){
                    Text("Toggle Activity")
                }
            }
        }
    }
}
```

The result should look as follows:

Figure 1.18 – UIKit ActivityIndicator in SwiftUI

How it works...

UIKit views can be implemented in SwiftUI by using the representable protocol to wrap the UIKit views. In this recipe, we implement a UIActivityIndicatorView by wrapping it with UIViewRepresentable.

To conform to the UIViewRepresentable protocol, we added a makeUIView and updateUIView function to our ActivityIndicator struct.

The makeUIView() function creates and prepares the view. In this case, it just returns the UIActivityIndicator view.

The `updateUIView` method updates the **UIView** when the animation state changes. The value of the animating variable in the struct is used to start or stop animating `UIActivityIndicator`.

> **Important note**
> If working on an iOS 14+ app, use `ProgressView` provided out of the box.

See also

Check out the recipe, *More views and controls*, at the end of this chapter for more information on `ProgressView`.

Adding SwiftUI to an existing app

In this recipe, we will learn how to navigate from a UIKit view to a SwiftUI view while passing a text as argument from our UIKit storyboard to our SwiftUI view.

A storyboard is a visual representation of the user interface in UIKit. The `Main.storyboard` file is to UIKit as the `ContentView.swift` file is to SwiftUI. They both are the default home views created when you start a new project.

The recipe begins with a UIKit project that contains a button.

Getting ready

To prepare for this recipe, perform the following steps:

1. Clone or download the GitHub project at `https://github.com/PacktPublishing/SwiftUI-Cookbook`.

2. Open the `StartingPoint` folder located at `SwiftUI-Cookbook/Chapter01 - Using the basic SwiftUI Views and Controls/10 - Adding SwiftUI to UIKit` and double-click on the `AddSwiftUIToUIKitApp.xcodeproj` file. It opens up the UIKit project in Xcode.

How to do it...

We will add a `NavigationController` to the UIKit `ViewController` that allows the app to navigate to the SwiftUI view when the button is clicked:

1. Open up the `Main.storyboard` file in Xcode by clicking on it. The display should look as follows:

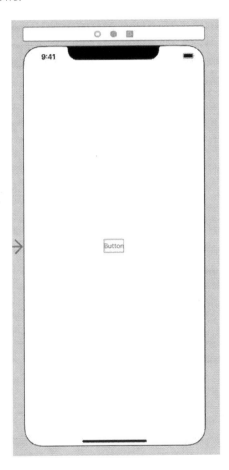

Figure 1.19 – UIKit ViewController

2. Click anywhere in `ViewController` to select it.

3. In the Xcode menu, click **Editor | Embed in | Navigation Controller**.

4. Add a new `ViewController` to the project.

5. Click on the + button, five buttons to the left of the top-right corner of Xcode.

6. In the pop-up menu that appears, type `hosting` and select the **Hosting View Controller**:

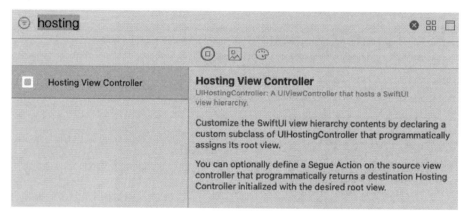

Figure 1.20 – Creating a UIKit ViewController

7. Hold down the *Ctrl* key, and then click and drag from the button in `ViewController` to the new hosting `ViewController` recently created.

8. In the pop-up menu, select the **Show** action segue.

9. Click the *Adjust Editor Options* button:

Figure 1.21 – Adjust Editor Options button

10. Click **Assistant**. This splits the view into two panes, as shown here:

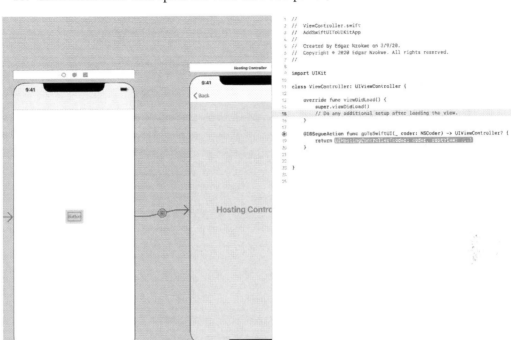

Figure 1.22 View when Assistant is opened

11. To create a segue action, hold the *Ctrl* key, and then click and drag from the segue button to the space after the `viewDidLoad()` function in `ViewController.swift`.

12. In the pop-up menu, name the segue `goToSwiftUI` and click **connect**. The following code will be added to the `ViewController.swift` file:

```
@IBSegueAction func goToSwiftUI(_ coder: NSCoder) ->
    UIViewController? {
        return <#UIHostingController(coder: coder,
            rootView: ...)#>
    }
```

13. Add a statement to import SwiftUI at the top of the `ViewController` page, next to `Import UIKit`:

```
Import SwiftUI
```

14. Within the `goToSwiftUI` segue action, create the string that will be passed to the SwiftUI view. Also create a `rootView` variable that indicates the SwiftUI view you would like to navigate to. Finally, return the `viewController` used to display the SwiftUI view. The resulting code should be as follows:

```
@IBSegueAction func goToSwiftUI(_ coder: NSCoder) ->
    UIViewController? {
    let greetings = "Hello From UIKit"
    let rootView = Greetings(randomText: greetings)
    return UIHostingController(coder: coder,
        rootView: rootView)
}
```

15. Create the **Greetings SwiftUI** view.

16. Within the Xcode menu, click **File | New | File** and select **SwiftUI** View.

17. Name the View `Greetings.swift`.

18. Add the code to display some text:

```
struct Greetings: View {
    var randomText = ""
    var body: some View {
        Text(randomText)
    }
}
```

Run the resulting program in a simulator or device.

How it works...

To host SwiftUI views in an existing app, you need to wrap the SwiftUI hierarchy in a `ViewController` or `InterfaceController`.

We started by performing core UIKit concepts, such as adding a `NavigationView` controller to the storyboard. We then proceeded to add `HostingController` as a placeholder for our SwiftUI view.

Lastly, an `IBSegueAction` function was created to present the SwiftUI view upon clicking a button.

More views and controls (iOS 14+)

Let's now take a look at some new SwiftUI views and controls introduced in iOS 14. We will look at the `ProgressView`, `Label`, `ColorPicker`, `Link`, `TextEditor`, and `Menu` views. We use ProgressViews to show the degree of completion of a task. There are two types of ProgressViews; indeterminate progress views show a spinning circle till a task is completed, and determinate progress views show a bar that gets filled up to show the progress of a task.

Labels provide an easy way to display a label and icon. ColorPickers expand when clicked and present the user with a wide range of colors to select from. `TextEditor` provides a multiline interface for the user to input text.

Finally, Menus present a list of items the user can chose from. Each item should perform a specific action.

Getting ready

Create a new SwiftUI app called `MoreViewsAndControls`.

How to do it...

Let's now implement all the new views and controls in the `ContentView.swift` file. To make the resulting app elegant, we will implement each item in a separate `Section` within a `List`. Let's proceed as follows:

1. Within the `ContentView` struct, just above the `body` variable, declare some state variables that we'll use later:

```
@State private var progress = 0.5
@State private var color   = Color.red
@State private var secondColor   = Color.yellow
@State private var someText = "Initial value"
```

2. Within the body view, let's add a `List` view and a `Section` view containing a `ProgressView`:

```
List{
    Section(header: Text("ProgressViews")) {
        ProgressView("Indeterminate progress
                        view")
        ProgressView("Downloading",value:
            progress, total:2)
        Button("More"){
            if(progress < 2){
                progress += 0.5
            }
        }
    }
}
```

3. Now, let's add another section that implements two Labels in two ways:

```
Section(header: Text("Labels")) {
    Label("Slow ", systemImage: "tortoise.
            fill")
    Label{
        Text ("Fast")
            .font(.title)
    }
    icon: {
        Circle()
            .fill(Color.orange)
            .frame(width: 40, height: 20,
                alignment: .center)
            .overlay(Text("F"))
    }
}
```

4. Add the `Link` section below the `ColorPicker` section:

```
Section(header: Text("Link")) {
    Link("Packt Publishing", destination:
    URL(string: "https://www.packtpub.com/")!)
}
```

5. Next, add a `TextEditor`:

```
Section(header: Text("TextEditor")) {
    TextEditor(text: $someText)
    Text("current editor text:\n\(someText)")
}
```

6. Next, add a `Menu`:

```
Section(header: Text("Menu")) {
    Menu("Actions") {
        Button("Set TextEditor text to
        'magic'") {
            someText = "magic"
        }
        Button("Turn first picker green") {
            color = Color.green
        }                              }
    }
}
```

7. Finally, let's improve the style by adding a `.listStyle()` modifier to our `List`:

```
List{
    ...
}.listStyle(GroupedListStyle())
```

Here is what the resulting app should look like:

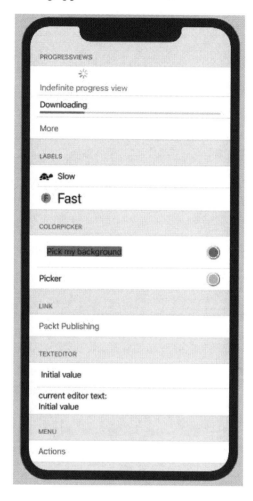

Figure 1.23 – MoreViewsAndControls app

Nice work! Run the app in Xcode preview and take some time to interact with the components to get a better appreciation for how they work.

How it works...

We've implemented multiple views in this recipe. Let's look at each one and discuss how they work.

Indeterminate ProgressViews require no parameter, just a label:

```
ProgressView("Indeterminate progress view")
ProgressView()
```

Determinate ProgressViews, on the other hand, require a `value` parameter that takes a state variable and displays the level of completion:

```
ProgressView("Downloading", value: progress, total:2)
```

The total parameter is optional, but defaults to 1.0 if not specified.

Labels are used to display some text and an icon. Labels can be implemented on a single line as follows:

```
Label("Slow ", systemImage: "tortoise.fill")
```

Alternatively, they can be implemented on multiple lines. This option is used when you need to customize how the `Label` text or icon is displayed:

```
Label{
    Text ("Fast")
        .font(.title)
}
icon: {
    Circle()
        .fill(Color.orange)
        .frame(width: 40, height: 20,
            alignment: .center)
        .overlay(Text("F"))
}
```

ColorPickers let you display a palate for users to pick colors from. We pass in an `@State` variable to the `ColorPicker` that stores the value of the selected color:

```
ColorPicker(selection: $color ){
                Text("Pick my background")
                    .background(color)
                    .padding()
        }
            ColorPicker("Picker", selection: $secondColor )
```

The `Link` view is used to display clickable links:

```
Link("Packt Publishing", destination: URL(string:
        "https://www.packtpub.com/")!)
```

`TextEditor` provides an easy way to allow the user to provide multiline input. The value entered is stored in the `@State` variable, `text`:

```
TextEditor(text: $someText)
```

`Menu` provides a convenient way of presenting a user with a list of actions to choose from:

```
Menu("Actions") {
            Button("Set TextEditor text to 'magic'"){
                someText = "magic"
            }
            Button("Turn first picker green") {
                color = Color.green
            }

        }
```

Menus can also be nested:

```
Menu("Actions") {
    Button("Set TextEditor text to 'magic'"){
        someText = "magic"
    }
    Button("Turn first picker green") {
        color = Color.green
    }
    Menu("Actions") {
        Button("Set TextEditor text to
            'magic'"){
            someText = "magic"
        }
        Button("Turn first picker green") {
            color = Color.green
        }
    }
}
```

You can add one or more buttons to a menu, each performing a specific action. Although menus can be nested, nesting them should be used sparingly as too much nesting may decrease usability.

2
Going Beyond the Single Component with Lists and Scroll Views

In this chapter, we'll learn how to display lists in SwiftUI. `List` views are similar to `UITableViews` in UIKit but are significantly simpler to use. No storyboards or prototype cells are required, and we do not need to know how many rows there are. SwiftUI's lists are designed to be modular so that you can build bigger things from smaller components.

We'll also look at lazy stacks and lazy grids, which are used to optimize the display of large amounts of data by loading only the subset of the content that is currently being displayed or is about to be displayed. Lastly, we'll take a look at how to present hierarchical data in an expanding list with sections that can be expanded or collapsed.

By the end of this chapter, you will understand how to display lists of static or dynamic items, add or remove rows from lists, edit lists, add sections to list views, and much more.

In this chapter, we will cover the following recipes:

- Using scroll views
- Creating a list of static items
- Using custom rows in a list
- Adding rows to a list
- Deleting rows from a list
- Editing a list
- Moving rows in a list
- Adding sections to a list
- Using `LazyHStack` and `LazyVStack` (iOS 14+)
- Using `LazyHGrid` and `LazyVGrid` (iOS 14+)
- Using `ScrollViewReader` (iOS 14+)
- Using expanding lists (iOS 14+)
- Using `DisclosureGroup` to hide and show content (iOS 14+)

Technical requirements

The code in this chapter is based on Xcode 12 and iOS 13. However, some recipes are only compatible with iOS 14 and higher.

You can find the code in the book's GitHub repository at `https://github.com/PacktPublishing/SwiftUI-Cookbook/tree/master/Chapter02%20-%20Lists%20and%20ScrollViews`.

Using scroll views

SwiftUI scroll views are used to easily create scrolling containers. They automatically size themselves to the area where they are placed. Scroll views are vertical by default and can be made to scroll horizontally or vertically by passing in the `.horizontal()` or `.vertical()` modifiers as the first parameter to the scroll view.

Getting ready

Let's start by creating a SwiftUI project called `ScrollViewApp`.

Optional: Download the **San Francisco (SF) Symbols** app here: `https://developer.apple.com/sf-symbols/`.

SF Symbols is a set of over 2,400 symbols provided by Apple. They follow Apple's San Francisco system font and automatically ensure optical vertical alignment for different sizes and weights.

How to do it...

We will add two scroll views to a `VStack` component: one horizontal and one vertical. Each scroll view will contain SF symbols for the letters A–L:

1. Between the `ContentView` struct declaration and its body, create an array of SF symbol names called `imageNames`. Add the strings for SF symbols A–L:

```
let imageNames = [
        "a.circle.fill",
        "b.circle.fill",
        "c.circle.fill",
        "d.circle.fill",
        "e.circle.fill",
        "f.circle.fill",
        "g.circle.fill",
        "h.circle.fill",
        "i.circle.fill",
        "j.circle.fill",
        "k.circle.fill",
        "l.circle.fill",
    ]
```

2. Add a `VStack` component and scroll views to the app:

```
var body: some View {
    VStack{
        ScrollView {
            ForEach(self.imageNames, id: \.self)
            { name in
                Image(systemName: name)
                    .font(.largeTitle)
                    .foregroundColor(Color.
                        yellow)
                    .frame(width: 50, height: 50)
                    .background(Color.blue)
            }
        }
        .frame(width:50, height:200)

        ScrollView(.horizontal, showsIndicators:
            false) {
            HStack{
                ForEach(self.imageNames, id: \.self)
                { name in
                    Image(systemName: name)
                        .font(.largeTitle)
                        .foregroundColor(Color.
                            yellow)
                        .frame(width: 50, height: 50)
                        .background(Color.blue)
                }
            }
        }
    }
}
```

The result is a view with a vertical and horizontal scroll view:

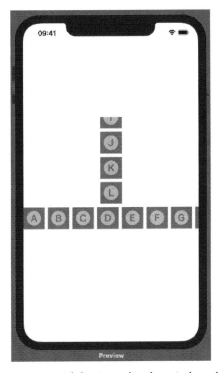

Figure 2.1 – App with horizontal and vertical scroll views

How it works...

VStack allows us to display multiple scroll views within the ContentView struct's body.

By default, scroll views display items vertically. The first ScrollView component in VStack displays items in a vertical way, even though no axis was specified.

Within the first ScrollView component, a ForEach loop is used to iterate over a static array and display the contents. In this case, the ForEach loop takes two parameters: the array we are iterating over and an identifier, id: \.self, used to distinguish between the items being displayed. The id parameter would not be required if the collection used conformed to the Identifiable protocol.

Two parameters are passed to the second ScrollView component: the axis and showIndicators (ScrollView(.horizontal, showsIndicators: false). The .horizontal axis parameter causes content to be horizontal, and showIndictors:false prevents the scrollbar indicator from appearing in the view.

See also

Refer to the Apple `ScrollView` documentation at `https://developer.apple.com/documentation/swiftui/scrollview`.

Creating a list of static items

Lists are similar to scroll views in that they are used to view a collection of items. Lists are used for larger datasets, whereas scroll views are used for smaller datasets; the reason being that list views do not load the whole dataset in memory at once and thus are more efficient at handling large data.

Getting ready

Let's start by creating a new SwiftUI app called `StaticList`.

How to do it...

We'll create a struct to hold weather information and an array of weather data. The data will then be used to create a view that provides weather information from several cities. Proceed as follows:

1. Before the `ContentView` struct, create a struct called `WeatherInfo` with four properties: `id`, `image`, `temp`, and `city`:

```
struct WeatherInfo: Identifiable {
    var id = UUID()
    var image: String
    var temp: Int
    var city: String
}
```

2. Within the `ContentView` struct, create a `weatherData` property as an array of `WeatherInfo`:

```
let weatherData: [WeatherInfo] = [
WeatherInfo(image: "snow", temp: 5, city:"New York"),
WeatherInfo(image: "cloud", temp:5, city:"Kansas
    City"),
WeatherInfo(image: "sun.max", temp: 80, city:"San
    Francisco"),
```

```
        WeatherInfo(image: "snow", temp: 5, city:"Chicago"),
        WeatherInfo(image: "cloud.rain", temp: 49,
          city:"Washington DC"),
        WeatherInfo(image: "cloud.heavyrain", temp: 60,
          city:"Seattle"),
        WeatherInfo(image: "sun.min", temp: 75,
          city:"Baltimore"),
        WeatherInfo(image: "sun.dust", temp: 65,
          city:"Austin"),
        WeatherInfo(image: "sunset", temp: 78,
          city:"Houston"),
        WeatherInfo(image: "moon", temp: 80, city:"Boston"),
        WeatherInfo(image: "moon.circle", temp: 45,
          city:"denver"),
        WeatherInfo(image: "cloud.snow", temp: 8,
          city:"Philadelphia"),
        WeatherInfo(image: "cloud.hail", temp: 5,
          city:"Memphis"),
        WeatherInfo(image: "cloud.sleet", temp:5,
          city:"Nashville"),
        WeatherInfo(image: "sun.max", temp: 80,
          city:"San Francisco"),
        WeatherInfo(image: "cloud.sun", temp: 5,
          city:"Atlanta"),
        WeatherInfo(image: "wind", temp: 88,
          city:"Las Vegas"),
        WeatherInfo(image: "cloud.rain", temp: 60,
          city:"Phoenix"),
    ]
```

3. Add the `List` view to the `ContentView` body. The list should display the information contained in our `weatherData` array. Also add the `font(size: 25)` and `padding()` modifiers:

```
List {
        ForEach(self.weatherData){ weather in
            HStack {
                Image(systemName: weather.image)
                    .frame(width: 50, alignment:
                                .leading)
```

```
              Text("\(weather.temp)°F")
                .frame(width: 80, alignment:
                          .leading)
              Text(weather.city)
          }
        .font(.system(size: 25))
      .padding()
    }
  }
```

The resulting preview should be as follows:

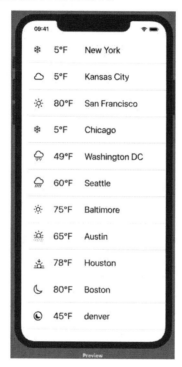

Figure 2.2 – List in the weather app

How it works...

We started the recipe by creating a `WeatherInfo` struct to hold and model our weather data. The `id = UUID()` property creates a unique identifier for each variable we create from the struct. Adding the `id` property to our struct allows us to later use it within a `ForEach` loop without providing `id: .\self` parameter as seen in the previous recipe.

The ForEach loop within the List view iterates through the items in our model data and copies one item at a time to the weather variable declared on the same line.

The ForEach loop contains HStack because we would like to display multiple items on the same line – in this case, all the information contained in the weather variable.

The font(.system(size: 25)) and padding() modifiers add some padding to the list rows to improve the design and readability of the information.

The images displayed are based on SF Symbols, explained in *Chapter 1, Using the Basic SwiftUI Views and Controls.*

Using custom rows in a list

The number of lines of code required to display items in a list view row could vary from one to several lines of code. A custom list row is used when working with several lines of code within a list view row. Implementing custom lists improves modularity and readability, and allows code reuse.

Getting ready

Let's start by creating a new SwiftUI app called CustomRows.

How to do it...

We will reuse part of the code in the static list and clean it up to make it more modular. We create a separate file to hold the WeatherInfo struct, a separate SwiftUI file for the custom WeatherRow, and finally, we implement the components in the ContentView. swift file. The steps are as follows:

1. Create a new Swift file called WeatherInfo by selecting **File | New | File | Swift File** or by pressing the ⌘ + *N* keys.

2. Define the WeatherInfo struct within the WeatherInfo.swift file:

```
struct WeatherInfo: Identifiable {
    var id = UUID()
    var image: String
    var temp: Int
    var city: String
}
```

3. Create a `weatherData` variable that holds an array of `WeatherInfo`:

```
let weatherData: [WeatherInfo] = [
    WeatherInfo(image: "snow", temp: 5,
        city:"New York"),
    WeatherInfo(image: "cloud", temp:5,
        city:"Kansas City"),
    WeatherInfo(image: "sun.max", temp: 80,
        city:"San Francisco"),
    WeatherInfo(image: "snow", temp: 5, city:"Chicago"),
    WeatherInfo(image: "cloud.rain", temp: 49,
        city:"Washington DC"),
    WeatherInfo(image: "cloud.heavyrain", temp: 60,
        city:"Seattle"),
    WeatherInfo(image: "sun.min", temp: 75,
        city:"Baltimore"),
    WeatherInfo(image: "sun.dust", temp: 65,
        city:"Austin"),
    WeatherInfo(image: "sunset", temp: 78,
        city:"Houston"),
    WeatherInfo(image: "moon", temp: 80, city:"Boston"),
    WeatherInfo(image: "moon.circle", temp: 45,
        city:"denver"),
    WeatherInfo(image: "cloud.snow", temp: 8,
        city:"Philadelphia"),
    WeatherInfo(image: "cloud.hail", temp: 5,
        city:"Memphis"),
    WeatherInfo(image: "cloud.sleet", temp:5,
        city:"Nashville"),
    WeatherInfo(image: "sun.max", temp: 80,
        city:"San Francisco"),
    WeatherInfo(image: "cloud.sun", temp: 5,
        city:"Atlanta"),
    WeatherInfo(image: "wind", temp: 88,
        city:"Las Vegas"),
    WeatherInfo(image: "cloud.rain", temp: 60,
        city:"Phoenix"),
    ]
```

4. Create a new SwiftUI file by selecting **File | New | File | SwiftUI View** or by pressing the ⌘ + *N* keys.

5. Name the file `WeatherRow`.

6. Add the following code to design the look and functionality of the weather row:

```
struct WeatherRow: View {
    var weather: WeatherInfo
    var body: some View {
        HStack {
            Image(systemName: weather.image)
                .frame(width: 50, alignment: .leading)
            Text("\(weather.temp)°F")
                .frame(width: 80, alignment: .leading)
            Text(weather.city)
        }
        .font(.system(size: 25))
        .padding()
    }
}
```

7. Add the following code to the `WeatherRow_Previews` struct to display information from a sample `WeatherInfo` struct instance:

```
static var previews: some View {
        WeatherRow(weather: WeatherInfo(image: "snow",
            temp: 5, city:"New York"))
    }
```

8. The resulting `WeatherRow.swift` canvas preview should look as follows:

Figure 2.3 – WeatherRow preview

9. Open the `ContentView.swift` file and create a list to display data using the custom `WeatherRow` component:

```
var body: some View {
        List {
            ForEach(weatherData) { weather in
                WeatherRow(weather: weather)
            }
        }
}
```

The resulting canvas preview should look as follows:

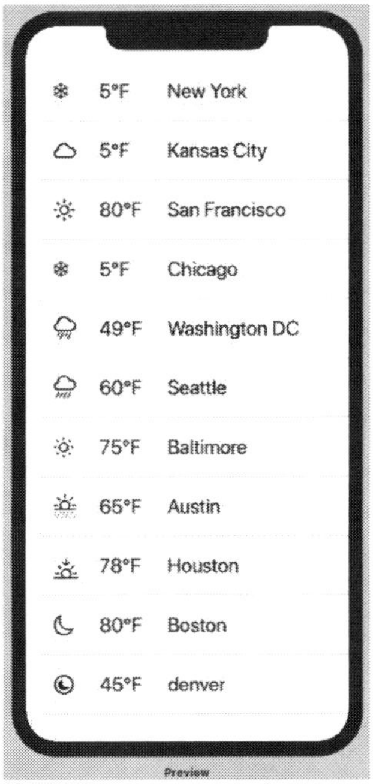

Figure 2.4 – CustomRowApp preview

Run the app live preview and admire the work of your own hands.

How it works...

The WeatherInfo Swift file contains the description of the WeatherInfo struct. Our dataset, an array of WeatherInfo variables, was also declared in the file to make it available to other sections of the project.

The WeatherRow SwiftUI file contains the design we will use for each weather row. The weather property within WeatherRow will hold the WeatherInfo arguments passed to the view. HStack in the body of WeatherRow is used to display data from weather variables since a SwiftUI view can only return one view at a time. When displaying multiple views – an image view and two text views, in this case – the views are all encased in an HStack component. The .frame(width: 50, alignment: .leading) modifier added to the image and first text view sets the width used by the element it modifies to 50 units and the alignment to the .leading parameter.

Finally, the `.font(.system(size: 25))` and `.padding()` modifiers are added to `HStack` to increase the text and image font sizes and add padding to all sides of `WeatherRow`.

Adding rows to a list

Lists are usually used to add, edit, remove, or display content from an existing dataset. In this section, we will go over the process of adding items to an already existing list.

Getting ready

Let's start by creating a new SwiftUI app called `AddRowsToList`.

How to do it...

To implement the add functionality, we will enclose the `List` view in `NavigationView`, and add a button to `navigationBarItems` that triggers the add function we will create. The steps are as follows:

1. Create a state variable in the `ContentView` struct that holds an array of integers:

   ```
   @State var numbers = [1,2,3,4]
   ```

2. Add a `NavigationView` component containing a `List` view to the `ContentView` body:

   ```
   NavigationView{
           List{
                   ForEach(self.numbers, id:\.self){
                   number in
                           Text("\(number)")
                   }
           }
   }
   ```

3. Add a `navigationBarItems` modifier to the list closing brace that contains a button that triggers the `addItemToRow()` function:

   ```
   .navigationBarItems(trailing: Button(action: {
                           self.addItemToRow()
                   }){
   ```

```
                              Text("Add")
                    })
```

4. Implement the `addItemToRow()` function, which appends a random integer to the numbers array. Place the function within the `ContentView` struct, immediately after the body variable's closing brace:

```
private func addItemToRow() {
        self.numbers.append(Int.random(in: 0 ..< 100))
    }
```

5. For the beauty and aesthetics, add a `navigationBarTitle` modifier to the end of the list so as to make it display a title at the top of the list:

```
.navigationBarTitle("Number List", displayMode: .inline)
```

6. The resulting code should be as follows:

```
struct ContentView: View {
    @State var numbers = [1,2,3,4]
    var body: some View {
        NavigationView{
            List{
                ForEach(self.numbers, id:\.self){
                    number in
                    Text("\(number)")
                }
            }.navigationBarTitle("Number List",
                displayMode: .inline)
                .navigationBarItems(trailing:
                    Button("Add", action: addItemToRow))
        }
    }
    private func addItemToRow() {
        self.numbers.append(Int.random(in: 0 ..< 100))
    }
}
```

The resulting preview should be as follows:

Figure 2.5 – AddRowToList preview

Run the app live preview and admire the work of your own hands!

How it works...

The array of numbers is declared as a `@State` variable because we want the view to be refreshed each time the value of the items in the array changes – in this case, each time we add an item to the numbers array.

The `.navigationBarTitle("Number List", displayMode: .inline)` modifier adds a title to the list using the `.inline display` mode parameter.

The .navigationBarItems(trailing: Button(...)...) modifier adds a button to the trailing end of the display, which triggers the addItemToRow function when clicked.

The addItemToRow function generates a random number in the range 0–99 and appends it to the numbers array.

Deleting rows from a list

In this section, we will display a list of countries and use a swipe motion to delete items from the list one at a time.

Getting ready

Let's start by creating a SwiftUI app called DeleteRowFromList.

How to do it...

We use the List view's .onDelete(perform: ...) modifier to implement list deletion. The process is as follows:

1. Add a state variable to the ContentView struct called countries. The variable should contain an array of countries:

```
@State var countries = ["USA", "Canada",
    "England","Cameroon", "South Africa", "Mexico" ,
    "Japan", "South Korea"]
```

2. Create a List view in the ContentView body that uses a ForEach loop to display the contents of the countries array:

```
List {
    ForEach(countries, id: \.self) { country in
        Text(country)
    }
}
```

3. Add a .onDelete(perform: self.deleteItem) modifier to the ForEach loop.

4. Implement the `deleteItem()` function. The function should be placed below the body variable's closing brace:

```
private func deleteItem(at indexSet: IndexSet){
    self.countries.remove(atOffsets: indexSet)
}
```

5. Optionally, enclose the `List` view in a navigation view and add a `.navigationBarTitle("Countries", displayMode: .inline)` modifier to the list. The resulting `ContentView` struct should be as follows:

```
struct ContentView: View {
    @State var countries = ["USA", "Canada",
        "England","Cameroon", "South Africa", "Mexico" ,
        "Japan", "South Korea"]
    var body: some View {
        NavigationView{
            List {
                ForEach(countries, id: \.self) {
                    country in
                    Text(country)
                }
                .onDelete(perform: self.deleteItem)
            }
            .navigationBarTitle("Countries",
                displayMode: .inline)
        }
    }
    private func deleteItem(at indexSet: IndexSet){
        self.countries.remove(atOffsets: indexSet)
    }
}
```

Run the canvas review by clicking the play button next to the canvas preview. A swipe from right to left on a row causes a **Delete** button to appear. Click on the button to delete the row:

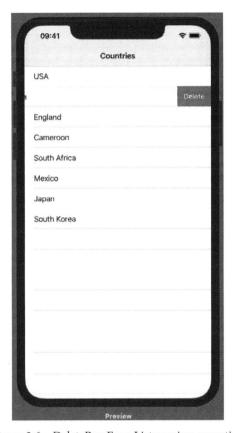

Figure 2.6 – DeleteRowFromList preview execution

Run the app live preview and admire the work of your own hands!

How it works...

Navigation views and list views were discussed earlier. Only the `.onDelete(...)` modifier is new. The `.onDelete(perform: self.deleteItem)` modifier triggers the `deleteItem()` function when the user swipes from right to left.

The `deleteItem(at indexSet: IndexSet)` function takes a single parameter, `IndexSet`, which represents the index of the row to be removed/deleted. The `.onDelete()` modifier automatically knows to pass the `IndexSet` parameter to `deleteItem(...)`.

There's more...

Deleting an item from a list view can also be performed by embedding the list in a navigation view and adding an `EditButton` component.

Editing a list

Implementing the `EditButton` component in a list is very similar to implementing the delete button in the previous recipe. An edit button offers the user the option to quickly delete items by clicking a minus sign to the left of each list row.

Getting ready

Let's start by creating a SwiftUI app called `EditListApp`.

How to do it...

We will reuse some of the code from the previous recipe to complete this project. Take the following steps:

1. Replace the `EditListApp` app's `ContentView` struct with the following content from the `DeleteRowFromList` app:

```
struct ContentView: View {
    @State var countries = ["USA", "Canada",
     "England","Cameroon", "South Africa", "Mexico" ,
     "Japan", "South Korea"]
    var body: some View {
        NavigationView{
            List {
                ForEach(countries, id: \.self) {
                    country in
                    Text(country)
                }
                .onDelete(perform: self.deleteItem)
            }
            .navigationBarTitle("Countries",
                displayMode: .inline)
        }
    }
    private func deleteItem(at indexSet: IndexSet){
```

```
        self.countries.remove(atOffsets: indexSet)
    }
}
```

2. Add a `.navigationBarItems(trailing: EditButton())` modifier to the `List` view, just below the `.navigationBarTitle("Countries", displayMode:.inline)` modifier.

    Run the preview and click the **Edit** button at the top-right corner of the screen. Minus (-) signs enclosed in red circles appear to the left of each row:

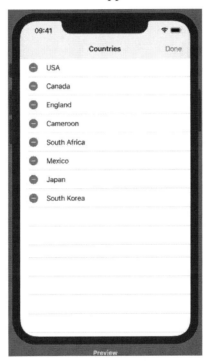

Figure 2.7 – EditListApp preview execution

Run the app live preview and admire the work of your own hands!

How it works...

The `.navigationBarItems(trailing: EditButton())` modifier adds an edit button to the right corner of the display that, once clicked, creates the view shown in the preceding screenshot. A click on the delete button executes the `.onDelete(perform: self.deleteItem)` modifier. The modifier then executes the `deleteItem` function, which removes/deletes the selected row.

There's more...

To move the edit button to the right of the navigation bar, change the modifier to `.navigationBarItems(leading: EditButton())`.

Moving rows in a list

In this section, we will create an app that implements a list view and allows the user to move/reorganize rows.

Getting ready

Let's start by creating a new SwiftUI app in Xcode called `MovingListRows`.

How to do it...

To allow users to move rows, we need to add a `.onMove(..)` modifier to the end of the list view's `ForEach` loop. We also need to embed the list in a navigation view and add a `navigationBarItems` modifier that implements an `EditButton` component. The steps are as follows:

1. Open `ContentView.swift`. Within the `ContentView` struct, add a `@State` variable in `Content` called `countries` that contains an array of countries:

   ```
   @State var countries = ["USA", "Canada",
      "England","Cameroon", "South Africa", "Mexico" ,
      "Japan", "South Korea"]
   ```

2. Replace the `Text` view in the body with a navigation view:

   ```
   NavigationView{
         }
   ```

3. Add a list and a ForEach loop within NavigationView that displays the content of the countries variable:

```
List {
    ForEach(countries, id: \.self) { country in
        Text(country)
    }.onMove(perform: moveRow)
}
```

4. Add a .onMove(...) modifier to the ForEach loop that calls the moveRow function:

```
ForEach(countries, id: \.self) { country in
    Text(country)
}.onMove(perform: moveRow)
```

5. Add the .navigationBarTitle("Countries", displayMode: .inline) and .navigationBarItems(trailing: EditButton()) modifiers to the end of the List view:

```
List {
    .
    .
    .
}
.navigationBarTitle("Countries",
    isplayMode: .inline)
.navigationBarItems(trailing: EditButton())
```

6. Implement the moveRow function at the end of the body variable's closing brace:

```
private func moveRow(source: IndexSet, destination: Int){
    countries.move(fromOffsets: source, toOffset:
        destination)
}
```

7.   The completed `ContentView` struct should be as follows:

```
struct ContentView: View {
    @State var countries = ["USA", "Canada",
        "England","Cameroon", "South Africa", "Mexico" ,
        "Japan", "South Korea"]
    var body: some View {
        NavigationView{
            List {
                ForEach(countries, id: \.self) {
                    country in
                    Text(country)
                }
                .onMove(perform: moveRow)
            }
            .navigationBarTitle("Countries",
                displayMode: .inline)
            .navigationBarItems(trailing: EditButton())
        }
    }
    private func moveRow(source: IndexSet,
        destination: Int){
        countries.move(fromOffsets: source,
            toOffset: destination)
    }
}
```

Run the application in the canvas, on a simulator, or on a physical device. A click on the **Edit** button at the top-right corner of the screen displays a hamburger symbol to the right of each row. Click and drag the symbol to move the row on which the country is displayed:

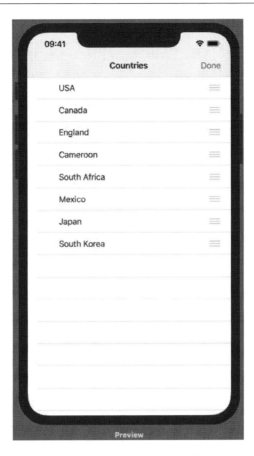

Figure 2.8 – MovingListRows preview when running

Run the app live preview and move the rows up or down. Nice work!

How it works...

To move list rows, you need to add the list to a navigation view, add the `.onMove(perform:)` modifier to the `ForEach` loop, and add a `.navigationBarItems(trailing: EditButton())` modifier to the list.

The `moveRow(source: IndexSet, destination: Int)` function takes two parameters: the source, an `IndexSet` argument representing the current index of the item to be moved, and the destination, an integer representing the destination of the row. The `.onMove(perform:)` modifier automatically passes those arguments to the function.

Adding sections to a list

In this section, we will create an app that implements a static list with sections. The app will display a partial list of countries grouped by continent.

Getting ready

Let's start by creating a new SwiftUI app in Xcode and name it `ListWithSections`.

How to do it...

We will add section views to our list view. We will then add a few countries to each of the sections. Proceed as follows:

1. (Optional) open the `ContentView.swift` file and replace the `Text` view in the body with a navigation view. Wrapping the list in a navigation view allows you to add a title and navigation items to the view:

```
NavigationView {
}
```

2. Add a list and section to the navigation view:

```
List {
    Section(header: Text("North America")){
        Text("USA")
        Text("Canada")
        Text("Mexico")
        Text("Panama")
        Text("Anguilla")
    }
}
```

3. Add a `listStyle(..)` modifier to the end of the list to change its style from the default plain style to `GroupedListStyle()`:

```
List {
    .
    .
    .
}
```

```
.listStyle(GroupedListStyle())
.navigationBarTitle("Continents and Countries",
   displayMode: .inline)
```

4. (Optional) add a `navigationBarTitle(..)` modifier to the list, just below the list style. Add this section if you included the navigation view in *step 1*.

5. Add more sections representing various continents to the navigation view. The resulting `ContentView` struct should look as follows:

```
struct ContentView: View {
   var body: some View {
      NavigationView{
         List {
            Section(header: Text("North America")){
               Text("USA")
               Text("Canada")
               Text("Mexico")
               Text("Panama")
               Text("Anguilla")
            }
            Section(header: Text("Africa")){
               Text("Nigeria")
               Text("Ghana")
               Text("Kenya")
               Text("Senegal")
            }
            Section(header: Text("Europe")){
               Text("Spain")
               Text("France")
               Text("Sweden")
               Text("Finland")
               Text("UK")
            }
         }
         .listStyle(GroupedListStyle())
         .navigationBarTitle("Continents and
            Countries", displayMode: .inline)
```

```
            }
        }
    }
```

The canvas preview should now show a list with sections, as follows:

Figure 2.9 – ListWithSections preview

Good work! Now, run the app live preview and admire the work of your own hands.

How it works...

SwiftUI's sections are used to separate items into groups. In this recipe, we used sections to visually group countries into different continents. Sections can be used with a header, as follows:

```
Section(header: Text("Europe")){
            Text("Spain")
            Text("France")
```

```
                    Text("Sweden")
                    Text("Finland")
                    Text("UK")
        }
```

They can also be used without a header:

```
Section {
                Text("USA")
                Text("Canada")
                Text("Mexico")
                Text("Panama")
                Text("Anguilla")
        }
```

When using a section embedded in a list, we can add a `.listStyle()` modifier to change the styling of the whole list.

Using LazyHStack and LazyVStack (iOS 14+)

SwiftUI 2.0 introduced the `LazyHStack` and `LazyVStack` components. These components are used in a similar way to regular `HStack` and `VStack` components but offer the advantage of lazy loading. Lazy components are loaded just before the item becomes visible on the device's screen during a device scroll, therefore reducing latency.

We will create an app that uses `LazyHStack` and `LazyVStack` and observe how it works.

Getting ready

Let's create a new SwiftUI app called `LazyStacks`:

1. Open Xcode and click **Create New Project**.

2. In the **Choose** template window, select **iOS** and then **App**.

3. Click **Next**.

4. Enter `LazyStacks` in the **Product Name** field and select **SwiftUI App** from the **Life Cycle** field.

5. Click **Next** and select a location on your computer where the project should be stored.

How to do it...

We will implement a `LazyHStack` and `LazyVStack` view within a single SwiftUI view file by embedding both in a `VStack` component. The steps are as follows:

1. Click on the `ContentView.swift` file to view its content in Xcode's editor pane.

2. Let's create a `ListRow` SwiftUI view that will have two properties: an ID and a type. `ListRow` should also print a statement showing what item is currently being initialized:

```swift
struct ListRow: View {
    let id: Int
    let type: String
    init(id: Int, type: String) {
        print("Loading \(type) item \(id)")
        self.id = id
        self.type = type
    }
    var body: some View {
        Text("\(type) \(id)").padding()
    }
}
```

3. Replace the initial `Text` view with `VStack`:

```swift
VStack {
}
```

4. Add a horizontal scroll view inside the `VStack` component and use a `.frame()` modifier to limit the view's height:

```swift
ScrollView(.horizontal){
}.frame(height: 100, alignment: .center)
```

5. Add `LazyHStack` inside the scroll view with a `ForEach` view that iterates through the numbers `1-10000` and displays them using our `ListRow` view:

```swift
LazyHStack {
    ForEach(1...10000, id:\.self){ item in
        ListRow(id: item, type: "Horizontal")
```

```
                    }
                  }
```

6. Add a second vertical scroll view to `VStack` with a `LazyVStack` struct that loops through numbers `1-10000`:

```
ScrollView {
  LazyVStack {
    ForEach(1...10000, id:\.self){ item in
      ListRow(id: item, type: "Vertical")
        }
      }
    }
```

7. Now, let's observe lazy loading in action. If the Xcode debug area is not visible, click on **View | Debug Area | Show Debug Area**:

Figure 2.10 – Show Debug Area

8. Select a simulator to use for running the app. The app should look as follows:

Figure 2.11 – Selecting the simulator from Xcode

9.   Click the play button to run the code in the simulator:

Figure 2.12 – The LazyStacks app running on the simulator

10. Scroll through the items in `LazyHStack` (located at the top). Observe how the `print` statements appear in the debug area just before an item is displayed on the screen. Each item is initialized just before it is displayed.

11. Scroll through the items in `LazyVStack`. Observe how the `print` statements appear in the debug area just before an item is displayed.

How it works...

We started this recipe by creating the `ListRow` view because we wanted to clearly demonstrate the advantage of lazy loading over the regular method where all items get loaded at once. The `ListRow` view has two properties: an ID and a string. We add a `print` statement to the `init()` function so that we can observe when each item gets initialized:

```
init(id: Int, type: String){
    print("Loading \(type) item \(id)")
    self.id = id
    self.type = type
}
```

The `ListRow` view body presents a `Text` view with the `ID` and `type` parameters passed to it.

Moving up to the `ContentView` struct, we replace the initial `Text` view in the body variable with a `VStack` component. This allows us to implement both `LazyHStack` and `LazyVStack` within the same SwiftUI view.

We implement `LazyHStack` by first wrapping it in a scroll view, then using a `ForEach` struct to iterate over the range of values we want to display. For each of those values, a new `ListRow` view is initialized just before it becomes visible when the user scrolls down:

```
ScrollView {
  LazyVStack {
    ForEach(1...10000, id:\.self){ item in
      ListRow(id: item, type: "Vertical")
            }
        }
    }
```

Run the app using a device emulator to view the `print` statements before each item is initialized. Nothing will be printed if the app is run in live preview mode on Xcode.

There's more...

Try implementing the preceding app using a regular `HStack` or `VStack` component and observe the performance difference. The app will be significantly slower since all the rows are initialized at once.

Using LazyHGrid and LazyVGrid (iOS 14+)

Just like lazy stacks, lazy grids use lazy loading to display content on the screen. They initialize only the subset of the items that would soon be displayed on the screen as the user scrolls. SwiftUI 2 introduced the `LazyVGrid` and `LazyHGrid` views. Let's implement a lazy grid that displays some text in this recipe.

Getting ready

Create a new SwiftUI iOS project and name it `UsingLazyGrids`.

How to do it...

We'll implement a `LazyVGrid` and `LazyHGrid` view inside a `Stack` view so as to observe both views in action on a single page. The steps are as follows:

1. Above the `ContentView` struct's body variable, let's create an array of `GridItem` columns. The `GridItem` struct is used to configure the layout of `LazyVGrid`:

    ```
    let columns = [
        GridItem(.adaptive(minimum: 100))
    ]
    ```

2. Create an array of `GridItem` rows that define the layout that would be used in `LazyHGrid`:

    ```
    let rows = [
        GridItem(.flexible()),
        GridItem(.flexible()),
        GridItem(.flexible())
    ]
    ```

3. Create an array of colors. This will be used for styling some items in our view:

    ```
    let colors: [Color] = [.green, .red, .yellow, .blue]
    ```

4. Replace the initial `Text` view in the body view with a `VStack` component and a scroll view.

5. Within the scroll view, add a `LazyVGrid` view and a `ForEach` struct that iterates over the numbers `1-999` and displays the number in a `Text` view:

    ```
    VStack {
        ScrollView {
            LazyVGrid(columns: columns, spacing:20) {
                ForEach(1...999, id:\.self) { index in
                Text("Item \(index)")
                }
            }
    ```

```
        }
    }
```

6. The resulting view displays the numbers in a grid, but the content looks very bland. Let's add some zest by styling the text.

7. Add a `padding()` modifier, a background modifier that uses the value of the current index to pick a color from our color array, and the `clipshape()` modifier to give each `Text` view a capsule shape:

```
...
ForEach(1...999, id:\.self){ index in
        Text("Item \(index)")
            .padding(EdgeInsets(top: 30, leading: 15,
                bottom: 30, trailing: 15))
            .background(colors[index % colors.count])
            .clipShape(Capsule())
        }
...
```

8. Now, let's add a scroll view and `LazyHStack`. You will notice that everything else is the same as the `LazyVGrid` view except for the `column` parameter that's changed to a `row` parameter:

```
VStack {
    ...
        ScrollView(.horizontal) {
            LazyHGrid(rows: rows, spacing:20) {
            ForEach(1...999, id:\.self){ index in
            Text("Item \(index)")
                .foregroundColor(.white)
                .padding(EdgeInsets(top: 30, leading:
                    15, bottom: 30, trailing: 15))
                .background(colors[index % colors.
                    count])
                .clipShape(Capsule())
            }
        }
    }
}
```

The resulting preview should look as follows:

Figure 2.13 – The UsingLazyStacks app

Run the app in the preview and vertically scroll through LazyVGrid and horizontally scroll through LazyHGrid. Observe how smoothly the scrolling occurs despite the fact that our data source contains close to 2,000 elements. Scrolling stays responsive because all our content is lazily loaded.

How it works...

One of the fundamental concepts of using lazy grids involves understanding how to define the `LazyVGrid` columns or the `LazyHGrid` rows. The `LazyVGrid` column variable was defined as an array containing a single `GridItem` component but causes three rows to be displayed. `GridItem(.adaptive(minimum: 80))` tells SwiftUI to use at least 80 units of width for each item and place as many items as it can along the same row. Thus, the number of items displayed on a row may increase when the device is changed from portrait to landscape orientation, and vice versa.

`GridItem(.flexible())`, on the other hand, fills up each row as much as possible:

```
let rows = [
        GridItem(.flexible()),
        GridItem(.flexible()),
        GridItem(.flexible())
    ]
```

Adding three `GridItem(.flexible())` components divides the available space into three equal rows for data display. Remove or add more `GridItem(.flexible())` components to the row array and observe how the number of rows decreases or increases.

We provide two parameters to our lazy grids: a `columns/rows` parameter that specifies the layout of the grid and a `spacing` parameter that defines the spacing between the grid and the next item in the parent view.

Using ScrollViewReader (iOS 14+)

`ScrollViewReader` can be used to programmatically scroll to a different section of a list that might not be currently visible. In this recipe, we will create an app that displays a list of characters from A to L. The app will also have a button at the top for programmatically scrolling to the last element in the list and a button at the bottom for programmatically scrolling to an element in the middle of the list.

Getting ready

Create a new SwiftUI app using the **UIKit App Delegate** life cycle:

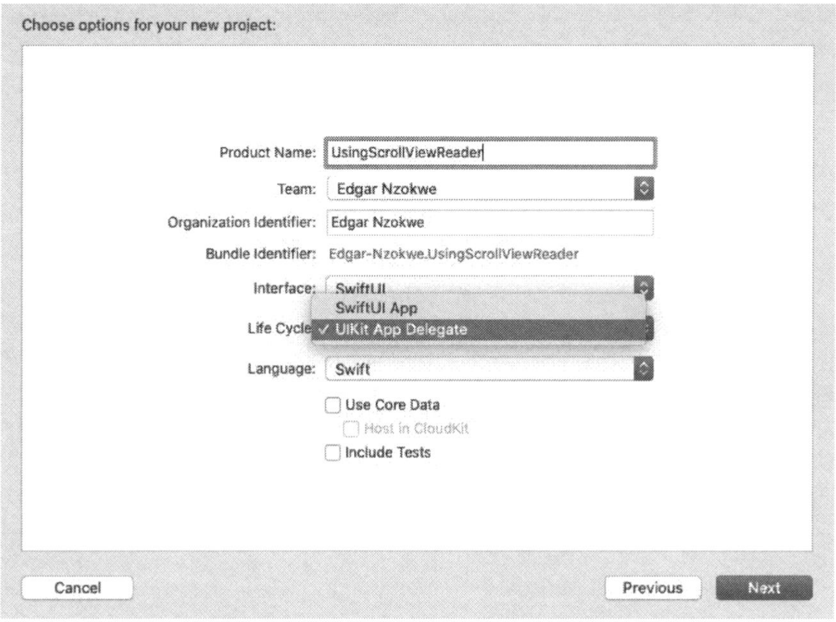

Figure 2.14 – UIKit App Delegate in Xcode

Name the app `UsingScrollViewReader`.

How to do it...

We will start by creating an array of structs with a name and an ID. The array will be used to display SF symbols for the characters A–L. We will then proceed to implement `ScrollViewReader` and programmatically move to the top or the bottom of the list.

The steps are as follows:

1. Create a struct called `ImageStore`, just above the `ContentView_Previews` struct. The struct should implement the `Identifiable` protocol:

```
struct ImageStore: Identifiable {
    var name: String
    var id: Int
}
```

2. Within the `ContentView` struct, just before the body variable, declare an array called `imageNames`. Initialize the array with `ImageStore` structs whose name parameters represent the letters A–Q from SF Symbols:

```
let imageNames = [
    ImageStore(name:"a.circle.fill",id:0),
    ImageStore(name:"b.circle.fill",id:1),
    ImageStore(name:"c.circle.fill",id:2),
    ImageStore(name:"d.circle.fill",id:3),
    ImageStore(name:"e.circle.fill",id:4),
    ImageStore(name:"f.circle.fill",id:5),
    ImageStore(name:"g.circle.fill",id:6),
    ImageStore(name:"h.circle.fill",id:7),
    ImageStore(name:"i.circle.fill",id:8),
    ImageStore(name:"j.circle.fill",id:9),
    ImageStore(name:"k.circle.fill",id:10),
    ImageStore(name:"l.circle.fill",id:11),
    ImageStore(name:"m.circle.fill",id:12),
    ImageStore(name:"n.circle.fill",id:13),
    ImageStore(name:"o.circle.fill",id:14),
    ImageStore(name:"p.circle.fill",id:15),
    ImageStore(name:"q.circle.fill",id:16),
]
```

3. Replace the `TextView` component in the body variable with a `ScrollView` component, `ScrollViewReader`, and a `Button` component to navigate to the letter Q in the list:

```
ScrollView {
    ScrollViewReader { value in
    Button("Go to letter Q") {
    value.scrollTo(16)
        }
    }
    }
```

4. Now use a `ForEach` struct to iterate over the `imageNames` array and display its content using the SwiftUI's `Image` struct:

```
ForEach(imageNames){ image in
    Image(systemName: image.name)
        .id(image.id)
        .font(.largeTitle)
        .foregroundColor(Color.yellow)
        .frame(width: 90, height: 90)
        .background(Color.blue)
        .padding()
}
```

5. Now, add another button at the bottom that causes the list to scroll back to the top:

```
Button("Go back to A") {
        value.scrollTo(0)
}
```

6. The app should be able to run now, but let's add some padding and background to the bottom and top buttons to improve their appearance:

```
Button("Go to letter Q") {
        value.scrollTo(0)
    }
    .padding()
    .background(Color.yellow)
    Button("Go to G") {
        value.scrollTo(6, anchor: .bottom)
    }
    .padding()
    .background(Color.yellow)
```

The resulting app preview should look as follows:

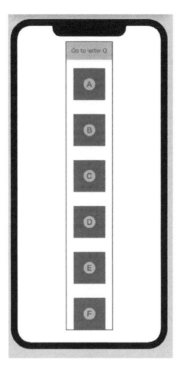

Figure 2.15 – The UsingScrollViewReader app

Run the app in Xcode live preview and tap the button at the top to programmatically scroll down to the letter **Q**.

Scroll to the bottom of the view and tap the button to scroll up to the view where the letter **G** is at the bottom of the visible area.

How it works...

We start this recipe by creating the `ImageStore` struct that defines the properties of each image we want to display:

```
struct ImageStore: Identifiable {
    var name: String
    var id: Int
}
```

The `id` parameter is required for `ScrollViewReader` as a reference for the location to scroll to, just like a house address provides the final destination for driving. By making the struct extend the `Identifiable` protocol, we are able to iterate over the `imageNames` array without specifying an `id` parameter to the `ForEach` struct:

```
ForEach(imageNames){ image in
                Image(systemName: image.name)
        ...
    }
```

`ScrollViewReader` should be embedded inside a scroll view. This provides a `scrollTo()` method that can be used to programmatically scroll to the item whose index is specified in the method:

```
ScrollViewReader { value in
            Button("Go to letter Q") {
                value.scrollTo(16)
        }
        ...
}
```

The `scrollTo()` method also has an `anchor` parameter that is used to specify the position of the item we are scrolling to; for example, `scrollTo(6, anchor: .top)`, in this case, causes the app to scroll until the `ImageStore` item with ID 6 at the bottom of the view.

Using expanding lists (iOS 14+)

Expanding lists can be used to display hierarchical structures within a list. Each list item can be expanded to view its contents. The expanding ability is achieved by creating a struct that holds some information and an optional array of items of the same type as the struct itself. Let's examine how expanding lists work by creating an app that displays the contents of a backpack.

Getting ready

Create a new SwiftUI app and name it `UsingExpandingLists`.

How to do it...

We start by creating the `Backpack` struct that describes the properties of the data we want to display. We'll then create a number of `Backpack` constants and display the hierarchical information using a `List` view containing a `children` property.

The steps are as follows:

1. At the bottom of the `ContentView.swift` file, define a `Backpack` struct that has an `id`, `name`, `icon`, and `content` property. The `content` property's type should be an optional array of `Backpack` structs:

```swift
struct Backpack: Identifiable {
    let id = UUID()
    let name: String
    let icon: String
    var content: [Backpack]?
}
```

2. Below the `Backpack` struct declaration, create three variables: two currency types and an array of currencies:

```swift
let dollar = Backpack(name: "Dollar", icon: "dollarsign.
    circle")
let yen = Backpack(name: "Yen",icon: "yensign.circle")
let currencies = Backpack(name: "Currencies", icon:
    "coloncurrencysign.circle", content: [dollar, yen])
```

3. Create a `pencil`, `hammer`, `paperclip`, and `glass` constant:

```swift
let pencil = Backpack(name: "Pencil",icon: "pencil.
    circle")
let hammer = Backpack(name: "Hammer",icon: "hammer")
let paperClip = Backpack(name: "Paperclip",icon:
    "paperclip")
let glass = Backpack(name: "Magnifying glass",
    icon: "magnifyingglass")
```

4. Create a `bin` Backpack constant that contains `paperclip` and `glass`, as well as a `tool` constant that holds `pencil`, `hammer`, and `bin`:

```
let bin  = Backpack(name: "Bin", icon: "arrow.up.bin",
    content: [paperClip, glass])
```

```
let tools = Backpack(name: "Tools", icon: "folder",
    content: [pencil, hammer,bin])
```

5. Going back to the `ContentView` struct, add an instance property; `items`, which contains an array of two items, the `currencies` and `tools` constants defined earlier:

```
struct ContentView: View {
    let items = [currencies,tools]
    ...
}
```

6. Within the body variable, replace the `Text` view with a `List` view that displays the content of the `items` array:

```
var body: some View {
    List(items, children: \.content){ row in
        Image(systemName: row.icon)
        Text(row.name)
    }
}
```

The resulting Xcode live preview should look as follows when expanded:

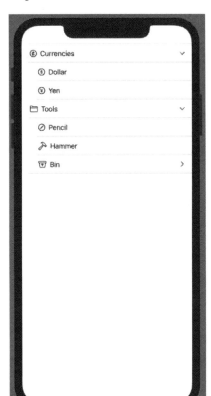

Figure 2.16 – Using expanding lists

Run the Xcode live preview and click on the arrows to expand and collapse the views.

How it works...

We start by creating a struct of the proper format for expanding lists. Expanding lists require one of the struct properties to be an optional array of the same type as the struct itself. Our Backpack content property holds an optional array of Backpack items:

```
struct Backpack: Identifiable {
    let id = UUID()
    let name: String
    let icon: String
    var content: [Backpack]?
}
```

The `UUID()` function generates a random identifier and stores it in the `id` property. We can manually provide the `name`, `icon`, and `content` variables for the items we add to the backpack.

We create our first hierarchical structure by creating the `Dollar` and `Yen` variables:

```
let dollar = Backpack(name: "Dollar", icon: "dollarsign.
    circle")
let yen = Backpack(name: "Yen",icon: "yensign.circle")
```

Observe that no `content` property has been provided for both variables. This is possible because the content is an optional parameter.

We then create a `currencies` constant that that has `name` and `icon`. The `Dollar` and `Yen` variables created earlier are added to its `content` array.

We use a similar composition to add elements to our `tool` constant.

After setting up the data we want to display, we create an `item` property in our `ContentView` struct that holds an array of `Backpack` constants created earlier:

```
let items = [currencies,tools]
```

Finally, we replace the `Text` view in the `ContentView` body with a `List` view that iterates over the items. The list is made expandable by adding the `children` parameter, which expects an array of the same time as the struct passed to the `List` view.

There's more...

The tree structure used for expandable lists can also be generated on a single line, as follows:

```
let tools = Backpack(name: "Tools", icon: "folder", content:
    [Backpack(name: "Pencil",icon: "pencil.circle"),
    Backpack(name: "Hammer",icon: "hammer"),
    Backpack(name: "Bin", icon: "arrow.up.bin", content:
        [Backpack(name: "Paperclip",icon: "paperclip"),
        Backpack(name: "Magnifying glass", icon:
            "magnifyingglass")
            ])
        ])
```

The SwiftUI `List` view provides out-of-the-box support for `OutlineGroup` in iOS 14. `OutlineGroup` computes views and disclosure groups on demand from an underlying collection.

See also

Refer to the WWDC20 video on stacks, grids, and outlines at `https://developer.apple.com/videos/play/wwdc2020/10031/`.

Refer to the Apple documentation on `OutlineGroup` at `https://developer.apple.com/documentation/swiftui/outlinegroup`.

Using disclosure groups to hide and show content (iOS 14+)

`DisclosureGroup` is a view used to show or hide content based on the state of a disclosure control. It takes two parameters: a label to identify its content and a binding to control whether its content is shown or hidden. Let's take a closer look at how it works by creating an app that shows and hides content in a disclosure group.

Getting ready

Create a new SwiftUI project and name it `UsingDisclosureGroup`.

How to do it...

We will create an app the uses `DisclosureGroup` views to reveal some planets in our solar system, continents on the Earth, and some surprise text. The steps are as follows:

1. Below the `ContentView` struct, add a state property called `showplanets`:

    ```
    @State private var showplanets = true
    ```

2. Replace the `Text` view in the body variable with a `DisclosureGroup` view that displays some planets:

    ```
    DisclosureGroup("Planets", isExpanded: $showplanets){
        Text("Mercury")
        Text("Venus")
    }
    ```

3. Review the result in Xcode's live preview, then nest another `DisclosureGroup` view for planet Earth. The group should contain the list of Earth's continents:

```
DisclosureGroup("Planets", isExpanded: $showplanets){
    ...
    DisclosureGroup("Earth"){
        Text("North America")
        Text("South America")
        Text("Europe")
        Text("Africa")
        Text("Asia")
        Text("Antarctica")
        Text("Oceania")
    }
}
```

4. Let's add another `DisclosureGroup` view using a different way of defining them. Since the body variable can't display two views, let's embed our parent `DisclosureGroup` view in a `VStack` component. Hold down the ⌘ key and click on the parent `DisclosureGroup` view and select **Embed in VStack** from the list of actions.

5. Below our parent `DisclosureGroup` view, add another one that reveals surprise text when clicked:

```
VStack {
    DisclosureGroup("Planets", isExpanded: $showplanets){
        Text("Mercury")
        Text("Venus")

        DisclosureGroup("Earth"){
            Text("North America")
            Text("South America")
            Text("Europe")
            Text("Africa")
            Text("Asia")
            Text("Antarctica")
            Text("Oceania")
        }
```

```
        }
    DisclosureGroup{
        Text("Surprise! This is an alternative
                way of using DisclosureGroup")
    } label : {
        Label("Tap to reveal", systemImage: "cube.box")
            .font(.system(size:25, design: .rounded))
            .foregroundColor(.blue)
        }
    }
```

The resulting preview should be as follows:

Figure 2.17 – The UsingDisclosureGroup app

Run the Xcode live preview and click on the arrows to expand and collapse the views.

How it works...

Our initial `DisclosureGroup` view presents a list of planets. By passing in a binding, we are able to read the state change and know whether the `DisclosureGroup` view is in an open or closed state:

```
DisclosureGroup("Planets", isExpanded: $showplanets){
    Text("Mercury")
    Text("Venus")
}
```

We can also use `DisclosureGroup` views without bindings, depending solely on the default UI:

```
DisclosureGroup("Earth"){
    Text("North America")
    Text("South America")
    ...
}
```

Lastly, we used the new Swift 5.3 closure syntax to separate the `Text` and `Label` portions into two separate views. This allows more customization of the `Label` portion:

```
DisclosureGroup{
    Text("Surprise! This is an alternative way of using
        DisclosureGroup")
} label : {
    Label("Tap to reveal", systemImage: "cube.box")
        .font(.system(size:25, design: .rounded))
        .foregroundColor(.blue)
}
```

`DisclosureGroup` views are very versatile as they can be nested and used to display content in a hierarchical way.

3
Viewing while Building with SwiftUI Preview

Developing an application requires several interactions between clients and developers. The clients may sometimes request minor changes, such as colors, fonts, and the position of items in the design. Previously, developers would need to update their design in Xcode and recompile all the code. iOS 13 solves this problem by introducing canvas previews. Previews allow the instant review and update of design changes without recompiling the whole code.

In this chapter, we will learn how to make effective use of Xcode previews to speed up the UI development time. The chapter includes the following recipes:

- Previewing the layout in dark mode
- Previewing the layout at different dynamic type sizes
- Previewing the layout in a navigation view
- Previewing the layout on different devices
- Using previews in UIKit
- Using mock data for previews

Technical requirements

The code in this chapter is based on Xcode 12 with iOS 13 as the minimum target version.

The code for this section can be found in `Chapter 3` of this book's GitHub repository: `https://github.com/PacktPublishing/SwiftUI-Cookbook`.

Previewing the layout in dark mode

SwiftUI has built-in functionality to support dark mode. Xcode previews allow users to change from light to dark mode without adding any extra code within the view. This is done by changing the `\.colorSheme` environment value in the preview.

In this section, we will create a simple app with a `Text` view and then preview it in dark mode.

Getting ready

Create a new SwiftUI app named `DarkModePreview`.

How to do it...

As of the time of writing this book, there is a bug in Xcode 11 that prevents dark mode previews of SwiftUI views that do not contain a navigation view. We need to enclose the content we want to view within a navigation view. The steps are as follows:

1. Open the `ContentView.swift` file.

2. Add a `NavigationView` component to the body variable of the `ContentView` view:

```
NavigationView {
        }
```

3. Add a `Text` view inside the `NavigationView` component. You can replace the `Text` view with any other view you would like to preview in dark mode:

```
Text("Quick journey to the dark side")
```

4. Within the `Content_Previews` struct, change the `ContentView` function call's color scheme to dark:

```
ContentView().colorScheme(.dark)
```

5. To also preview the light mode version, we'll enclose `ContentView().colorScheme(.dark)` within a `Group` view and add a light mode `ContentView` view, resulting in the following preview:

```
Group {
        ContentView().colorScheme(.dark)
        ContentView().colorScheme(.light)
    }
```

The resulting preview should look as follows:

Figure 3.1 – Dark mode preview

The light mode preview will be displayed just below the dark mode preview and should look as follows:

Quick journey to the dark side

Preview

Figure 3.2 – Light mode preview

Little to no font color change is required in dark mode since Xcode handles the changes by default.

How it works...

The process of previewing content in dark mode is self-explanatory. The preview displays content from the ContentView view. If no color scheme is provided to the preview, it uses .light as the default color scheme.

> **Important note**
>
> Later versions of Xcode may not require a navigation view to preview content in dark mode.

Previewing the layout at different dynamic type sizes

Some people use small font sizes to have a higher information density, while others use large text. It is therefore important to make sure that layouts work great with all ranges of dynamic type sizes.

In this recipe, we will create an app that allows the developer to preview their designs on different dynamic type sizes.

Getting ready

Let's start by creating a SwiftUI app called `DynamicTypeSizesPreview`.

How to do it...

We will create a view to display news articles. The view will contain an image, a title, and description text. We will then modify the preview to observe the view we created in different dynamic type sizes. The steps are as follows:

1. Expand the **Preview Content** folder in the Xcode navigation pane.

2. Click on **Preview Assets.xcassets** to view the page:

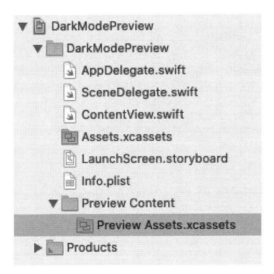

Figure 3.3 – The Preview Content folder in the navigation pane

3. Click **Import** and select the `reading.jpg` file from this recipe's resources file downloaded from GitHub. It can be found at `https://github.com/ PacktPublishing/SwiftUI-Cookbook/tree/master/Resources/ Chapter03`.

4. Create a struct to model news articles:

    a. Create a new Swift source file by pressing the ⌘ + *N* keys.

    b. Select **Swift file** and click **Next**.

    c. In the **Save As** field, enter `Article`.

    d. Click **Create**.

5. Create an `Article` struct. The struct should have three string properties: `imageName`, `title`, and `description`:

```
struct Article {
    var imageName:String
    var title:String
    var description:String
}
```

6. Create two sample articles below the struct definition. These variables can be used when building SwiftUI views:

```
let sampleArticle1 = Article(imageName: "reading", title:
    "Love reading", description: "Reading is essential to
        success")
let sampleArticle2 = Article(imageName: "naptime", title:
    "Nap time", description: "Take naps when tired.
        Improves performance
```

7. Create a SwiftUI view called `ArticleView`. This view will be used to design the UI of an article view:

    a. Press the ⌘ + *N* keys to create a new file.

    b. Select **SwiftUI View** and click **Next**.

    c. Save it as `ArticleView`.

8. Add an `article` property of the `Article` type to `ArticleView` (before the body property):

```
var article: Article
```

9. Add an `HStack` component containing an image to the `ArticleView` body:

```
HStack{
        Image(article.imageName)
        .resizable()
        .aspectRatio(contentMode: .fit)
        .frame(width:150, height:100)
        .clipShape(Ellipse())
```

10. Add a `VStack` component below the image modifiers. The `VStack` component should display the article title and description:

```
VStack {
        Text(article.title)
        .font(.title)
        Text(article.description)
        .padding()
    }
```

11. To preview the UI, pass a sample article to the `ArticleView()` struct in `ArticleView_Previews`:

```
ArticleView(article: sampleArticle1)
```

Now, the `ArticleView` preview within the canvas should look as follows:

Figure 3.4 – ArticleView preview

12. Now, click on the `ContentView.swift` file and view it in the Xcode editor pane (the middle section of the Xcode window).

13. Add `ArticleView` to the `ContentView` body and pass in `sampleArticle2` as an argument (the constant created in the `Article.swift` file):

```
ArticleView(article: sampleArticle2)
```

14. Run/resume the canvas preview. It should display the content of
    `sampleArticle2`:

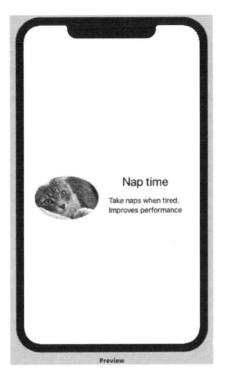

Figure 3.5 – ContentView preview

15. To view the results at different dynamic type sizes, we need to modify the
    `ContentView_Previews` struct. Let's start by enclosing the `ContentView()`
    function call in a group (groups are used to display 1–10 views):

```
Group {
        ContentView()
    }
```

16. Add a second `ContentView()` function call to the group, but this time, also add
    `.environment(\.sizeCategory, .extraSmall)`:

```
ContentView()
        .environment(\.sizeCategory, .extraSmall)
```

17. Observe the current result in the canvas, then add a `.previewLayout(.sizeThatFits)` modifier to the `Group` view:

```
Group {
    ContentView()
    ContentView()
        .environment(\.sizeCategory, .extraSmall)
}.previewLayout(.sizeThatFits)
```

18. Add a third `ContentView()` function call to the group with a `.environment(\.sizeCategory, .accessibilityExtraExtraExtraLarge)` modifier:

```
ContentView()
    .environment(\.sizeCategory,
        .accessibilityExtraExtraExtraLarge)
```

The preview should look as follows:

Figure 3.6 – Dynamic type sizes preview

Click on the play button at the top of each of the size categories to preview how it would be displayed on a device.

How it works...

We modularize this program by separating the model from the view. We first start by creating the `Article.swift` file. This file contains the models for articles we would like to display. The `Article` struct that we defined contains three strings: the image name, the title, and descriptions. We also create two article variables, `sampleArticle1` and `sampleArticle2`, to be used in other pages when building the UI.

The `ArticleView.swift` file contains the design for displaying articles. It uses a combination of `HStack` and `VStack` to build the design (refer to *Chapter 1, Using the Basic SwiftUI Views and Controls*, for more information on `HStack` and `VStack`).

Finally, the `ContentView` struct in the `ContentView.swift` file calls `ArticleView` and passes on the sample article variables we created as an argument. The `ContentView_Previews` struct handles the code related to previewing the design on multiple dynamic type sizes. The first step in previewing the layout on multiple dynamic types is to embed the `ContentView()` function in a `Group` view to allow the simultaneous display of multiple different views. The `.previewLayout(.sizeThatFits)` modifier should also be added to restrict the view to the amount of space it needs. Otherwise, each new `ContentView()` call would cause the canvas to display the new `ContentView` view in a new device below the current one.

The `.environment(...)` modifier uses a `ContentSizeCategory` enumerator to change the size of the content being displayed.

See also

Refer to the following list of possible `ContentSizeCategory` values: `https://developer.apple.com/documentation/swiftui/contentsizecategory`.

Previewing the layout in a navigation view

Some views are designed to be presented in a navigation stack but are not themselves part of a navigation view. One solution to this problem would be to run the application and navigate to the view in question. However, previews provide a time-saving way to figure out how the view would be displayed without running the app.

In this recipe, we will create an app with a view that is part of the navigation stack and preview it in a navigation view.

Getting ready

Let's create a SwiftUI app called `PreviewingInNavigationView`.

How to do it...

We will add a `NavigationView` and `NavigationLink` components to `ContentView` that lead to a second view. The second view will not contain a navigation view but will be previewed in one. The steps are as follows:

1. Replace the `Text` view in `ContentView` with a navigation view containing a `VStack` component and `NavigationLink` to a view called `SecondView`:

```
NavigationView {
    VStack {
        NavigationLink(destination: SecondView(someText:
            "Sample text")){
            Text("Go to second view")
                .foregroundColor(Color.white)
                .padding()
                .background(Color.black)
                .cornerRadius(25)
        }
        }.navigationBarTitle("Previews", displayMode:
            .inline)
    }
}
```

2. Create a new SwiftUI view called `SecondView`:

   a. Press ⌘ + N.

   b. Select **SwiftUI View** from the **User Interface** section.

   c. Enter `SecondView` in the **Save As** field.

3. Add a variable called `someText` to `SecondView`, above the body variable:

```
var someText:String
```

4. Add a `Text` view and a `.navigationBarTitle(..)` modifier to the
    `Text` view:

```
Text(someText)
        .navigationBarTitle("Second View ", displayMode:
            .inline)
```

Observe the canvas preview. No navigation bar title is present:

Figure 3.7 – SecondView with no navigation bar

5. Click on the `ContentView.swift` file located in the navigation pane of Xcode.

6. Run/resume the canvas preview and click the play button.

7. Click the `NavigationLink` text to navigate to the second view.

8. The second view displays text with navigation, as follows:

Figure 3.8 – The SecondView UI after navigating from ContentView

9. Click on `SecondView.swift` and enclose the `SecondView` call in a
    navigation view:

```
NavigationView{
    SecondView(someText: "Testing")
}
```

When views are accessible from `NavigationLink`, enclosing the preview in a
`NavigationView` component provides a quick and easy way to update the style and
display without running the app multiple times.

How it works...

Pages containing a `.navigationBarTitle(..)` modifier but no `NavigationView` will be displayed with navigation views if they are a part of the navigation stack.

Enclosing the preview of such pages in a `NavigationView` component allows the developers to preview the UI in a navigation view without running the app in the simulator or through the canvas.

Previewing the layout on different devices

SwiftUI allows developers to preview designs on multiple screen sizes and device types at the same time using the `.previewDevice()` modifier. In this recipe, we will create a simple app that displays an image and some text on multiple devices.

Getting ready

Let's create a SwiftUI app called named `PreviewOnDifferentDevices`.

How to do it...

We will add an image and some text to the `ContentView` struct and modify the preview struct to show the content on multiple devices. The steps are as follows:

1. Click on the **Preview Content** folder in the Xcode navigation pane.

2. Import the `friendship.png` image from the `Chapter 3` resource files (it can be found at `https://github.com/PacktPublishing/SwiftUI-Cookbook/tree/master/Resources/Chapter03/recipe%202O2`).

3. Click on the `ContentView.swift` file from the navigation pane to open it in the editor window.

4. Replace the initial `Text` view in `ContentView` struct's body variable with `VStack`:

```
VStack{

}
```

5. Add an `Image` view to the `VStack` component with modifiers to correctly display the image:

```
Image("friendship")
    .resizable()
    .aspectRatio(contentMode: .fit)
```

6. Add two `Text` views below the `Image` view to display the title and content related to the image:

```
Text("Importance of Friendship").font(.title)
Text("Friends helps us deal with stress and make better
    life choices").multilineTextAlignment(.center).
    padding()
```

Now, let's begin modifying the preview to view the content on multiple devices. The next steps will be performed within the `ContentView_Previews` struct.

7. First, embed the `ContentView()` call in a `Group` view:

```
Group {
    ContentView()
}
```

8. Modify the first `ContentView()` call to preview it on an iPhone 11 Pro Max:

```
ContentView().previewDevice("iPhone 11 Pro Max")
```

9. Add a display name to the preview to distinguish it from the other previews we will create:

```
.previewDisplayName("Iphone 11 Pro Max")
```

The resulting canvas preview should display our design on an iPhone 11, as shown here:

Figure 3.9 – Preview on iPhone 11 Pro Max

10. Add a second `ContentView` call together with `.previewDevice(...)` and a `.previewDisplayName(...)` modifier to view the design on an iPhone 8:

```
ContentView()
    .previewDevice("iPhone 8")
    .previewDisplayName("iPhone 8")
```

11. Add a third `ContentView` call together with `.previewDevice(...)` and a `.previewDisplayName(...)` modifier. This time, use a custom width and height for the preview layout:

```
ContentView()
    .previewLayout(.fixed(width: 568, height: 320))
    .previewDisplayName("Custom Size to infer landscape
      mode")
```

Congrats on adding one more tool to your toolbox! Xcode previews help you save time by quickly viewing design changes across multiple devices.

How it works...

The `.previewDevice()` modifier lets you select a device to display your design. The device name provided to the modifier should be the exact same name as a device available in the Xcode **Destination** menu:

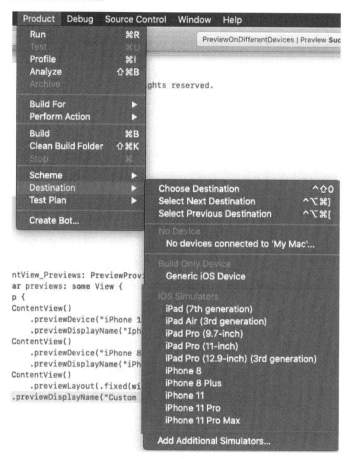

Figure 3.10 – List of available devices in the Xcode Destination menu

At the time of writing, Xcode 12 previews do not allow viewing devices in landscape mode. The workaround is to specify the preview width and height using a frame modifier.

Using previews in UIKit

Xcode previews provide a fast and easy way to quickly preview the current state of your view. Previews were introduced in Xcode 11 together with SwiftUI. You might think previews can only be used on SwiftUI apps, but you'll be wrong. UIKit apps can also make use of this great new feature!

In this recipe, we will set up a UIKit view to make it "previewable" in the Xcode canvas.

Getting ready

If you have not yet done so, download the GitHub repository for this book from `https://github.com/PacktPublishing/SwiftUI-Cookbook`.

How to do it...

We will change the build settings of UIKit to add iOS 13+ capabilities to the debug build, and then set up the UIKit page to preview our code during design and debugging. The steps are as follows:

1. Open the initial iOS 12 XCode project located at `https://github.com/PacktPublishing/SwiftUI-Cookbook/tree/master/Chapter03%20-%20Viewing%20while%20building%20with%20SwiftUI%20Preview/05%20-%20Previewing%20UIKit%20Views`

2. Click the **PreviewUIKItViews** project file on the Xcode navigation pane located at the left of the screen:

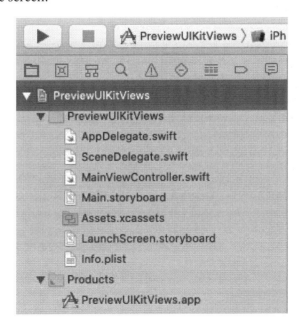

Figure 3.11 – Xcode navigation pane with the project file

3. Click on **Build Settings**, scroll down to the **Deployment** section, open the **iOS Deployment Target** drop-down menu, and change the iOS debug version to iOS 13.4 and the release version to iOS 12.4 (it will also work if the debug version is set to iOS 14):

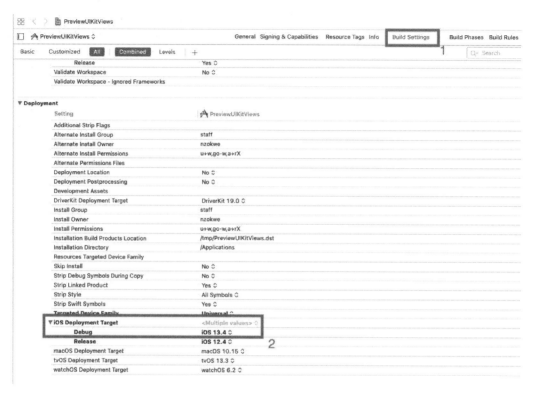

Figure 3.12 – Xcode build settings with deployment targets highlighted

4. Click on the **Main.storyboard** file on the navigation pane. The storyboard file holds the UIKit app designs. You should see `ViewController` with some text displayed:

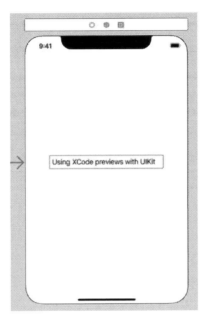

Figure 3.13 – Main storyboard

5. Click the `MainViewController.swift` file on the navigation pane. This opens it up in the editor view.

6. Below the `MainViewController` class, add a statement to run previews in canvas when in debug mode to be used if SwiftUI is supported by the version of Xcode. The next steps will all involve adding code within the `#if` block created here:

```
#if canImport(SwiftUI) && DEBUG
//The rest of the code goes here
#endif
```

7. Import SwiftUI and create a `MainViewRepresentable` struct that extends `UIViewRepresentable`:

```
Import SwiftUI
struct MainViewRepresentable: UIViewRepresentable {
}
```

8. Within `MainViewRepresentable`, implement the `makeUIView` and `updateUIView` functions, required to conform to `UIViewRepresentable`. The `makeUIview` function should return the UIKit view configuration:

```
func makeUIView(context: Context) -> UIView {
    return UIStoryboard(name: "Main", bundle: Bundle.main).
        instantiateInitialViewController()!.view
}


func updateUIView(_ view: UIView, context: Context) {

}
```

9. Before implementing the `MainViewController_Preview` struct, let's add a statement to only run this section if the project's iOS version is greater than iOS 13.0:

```
@available(iOS 13.0, *)
```

10. To preview the design in the canvas, add a `MainViewController_Preview` struct that extends `PreviewProvider`. The struct's preview variable should call the `MainViewRepresentable()` struct created earlier:

```
struct MainViewController_Preview: PreviewProvider {
    static var previews: some View {
        MainViewRepresentable()
    }
}
```

11. If the canvas is not visible, click on the adjust editor options below the top-right corner of the Xcode editor (or press the ⌥ + ⌘ + ⏎ keys):

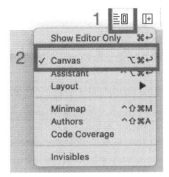

Figure 3.14 – Opening the canvas in Xcode

The resulting canvas preview should be as follows:

Figure 3.15 – Preview of UIKit UIViewController

Skill gained! You can now use the power of SwiftUI previews on UIKit apps. Such a setup is useful when previewing dynamic type sizes on different devices or testing UI changes on multiple devices at once.

How it works...

Previews are only available in iOS 13+. In order to use them in UIKit, you first have to change the debug version of the code to iOS 13.0 or above. Changing the debug version allows the app to be built with SwiftUI functionalities while in debug mode. In this recipe, we intend to use it for previews only–we are not adding functionalities to the app.

Before previewing `UIViewController`, we first need to make sure we are in debug mode and the version of Xcode being used supports SwiftUI. We achieve this by adding a preprocessor directive that checks whether both conditions are met:

```
#if canImport(SwiftUI) && DEBUG

#endif
```

`MainViewRepresentable` is our wrapper that converts `UIView` into a SwiftUI view. The `makeUIView` method instantiates the SwiftUI view.

Lastly, `MainViewController_Preview` implements the `PreviewProvider` protocol and automatically enables the preview canvas in Xcode. We add the `@ available` code before the preview definition to make sure the code still builds if the debug iOS version is changed to an unsupported version.

Using mock data for previews

So far, we've built apps using our own data. However, when building an app for a client, you may want to use mock data that closely resembles client data. Using API calls early on in development may be a bottleneck. In this recipe, we will introduce a faster option, using JSON data stored in a file.

In this recipe, we will read `Insect` data from a JSON file and display the content in a SwiftUI view.

Getting ready

Let's create a new project called `UsingMockDataForPreviews`.

If not yet done, clone this book's GitHub repository from `https://github.com/ PacktPublishing/SwiftUI-Cookbook`.

How to do it...

We will add our mock data to the Xcode project, then proceed to design a SwiftUI view that elegantly displays the data. The steps are as follows:

1. From the cloned GitHub repository, open the Resources file, then drag and drop the insectData.json file into the Preview Content folder of the Xcode project:

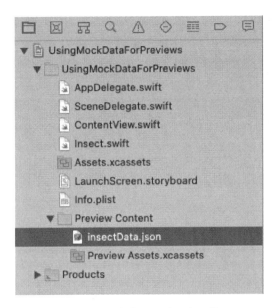

Figure 3.16 – Mock data in Preview Content

2. Click on the insectData.json file to view its content.

3. Create a struct that models the expected data:

   a. Press the ⌘ + N keys to create a new file.

   b. Select **Swift File** and click **Next**.

   c. Enter Insect in the **Save As** field on the next window and click **Create**.

4. Define a struct that models the data in the JSON file:

```
struct Insect : Decodable, Identifiable{
    var id: Int
    var imageName:String
    var name:String
    var habitat:String
    var description:String
}
```

5. Create a variable from the model (to be used as default if reading data from the JSON file fails):

```
let testInsect = Insect(id: 1, imageName: "grasshopper",
    name: "grass", habitat: "bod", description: "sije")
```

6. Click the `ContentView.swift` file to open it in the editor pane.

7. Add a variable to hold an array of `Insect`, just above the `body` variable:

```
var insects:[Insect] = []
```

8. Add `NavigationView` and a `List` view that loops through all the `insect` variables passed to the `ContentView` struct and displays them:

```
NavigationView {
    List {
        ForEach(insects) {insect in
            HStack{
                Image(insect.imageName)
                    .resizable()
                    .aspectRatio(contentMode: .fit)
                    .clipShape(Rectangle())
                    .frame(width:100, height: 80)

                VStack(alignment: .leading){
```

```
                Text(insect.name).font(.title)
                Text(insect.habitat)
            }.padding(.vertical)
        }
    }
}.navigationBarTitle("Insects")
}
```

9. Let's move to the `ContentView_Previews` struct now and make the changes
    required to read and use our mock data. Below the `previews` variable, create
    a variable that reads the data from the JSON file and converts it into an array of
    `Insect` variables:

```
static var testInsects : [Insect]{
    guard let url = Bundle.main.url(forResource:
        "insectData", withExtension: "json"),
        let data = try? Data(contentsOf: url)
            else{
                return[]
        }
        let decoder = JSONDecoder()
        let array = try?decoder.decode([Insect].self,
            from: data)
        print("test")
        return array ?? [testInsect]
}
```

10. With the `ContentView_Previews` code block, update the `ContentView` call
    to pass the array of `Insect` variables read from our mock data:

```
ContentView(insects: Self.testInsects)
```

The resulting preview should look as follows:

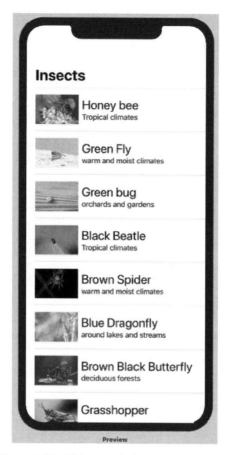

Figure 3.17 – Using mock data project preview

How it works...

The new concept in this recipe involves modeling the Insect struct and converting data from JSON into an array of objects.

The insect struct extends the decodable protocol so that you can use it to decode JSON objects into the struct. Extending Identifiable permits the struct to be used in a ForEach loop without requiring an id: parameter.

In `ContentView_Previews`, we perform a number of steps to convert our data into an array of `Insect`.

We first get the data from the file:

```
guard let url = Bundle.main.url(forResource: "insectData",
    withExtension: "json"),


        let data = try? Data(contentsOf: url)
            else{
                return[]
        }
```

Then, we decode the data into an array of `Insect` structs and return the result:

```
let decoder  = JSONDecoder()
let array = try?decoder.decode([Insect].self, from: data)
return array ??  [testInsect]
```

The `return` statement returns the decoded array if it is not nil. Otherwise, an array of one object, `testInsect` created in `Insect.swift`, is returned.

4

Creating New Components and Grouping Views in Container Views

In this chapter, we will focus on grouping views using `Form` and `TabView` views.

`Form` views are one of the best ways to get input from prospective clients or current users. Proper implementation of Forms improves the user experience and increases the chances of retention, whereas complex or frustrating forms lead to negative user experiences. We used forms and containers in the earlier chapters but in this chapter, we will learn additional ways to use forms.

SwiftUI's `TabView` is similar to UIKit's `UITabBarController`. It provides an easy and intuitive way to present multiple views to the user and allow them to easily navigate between each of those views.

The following concepts will be discussed in this chapter:

- Showing and hiding sections in forms
- Disabling and enabling items in a form
- Navigating between multiple views with `TabView`
- Using gestures with `TabView`

Technical requirements

The code in this chapter is based on Xcode 12 but all the recipes are compatible with iOS 13 and 14.

The code for this section can be found in the folder for `Chapter 4` of this book's GitHub repository, at `https://github.com/PacktPublishing/SwiftUI-Cookbook`.

Showing and hiding sections in forms

Forms provide a means of getting information from the user. Long forms can, however, discourage users from providing information. Users not completing a form may mean fewer people signing up for your app or providing payment information.

In this recipe, we will learn how to show/hide an additional address section of a form based on user input.

Getting ready

Create a SwiftUI Project named `SignUp`.

How to do it...

We will create a signup form with sections for various user input. The additional address sections will be shown or hidden based on how long the user has lived at their current address. Use the following steps:

1. Create a new SwiftUI View called `signUpView`:

   a. Press ⌘ + *N*.

   b. Select **SwiftUI View**.

   c. Click **Next**.

d. Click on the **Save As** field and enter the text `signUpView`.

e. Click **Finish**.

2. Declare and initialize the `@State` variables that will be used in the form:

```
@State private var fname = ""
@State private var lname = ""
@State private var street = ""
@State private var city = ""
@State private var zip = ""
@State private var lessThanTwo = false
@State private var username = ""
@State private var password = ""
```

3. Open the `signUPView.swift` file and add a `NavigationView` and a `Form` view to the body variable:

```
NavigationView{
   Form{
     }.navigationBarTitle("Sign Up")
   }
```

4. Let's add a `.navigationBarTitle` modifier to the `Form` view:

```
Form{
   }.navigationBarTitle("Sign Up")
```

5. Add a `Section` to the form with two `TextField` structs to store the user's first and last names:

```
Section(header: Text("Names")){
        TextField("First Name", text: $fname)
        TextField("Last Name" , text: $lname)
       }
```

6. Below the `"Names"` section, add another section with `TextField` structs to hold the user's current address:

```
Section(header: Text("Current Address")){
        TextField("Street Address" , text: $street)
        TextField("City" , text: $city)
        TextField("Zip" , text: $zip)
    }
```

7. Add a `Toggle` field to the preceding form to inquire whether the user has been at their current address for at least 2 years. Place the `Toggle` field below the `TextField` where we request the user's zip code:

```
Toggle(isOn: $lessThanTwo){
Text("Have you lived here for 2+ years")
    }
```

8. Add an `if` statement and a form section that will be shown if the user has been at their current address for less than two years and hidden otherwise:

```
if !lessThanTwo{
Section(header:Text("Previous Address")){
        TextField("Street Address" , text: $street)
        TextField("City" , text: $city)
        TextField("Zip" , text: $zip)
    }
}
```

9. Add a Section to the form with a `TextField` struct for the username and a `SecureField` struct to store the password:

```
Section(header:Text("Create Account Info")) {
        TextField("Create Username" , text: $username)
        SecureField("Password", text: $password)
    }
```

10. Finally, let's add a submit button. The `Button` should display text that says **Submit**, but no action will be provided:

```
Button("Submit") {
    print("Form submit action here")
}
```

Your resulting preview should be similar to the following image:

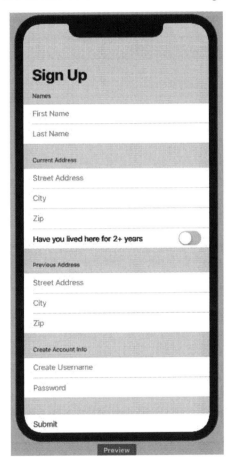

Figure 4.1 – Sign Up form

How it works...

Showing or hiding sections or fields in a form is performed using the `if` conditional statement. The **Previous Address** section of the form gets displayed only when the value stored in the `Toggle` field is set to `True`.

We also added sections in the form to group related fields together such as addresses, names, and the section to create login information. Some of the sections had headers describing the contents they hold while others did not.

Using sections in forms is optional. The form created in this recipe could have been created as a single block of input without any sections.

There's more

If you ran the code and clicked the **Submit** button, you might have noticed that the print statement does not show up anywhere. To see the `print` statement used in the code, you need to do two things:

Make sure that the debug area of Xcode is visible. In the Xcode menu, click **View | Debug Area**:

Figure 4.2 – Debug Area toggle

Run the app on an Xcode simulator, *not* using the canvas preview.

The `print` statement should now be displayed when the submit button is clicked.

Disabling/enabling items in a form

Forms may contain required and optional fields. Some fields may have additional requirements that need to be met. For example, the password fields may be required to contain at least eight characters. When developing an app, we may want to enable or disable the submit button based on the form requirements, thus allowing the users to submit a form only when it meets all our requirements.

In this recipe, we will create a sign-in page where the submit button gets enabled only if the user enters some content in the username and password fields.

Getting ready

Create a SwiftUI project and name it `FormFieldDisable`.

How to do it...

We will create a SwiftUI view with a username field, password field, and a submit button. The submit button will be disabled unless the user enters some text in the username and password fields. The steps are as follows:

1. Create a new SwiftUI view file named `LoginView`:

   a. Press ⌘ + *N*.

   b. Select **SwiftUI View**.

   c. Click **Next**.

   d. Click on the **Save as** field and enter the text `LoginView`.

   e. Click **Finish**.

2. Open the `LoginView.swift` file by clicking on it.

3. Add `@State` variables for `username` and `password` above the `LoginView` struct's body variable:

```
@State private var username = ""
@State private var password = ""
```

4. Add a `VStack` component and a `Text` struct that displays the app name, `"Amazing Games"`. Add the included modifiers one at a time to observe their effect on the UI:

```
VStack{
     Text("Amazing Games")
          .fontWeight(.heavy)
          .foregroundColor(.blue)
          .font(.largeTitle)
          .padding(.bottom, 30)
}
```

5. Add an `Image` struct with a person **San Francisco (SF)** symbol below the `Text` struct (still in `VStack`):

```
Image(systemName: "person.circle")
    .font(.system(size: 150))
    .foregroundColor(.gray)
    .padding(.bottom, 40)
```

6. Add a `Group` view containing a `TextField` for the username and a `SecureField` for the password:

```
Group{
    TextField("Username", text: $username)
    SecureField("Password", text: $password)
}
    .padding()
    .overlay(
        RoundedRectangle(cornerRadius: 10)
            .stroke(Color.black, lineWidth: 2)
    )
```

7. Add a `Submit` button that stays disabled when either of the username or password fields are empty:

```
Button(action: {
        print("Submit clicked")
    }){
        Text("Submit")
    }.padding()
    .background(Color.blue)
    .foregroundColor(Color.white)
    .clipShape(Capsule())
    .disabled(username.isEmpty || password.isEmpty)
```

8. Click on the `ContentView.swift` file and replace `Text(...)` with `LoginView()`:

```
var body: some View {
        LoginView()
}
```

The resulting preview should look as follows:

Figure 4.3 – FormFieldDisable preview

To test the app, first activate the debug console (if it has not yet been opened.) This can be done with the ⇧ + ⌘ + C key combination or through the Xcode menu via **View | Debug Area | Activate Console**:

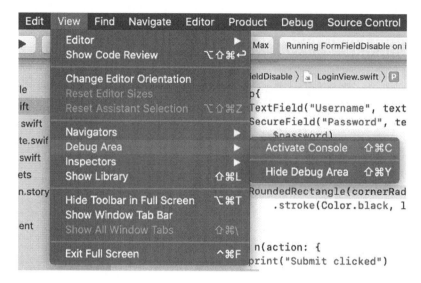

Figure 4.4 – Activate Debug Console on Xcode

Now run the app in an emulator. The text `Submit clicked` will be printed in the debug console only when some text has been entered in the username and password fields.

How it works

The `.disable()` modifier can be used to disable a button and prevent users from submitting a form until certain conditions have been met. The `.disable()` modifier takes a Boolean parameter and disables the button if the condition executes to `true`. In this example, we check whether our `@State` variables and the username and password fields are not empty. The **Submit** button is disabled if any of the fields are left empty.

We also learned that we can apply modifiers to multiple items at once without repeating ourselves by applying the modifiers to the `Group` view.

There's more

You can use a wider range of colors by using color literals instead of `Color.white`, `Color.blue`, and the others used thus far. To use color literals, start by typing the word `Color`, and then select **Color Literal** from the Xcode auto-complete popup:

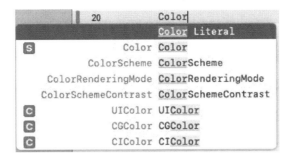

Figure 4.5 – Selecting a color literal

You can now click on the **Color Literal** object displayed to view a larger palette of colors:

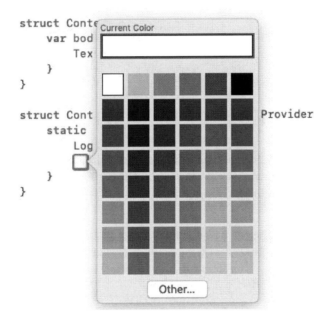

Figure 4.6 – Color literal palette

Navigating between multiple views with TabView

Navigation views are ideal for displaying hierarchical data because they allow users to drill down into the data. Navigation views, however, don't work well with unrelated data. We use SwiftUI's TabView struct for that purpose.

Getting ready

Create a new SwiftUI iOS app named `UsingTabViews`.

How to do it

We will create an app with two `TabView` structs where one displays the top games of 2020, while the other displays some world currencies. The steps are as follows:

1. Create a SwiftUI view called `HomeView`:

   a. Press ⌘ + N.

   b. Select **SwiftUI View**.

   c. Click **Next**.

   d. Click on the **Save as** field and enter the text `HomeView`.

2. Before the `struct HomeView` line, create a string array containing the various games:

```
let games = ["Doom", "Final F","Cyberpunk", "avengers",
    "animal trivia", "sudoku", "snakes and ladders", "Power
        rangers", "ultimate frisbee", "football", "soccer",
        "much more"]
```

3. Replace the `Text` view in the body with a `NavigationView` component that displays the content of our array in a list:

```
NavigationView{
        List {
                ForEach(games, id: \.self){ game in
                    Text(game).padding()
                }
            }.navigationBarTitle("Best Games for 2020",
                displayMode: .inline)
    }
```

The preview of the `HomeView.swift` file should look as follows:

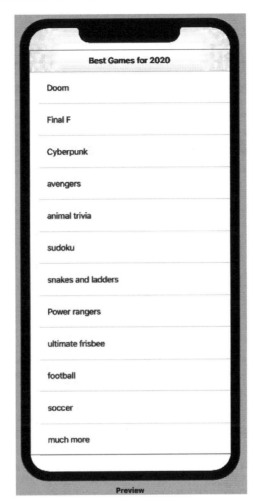

Figure 4.7 – HomeView preview

4. Create a new SwiftUI view called `CurrenciesView`:

    a. Press ⌘ + *N*.

    b. Select **SwiftUI View**.

    c. Click **Next**.

    d. Click on the **Save as** field and enter the text `CurrenciesView`.

    e. Click **Finish**.

5. We would like to display some currency names and their symbols within the
    `CurrenciesView`. Let's start by creating a model for the currency. Create a new
    Swift file called `Currency`:

    a. Press ⌘ + *N*.

    b. Select **Swift File**.

    c. Click **Next**.

    d. Click the **Save as** field and enter the text `Currency`.

    e. Click **Finish**.

6. In the `Currency.swift` file, create a struct that represents the currency
    information. A currency should have a name and an image variable. Make the
    `Currency` struct `Identifiable` so that it can be used in a `ForEach` loop
    without providing an `id` argument:

    ```swift
    struct Currency: Identifiable {
        let id = UUID()
        var name:String
        var image:String
    }
    ```

7. Below the currency definition, create a sample array of various currencies:

    ```swift
    var currencies = [Currency(name: "Dollar", image:
            "dollarsign.circle.fill"),
                Currency(name: "Sterling", image:
                    "sterlingsign.circle.fill"),
            Currency(name: "Euro", image: "eurosign.
                circle.fill"),
            Currency(name: "Yen", image: "yensign.
                circle.fill"),
            Currency(name: "Naira", image:
                "nairasign.circle.fill")]
    ```

8. In the navigation pane, click the `CurrenciesView.swift` file to open it up on the editor view.

9. Replace the `Text` view with a `NavigationView` and a `VStack` component containing a `.navigationBarTitle` modifier that displays the view's title:

```
NavigationView{
        VStack{
}.navigationBarTitle("Currencies")
}
```

10. We would like to loop through our list of currencies and display the name and image side by side. Within the `VStack` component, let's add a `ForEach` loop to iterate through the currencies and an `HStack` component that displays the name and image side by side:

```
ForEach(currencies){ currency in
        HStack{
            Group{
                Text(currency.name)
                Spacer()
                Image(systemName: currency.image)
            }.font(Font.system(size: 40, design:
            .default))
            .padding()
        }
}
```

The `CurrenciesView` preview should look as follows:

Figure 4.8 – CurrenciesView preview

11. Now that we have set up the sub-views, click on `ContentView.swift` to open the file in the editor window.

12. Replace the `Text` view in the `ContentView` struct with the `TabView` struct that displays `HomeView` and `CurrenciesView` as tabs:

```
TabView {
    HomeView()
        .tabItem{
            Image(systemName: "house.fill")
            Text("Home")
        }
    CurrenciesView()
        .tabItem{
            Image(systemName: "coloncurrencysign.circle.
                fill")
            Text("Currencies")
        }
}
```

The `ContentView` preview should look as follows:

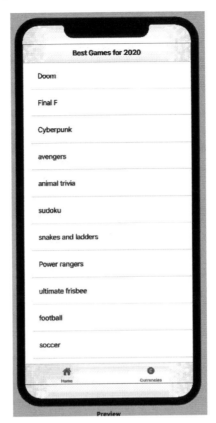

Figure 4.9 – UsingTabViews app's ContentView preview

You can now run the app to test the code and navigate between tabs.

How it works

Let's begin with a discussion about the `ContentView.swift` file because it contains the main login for displaying tabs.

In its most basic version, a `TabView`, just like a Group view can hold multiple views. The following code will display an app with two tabs (though without a tab name or image):

```
TabView{
    Text("First")
    Text("Second")
}
```

However, most client apps would require the developer to display more information on each tab. The `.tabItem` modifier can be added to each view to set up the view in a new tab. In `ContentView.swift`, we have added `.tabItem` modifiers to the `HomeView` and `CurrenciesView` structs. We also passed an `Image` and some text to serve as `TabItem` labels.

Now let's take a closer look at the `HomeView` and `CurrenciesView` structs.

The `HomeView` struct is defined in the `HomeView.swift` file. It displays an array of games using a `List` (review *Chapter 2, Going Beyond the Single Component with Lists and Scroll Views,* for more information on `List` views).

The `CurrenciesView` struct displays a few currency names and their symbols using a `Vstack` component, a `ForEach` loop, and an `Hstack` component. The data displayed is based on the `Currency` model and the currencies sample array defined in the `Currency.swift` file.

There's more

In iOS 14, SwiftUI's `TabView` also doubles up as a `UIPageVieweController`. You can allow swiping through multiple screens using paging dots. To implement this, add a `.tabViewStyle()` modifier to the `TabView` and pass the `PageTabViewStyle()` as follows:

```
TabView {
    ...
}.tabViewStyle(PageTabViewStyle())
```

> **Important note**
> If you're using `TabView` and `NavigationView` at the same time, make sure `TabView` is the parent, and `NavigationView` is nested in `TabView`.

Using gestures with TabView

In the preceding recipe, we learned how to switch between tabs using the navigation pane at the bottom of the screen. However, when building an app, the client may want something else to trigger the navigation. Navigation between `TabView` tabs can be performed programmatically. In this recipe, we will use a tap gesture to trigger the transition from one tab to another, but the concept can be generalized to any other programmatic trigger.

Getting ready

Create a SwiftUI app for iOS and name it `TabViewWithGestures`.

How to do it

We will implement a screen with two `TabView` structs where the user would be able to transition between tabs by using the tab bar at the bottom of the screen or by clicking on some text. The steps are as follows:

1. Click on the `ContentView.swift` file to open it in the editor window.

2. Add an `@State` variable that holds the value of the currently selected tab. The variable should be located just above the `body` variable:

```
@State private var tabSelected = 0
```

3. Replace the `Text` view in the `body` variable with `TabView`. The `TabView` should take an argument, `selection`, that binds to the `tabSelected` `@State` variable mentioned in the preceding step:

```
TabView(selection: $tabSelected){
}
```

4. Within the `TabView`, add a `Text` view for the left tab with a `.onTapGesture` modifier that changes the value of the tab selected:

```
Text("Left Tab")
        .onTapGesture {
            self.tabSelected = 1
}
```

5. Add a `.tag` modifier that specifies this tab's value. Also add a `.tabItem` modifier with an l character as the tab image and a `Text` struct that contains the text `"Left"`.:

```
.tag(0)
        .tabItem{
            Image(systemName: "1.circle.fill")
            Text("Left")
}
```

6. Still within `TabView`, add the `Text` struct for the right tab together with the `.onTapGesutre`, `.tabItem`, and `.tag` modifiers:

```
Text("Right Tab")
        .onTapGesture {
            self.tabSelected = 0
        }
        .tabItem{
            Image(systemName: "r.circle.fill")
            Text("Right")
}.tag(1)
```

The resulting preview should be as follows:

Figure 4.10 – TabViewWithGesture preview

Run the app's live preview. You can now switch between tabs by clicking on the tab buttons at the bottom of the display or just by clicking on the text in each tab.

How it works

There are four steps involved to allow programmatic `TabView` navigation:

1. Create a `@State` variable to hold the currently selected tab.

2. Add the selection argument to the `TabView` struct and bind it to the variable created in *step 1*.

3. Add an `.onTabGesture` modifier or any other trigger to the item you want to use for programmatic tab navigation.

4. Add a `.tag` modifier to each of the tabs to uniquely identify each tab.

Each of the four preceding steps is required to programmatically switch between tabs. Since actions in SwiftUI are performed based on the state of the application, we need to change the value of the `@State` variable when we want to move to a new tab. In this recipe, the value of the `@State` variable is changed based on a tap gesture, but this could be substituted for any other event such as a left- or right-swipe gesture.

Tab numbers could however be confusing if there were several tabs or the tabs were moved around when making changes. For this reason, when programmatically switching between tabs, it is important to add the `.tag()` modifier to each tab and to specify the tab number.

5

Presenting Extra Information to the User

In this chapter, we shall look at how to present extra information to the user using alerts, modals, context menus, and popovers.

When interacting with mobile applications, we expect a certain level of handholding. If we are about to perform an irreversible action such as delete a file, we expect an alert to pop up and ask for confirmation if we want to perform the requested action. Depending on our response, the file may be deleted or not. We also expect to click on certain buttons/ links to see extra information regarding a topic.

Since SwiftUI is a declarative programming language, presenting extra information to the user involves adding modifiers to already existing views. It is possible to add one or several such modifiers to a view and set the conditions for each to be triggered.

The list of topics for this chapter is as follows:

- Presenting alerts
- Adding actions to alert buttons
- Presenting multiple alerts
- Presenting ActionSheet views
- Showing a sheet modally
- Creating a context menu
- Implementing a popover

Technical requirements

The code in this chapter is based on Xcode 12, but all the apps here are compatible with iOS 13 and 14.

You can find the code in the book's GitHub repository at `https://github.com/PacktPublishing/SwiftUI-Cookbook/tree/master/Chapter05%20-%20Presenting%20Extra%20information%20to%20the%20user`.

Presenting alerts

A common way of letting the user know that something important happened is to present an alert with a message and an **OK** button. In this recipe, we will create a simple alert that gets displayed when a button is pressed.

Getting ready

Create a SwiftUI application named `PresentingAlerts`.

How to do it

We display alerts by creating an `Alert` and setting up the condition for when it should be displayed using a `@State` variable. The alert will contain a title, text, and dismiss button.

The process is as follows:

1. Create a `@State` variable whose value determines if the alert is shown or not:

    ```
    @State private var showSubmitAlert = false;
    ```

2. Replace the `Text` struct in `ContentView` with a `Button` with the label `"Submit"`:

    ```
    Button(action: {
    //button action
            }){
                Text("Submit")
            }
    ```

3. Add an `.alert()` modifier to the end of the button. The modifier takes the `showSubmitAlert` state variable as a parameter and the `Alert` as content:

    ```
    .alert(isPresented: $showSubmitAlert ){
            //Alert Goes here
        }
    ```

4. Within the `.alert()` modifier, create an `Alert` with a `title`, `message`, and `dismiss` button:

    ```
    Alert(title: Text("Confirm Action"),
            message: Text("Are you sure you want to submit the
                form"),
            dismissButton: .default(Text("OK"))
        )
    ```

5. At this point, if you run the canvas preview and click on the **Submit** button, nothing happens. We need to change the `showSubmitAlert` state variable to true when we want the alert to be presented. Within the Buttons action placeholder, add the following code to change the `showSubmitAlert` variable to `true` when the button is clicked:

    ```
    self.showSubmitAlert=true
    ```

6. Now run the canvas preview and click on the **Submit** button to see the alert. Then click the **OK** button to dismiss it.

7. Lastly, let's add some styling to the button's text to make it look fancier:

```
Text("Submit")
    .padding()
     .background(Color.blue)
    .foregroundColor(.white)
   .clipShape(Capsule())
```

The resulting canvas preview should look as follows:

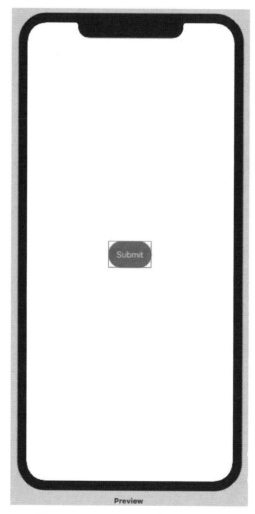

Figure 5.1 – PresentingAlerts preview

Run the app in the live preview and confirm that the alert appears on the screen. Click the **OK** button to close the alert and return to the view.

How it works

Displaying alerts is a three-step process. First, we create an `@State` variable that triggers the displaying or hiding of the variable; then, we add an `.alert()` modifier to the view we are modifying; and finally, we add the `Alert` view inside the `.alert()` modifier.

The `showSubmitAlert` state variable is passed to the modifier's `isPresented` argument. The alert gets displayed when the `showSubmitAlert` variable is set to `true`. The value changes back to false when the user clicks on the **OK** or **Dismiss** button (thanks to two-way binding).

The `Alert` used here contains three parameters. The title and message are text, while the `dismissButton` is of the `Alert.Buttons` type.

See also

- Types of alert buttons: `https://developer.apple.com/documentation/swiftui/alert/button`
- Apple Human Interface guidelines regarding alerts: `https://developer.apple.com/design/human-interface-guidelines/macos/windows-and-views/alerts/`

Adding actions to alert buttons

We may want to display alerts with more than just an **OK** button to confirm the alert has been read. In some cases, we may want to present a *Yes* or *No* choice to the user. For example, if the user wanted to delete an item in a list, we may want to present an alert where clicking on **yes** deletes the item and clicking on **no** does not change anything.

In this recipe, we will look at how to add a secondary button to alerts.

Getting ready

Create a SwiftUI app named `AlertsWithActions`.

How to do it

We will implement an alert with two buttons and an action. The alert will get triggered by a tap gesture on some text. The steps are as follows:

1. Create a @State variable that determines if the alert is displayed or not. Place the variable just below the ContentView struct declaration:

```
@State private var changeText = false
```

2. Create a @State variable to hold the text to be displayed on the screen. Give it an initial value of Tap to Change Text:

```
@State private var displayText = "Tap to Change Text"
```

3. Modify the Text view to display the content of our @State variable, displayText:

```
Text(displayText)
```

4. Add an onTapGesture modifier to the Text that changes the value of the changeText state variable to true:

```
.onTapGesture {
    self.changeText = true
}
```

5. Add am .alert() modifier after the tap gesture. The modifier takes the Boolean binding parameter, changeText, which was declared earlier:

```
.alert(isPresented: $changeText){
    //place alert here
}
```

6. Add an Alert view inside the .alert() modifier. The alert's message and title parameter are of the Text type, while the primaryButton and secondaryButton parameters are of the Alert.Button type:

```
Alert(title: Text("Changing Text"),
    message: Text("Do you want to change the displayed
        text"),
    primaryButton: .cancel(),
    secondaryButton: .default(Text("OK"))
```

```
        //secondaryButton Action
)
```

7. Running the code in canvas now should display an alert with two buttons. Nothing happens when we click **OK** or **Cancel**. Let's fix this by adding an action to our `secondaryButton`. Let's add a closure to the `secondaryButton` that performs an action:

```
secondaryButton: .default(Text("OK")){
    self.displayText = (self.displayText == "Stay Foolish") ?
        "Stay Hungry" : "Stay Foolish"
}
```

8. Try running the code using the canvas preview. Each click on the text should display an alert. A click on **OK** changes the text, whereas nothing happens when **Cancel** is clicked.

The resulting canvas preview should be as follows:

Figure 5.2 – AlertsWithActions preview

The alert with two actions (*Figure 5.3*) will be displayed when the **Tap to Change Text** button is pressed.

Figure 5.3 – Alert message AlertsWithActions app

How it works

The .onTapGesture() modifier gets triggered when the user taps on the Text struct displayed on the screen. Once it's triggered, we change the value of our @State variable, changeText. Since our .alert() modifier presents the alert based on the value of the changeText variable, a tap on the Text struct causes the alert to be displayed.

The `Alert` struct contains a title and a message parameter, as seen in the previous recipe. Instead of using the `dismissButton` as in the previous recipe, we introduced two new alert buttons, `primaryButton` and `secondaryButton`. Both buttons can either accept a `Label` struct only, or a `Label` and an `Action` struct. We pass the `cancel()` function to the `primaryButton` parameter because we do not want to take action if that button is clicked. By default the `cancel()` function also causes the text **Cancel** to be displayed within that button.

If the user instead clicks on the `secondaryButton`, we pass in the `.default()` function and a closure. The `.default()` function displays the text in the button, while the closure performs an action when the button is clicked. The closure changes the text displayed on the screen to **Stay Foolish** or **Stay Hungry**.

See also

- Types of alert buttons: `https://developer.apple.com/documentation/swiftui/alert/button`

- Apple Human Interface guidelines regarding alerts: `https://developer.apple.com/design/human-interface-guidelines/macos/windows-and-views/alerts/`

Presenting multiple alerts

We have reviewed the process for displaying single alerts in a view. What happens if we have multiple alerts in a single view? When multiple alerts are attached to a view, only one of them works. To create a view with multiple alerts that work, we need to make sure each alert is tied to a different view.

Getting ready

Create a SwiftUI app named `PresentingMultipleAlerts`.

How to do it

We will create a `VStack` that holds two structs, with a `.alert()` modifier attached to each struct. We will use a button click and a `Toggle` struct to display alerts. The steps are as follows:

1. Create the `@State` variable that will trigger the alerts. The variables should be declared immediately below the `ContentView` struct declaration and before the `body` variable:

```
@State private var showTwoButtonsAlert = false
@State private var showSimpleAlert = false
```

2. Replace the `Text` struct with a `VStack` to hold the other structs. We will add the following:

```
VStack{
//The rest of the program goes here
}
```

3. Let's add a `Toggle` struct and pass the `showTwoButtonsAlert` variable to its `isOn` argument. The `Text` view in the `Toggle` struct should say `"Display Alert"`. Also add some padding to the `Toggle` struct:

```
Toggle(isOn: $showTwoButtonsAlert) {
        Text("Display alert")
                    }.padding()
```

4. Add a `.alert()` modifier to the Toggle struct. The modifier contains a two- button alert, as seen in the *Adding actions to alert buttons* recipe we implemented earlier in this chapter. A click on the primary button keeps the `showTwoButtonsAlert` variable as `true` instead of resetting it before the alert popup disappears:

```
.alert(isPresented: $showTwoButtonsAlert){
            Alert(title: Text("Turn on the Switch?"),
                message:Text("Are you sure"),
            primaryButton: .default(Text("Yes"),
        action: {
                    self.showTwoButtonsAlert.toggle()
                }), secondaryButton: .cancel(Text("No"))
    )
```

5. Create a `Button` that changes the value of our `showSimpleAlert` variable to `true`:

```
Button("Display other alert"){
    self.showSimpleAlert = true
}
```

6. Add an alert modifier with a simple `Alert` that displays a message in its title:

```
.alert(isPresented: $showSimpleAlert){
    Alert(title: Text("Minimalist Alert"))
}
```

The resulting preview should look as follows:

Figure 5.4 – PresentingMultipleAlerts preview

7. Click the **Display alert** toggle to see the following alert:

Figure 5.5 – PresentingMultipleAlerts with Display alert clicked

8. Click the **No** button on the **Turn on the Switch?** alert to keep the switch off. Then click the **Display other alert** button to see the second alert as shown in the following screenshot:

Figure 5.6 – PresentingMultipleAlerts with Display other alert clicked

Click **OK** to close the alert. Nice work! You can now build apps using multiple alerts.

How it works

Adding multiple alerts to a single view requires each alert to be attached to a separate struct. Chaining multiple alerts on a single struct would cause just one of the alerts to be executed.

As mentioned in the previous recipes, alerts are triggered when the binding variable passed to the `.alert()` modifier is changed from `false` to `true`. In the `Toggle` view, we use the `primaryButton()` function to set the value of `showTwoButtonsAlert` to `true`. Otherwise, its value gets changed back to `false` before the alert is displayed.

The `cancel()` function also does something new. It contains a custom `Text` struct that provides some custom text to be displayed in the **Cancel** button. If the `Text` struct is left out, the default text, "**Cancel**" will be displayed in the cancel button.

Presenting ActionSheet views

The SwiftUI `ActionSheet` and `Alert` views are both used to request additional information from the user by interrupting the normal flow of the app to display a message. `ActionSheet` provides the user with additional choices related to an action they are currently taking, whereas the `Alert` view informs the user if something unexpected happens or they are about to perform an irreversible action.

In this recipe, we will create an action sheet that gets displayed when the user taps some text in the view.

Getting ready

Create a SwiftUI app named `PresentingActionSheet`.

How to do it

We will implement an action sheet by adding a `.actionSheet()` modifier to a view as well as a trigger that changes the value of a variable used to determine if the sheet is shown or not. The steps are as follows:

1. Below the `ContentView` struct but above the `body` variable, add an `@State` variable to store the state of the action sheet:

    ```
    @State private var showSheet = false
    ```

2. Modify the `Text` in the body variable to display the words `"Present Sheet"` and also add a `.onTapGesture()` modifier to the struct. The latter modifier should set our `showSheet` state variable, which was earlier declared as `true`:

```
Text("Present Sheet")
       .onTapGesture {
       self.showSheet = true
   }
```

3. Finally, add the `.actionSheet()` modifier containing an `ActionSheet`:

```
.actionSheet(isPresented: $showSheet){
   ActionSheet(
     title: Text("ActionSheet"),
     message: Text("Use Action sheet to give users
       alternatives to completing a task").font(.
         largeTitle),
     buttons: [
         .default(Text("Dismiss Sheet")),
         .default(Text("Save")),
         .destructive(Text("Cancel")),
         .default(Text("Print to console")){
             print("Print button clicked")
         }
     ])
   }
```

The resulting preview should look as follows:

Figure 5.7 – PresentingActionSheet preview

4.   Click on **Present Sheet** to display the action sheet:

Figure 5.8 – PresentingActionSheet live preview with the sheet displayed

To view the result of the **Print to console** action, press ⌘ + ⇧ + C to activate the debug console, run the app in an emulator, and press the **Print to console** button. The **Print button clicked** statement should appear in the console when you click the button.

How it works

Displaying or hiding content in SwiftUI is based on the current state of the variables in the view. To display an action sheet, we create a state variable to hold the state of the sheet, a condition that triggers the switch to be displayed, and a view modifier containing the details of the action sheet. In this recipe, our state variable is showSheet, the trigger to change its value is the .onTapGesture() modifier, and the .actionSheet() view modifier contains the details regarding the action sheet. Let's take a closer look at the .actionSheet() modifier and its contents.

The `.actionSheet()` modifier's `isPresented` parameter accepts a binding variable, `showSheet`. This means the action sheet will get displayed when the value of `showSheet` becomes `true`. By using a binding variable, the modifier is also able to change the value of `showSheet` back to `false` after the user makes their choice.

The `ActionSheet` struct in the `.actionSheet()` modifier contains variables for the title and message, and an array of `Alert.Buttons`.

Showing a sheet modally

The Modality design technique can be used to present content in a temporary mode that's separate from the user's previous content and requires an explicit action to exit. Modals can help focus on a self-contained task or set of closely related tasks.

In this recipe, we will learn how to present a sheet modally and how to add navigation items to the modal.

Getting ready

Create a SwiftUI app named `ModalViewApp`.

How to do it

We shall create two SwiftUI views named `ModalView` and `ModalWithNavView` that would be displayed modally when a button is clicked. The steps are as follows:

1. In `ContentView.swift`, between the struct declaration and the body variable, add two state variables, `showModal` and `sheetWithNav`. The state variables will be used to trigger the sheet presentation:

```
@State private var showModal = false
@State private var sheetWithNav = false;
```

2. Add a `VStack` and a button that changes the value of our `showModal` variable to `true` when clicked:

```
VStack {
    Button("Display Sheet"){
        self.showModal = true
    }.sheet(isPresented: $showModal){
```

```
        ModalView()
    }
}
```

3. Add a `.sheet()` modifier to the end of the button. Pass the `showModal` binding to the modifier's `isPresented` argument. Your `Button` struct should now be as follows:

```
Button("Dislay Sheet"){
    self.showModal = true
}.sheet(isPresented: $showModal){
    ModalView()
}
```

4. Now let's create the `ModalView()` SwiftUI view mentioned in the `Button` struct:

   a. Create a new SwiftUI view by pressing the ⌘ + N keys.

   b. Select **SwiftUI View** and click **Next**.

   c. In the **Save As:** field, enter `ModalView`.

   d. Click **Create**.

5. In `ModalView.swift`, change the `Text` struct to display `"Modal Window View"`:

```
Text("Modal Window View")
```

6. Now navigate back to the `ContentView.swift` file and run the canvas Live Preview. Click on the **Display Sheet** button to present the modal. Swipe down to hide the modal.

7. Now let's add a `Button` struct and `.sheet()` modifier to display a modal with navigation items:

```
Button("SheetWithNavigationBar"){
    self.sheetWithNav = true
}.sheet(isPresented: $sheetWithNav){
    ModalWithNavView(sheetWithNav: self.$sheetWithNav)
}
```

8. Let's create the `ModalWithNavView()` SwiftUI view mentioned in the `Button` struct:

   a. Create a new SwiftUI view by pressing the ⌘ + *N* keys.

   b. Select **SwiftUI View** and click **Next**.

   c. In the **Save As:** field, enter `ModalWithNavView`.

   d. Click **Create**.

9. In `ModalWithNavView`, add an `@Binding` variable named `sheetWithNav`:

   ```
   @Binding var sheetWithNav: Bool
   ```

10. Change the `Text` struct string to `"Sheet with navigation"`:

    ```
    Text("Sheet with navigation")
    ```

11. Add a `.navigationBarTitle()` modifier to the text and set the `displayMode` to `.inline`:

    ```
    .navigationBarTitle(Text("Sheet title"), displayMode:
    .inline)
    ```

12. Add a `.navigationBarItems()` modifier to the `Text` struct. The navigation modifier should contain a `Button` struct trailing item that changes our `sheetWithNav` binding back to `false`:

    ```
    .navigationBarItems(trailing: Button(action:{
        self.sheetWithNav = false;
    }){
        Text("Done")
    })
    ```

13. We can't build or run the program at this point because we need to pass a value to the `ModalWithNavView()` located in the preview. To fix the problem, update the view to pass in a binding with an immutable value of `true`:

    ```
    ModalWithNavView(sheetWithNav: .constant(true))
    ```

14. Finally, navigate back to `ContentView.Swift` and run the canvas Live Preview. A click on the `"sheetWithNavigationBar"` button should display the following:

Figure. 5.9 – ModalViewApp preview

How it works

We display the first sheet modally by using the same pattern as in the earlier recipes. First, we create an `@State` variable, `showModal`, that tracks whether the sheet should be visible or not. Then we create a button that changes the value of our state variable when clicked, and finally we add a modifier, `.sheet()`, whose `isPresented` parameter takes our state variable and displays some content when the value turns to `true`.

The second sheet follows a similar pattern to the first sheet but takes a `@Binding` as a parameter. To find out why we use the binding, let's take a look at the view displayed by the second sheet, `ModalWithNavView()`.

The `ModalWithNavView` struct, unlike earlier structs we've used, has an `@Binding` property where we've usually used a `@State` property.

```
@Binding var sheetWithNav: Bool
```

The `@Binding` property lets us declare that a value comes from elsewhere and should be shared between both places. In this case, we want to share the value of the `sheetWithNav` variable declared in `ContentView.swift`. Changing the value in `ModalNavView` struct should change the value in the `ContentView` struct and vice versa.

The content of the `ModalWithNavView` body variable contains a `NavigationView` struct and a `Text` struct with two modifiers. The `.navigationBarTitle()` modifier adds the title to the view, while the `.navigationBarItems()` modifier adds a trailing button that sets our binding variable, `sheetWithNav`, back to `false` when clicked. When clicked, the latter button sets the `ModalWithNavView` back to invisible.

Finally, the `ModalWithNavView` preview expects a `@Binding` for the preview to run. The `ModalWithNavView(sheetWithNav: true)` statement will cause an error because the preview expects a binding to be passed to the view. This can be solved by passing in a binding with an immutable value, `.constant(true)`. Your resulting preview statement should be as follows:

```
ModalWithNavView(sheetWithNav: .constant(true))
```

See also

Apple Human Interface guidelines regarding sheets: `https://developer.apple.com/design/human-interface-guidelines/macos/windows-and-views/sheets/`

Creating a context menu

A context menu is a pop-up menu used to display actions that the developer anticipates the user might want to take. SwiftUI context menus are triggered using 3D Touch on iOS and a right-click on macOS.

A context menu consists of a collection of buttons displayed horizontally in an implicit `HStack`.

In this recipe, we will create a context menu to change the color of an SF symbol.

Getting ready

Create a new SwiftUI project named `ContextMenuApp`.

How to do it

We will display a light bulb in our view and change its color using a context menu. To achieve this, we'll need to create an `@State` variable to hold the current color of the bulb and change its value within the context menu. The steps are as follows:

1. Just above the body variable in `ContentView.swift`, add an `@State` variable to hold the color of the bulb. Initialize it to `red`:

```
@State private var bulbColor = Color.red
```

2. Within the body variable, change the `Text` struct to an `Image` struct that displays a light bulb from SF Symbols:

```
Image(systemName: "lightbulb.fill")
```

3. Add `.font()` and `.foregroundColor()` modifiers to the image. Change the font size to `60` and the foreground color to our `bulbColor` variable:

```
.font(.system(size: 60))
.foregroundColor(bulbColor)
```

4. Add a `.contextMenu()` modifier with three buttons. Each `Button` changes the value of our `bulbColor` variable to a new color:

```
.contextMenu{

        Button("Yellow Bulb"){
            self.bulbColor = Color.yellow
        }
        Button("Blue Bulb"){
            self.bulbColor = Color.blue
        }
        Button("Green Bulb"){
            self.bulbColor = Color.green
        }
    }
```

The resulting preview should look as follows:

Figure 5.10 – ContextMenuApp preview

To test the app, run the canvas live preview, long press on the bulb to display the context menu, and select a new bulb color. The bulb color changes to the selected value.

How it works

The `.contextMenu()` modifier can be attached to any view. In this recipe, we attached it to an `Image` view such that a long press on the view displays the context menu. The `.contextMenu()` modifier contains buttons whose action closure performs a particular function. In our case, each `Button` changes our `bulbColor` `@State` variable to a new color, thereby updating our view.

See also

Apple Human Interface guidelines regarding contextual menus: `https://developer.apple.com/design/human-interface-guidelines/macos/menus/contextual-menus/`

Implementing a popover

A popover is a transient view that appears above other content onscreen when you tap a control area. Popovers typically include an arrow pointing to the location from where it emerged and are dismissed by tapping another part of the screen or a button on the popover.

Popovers are typically used on larger screens and can contain a wide variety of elements. Anything from navigation bars, tables collections, or any other views. The Apple Human Interface guidelines recommend using popovers on iPads only and not iPhones.

In this recipe, we will create a simple popover with a text and display it on an iPad.

Getting ready

Create a new SwiftUI app named `PopoverApp`.

How to do it

Following the pattern we've used so far in this chapter, we shall first create an `@State` variable whose value triggers the displaying or hiding of a popover, and then add a `.popover()` modifier that displays the popover when the `@State` variable is `true`. The steps are as follows:

1. Just above the `body` variable in the `ContentView.swift` file, add a state variable that will be used to trigger the popover:

    ```
    @State private var showPopover = false
    ```

2. Within the `body` variable, replace the `Text` struct with a `Button` that changes the value of `showPopover` to `true` when clicked:

    ```
    Button(action: {
        self.showPopover = true
    }) {
        Text("Show popover").font(.system(size: 40))
    }
    ```

3. Add the `.popover()` modifier to the end of the `Button`:

```
.popover(
        isPresented: self.$showPopover,
        arrowEdge: .bottom
) {
        Text("Popover content displayed here")
    }
```

4. Since popovers should be used on iPads, let's change the canvas preview to display an iPad. Click on the *set the active scheme* button located in the Xcode toolbar area, highlighted in the following screenshot :

Figure 5.11 – Set the active scheme button on Xcode

5. Select any of the iPads in the list (or add a simulator if no iPads are on the list):

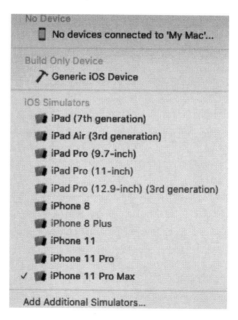

Figure 5.12 – List of Xcode simulators

6. Run the code in the canvas Live Preview and click on the **Show popover** button to display the popover. The resulting view should be as follows:

Figure. 5.13 – PopoverApp preview

Click on the **Show popover** text to display the popover.

How it works

A .popover() modifier takes four possible arguments, although three were used here. Possible arguments are isPresented, attachmentAnchor, arrowEdge, and content.

The isPresented argument takes a binding that's used to trigger the display of the popover, showPopover.

We did not use an attachment anchor in this recipe. attachmentAnchor is a positioning anchor that defines where the popover is attached.

The `arrowEdge` argument represents where the popover arrow should be displayed. It takes four possible values, `.bottom`, `.top`, `.leading`, and `.trailing`. We used the `.bottom` value to display our arrow edge at the bottom of the popover, just above our text.

The `content` argument is a closure that returns the content of the popover. In this recipe, a `Text` struct was used as content, but we could also use a separate SwiftUI view in the content closure, such as an image or a view from another SwiftUI View file.

See also

Apple Human Interface guidelines regarding popovers: `https://developer.apple. com/design/human-interface-guidelines/macos/windows-and-views/ popovers/`

6
Drawing with SwiftUI

One of the strongest points of SwiftUI is that all the components are uniform, and they can be used in an interchangeable and mixed way, whereas in UIKit, intermixing labels, buttons, and custom shapes was a bit cumbersome. In this chapter, we'll see how to use the basic shapes offered out of the box by SwiftUI and how to create new shapes using the `Path` class. We'll see how simple and natural it is to deal with, extend, and use them with standard components such as text and sliders.

At the end of the chapter, you'll be able to create a view from a custom path, add a gradient to fill it or to act as a border, and will know how to write a Tic-Tac-Toe game using basic shapes.

In this chapter, we will cover the following recipes:

- Using SwiftUI's built-in shapes
- Creating a dashed border in SwiftUI
- Drawing a custom shape
- Drawing a curved custom shape
- Using `UIBezierPath` with SwiftUI
- Implementing a progress ring

- Implementing a Tic-Tac-Toe game in SwiftUI

- Rendering a gradient view in SwiftUI

- Rendering a border with a gradient

- Filling a border with an image

- Building a bar chart

- Building a pie chart

Technical requirements

The code in this chapter is based on Xcode 12 and iOS 14, but all the recipes support iOS 13 as well.

You can find the code in the book's GitHub repo at `https://github.com/PacktPublishing/SwiftUI-Cookbook/tree/master/Chapter06%20-%20Drawing%20with%20SwiftUI`.

Using SwiftUI's built-in shapes

SwiftUI contains a few basic shapes such as rectangles, circles, and so on that can be used to create more complex shapes by combining them.

In this recipe, we'll explore how to create them, add a border and a fill, and how to lay out the shapes.

There will be more than we can show here, but with this recipe as a starting point, you can modify the shapes to discover all the potential of the built-in shapes of SwiftUI.

Getting ready

As usual, let's start by creating a new SwiftUI project with Xcode, calling it `BuiltInShapesApp`.

How to do it...

SwiftUI has five different basic shapes:

- `Rectangle`

- `RoundedRectangle`

- `Capsule`

- Circle

- Ellipse

In the `ContentView` body, we add a vertical stack to contain all of them:

1. Create a `VStack` component with a spacing of `10` and horizontal padding of `20`:

```
var body: some View {
    VStack(spacing: 10) {

    }
    .padding([.horizontal], 20)
}
```

2. Add the shapes inside the stack:

```
var body: some View {
    VStack(spacing: 10) {
        Rectangle()
            .stroke(Color.orange,
                    lineWidth: 15)
        RoundedRectangle(cornerRadius: 20)
            .fill(Color.red)
        Capsule(style: .continuous)
            .fill(Color.green)
            .frame(height: 100)
        Capsule(style: .circular)
            .fill(Color.yellow)
            .frame(height: 100)
        Circle()
            .strokeBorder(Color.blue,
                          lineWidth: 15)
        Ellipse()
            .fill(Color.purple)
    }
    .padding(.horizontal, 20)
}
```

This renders the following preview:

Figure 6.1 – SwiftUI's built-in shapes

How it works

Thanks to SwiftUI, the code is pretty self-explanatory, but there are a couple of notes to make. Firstly, `capsule` can have two types of curvatures for the rounded corners:

- Continuous
- Circular

In the following diagram, you can see the difference between the corners of the two capsules when taken in isolation:

Figure 6.2 – Capsule corners style

The shape at the top is a capsule with the continuous style, and the capsule at the bottom has a circular style.

In the case of the circular style, the sides of the capsule are two perfect semi-circles, while with the continuous style, the corners smoothly transition from a line to a curve.

The other thing to note is that the rectangles are closer to each other than the other shapes: the gap is narrower than the one between the circle and the ellipse.

The difference lies in the way the borders are applied to the shapes.

The rectangle uses the `.stroke()` modifier, which creates a border centered in the frame, as shown in the following diagram:

Figure 6.3 – stroke applied to a shape

On the other hand, the circle uses the `.strokeBorder()` modifier, which creates a border contained inside the frame:

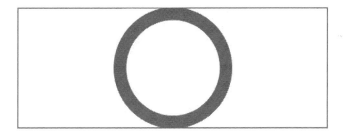

Figure 6.4 – strokeBorder applied to a shape

Depending on where you want to lay the shapes down, you can use either one of the View modifiers.

Creating a dashed border in SwiftUI

SwiftUI permits you to create sophisticated strokes around the border of a View. The strokes can be customized as much as we want, changing the color, thickness, and the style it's drawn in – either continuous or dashed.

Using this functionality, in this recipe, we'll see how to build a dashed border for an Instagram avatar-like image.

Getting ready

Let's implement a new SwiftUI project called `DashedBorderShapeApp`. The recipe requires an image as the base for the avatar – feel free to add your own image or use the one you can find in the GitHub repository in the `Resources` folder (`https://github.com/PacktPublishing/SwiftUI-Cookbook/blob/master/Resources/Chapter06/recipe2/mountainbike.jpg`), courtesy of the *Pixabay* user *David Mark* (`https://pixabay.com/users/tpsdave-12019`). Add the image in the `Assets` catalog, calling it `mountainbike`.

How to do it...

In this recipe, we'll see how adding a dashed border is as easy as adding an overlay to an image:

1. Add an `Image` component in the body of the `ContentView` struct, and then we clip it with a `Circle` shape. In this way, we cut out everything outside the border of the `Circle` shape, creating a spherical image:

```
struct ContentView: View {
    var body: some View {
        Image("mountainbike")
            .resizable()
            .aspectRatio(contentMode: .fit)
            .clipShape(Circle())
            .shadow(radius: 10)
            .padding(.horizontal, 20)
    }
}
```

2. Add an overlay View modifier with `Circle` whose border has a custom `StrokeStyle` applied, with a dashed list:

```
.overlay(
    Circle()
        .strokeBorder(Color.black,
                      style: StrokeStyle(
```

```
                              lineWidth: 10,

                              dash: [15]

            ))

    )
```

This renders a nice dashed border around the avatar, like so:

Figure 6.5 – A simple dashed border around an image

How it works

The `StrokeStyle` class creates a custom line that can be applied everywhere a line can be drawn.

The `dash` parameter defines the size of each element of the line, so it is possible to have a more complex dashed line:

Figure 6.6 – Complex dashed border

The preceding image is what you get with a border with the following parameters:

```
.strokeBorder(Color.black,
                style: StrokeStyle(
                    lineWidth: 10,
                    dash: [15, 5, 25]
))
```

As usual with SwiftUI, this only scratches the surface of the possibilities, and the best way of learning is to try fiddling with the parameters in an example app.

Drawing a custom shape

SwiftUI's drawing functionality permits more than just using the built-in shapes: creating a custom shape is just a matter of creating a `Path` component with the various components and then wrapping it in a `Shape` object.

In this recipe, we will work through the basics of custom shape creation, implementing a simple rhombus, which is a geometric shape with four equal straight sides that resembles a diamond.

To create a custom shape in SwiftUI, our class must conform to the `Shape` protocol, whose only function, `path(in: CGRect)`, provides a rectangle that represents the frame where the shape will be rendered as a parameter, and returns a `Path` struct that is the description of the outline of the shape.

The `Path` struct has several drawing primitives that permit us to move the point, add lines and arcs, and so on. This allows us to define the outline of the shape.

Using a `Path` object resembles a bit of the old educative language, **Logo**, where you are in charge of guiding a turtle that draws a line onto the screen, and you can give only simple commands: go to location A, draw a line until location B, draw an arc up to location C, and so on.

Getting ready

Create a new single-view app with SwiftUI, called `RhombusApp`.

How to do it...

As we mentioned in the introduction, we are going to implement a `Shape` object that defines the way our custom view must be visualized:

1. Let's add a `Rhombus` struct:

```
struct Rhombus: Shape {
    func path(in rect: CGRect) -> Path {
        Path() { path in
            path.move(to: CGPoint(x: rect.midX,
                                  y: rect.minY))
            path.addLine(to: CGPoint(x: rect.maxX,
                                     y: rect.midY))
            path.addLine(to: CGPoint(x: rect.midX,
                                     y: rect.maxY))
            path.addLine(to: CGPoint(x: rect.minX,
                                     y: rect.midY))
            path.closeSubpath()
        }
    }
}
```

2. Use the `Rhombus` struct inside the `body` of the `ContentView` struct:

```
struct ContentView: View {
    var body: some View {
        Rhombus()
            .fill(Color.orange)
            .aspectRatio(0.7, contentMode: .fit)
            .padding(.horizontal, 10)
    }
}
```

A nice orange rhombus is then displayed in the preview:

Figure 6.7 – A rhombus as a custom SwiftUI shape

How it works

As mentioned in the introduction to the recipe, to create a shape we must give commands to a Path object. In this case, it is important to note that the coordinates system of SwiftUI has its origin in the top-left corner of the screen, with the x axis from left to right, and the y axis from top to bottom.

The following diagram shows the coordinates system and the shortcuts defined in iOS for the most important points:

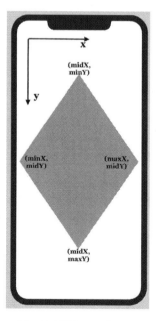

Figure 6.8 – SwiftUI coordinates system

As mentioned in the introduction, the `rect` parameter is the container frame, and by exploiting a few of the convenient properties it exposes, we initially set our starting point in the top vertex of the rhombus, from where we added lines in an anti-clockwise direction connecting the other three corners.

Finally, we close the path, which creates a complete line from the last point to the first point.

SwiftUI recognizes the closed shape and intuitively knows the space that needs to be filled inside the boundaries of the shape.

Drawing a curved custom shape

Following up on the previous *Drawing a custom shape* recipe, what if we want to define a shape that is made up not only of straight lines, but also has a curved line in it? In this recipe, we'll build a heart-shaped component using the arc and curve primitives of `Path`.

Getting ready

As usual, create a SwiftUI app called `HeartApp`.

How to do it...

We are going to follow the same steps we implemented in the previous *Drawing a custom shape* recipe, adding curves and an arc from one point to another.

Since the control points of a heart shape are in the mid point of each side, we must add some convenient properties to the `CGRect` struct.

Let's do this with the following steps:

1. Let's add the properties to return the coordinates from each of the quarters:

```
extension CGRect {
    var quarterX: CGFloat {
        minX + size.height/4
    }
    var quarterY: CGFloat {
        minY + size.height/4
    }
    var threeQuartersX: CGFloat {
        minX + 3*size.height/4
```

```
        }
    var threeQuartersY: CGFloat {
        minY + 3*size.height/4
    }
}
```

2. Implement the `Heart` shape:

```
struct Heart: Shape {
    func path(in rect: CGRect) -> Path {
        Path { path in
            path.move(to: CGPoint(x: rect.midX,
                                  y: rect.maxY))
            path.addCurve(to: CGPoint(x: rect.minX,
                                      y: rect.quarterY),
                          control1: CGPoint(x: rect.midX,
                                  y: rect.threeQuartersY),
                          control2: CGPoint(x: rect.minX,
                                      y: rect.midY))
            path.addArc(center: CGPoint(x: rect.quarterX,
                                        y: rect.quarterY),
                        radius: rect.size.width/4,
                        startAngle: .radians(.pi),
                        endAngle: .radians(0),
                        clockwise: false)
            path.addArc(center: CGPoint(x: rect.
                threeQuartersX, y: rect.quarterY),
                        radius: rect.size.width/4,
                        startAngle: .radians(.pi),
                        endAngle: .radians(0),
                        clockwise: false)

            path.addCurve(to: CGPoint(x: rect.midX,
                                      y: rect.maxY),
                          control1: CGPoint(x: rect.maxX,
                                      y: rect.midY),
                          control2: CGPoint(x: rect.midX,
```

```
                                      y: rect.threeQuartersY))

            path.closeSubpath()
        }
    }
}
```

3. Finally, the `Heart` shape is ready to be added to the body, where we fill it with red and add an orange border:

```
struct ContentView: View {
    var body: some View {
        Heart()
            .fill(Color.red)
            .overlay(Heart()
                .stroke(Color.orange, lineWidth: 10))
            .aspectRatio(contentMode: .fit)
            .padding(.horizontal, 20)
    }
}
```

The following screenshot shows a really nice heart shape as a result of our code:

Figure 6.9 – Custom heart-shaped component

How it works

Like in the *Drawing a custom shape* recipe, we initially set the starting point to be the top tip of the shape, and then added the curves and arcs clockwise.

You can see that the `arc()` function has a `clockwise` parameter, which is set to `false` in our example. However, the arcs are drawn in a clockwise direction: how is this possible?

The thing is that SwiftUI, like UIView, uses a flipped coordinate system, so clockwise for SwiftUI means counterclockwise for the user, and vice versa. You can imagine a flipped coordinate system as a coordinates system flipped around the *y* axis, so if it is reverted to the original position, you can see how a clockwise movement is then clockwise for the observer too.

The following figure should help you to visualize this:

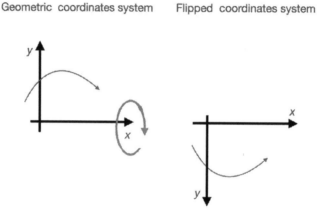

Figure 6.10 – Relation to the clockwise direction – drawing an arc in the geometric and flipped coordinate systems

Using UIBezierPath with SwiftUI

In the preceding *Drawing a custom shape* and *Drawing a curved custom shape* recipes, we saw how to build a path using points relative to the container frame, but what if we have a figure built using absolute coordinates in `UIBezierPath`, maybe from a previous UIKit project?

It turns out that we can translate `UIBezierPath` into a `Path` object, and then adapt it to the contained frame, scaling it to fill it.

Getting ready

For this recipe, we are going to use a pretty long `UIBezierPath` definition of an *ace of spades* shape, so I won't add the full description here, but you can find it in the repo at `SwiftUI-Cookbook/Chapter06 - Drawing with SwiftUI/05 - Using UIBezierPath with SwiftUI/AceOfSpadeApp/AceOfSpadeApp/AceOfSpade+UIBezierPath.swift`.

Let's create a project called `AceOfSpadeApp` and add that file to it.

How to do it...

This recipe is really straightforward; the only thing to take note of is to calculate the scale factor in the correct way:

1. Add the definition of the symbol as an extension of `UIBezierPath`. You can find the full definition of the file in the repo and mentioned in the *Getting ready* section:

```swift
extension UIBezierPath {
    static var spade: UIBezierPath {
        let rightPath = UIBezierPath()
        rightPath.move(to: CGPoint(x: 0.472915, y:
            0.13958))
        //... Code
        rightPath.close()


        let leftPath = UIBezierPath()
        leftPath.move(to: CGPoint(x: 0.472915, y:
            0.139584))
        //... Code
        leftPath.close()


        let path = UIBezierPath()
        path.append(rightPath)
        path.append(leftPath)
        return path
    }
}
```

2. Create a struct that conforms to `Shape` where we pass a `UIBezierPath` class that will be rescaled to fit the frame:

```
struct BezierShape: Shape {
    let bezierPath: UIBezierPath

    func path(in rect: CGRect) -> Path {
        let ratio = min(rect.width, rect.height)
        let transform = CGAffineTransform(scaleX: ratio,
                                          y: ratio)
        return Path(bezierPath.cgPath).
            applying(transform)
    }
}
```

3. Render the shape in the body of the `ContentView` struct:

```
struct ContentView: View {
    var body: some View {
        BezierShape(bezierPath: .spade)
            .aspectRatio(contentMode: .fit)
    }
}
```

Previewing the screen, we can see a nice ace of spades in the center of the simulator:

Figure 6.11 – Ace of spades rendered as UIBezierPath

How it works

Depending on the way the original shape is described, we need to scale the resulting **Path** object in a way to be visible onscreen.

In this recipe, the original image has all its points between 0 and 1, so we need to scale the size of the path using the minimum between the width and height of the resulting frame as a multiplier for each point. In this way, the image will be perfectly contained in the frame.

In the case that your path is bigger than 1, you should scale it down, either hardcoding the largest x or y value, or preprocessing the path to make it contained in the box between 0 and 1.

There's more

If you look carefully at the spade shape, you can see that there is a thin transparent line between the two halves: this is because of the approximation of the points that slightly overlap.

Would you be able to convert the two original paths to a single and closed one?

This is a good exercise that is left to you, the reader, in order to further understand how the drawing of a path works.

Implementing a progress ring

Admit it – since you bought your Apple Watch, you are getting fitter, aren't you?

I bet it is because of the activity rings you want to close every day – am I right?

In this recipe, we'll implement a progress ring similar to those on the Apple Watch, and we'll drive them via some sliders.

Getting ready

There's nothing in particular that needs preparing for this recipe; just create a SwiftUI project called ProgressRingApp.

How to do it...

We are going to implement two components:

- A single `ProgressRing` View
- A composite `RingsView`

We'll add the latter to `ContentView`, and we'll simulate the progress using three sliders:

1. Implement a ring view using a `Shape` object and an arc:

```swift
struct ProgressRing: Shape {
    private let startAngle = Angle.radians(1.5 * .pi)

    @Binding
    var progress: Double

    func path(in rect: CGRect) -> Path {
        Path() { path in
            path.addArc(
                center: CGPoint(x: rect.midX, y: rect.
                    midY),
                radius: rect.width / 2,
                startAngle: startAngle,
                endAngle: startAngle +
                            Angle(radians: 2 * Double.pi *
                                progress),
                clockwise: false
            )
        }
    }
}
```

2. Create a `RingsView` view with three concentric `ProgressRingView` structs:

```swift
struct ProgressRingsView: View {
    private let ringPadding: CGFloat = 5
    private let ringWidth: CGFloat = 40
    private var ringStrokeStyle: StrokeStyle {
        StrokeStyle(lineWidth: ringWidth,
```

```
                        lineCap: .round,
                        lineJoin: .round)

    }

    @Binding
    var progressExternal: Double
    @Binding
    var progressCentral: Double
    @Binding
    var progressInternal: Double

    var body: some View {
        ZStack {
            ProgressRing(progress: $progressInternal)
                .stroke(Color.blue,
                    style: ringStrokeStyle)
                .padding(2*(ringWidth + ringPadding))
            ProgressRing(progress: $progressCentral)
                .stroke(Color.red,
                    style: ringStrokeStyle)
                .padding(ringWidth + ringPadding)
            ProgressRing(progress: $progressExternal)
                .stroke(Color.green,
                    style: ringStrokeStyle)

        }
        .padding(ringWidth)
    }
}
```

3. Finally, add `RingsView` and three sliders in the `ContentView` struct:

```
struct ContentView: View {
    @State
    private var progressExternal: Double = 0.3
    @State
    private var progressCentral: Double = 0.7
    @State
    private var progressInternal: Double = 0.5

    var body: some View {
        VStack(spacing: 10) {
            Spacer()
                ProgressRingsView(
                    progressExternal: $progressExternal,
                    progressCentral: $progressCentral,
                    progressInternal: $progressInternal)
                .aspectRatio(contentMode: .fit)
            Spacer()
            Slider(value: $progressInternal,
                    in: 0...1, step: 0.01)
            Slider(value: $progressCentral,
                    in: 0...1, step: 0.01)
            Slider(value: $progressExternal,
                    in: 0...1, step: 0.01)
        }
        .padding(30)
    }
}
```

Previewing the app after pressing the play button, we can play with the ring and even close all of them without doing any activities! You can see the rings in the following screenshot:

Figure 6.12 – Our three progress rings

How it works

ProgressRing is a simple Path object with an arc.

The origin of an arc in Path is from the horizontal right axis. Since we want to make the ring start at the vertical axis, we set our initial arc as $3/2* \pi$ because the angle grows clockwise. Even though the direction of the angle is clockwise, you will notice that we set false in the parameter of the arc: this is because SwiftUI has a flipped coordinate system, as discussed earlier, where the y axis points downward instead of upward, so the clock direction is inverted.

The various progress variables are decorated with @Binding in the ProgressRing and RingsView components, because they are injected and controlled by an external class, and they are decorated with @State in ContentView because they are mutated in the same component by the sliders.

When we change the value of a slider, the mutation is reflected in the rendering of ContentView and then mirrored down to the child components that update the arc length.

Implementing a Tic-Tac-Toe game in SwiftUI

SwiftUI's drawing primitives are powerful, and it is even possible to implement a game using these only.

In this recipe, we'll see how to build a simple touchable and playable Tic-Tac-Toe game, in which the game alternates between inserting a cross and a nought every time you put your finger on a cell of the board.

For those who are unfamiliar with the game, Tic-Tac-Toe is a paper-and-pencil game where two players take turns to mark either a cross or a circle, also called a *nought*, in a 3x3 grid. The player who is able to place three of their marks in a line horizontally, vertically, or diagonally, wins.

Getting ready

For this recipe, we don't need any external resources, so it is enough just to create a SwiftUI project in Xcode called `TicTacToeApp` to hit the ground running.

How to do it...

As you know, Tic-Tac-Toe is composed of three components:

- A nought (circle)
- A cross
- The game grid

Using SwiftUI, we can precisely model these components, splitting each one in two – a shape that renders the design and a view that manages the business logic:

1. Let's start with the nought, which is just a circle:

```
struct Nought: View {
    var body: some View {
        Circle()
            .stroke(Color.red, lineWidth: 10)
    }
}
```

2. Next, implement the shape of a cross:

```swift
struct CrossShape: Shape {
    func path(in rect: CGRect) -> Path {
        Path() { path in

            path.move(to: CGPoint(x: rect.minX,
                                  y: rect.minY))
            path.addLine(to: CGPoint(x: rect.maxX,
                                     y: rect.maxY))

            path.move(to: CGPoint(x: rect.maxX,
                                  y: rect.minY))
            path.addLine(to: CGPoint(x: rect.minX,
                                     y: rect.maxY))
        }
    }
}
```

3. Now, we implement a `Cross` view that renders the shape of the `CrossShape` struct with a green stroke:

```swift
struct Cross: View {
    var body: some View {
        CrossShape()
            .stroke(Color.green, style:
                StrokeStyle(lineWidth: 10,
                            lineCap: .round,
                            lineJoin: .round))
    }
}
```

4. Next, we add the `Cell` view, which can be either a nought or a cross, visible or hidden. It also manages to change itself by detecting when the user taps on it:

```
struct Cell: View {
    @State private var isVisible = false
    @State private var isNought = false
    @Binding var isNextNought: Bool

    var body: some View {
        ZStack {
            Nought()
                .opacity((isVisible && isNought) ? 1 : 0)
            Cross()
                .opacity((isVisible && !isNought) ? 1 : 0)
        }
        .padding(20)
        .contentShape(Rectangle())
        .onTapGesture {
            guard !isVisible else {
                return
            }
            isVisible = true
            isNought = self.isNextNought
            isNextNought.toggle()
        }
    }
}
```

5. Let's now implement the grid, starting from its shape:

```
struct GridShape: Shape {
    func path(in rect: CGRect) -> Path {
        Path() { path in

            path.move(to: CGPoint(x: rect.width/3,
                                  y: rect.minY))
            path.addLine(to:
                         CGPoint(x: rect.width/3,
```

```
                                        y: rect.maxY))

        path.move(to: CGPoint(x: 2*rect.width/3,
                                y: rect.minY))
        path.addLine(to: CGPoint(x: 2*rect.width/3,
                                  y: rect.maxY))

        path.move(to: CGPoint(x: rect.minX,
                                y: rect.height/3))
        path.addLine(to: CGPoint(x: rect.maxX,
                                  y: rect.height/3))

        path.move(to: CGPoint(x: rect.minX,
                                y: 2*rect.height/3))
        path.addLine(to: CGPoint(x: rect.maxX,
                                  y: 2*rect.height/3))
        }
      }
    }
```

6. At this point, we could create a `Grid` view with 9 nested cells, but it is better to introduce the concept of `Row`, which contains three cells horizontally:

```
struct Row: View {
    @Binding
    var isNextNought: Bool

    var body: some View {
      HStack {
        Cell(isNextNought: $isNextNought)
        Cell(isNextNought: $isNextNought)
        Cell(isNextNought: $isNextNought)
      }
    }
}
```

7. The `Grid` view we add in the following code has three vertically stacked
    `Row` structs:

```swift
struct Grid: View {
    @State
    var isNextNought: Bool = false

    var body: some View {
        ZStack {
            GridShape()
                .stroke(Color.blue, lineWidth: 15)
            VStack {
                Row(isNextNought: $isNextNought)
                Row(isNextNought: $isNextNought)
                Row(isNextNought: $isNextNought)
            }
        }
        .aspectRatio(contentMode: .fit)
    }
}
```

8. The last thing to add is the `Grid` view to the `ContentView` struct:

```swift
struct ContentView: View {
    var body: some View {
        Grid()
            .padding(.horizontal, 20)
    }
}
```

It's been quite a long recipe, but when you preview the screen, you can see how we can play almost as if we have a pencil and paper in front of us:

Figure 6.13 – Playing Tic-Tac-Toe with SwiftUI

How it works

This simple game is a perfect example of how it is possible to create quite sophisticated interactions by composing simple components.

The isNextNought variable defines which type of mark will be the next one placed, and it is set to false in the Grid component, meaning that the first mark will always be Cross. When tapping on a cell, the isNextNought variable will be toggled, alternating the type of mark, a cross or a nought, placed each time.

It is interesting to note that before applying the view modifier for the `onTapGesture` gesture, we must set a `contentShape()` modifier. The reason for that is because the default tappable area is given by the visible part of the component, but at the start, all the cells are hidden, and so the area is empty!

The `contentShape()` modifier then defines the hit test area in which a touch can be detected. In this case, we want that to occupy the whole area, so `Rectangle` is used, but we could use `Circle`, `Capsule`, or even a custom shape.

There's more

The game is almost complete, but it is missing at least a couple of things:

- Selecting the first mark
- Detecting when a player has won

Use the task of creating these features to further explore SwiftUI and the way it manages shapes. Adding these two features would help you to better understand how the components work together, and with these features added, you can create a complete **Tic-Tac-Toe** game app you could even release in the App Store!

Rendering a gradient view in SwiftUI

SwiftUI has several ways of rendering gradients. A gradient can be used to fill a shape, or even fill a border, as you will see in the *Rendering a border with a gradient* recipe later in this chapter.

In this recipe, we will be focused on understanding what types of gradients we can use with SwiftUI and how to define them.

Getting ready

Create a SwiftUI app called `GradientViewsApp`.

How to do it...

SwiftUI has three different types of gradients:

- Linear gradients
- Radial gradients
- Angular gradients

In each one, we can define the list of the colors that will smoothly transform into each other and, depending on the type of gradient, we can also define some additional properties such as the direction, radius, and angles of the transformation.

To explore all of them, we are going to add a a `Picker` component to select the type of gradient.

The `ContentView` struct will have a `Text` component that shows the selected gradient. We can do this with the following steps:

1. Let's start by adding a style to our `Text` component:

```swift
extension Text {
    func bigLight() -> some View {
        self
            .font(.system(size: 80))
            .fontWeight(.thin)
            .foregroundColor(.white)
    }
}
```

2. The first gradient we add is the linear one, where the color transitions in a linear direction:

```swift
struct LinearGradientView: View {
    var body: some View {
        ZStack {
            LinearGradient(
                gradient: Gradient(colors:
                    [.orange, .green, .blue, .black]),
                startPoint: .topLeading,
                endPoint: .bottomTrailing)
            Text("Linear Gradient")
                .bigLight()
        }
    }
}
```

3. The second is the radial gradient, where the colors transitions through concentric circles:

```
struct RadialGradientView: View {
    var body: some View {
        ZStack {
            RadialGradient(gradient: Gradient(colors:
                           [.orange, .green, .blue, .black]),
                           center: .center,
                           startRadius: 20,
                           endRadius: 500)
            Text("Radial Gradient")
                .bigLight()
        }
    }
}
```

4. The last one is the angular gradient, where the transition rotates in a complete rotation:

```
struct AngularGradientView: View {
    var body: some View {
        ZStack {
            AngularGradient(gradient: Gradient(
                colors: [.orange, .green, .blue, .black,
                         .black, .blue, .green, .orange]),
                         center: .center)
            Text("Angular Gradient")
                .bigLight()
        }
    }
}
```

5. Finally, we add the three different gradients to the ContentView struct, selecting the one to present using Picker:

```swift
struct ContentView: View {
    @State
    private var selectedGradient = 0

    var body: some View {
        ZStack(alignment: .top) {
            Group {
                if selectedGradient == 0 {
                    LinearGradientView()
                } else if selectedGradient == 1 {
                    RadialGradientView()
                } else {
                    AngularGradientView()
                }
            }.edgesIgnoringSafeArea(.all)

            Picker(selection: self.$selectedGradient,
                   label: Text("Select Gradient")) {
                Text("Linear").tag(0)
                Text("Radial").tag(1)
                Text("Angular").tag(2)
            }
            .pickerStyle(SegmentedPickerStyle())
            .padding(.horizontal, 32)
        }
    }
}
```

Running the app, we can see the different types of gradients, and you may be amazed by how such a beautiful effect can be achieved with so few lines of code:

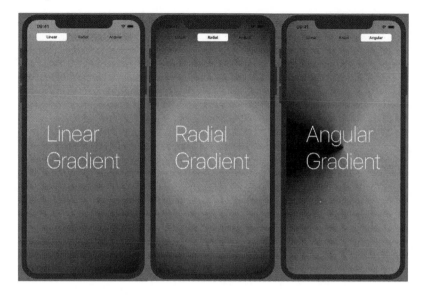

Figure 6.14 – Linear, radial, and angular gradients

How it works

Each type of gradient has a list of colors as parameters, and this provides great flexibility. We have seen in this recipe that there are three different ways of representing a gradient: linear, radial, and angular.

For each of them, we defined a list of the colors it draws from the origin to the destination.

It is worth noting that the colors don't need to be just the original and destination colors; rather, we can have as many as we want. The Gradient SwiftUI view will take care of creating a smooth transition between each pair of colors.

Each different gradient type then offers further possibilities for customization:

- In the case of a **linear** gradient, you can define the direction in which the gradient changes (for example, top to bottom or top-leading to bottom-trailing).

- For the **radial** gradient, you can set the radius of the concentric circles for each of the transitions.

- In the **angular** gradient, you can define the center where the angle of the color transition starts, as well as the start and end angles. If you omit the angles, a full rotational gradient will be created.

There's more

In the following *Rendering a border with a gradient* recipe, we'll see how the gradient can be applied to borders as well.

Rendering a border with a gradient

A gradient can be a powerful way to fill the border of a geometric shape.

In this recipe, we'll see how to change the border of a progress ring with the different types of gradient.

Getting ready

This recipe doesn't require any resources, so let's just create a SwiftUI project called `GradientBorderApp`.

How to do it...

Adding a gradient to a shape is like having a gradient in a view and using that shape as a cutout.

We'll reuse the progress ring made in the *Implementing a progress ring* recipe, using a slider to change the progress and a picker to change the type of gradient:

1. First, let's add the `ProgressRing` View:

```
struct ProgressRing: Shape {
    private let startAngle = Angle.radians(1.5 * .pi)

    @Binding
    var progress: Double

    func path(in rect: CGRect) -> Path {
        Path() { path in
            path.addArc(
                center: CGPoint(x: rect.midX, y: rect.
                    midY),
                radius: rect.width / 2,
                startAngle: startAngle,
                endAngle: startAngle +
```

```
                    Angle(radians: 2 * Double.pi *
                        progress),
              clockwise: false
          )
        }
      }
    }
```

2. The gradients will be part of an enum constant to wrap them in a namespace:

```
enum Gradients {
    static var linearGradient: some ShapeStyle {
        LinearGradient(
            gradient: Gradient(colors:
                [.orange, .yellow, .red]),
            startPoint: .top,
            endPoint: .bottom)
    }

    static var radialGradient: some ShapeStyle {
        RadialGradient(gradient:
            Gradient(colors:[.orange, .green]),
                center: .center,
                startRadius: 35,
                endRadius: 450)
    }

    static var angularGradient: some ShapeStyle {
        AngularGradient(gradient: Gradient(
            colors: [.orange, .yellow, .red,
                .yellow, .orange]),
                center: .center)
    }
}
```

3. Finally, let's add `RingView` to the `ContentView` struct, to simulate the progress with a moving `Slider` component, and select the type of gradient we want with a picker. First, add a property to return the right progress ring:

```
struct ContentView: View {
    @State
    private var selectedGradient = 0
    @State
    private var progressInternal: Double = 0.7

    private let strokeStyle = StrokeStyle(lineWidth: 60,
                                          lineCap: .round,
                                          lineJoin: .round)

    @ViewBuilder
    var progressRing: some View {
        if selectedGradient == 0 {
            ProgressRing(progress: $progressInternal)
                .stroke(Gradients.linearGradient,
                    style: strokeStyle)
        } else if selectedGradient == 1 {
            ProgressRing(progress: $progressInternal)
                .stroke(Gradients.radialGradient,
                    style: strokeStyle)
        } else {
            ProgressRing(progress: $progressInternal)
                .stroke(Gradients.angularGradient,
                    style: strokeStyle)
        }
    }

    var body: some View {
        // ...
    }
}
```

4. Finally, let's add the progress ring to the body in the following code, alongside the picker and the slider:

```swift
struct ContentView: View {
    // ...

    var body: some View {
        VStack() {
            Picker(selection: self.$selectedGradient,
                   label: Text("Select Gradient")) {
                Text("Linear").tag(0)
                Text("Radial").tag(1)
                Text("Angular").tag(2)
            }
            .pickerStyle(SegmentedPickerStyle())
            Spacer()
            progressRing
            .aspectRatio(contentMode: .fit)
            Spacer()
            Slider(value: $progressInternal,
                   in: 0...1,
                   step: 0.01)
        }
        .padding(.horizontal, 60)
    }
}
```

Running the app, we can see how the gradients apply to the stroke:

Figure 6.15 – Stroke with linear, radial, and angular gradient

How it works

To use a struct as a stroke, it must conform to the ShapeStyle protocol.

In this recipe, we implemented three types of gradient components, conforming to the ShapeStyle protocol.

We then created a tab bar component to select which Gradient style will be applied to the progress ring. To make clear how the gradient border applies to the progress ring, the size of it is handled by a slider component.

It is interesting to note that the @ViewBuilder property wrapper states that the property can be used as a view builder inside other view builders. We use this statement to reduce the code inside ContentView's body method.

Filling a border with an image

We know that filling a border with color is pretty easy, but what about an image?

It turns out that, like gradients in the *Rendering a border with a gradient* recipe, using an image for styling a stroke is straightforward.

Getting ready

We are going to use an image to fill the border, and you can either use JesterBackground, provided for you in the GitHub repo in the Resources folder (https://github.com/PacktPublishing/SwiftUI-Cookbook/blob/master/Resources/Chapter06/recipe10/JesterBackground.png), or add one of your choice.

Create a SwiftUI project called ImageBorderApp and add the image to the Assets folder.

How to do it...

In this recipe, we are going to render a simple Circle and add an image in the strokeBorder() modifier:

1. Let's add Circle inside the body of the ContentView struct and make it central on the screen with some padding:

    ```
    struct ContentView: View {
        var body: some View {
            Circle()
                .aspectRatio(contentMode: .fit)
                .shadow(radius: 10)
                .padding(.horizontal, 30)
        }
    }
    ```

2. Add a strokeBorder() modifier with an image as StrokeStyle:

    ```
    var body: some View {
        Circle()
            .strokeBorder(ImagePaint(image:
                Image("JesterBackground"),
                                scale: 0.1),
    ```

```
                        lineWidth: 50)
    //...
}
```

In the live preview, we can see the circle with our image as a background:

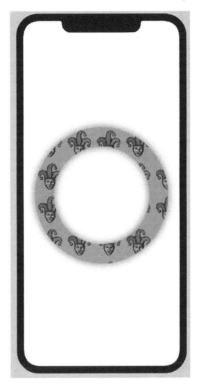

Figure 6.16 – Image as a stroke background

How it works

ImagePaint is a struct that encapsulates an image, and it also conforms to ShapeStyle, so that it can be used as a parameter in strokeBorder().

It has a parameter to set the scale, and also another parameter that you can use to restrict to only a part of the image, defining a rectangle to crop.

Building a bar chart

Using simple shapes, it is possible to build some nice features. For example, using just a bunch of rectangles, we can create a nice bar chart.

We are going to present the average monthly precipitation for three European cities: Dublin, Milan, and London. The data that we'll use is from https://www.climatestotravel.com/.

Getting ready

This recipe doesn't need any external resources, so it's enough to create a SwiftUI project called BarChartApp.

How to do it...

The data we have represents the average quantity of rain in centimeters. Looking at the data, we can see that the maximum rainfall is one centimeter, so we can adapt the bars to have a full shape for that value.

Let's implement our bar chart as follows:

1. Add enum to represent the months and a datapoint value type to hold the values to plot on the bar chart:

```
enum Month: String, CaseIterable {
    case jan, feb, mar, apr, may, jun,
    jul, aug, sep, oct, nov, dec
}


struct MonthDataPoint: Identifiable {
    let id = UUID()
    let month: Month
    let value: Double
    var name: String {
        month.rawValue.capitalized
    }
}
```

2. To simplify how we save the raw data, let's introduce an extension to an Array of `Double` to transform it into an array of `MonthDataPoint`:

```
extension Array where Element == Double {
    func monthDataPoints() -> [MonthDataPoint] {
        zip(Month.allCases, self).map { (month, value) in
            MonthDataPoint(month: month, value: value)
        }
    }
}
```

3. The data for the average precipitation is collected from `https://www.climatestotravel.com`, and we save it as a series of static constants:

```
struct DataSet {
    static let dublin = [
        0.65, 0.50, 0.55, 0.55, 0.60, 0.65,
        0.55, 0.75, 0.60, 0.80, 0.75, 0.75
    ].monthDataPoints()

    static let milan = [
        0.65, 0.65, 0.80, 0.80, 0.95, 0.65,
        0.70, 0.95, 0.70, 1.00, 1.00, 0.60
    ].monthDataPoints()

    static let london = [
        0.55, 0.40, 0.40, 0.45, 0.50, 0.45,
        0.45, 0.50, 0.50, 0.70, 0.60, 0.55,
    ].monthDataPoints()
}
```

4. Let's now implement the bar chart starting from the single `BarView` struct:

```
struct BarView: View {
    var dataPoint: MonthDataPoint
    var body: some View {
        VStack {
            ZStack(alignment: .bottom) {
                Rectangle()
```

```
                          .fill(Color.blue)
                        .frame(width: 18,
                               height: 180)
                 Rectangle()
                          .fill(Color.white)
                        .frame(width: 18,
                               height:
                                  CGFloat(dataPoint.value *
                                  180.0))
   }
             Text(dataPoint.name)
                  .font(.system(size: 12))
                 .rotationEffect(.degrees(-45))
       }
    }
}
```

5. `BarChartView` is simply a horizontal stack that we populate using a `ForEach` loop, explaining the reason for having the datapoints conforming to `Identifiable`:

```
struct BarChartView: View {
    var dataPoints: [MonthDataPoint]

    var body: some View {
        HStack (spacing: 12) {
            ForEach(dataPoints) {
                BarView(dataPoint: $0)
            }
        }
    }
}
```

6. Finally, we add `BarChartView` into the body of `ContentView`, alongside a title and a segmented picker view to allow us to select the city:

```
struct ContentView: View {
    @State
```

```
    var dataSet = [
        DataSet.dublin, DataSet.milan, DataSet.london
    ]


    @State
    var selectedCity = 0


    var body: some View {
        ZStack {
            Color.blue.opacity(0.4)
                .edgesIgnoringSafeArea(.all)
            VStack (spacing: 24) {
                Spacer()
                Text("Average Precipitation")
                    .font(.system(size: 32))

                Picker(selection: self.$selectedCity,
                    label: Text("Average Precipitation")) {
                    Text("Dublin").tag(0)
                    Text("Milan").tag(1)
                    Text("London").tag(2)
                }
                .pickerStyle(SegmentedPickerStyle())

                BarChartView(dataPoints:
                    dataSet[selectedCity])
                Spacer()
            }.padding(.horizontal, 10)
        }
    }
}
```

Running the app, we can see how, when selecting the different cities, the bars nicely change to represent their values:

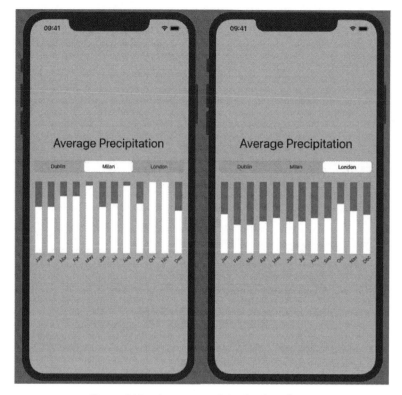

Figure 6.17 – Average precipitation bar charts

How it works

As you've seen, the code of the bars is really simple. A bar is simply two rectangles: an empty rectangle for the background, and a rectangle that represents the percentage of the value as a proportion of the full length of the bar.

Below each bar, we added a `Text` component that shows the name of the month that the given bar represents, and rotated it 45 degrees for readability.

Unrelated to SwiftUI, the extended `monthDataPoints()` function shows a nice trick to join two sequences: the list of the months is a sequence, the array of the values is a sequence, and the `zip()` function joins the two sequences together as if it were a sequence of tuples, so that we can iterate and create a new `MonthDataPoint` struct from each tuple.

Pretty neat!

There's more

Bars are scaled to have a full bar for one centimeter, but what if the maximum rainfall is less than or greater than one centimeter?

A good exercise would be to adapt the code we just wrote to have a flexible and configurable maximum height, depending on the maximum value in the dataset.

Another nice feature could be adding a label for each bar representing the value: could you do it while taking into account when the value is the maximum or is the minimum? Give it a try!

Building a pie chart

We know that a pie chart is a way to represent proportional numeric values, using slices that form a circle—a pie.

With a pie chart being made up of a slice and a circle – simple geometric shapes – it is simple enough to implement them in SwiftUI.

This recipe will use a dataset on the number of pets in three different European cities.

Getting ready

This recipe doesn't have any external resources, so it is enough just to create a SwiftUI project called `PieChartApp`.

How to do it...

This recipe is slightly more complicated than usual because it has two main parts:

- Manipulating datapoints
- Visualizing datapoints

Regarding the datapoints, given the list of data, we must scale the value to adapt to the maximum, meaning that we must calculate the maximum value in the series and then scale the other values so that each value can fit the pie chart. Also, we must calculate the angles for each slice – the starting angle (which is the ending angle of the previous slice) and the ending angle, both of which are proportional to the value of that slice.

Regarding the actual shapes, we implement a single slice as an arc with the stroke size equal to half the size of the container frame.

Let's start to write the code, and you'll see that it is less complicated than it sounds:

1. First of all, we implement enum to define the pet we want to track, with a function that returns its associated color to present it in the pie chart:

```
enum Animal: String {
    case cat
    case dog
    case fish
    case horse
    case hamster
    case rabbit
    case bird

    var color: Color {
        switch self {
        case .cat:
            return .red
        case .dog:
            return .blue
        case .fish:
            return .green
        case .horse:
            return .orange
        case .hamster:
            return .purple
        case .rabbit:
            return .gray
        case .bird:
            return .yellow
        }
    }
}
```

2. Then, add a simple struct to contain the raw data:

```swift
struct PetData {
    let value: Double
    let animal: Animal
    var color: Color {
        animal.color
    }

    var name: String {
        animal.rawValue.capitalized
    }
}
```

3. For simplicity, we set the raw data as static variables in a `DataSet` struct:

```swift
struct DataSet {
    static let dublin: [PetData] = [
        .init(value: 2344553, animal: .cat),
        .init(value: 1934345, animal: .dog),
        .init(value: 323454, animal: .fish),
        .init(value: 403400, animal: .rabbit),
        .init(value: 1003445, animal: .horse),
        .init(value: 1600494, animal: .hamster),
    ]
    static let milan: [PetData] = [
        .init(value: 3344553, animal: .cat),
        .init(value: 2004345, animal: .dog),
        .init(value: 923454, animal: .fish),
        .init(value: 803400, animal: .rabbit),
        .init(value: 1642345, animal: .bird),
        .init(value: 804244, animal: .hamster),
    ]
    static let london: [PetData] = [
        .init(value: 3355553, animal: .cat),
        .init(value: 4235345, animal: .dog),
        .init(value: 1913454, animal: .fish),
        .init(value: 1103400, animal: .rabbit),
```

```
            .init(value: 683445, animal: .horse),
         .init(value: 3300494, animal: .hamster),
      ]
   }
```

4. Each point needs certain information to be presented; notably the start angle and the percentage value. Also, a convenient formatting function will be used to build the legend that explains the data represented in the chart:

```
struct DataPoint: Identifiable {
    let id = UUID()
    let label: String
    let value: Double
    let color: Color
    var percentage: Double = 0
    var startAngle: Double = 0

    var formattedPercentage: String {
        String(format: "%.2f %%", percentage * 100)
    }
}
```

5. To calculate and adapt the points, we introduce a `DataPoints` struct that holds the points, and every time a new point is added, it calculates the maximum value and scales the percentages of the datapoints and moves the angles accordingly:

```
struct DataPoints {
    var points = [DataPoint]()

    mutating func add(value: Double,
                label: String, color: Color) {
        points.append(DataPoint(label: label,
                        value: value, color: color))
        let total = points.reduce(0.0) { $0 + $1.value }

        points = points.map {
            var point = $0
            point.percentage = $0.value / total
```

```
                return point
        }

        for i in 1..<points.count {
            let previous =  points[i - 1]
            let angle = previous.startAngle +
                previous.value*360/total
            var current = points[i]
            current.startAngle = angle
            points[i] = current
        }
    }
}
```

6. With all the data in place, it is now time to prepare the drawing part of our project, starting with a single slice. As you can see, the slice conforms to `InsettableShape`. We'll explain the reason in the next section:

```
struct PieSliceShape: InsettableShape {
    var percent: Double
    var startAngle: Angle
    var insetAmount: CGFloat = 0

    func inset(by amount: CGFloat) -> some
      InsettableShape {
        var slice = self
        slice.insetAmount += amount
        return slice
    }

    func path(in rect: CGRect) -> Path {
        Path() { path in
            path.addArc(center: CGPoint(x: rect.size.
                                        width/2,

                                        y: rect.size.
                                        width/2),
```

```
                     radius: rect.size.width/2 -
                           insetAmount,
               startAngle: startAngle,
               endAngle: startAngle +
                     Angle(degrees: percent * 360),
               clockwise: false)
       }
    }
}
```

7. Given the shape defined in the preceding code, we wrap it in a view using a `GeometryReader` component, where we render it with a stroke of a size that is half of the width of the frame:

```
struct PieSlice: View {
    var percent: Double
    var degrees: Double
    var color: Color

    var body: some View {
        GeometryReader { geometry in
            PieSliceShape(percent: percent,
                        startAngle: Angle(degrees:
                           degrees))
              .strokeBorder(color,
                          lineWidth: geometry.size.
                             width/2)
              .rotationEffect(.degrees(-90))
              .aspectRatio(contentMode: .fit)
        }
    }
}
```

8. The `PieChart` view consists of two other views: a legend that describes the percentage of pet owners for each type of pet, and a list of pie slices. Since we want to show what each slice represents, a legend with the color and the related percentage is the simplest way to achieve that result. Each slice is then rendered on top of the others, to create the effect of a pie:

```swift
struct PieChart: View {
    var dataPoints: DataPoints

    var body: some View {
        VStack(alignment: .leading, spacing: 30) {
            VStack(alignment: .leading) {
                ForEach(dataPoints.points) { p in
                    HStack(spacing: 16) {
                        Rectangle()
                            .foregroundColor(p.color)
                            .frame(width: 16, height: 16)
                        Text("\(p.label): \
                            (p.formattedPercentage)")
                    }
                }
            }
            ZStack {
                ForEach(dataPoints.points) { point in
                    PieSlice(percent: point.percentage,
                             degrees: point.startAngle,
                             color: point.color)
                }
            }
            .aspectRatio(contentMode: .fill)
        }
    }
}
```

9. Finally, the `ContentView` view has the dataset to be presented and a variable to select the city:

```
struct ContentView: View {
    @State var dataSet: [DataPoints] = [
        DataSet.dublin.reduce(into: DataPoints()) {
            $0.add(value: $1.value,
                   label: $1.name,
                   color: $1.color)
        },
        DataSet.milan.reduce(into: DataPoints()) {
            $0.add(value: $1.value,
                   label: $1.name,
                   color: $1.color)
        },
        DataSet.london.reduce(into: DataPoints()) {
            $0.add(value: $1.value,
                   label: $1.name,
                   color: $1.color)
        },
    ]
    @State var selectedCity = 0
    var body: some View {
        // ...
    }
}
```

10. Last but not least, the body lays out the segmented control and the pie chart:

```
struct ContentView: View {
    //...

    var body: some View {
        VStack (spacing: 50) {
            Text("Most Popular Pets")
                .font(.system(size: 32))

            Picker(selection: self.$selectedCity,
```

```
            label: Text("Most Popular Pets")) {
            Text("Dublin").tag(0)
            Text("Milan").tag(1)
            Text("London").tag(2)
        }
        .pickerStyle(SegmentedPickerStyle())
        PieChart(dataPoints: dataSet[selectedCity])
            .aspectRatio(1, contentMode: .fit)
        Spacer()
    }
    .padding(.horizontal, 20)
    }
}
```

Running the app, we can see how the pie chart is rendered and how it changes its values when selecting a different city:

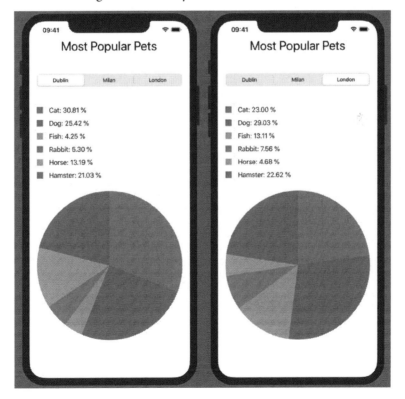

Figure 6.18 – Most popular pets pie chart

How it works

In general, this recipe is not complicated, but there are a few caveats to take into consideration.

First, let's analyze the `DataPoints` struct, whose objective it is to hold a list of ready-to-render datapoints.

To do this, every time a new point is added, the total is calculated with the following line of code:

```
let total = points.reduce(0.0) { $0 + $1.value }
```

Then the percentage of each point is updated:

```
points = points.map {
        var point = $0
        point.percentage = $0.value / total
        return point
    }
```

Finally, the angles are updated, considering the starting angle as the ending angle of the previous slice:

```
for i in 1..<points.count {
    let previous =  points[i - 1]
    let angle = previous.startAngle +
        previous.value*360/total
    var current = points[i]
    current.startAngle = angle
    points[i] = current
}
```

Another nice tip is the use of the `InsettableShape` protocol, which allows us to use `strokeBorder()` instead of `stroke()`:

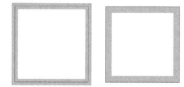

Figure 6.19 – stroke() and strokeBorder() applied to two shapes

The difference is that in the case of `stroke()`, the yellow border grows beyond the outline of the shape, which remains in the middle of the border; whereas in the case of `strokeBorder()`, the yellow border is completely contained in the outline.

To conform to the `InsettableShape` protocol, a shape must implement an `inset(by)` function that is called when `strokeBorder()` is invoked, passing the size of the inset to be applied. In our pie slice, we save it in a property called `insetAmount`, which will be used to reduce the radius of the arc to be drawn:

```
path.addArc(center: CGPoint(x: rect.size.width/2,
                            y: rect.size.width/2),
            radius: rect.size.width/2 - insetAmount,
            startAngle: startAngle,
```

Finally, the use of the `GeometryReader` object in the `PieSlice` view is interesting, as it basically reads the frame in which it is encapsulated, and explicitly creates a `geometry` object that contains the information of the frame that we use to define the size of the stroke for that slice:

```
GeometryReader { geometry in
              //...
              .strokeBorder(color,
lineWidth: geometry.size.width/2)
              //...
       }
```

It's been a quite long recipe, but we created quite a sophisticated component, and we learned a few tricks that we can reuse in other components.

7

Animating with SwiftUI

SwiftUI has introduced not only a new way of describing the UI elements and components but also a new way of implementing animations. In the case of animations, it needs an even more complex change of thinking. Whereas the layout concept is inherently declarative, the animation concept is inherently imperative.

When creating an animation in UIKit, for example, it is normal to describe it as a series of steps: when *this* happens, do *that* animation for 1 second, then *another* animation for 2 seconds.

Animation in the SwiftUI way requires us to define three parts:

- A trigger
- A change of data
- A change of UI

A trigger is an event that *happens*, such as a button click, a slider, a gesture, and so on.

A change of data is a change of an @State variable, such as a Boolean flag.

A change of UI is a change of something that is represented visually following the change of data – for example, a vertical or horizontal offset, or the size of a component that has one value when the flag is false and another value when the flag is true.

In the following recipes, we'll learn how to implement basic and implicit animations, how to create custom animations, and also how to recreate some effects we experience every day in the most used apps we have on our devices.

At the end of the chapter, we'll know a set of techniques that will allow us to create the most compelling animations in the SwiftUI way.

In this chapter, we will cover the animations in SwiftUI through the following recipes:

- Creating basic animations
- Transforming shapes
- Creating a banner with a spring animation
- Applying a delay to a view modifier animation to create a sequence of animations
- Applying a delay to a `withAnimation` function to create a sequence of animations
- Applying multiple animations to a view
- Creating custom view transitions
- Creating a hero view transition with `.matchedGeometryEffect`
- Creating an animated pressable button
- Lottie animations in SwiftUI
- Implementing a stretchable header in SwiftUI
- Creating floating hearts in SwiftUI
- How to implement a swipeable stack of cards in SwiftUI

Technical requirements

The code in this chapter is based on Xcode 12 and iOS 14. Apart from the *Creating a hero transition with .matchedGeometryEffect* recipe, the other recipes are compatible with iOS 13 as well.

You can find the code in the book's GitHub repo under the `https://github.com/PacktPublishing/SwiftUI-Cookbook/tree/master/Chapter07%20-%20Animating%20with%20SwiftUI` path.

Creating basic animations

Let's introduce the way to animate in SwiftUI with a simple app that moves a component on the screen.

SwiftUI brings a few predefined temporal curves: `.easeInOut`, `.linear`, `.spring`, and so on. In this recipe, we'll compare them against the default animation.

We are going to implement two circles that move to the top or the bottom of the screen. One circle moves using the default animation, and the other with the selected animation; we can then select the other animation using an action sheet, which is a modal view that appears from the bottom.

Getting ready

Let's implement a SwiftUI app called `BasicAnimationsApp`.

How to do it...

This is a super simple app where we are going to render two circles, a red and a blue one, and an action sheet to choose the animation for the red circle, while the animation for the blue circle is always the default one.

We will select the animation for the red circle with a button that presents an action sheet with a list of the possible animations.

Finally, the animation is triggered by a default button with the text **Animate**:

1. Let's start the recipe by adding a type for the animation to be able to list all of the possible animations and then select one:

```swift
struct AnimationType {
    let name: String
    let animation: Animation

    static var all: [AnimationType]  = [
        .init(name: "default", animation: .default),
        .init(name: "easeIn", animation: .easeIn),
        .init(name: "easeOut", animation: .easeOut),
        .init(name: "easeInOut", animation: .easeInOut),
        .init(name: "linear", animation: .linear),
        .init(name: "spring", animation: .spring()),
    ]
}
```

2. Then, add three `@State` variables to drive the animation and the components to show in the view:

```
struct ContentView: View {
    @State
    private var onTop = false
    @State
    private var type =
        AnimationType(name: "default", animation:
            .default)
    @State
    private var showSelection = false
    //...
}
```

3. The next step is to add two circles of the same size but of different colors:

```
struct ContentView: View {
    //...

    var body: some View {
        VStack(spacing: 12) {
            GeometryReader { geometry in
                HStack {
                    Circle()
                        .fill(Color.blue)
                        .frame(width: 80, height: 80)
                        .offset(y: onTop ?
                            -geometry.size.height/2 :
                            geometry.size.height/2)
                        .animation(.default)
                    Spacer()
                    Circle()
                        .fill(Color.red)
                        .frame(width: 80, height: 80)
                        .offset(y: onTop ?
                            -geometry.size.height/2 :
                            geometry.size.height/2 )
```

```
                               .animation(type.animation)
                }
            .padding(.horizontal, 30)
        }
        //...
            }
        }
    }
```

4. The code for the UI and the animation is there; let's just add the `ActionSheet` component with the list of the available animations:

```
struct ContentView: View {
    //...
    var actionSheet: ActionSheet {
        ActionSheet(title: Text("Animations"),
                    buttons: AnimationType
                        .all.map { type in
                            .default(Text(type.
                                name),
                            action:   {
                                self.type = type
                        })
                    } + [ .destructive(Text("Cancel")) ],
        )
    }
    //...
}
```

5. Finally, after adding the buttons to trigger the animation and the selection of the animation, we are ready to test it:

```
struct ContentView: View {
    //...
    var body: some View {
        VStack(spacing: 12) {
            GeometryReader { geometry in
                //...
            }
            Button { onTop.toggle() } label: {
                Text("Animate")
            }
            Button { showSelection = true } label: {
                Text("Choose Animation")
            }
            .actionSheet(isPresented:
                            $showSelection,
                          content: { actionSheet }
            )
            Text("Current: \(type.name)")
        }
    }
}
```

Running the app, we can now see how the different animations run compared to each other:

Figure 7.1 – Basic animations in SwiftUI

How it works...

As you can see, the result is pretty neat considering that we have used just a couple of lines to add an animation.

In our code, we can see the three steps we mentioned in the introduction:

- The trigger is the tap on the **Animate** button.
- The change of data is the change of the @State variable onTop.
- The change of UI is the vertical position of the circle, which is guided by the onTop variable.

When given the three previous steps, and after adding the animation() view modifier, SwiftUI will then apply that animation.

In practical terms, this means that for the duration of the animation, SwiftUI calculates the position of the circle using the selected curve.

For .easeInOut, for example, the animation starts and finishes slowly, but it is fast in between, whereas for .linear, the speed is always constant.

If you want to slow down the animation to see the difference, you can apply a `.speed()` modifier to the animation, such as the following:

```
//...
.animation(Animation.default.speed(0.1))
//...
.animation(self.type.animation.speed(0.1))
//...
```

By playing around with that, you should better understand the difference between the different animations.

There's more...

Changing the offset is just one of the possible changes of the UI. What about experimenting with changing other things—for example, the fill colors or the size of the circles? Does the animation work for every modification? Feel free to experiment and get familiar with the way SwiftUI manages the animations.

See also

If you want to have a visualization of the different curves, you will find a graph for the most common easing functions here: `https://easings.net/en`.

Bear in mind that that site is not SwiftUI-related, so the names are slightly different.

Transforming shapes

In the previous recipe, *Creating basic animations*, you can see that SwiftUI is able to animate the change of common characteristics, such as position, color, size, and so on. But what if the feature we want to animate is not one that is part of the framework?

In this recipe, we'll create a triangular shape whose height is equal to the width times a fraction of the width; when we tap on the triangle, we set that multiplier to a random number, making the height change.

How can we instruct SwiftUI to animate the change of the multiplier? We'll see that the code needed is simple, but that the underlying engine is quite sophisticated.

Getting ready

This recipe doesn't need any external resources, so let's just create a SwiftUI project called `AnimateTriangleShape` in Xcode.

How to do it...

We are going to implement a triangle shape where the height is equal to the width times a multiplier.

Tapping on the shape, the multiplier changes:

1. Let's start with adding a `Triangle` view:

```swift
struct Triangle: Shape {
    var multiplier: CGFloat

    func path(in rect: CGRect) -> Path {
        Path { path in
            path.move(to: CGPoint(x: rect.minX,
                                  y: rect.maxY))
            path.addLine(to: CGPoint(x: rect.maxX,
                                     y: rect.maxY))
            path.addLine(to: CGPoint(x: rect.midX,
                                     y: rect.maxY
                                     - multiplier * rect.
                                       width))
            path.closeSubpath()
        }
    }
}
```

2. Then, add the shape to `ContentView` and a gesture that changes the multiplier:

```
struct ContentView: View {
    @State
    var multiplier: CGFloat = 1

    var body: some View {
        Triangle(multiplier: multiplier)
            .fill(Color.red)
            .frame(width: 300, height: 300)
            .onTapGesture {
                withAnimation(.easeOut(duration: 2)) {
                    multiplier = CGFloat
                        .random(in: 0.3...1.5)
                }
            }
    }
}
```

3. This looks like all the code we need, but if we run the app now, we can see that although the triangle changes if we tap on it, the change is not animated.

    This is because SwiftUI doesn't know which data it has to animate. To instruct it, what we have to do is to add a property called `animatableData` to the shape:

```
struct Triangle: Shape {
    var animatableData: CGFloat {
        get { multiplier }
        set { multiplier = newValue }
    }
    //...
}
```

Running the app now, the height changes smoothly when we tap on the triangle:

Figure 7.2 – Shape animated transformation

How it works...

SwiftUI can only animate components that conform to `Animatable`, meaning that they should have a property called `animatableData` so that SwiftUI can save and retrieve the intermediate steps during an animation.

To inspect the behavior, let's add `print` to the setter:

```
var animatableData: CGFloat {
    get { multiplier }
    set {
        multiplier = newValue
        print("value: \(multiplier)")
    }
}
```

Running the app, the Xcode console will print something like the following:

```
value: 1.0
value: 1.0
value: 1.0000194373421276
value: 1.0025879432661413
value: 1.0051161861243192
value: 1.0076164878031886
value: 1.0100930134474908
value: 1.0125485398203875
value: 1.0149842817557613
value: 1.0174018011828905
value: 1.0198019658402626
value: 1.0221849492755757
value: 1.0245516192273172
value: 1.02690249633858
value: 1.0292379277047592
value: 1.03155826042125
value: 1.0338634944880523
value: 1.0361541505482588
```

Figure 7.3 – Intermediate value of animatableData

For every step, SwiftUI calculates where the `animatableData` value must be for that step, sets it in the shape, and then renders the shape.

The shape already conforms to `Animatable`, so the only thing we have to do is define the `animatableData` property, specifying the characteristic we want to animate.

Another thing to note is the way we are triggering the animation. In the gesture action, we are wrapping the change of the `@State` variable with a `withAnimation` function:

```
withAnimation(.easeOut(duration: 2)) {
                multiplier = CGFloat.random(in: 0.3...1.5)
}
```

This is like saying to SwiftUI "everything that changes inside this function must be animated using the animation configuration passed as a parameter."

Creating a banner with a spring animation

A really nice and configurable easing function is the spring, where the component bounces around the final value.

We are going to implement a banner that is usually hidden, and when it appears, it moves from the top with a spring animation.

Getting ready

No external resources are needed, so let's just create a SwiftUI project in Xcode called `BannerWithASpringAnimationApp`.

How to do it...

This is a really simple recipe, where we create a banner view that can be animated when we tap on a button:

1. Let's implement `Banner`:

```swift
struct Banner: View {
    let message: String
    var show: Bool

    var body: some View {
        Text(message)
            .font(.title)
            .frame(width:UIScreen.main.bounds.width - 20,
                   height: 100)
            .foregroundColor(.white)
            .background(Color.green)
            .cornerRadius(10)
            .offset(y: show ?
                -UIScreen.main.bounds.height / 3 :
                -UIScreen.main.bounds.height)
            .animation(.interpolatingSpring(mass: 2.0,
                                            stiffness: 100.0,
                                            damping: 10,
                                            initialVelocity: 0))
    }
}
```

2. Then, we add the banner and a button to trigger the visibility in `ContentView`:

```swift
struct ContentView: View {
    @State
    var show = false

    var body: some View {
        VStack {
            Banner(message: "Hello, World!", show: show)
            Button {
                show.toggle()
            } label: {
                Text(show ? "Hide" : "Show")
                    .padding()
                    .frame(width: 100)
                    .foregroundColor(.white)
                    .background(show ? Color.red : Color.
                        blue)
                    .cornerRadius(10)
            }
        }
    }
}
```

When we run the app, we can see that the banner nicely bounces when it appears:

Figure 7.4 – A bouncing banner view

How it works...

To reiterate what we mentioned in the introduction, the trigger is the tap on the button, the change in data is the show variable, and the change in the UI is the position of the banner.

The curve is a spring curve, which has a few parameters:

- mass: This is the mass of the object attached to the spring; the bigger it is, the more inertia it gains when it reaches the speed, so it bounces more.

- stiffness: This is how much the spring resists when a force is applied; the more resistance, the more rigid the spring is.

- damping: This is how much the spring resists to changes; the more resistance, the less bouncing of the spring.

- initialVelocity: This is the velocity when the animation starts.

Feel free to change the parameters and see how the animation changes.

Applying a delay to a view modifier animation to create a sequence of animations

In the current version of SwiftUI, there is no way of joining different animations together to create a sequence of animations.

This will surely be fixed in a later SwiftUI version, but at the moment, we can implement a sequence of animations using a delay.

As you should know, there are two ways of defining an animation:

- Using the `.animation()` view modifier
- Using the `withAnimation` function

In this recipe, we'll see how to use the `.animation()` view modifier, and we'll cover the `withAnimation` function in the next recipe, *Applying a delay to a withAnimation function to create a sequence of animations*.

Getting ready

Let's create a SwiftUI project in Xcode called `DelayedAnimationsApp`.

How to do it...

In our app, we will create a sequence of three animations on a rectangle:

- A change of the vertical offset
- A change of scale
- A 3D rotation around the *X* axis

Since we cannot create an animation with these sub-animations, we are going to use a delay to reach the same effect:

1. Let's start by adding an `@State` variable to activate the animation, as well as the rectangle with the three animations:

```
struct ContentView: View {
    @State
    var change = false

    var body: some View {
        VStack(spacing: 30) {
```

```
            Rectangle()
                .fill(Color.blue)

                .offset(y: change ? -300 : 0)
                .animation(Animation
                    .easeInOut(duration: 1).delay(0))

                .scaleEffect(change ? 0.5 : 1)
                .animation(Animation
                    .easeInOut(duration: 1).delay(1))

                .rotation3DEffect(
                    change ? .degrees(45) : .degrees(0),
                            axis: (x: 1, y: 0, z: 0))
                .animation(Animation
                    .easeInOut(duration: 1).delay(2))

                .frame(width: 200, height: 200)
        }
    }
}
```

2. Then, let's add the button to trigger the animation:

```
var body: some View {
    VStack(spacing: 30) {
//...
        Button {
            change.toggle()
        } label: {
            Text("Animate")
                .fontWeight(.heavy)
                .foregroundColor(.white)
                .padding()
                .background(Color.green)
            .cornerRadius(5)
```

```
        }
      }
    }
```

Running the app, we can see the animations joining together as if they were a single animation:

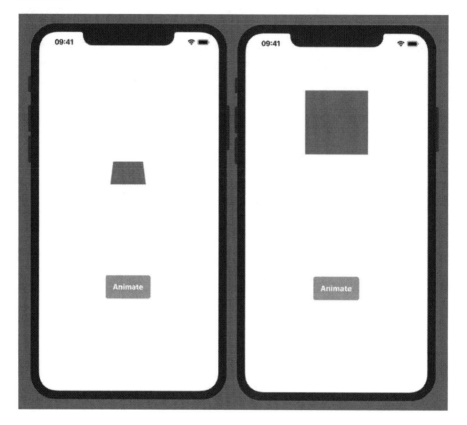

Figure 7.5 – Chaining animations with a delay

How it works...

When defining an animation, you can add a delay to make it start after a while.

You will notice that every animation is related to the previous change, so you can have multiple changes that happen at the same time.

Also, even though the technique is pretty simple, it doesn't work for all the view modifiers, so play around with and test them to find the correct sequence of animations.

Applying a delay to a withAnimation function to create a sequence of animations

As we mentioned in the previous recipe, SwiftUI doesn't have a way to define a chain of animations yet, but this can be simulated using delay animations.

As mentioned in the previous recipe, there are two ways of defining an animation:

- Using the `.animation()` view modifier
- Using the `withAnimation` function

In this recipe, we'll see how to use the `withAnimation` function. We covered the `.animation` view modifier in the previous recipe, *Applying a delay to a view modifier animation to create a sequence of animations.*

Getting ready

This recipe doesn't need any external resources, so let's just create a SwiftUI project called `DelayedAnimationsApp`.

How to do it...

To illustrate the delay applied to the `withAnimation` function, we are going to implement an app that presents three text elements that appear and disappear in sequence when tapping on a button:

1. To add a nice look, we define a custom modifier for `Text`:

```
struct CustomText: ViewModifier {
    let foregroundColor: Color
    let backgroundColor: Color
    let cornerRadius: CGFloat

    func body(content: Content) -> some View {
        content
            .foregroundColor(foregroundColor)
            .frame(width: 200)
            .padding()
```

```
            .background(backgroundColor)
            .cornerRadius(cornerRadius)
    }
}
```

2. We can now add three @State variables to drive the visibility of each Text component:

```
struct ContentView: View {
    @State var hideFirst = true
    @State var hideSecond = true
    @State var hideThird = true
    var body: some View {
        VStack {
            VStack(spacing: 30) {
                Text("First")
                    .modifier(CustomText(foregroundColor:
                        .white, backgroundColor: .red,
                        cornerRadius: 10))
                    .opacity(hideFirst ? 0 : 1)
                Text("Second")
                    .modifier(CustomText(foregroundColor:
                        .white, backgroundColor: .blue,
                        cornerRadius: 10))
                    .opacity(hideSecond ? 0 : 1)

                Text("Third")
                    .modifier(CustomText(foregroundColor:
                        .white, backgroundColor: .yellow,
                        cornerRadius: 10))
                    .opacity(hideThird ? 0 : 1)
            }
        }
    }
}
```

3. Finally, let's add the trigger button:

```
var body: some View {
    VStack {
        VStack(spacing: 30) {
            //...
        }


        Spacer()
        Button {
            withAnimation(Animation.easeInOut) {
                hideFirst.toggle()
            }
            withAnimation(Animation.easeInOut.delay(0.3))
            {
                hideSecond.toggle()
            }
            withAnimation(Animation.easeInOut.delay(0.6))
            {
                hideThird.toggle()
            }
        }) {
            Text("Animate")
                .fontWeight(.heavy)
                .modifier(CustomText(foregroundColor:
                    .white, backgroundColor: .green,
                    cornerRadius: 5))
        }
    }
}
```

Running the app, we can see how the opacity of the components changes in sequence, simulating a single animation:

Figure 7.6 – Delayed animations to create a sequential appearing of components

How it works...

Remember that with the `withAnimation` function, we are telling SwiftUI to animate what is inside the function that we pass as the last parameter; it is pretty obvious that applying a delay to the same animation will cause it to start later.

Although the current and previous recipes are two working solutions, I think you'll agree that they are more a workaround than a proper pattern.

Let's hope that the next version of SwiftUI will bring us a proper way to chain animations together.

Applying multiple animations to a view

SwiftUI allows us to animate multiple features at the same time, and also, they can be animated using different durations and different animation curves.

In this recipe, we'll learn how to animate two sets of features, and how to make the result look like one single, smooth animation.

Getting ready

Let's create a SwiftUI project called `MultipleAnimationsApp`.

How to do it...

To illustrate how you can apply multiple animations to a view, we are going to create a rectangle that has two sets of animations:

- One set with the color, the vertical offset, and the rotation around the X axis
- One set with the scale, and a rotation around the Z axis

We are using a `.easeInOut` curve for the former, and `.linear` for the latter:

1. Let's start by adding the rectangle and the button to trigger the change:

```swift
struct ContentView: View {
    @State
    var initialState = true

    var body: some View {
        VStack(spacing: 30) {
            Rectangle()
            Button {
                initialState.toggle()
            } label: {
                Text("Animate")
                    .fontWeight(.heavy)
                    .foregroundColor(.white)
                    .padding()
                    .background(Color.green)
                    .cornerRadius(5)
            }
        }
```

```
            }
        }
    }
```

2. We can now add the first set of changes, with a `.easeInOut` animation:

```
///...
Rectangle()
    .fill(initialState ? Color.blue : Color.red)
    .cornerRadius(initialState ? 50 : 0)
    .offset(y: initialState ? 0 : -200)
    .rotation3DEffect(initialState ? .degrees(0)
                                    : .degrees(45),
                axis: (x: 1, y: 0, z: 0))
    .animation(.easeInOut(duration: 2))
```

3. Finally, we add the second set of changes, with a `.linear` animation:

```
Rectangle()
//...
    .scaleEffect(initialState ? 1 : 0.8)
    .rotationEffect(initialState ?
Angle(degrees:0) :
Angle(degrees:-90))
    .animation(.linear(duration: 1))
    .frame(width: 300, height: 200)
```

Running the app, we can see how the two animation sets interact:

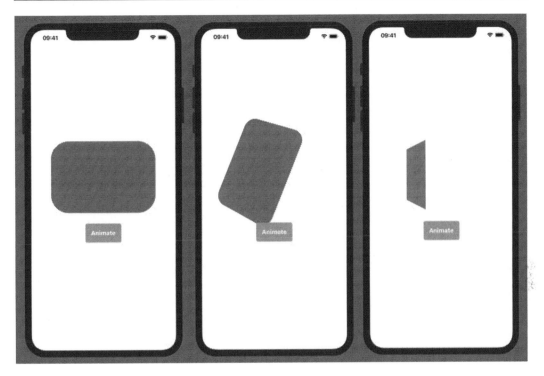

Figure 7.7 – Multiple animations on the same components

How it works...

Remember in the introduction how we mentioned the three steps of an animation – a trigger, a change of data, and a change of UI?

Basically, changing multiple features of a component is considered as a single change for SwiftUI, which for each step, calculates the intermediary value for each of them, and then applies all the changes at the same time for every single step.

Creating custom view transitions

SwiftUI has a nice feature that gives us the possibility to add an animation when a view appears or disappears.

It is called *Transition*, and it can be animated with the usual degree of customization.

In this recipe, we'll see how to create custom appearing and disappearing transitions, combining different transitions.

Getting ready

This recipe uses two images courtesy of *Erika Wittlieb* (`https://pixabay.com/users/erikawittlieb-427626/`) from *Pixabay* (`https://pixabay.com/`).

You can find the images in the GitHub repo at `https://github.com/PacktPublishing/SwiftUI-Cookbook/tree/master/Resources/Chapter07/recipe7`, but you can also use your own images for this recipe.

Create a new SwiftUI project in Xcode called `CustomViewTransitionApp`, and copy the `ch7-r7-i1.jpg` and `ch7-r7-i2.jpg` images in the **Assets** catalog:

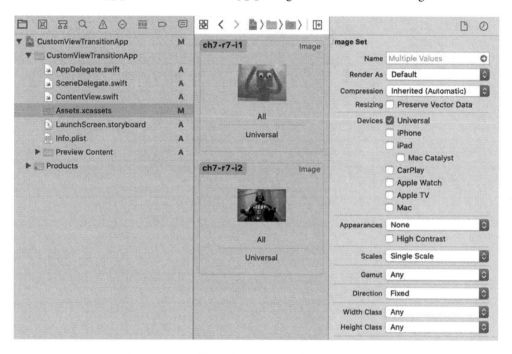

Figure 7.8 – Adding the images to the Assets catalog

How to do it...

We are going to implement a simple app where we are switching two views when we tap on a button.

For simplicity, the two components are just wrappers around an `Image` component, but this will work for any kind of component:

1. Firstly, we will implement the two views that wrap around an `Image` component:

```
extension Image {
    func custom() -> some View {
        self
            .resizable()
            .aspectRatio(contentMode: .fit)
            .cornerRadius(20)
            .shadow(radius: 10)
    }
}

struct FirstComponent: View {
    var body: some View {
        Image("ch7-r7-i1")
            .custom()
    }
}

struct SecondComponent: View {
    var body: some View {
        Image("ch7-r7-i2")
            .custom()
    }
}
```

2. Let's now put the components in `ComponentView`, selecting which one to present depending on a flag that will be toggled by a button:

```
struct ContentView: View {
    @State var showFirst = true
    var body: some View {
        VStack(spacing: 24) {
            if showFirst {
                FirstComponent()
            } else {
                SecondComponent()
            }
            Button {
                showFirst.toggle()
            } label: {
                Text("Change")
            }
        }
        .animation(Animation.easeInOut(duration: 1))
        .padding(.horizontal, 20)
    }
}
```

3. If you run the app now, the two images will be swapped using a crossfade animation, which is the default animation for the images.

Let's introduce the concept of transitions, creating a new type of transition and modifying the images to respect the transition animation when appearing or disappearing:

```
extension AnyTransition {
    static var moveScaleAndFade: AnyTransition {
        let insertion = AnyTransition
            .scale
            .combined(with: .move(edge: .leading))
            .combined(with: .opacity)
        let removal = AnyTransition
            .scale
```

```
                .combined(with: .move(edge: .top))
            .combined(with: .opacity)
        return .asymmetric(insertion: insertion,
                        removal: removal)
    }
}
struct ContentView: View {
    // ...
        FirstComponent()
            .transition(.moveScaleAndFade)
    // ...
        SecondComponent()
            .transition(.moveScaleAndFade)
    // ...
}
```

Running the app now, we can see that the components appear by scaling up and moving from the left, and disappear by scaling down and moving to the top:

Figure 7.9 – Custom view transitions

How it works...

Transition is basically a list of transformations that can be applied when a view appears or disappears.

Using the `.combine` function, a transition can be combined with others to create more sophisticated animations.

In our example, we used a `.asymmetric` transition, meaning that the removal will look different than the insertion, but of course, we could have a symmetric transition returning the `insertion` or `removal` transition: try it and see how the app behaves.

There's more...

You probably noticed that the components are just a wrapper around an `Image` components – why is that? Couldn't you just use two different images in the body of `ContentView`?

Try to replace `FirstComponent` and `SecondComponent` with two `Image` components and see what happens.

Can you give an explanation for this unexpected behavior?

Creating a hero view transition with .matchedGeometryEffect

Do you know what a hero transition is? If you don't know the term, you have still probably seen it many times.

Maybe in an e-commerce app, where with a list of products where each product has a thumbnail to show the product, selecting an item flies it to a details page, with a big image of the same product. The smooth animation from the thumbnail to the big image is called a "hero transition."

Another example is the cover image animation in the Apple Music player, transitioning from the mini-player to the full-player.

In iOS 14, SwiftUI introduced a modifier, `.matchedGeometryEffect`, which makes it very easy to implement this kind of animation almost without any effort.

Getting ready

This recipe uses a few images courtesy of *Pixabay* (https://pixabay.com/).

You can find the images in the GitHub repo at https://github.com/PacktPublishing/SwiftUI-Cookbook/tree/master/Resources/Chapter07/recipe8, but you can also use your own images for this recipe.

Create a new SwiftUI project in Xcode called HeroViewTransitionApp, and copy the images in the **Assets** catalog:

Figure 7.10 – Adding the images to the Assets catalog

How to do it...

We are going to implement a simple app with a list of holiday destinations. When the user selects one destination, the thumbnail flies to the details page. A cross mark button on the page allows the user to close it. When the page is closing, the big image flies back to the original position in the list view:

1.   Firstly, we implement the model for our holiday destination app:

```
struct Item: Identifiable {
    let id = UUID()
    var image : String
    var title : String
    var details : String
}
```

2.   With this model, we create an array of items:

```
let data = [
    Item(image: "california", title: "California",
        details: "California, the most populous state
            in the United States and the third most extensive
            by area, is located on the western coast of the
            USA and is bordered by Oregon to the north,
            Nevada, to the east and northeast, Arizona to the
            southeast and it shares an international border
            with the Mexican state of Baja California to
            the south."),
    Item(image: "miami", title: "Miami", details: "Miami
        is an international city at Florida's south-eastern
        tip. Its Cuban influence is reflected in the
        cafes")
    //...
    ]
```

3.   Since this code is long and not so interesting, you can find the `Data.swift` file with it in the GitHub repo: `https://github.com/PacktPublishing/SwiftUI-Cookbook/tree/master/Resources/Chapter07/recipe8/Data.swift`. Copy this into your project.

4. We will move now to the `ContentView` component, where we add the property to drive the animation:

```
struct ContentView: View {
    @State
    private var selectedItem: Item!
    @State
    private var showDetail = false
    @Namespace
    var animation
    var body: some View {
        //....
    }
}
```

5. Inside the body, we present the two components: `DestinationListView`, with the list of the holiday destinations, and `DestinationDetailView`, with the information for the selected item:

```
var body: some View {
    ZStack {
        DestinationListView(selectedItem: $selectedItem,
                            showDetail: $showDetail,
                            animation: animation)
            .opacity(showDetail ? 0 : 1)
        if showDetail {
            DestinationDetailView(selectedItem:
                selectedItem, showDetail: $showDetail,
                animation: animation)
        }
    }
}
```

6. Let's start implementing `DestinationListView`, defining the properties to drive its layout:

```
struct DestinationListView: View {
    @Binding
    var selectedItem: Item!
    @Binding
    var showDetail: Bool
    let animation: Namespace.ID

    var body: some View {
    }
}
```

7. In the body function, we add `ScrollView`, where we iterate on the data array to show the thumbnails:

```
var body: some View {
    ScrollView(.vertical) {
        VStack(spacing: 20) {
            ForEach(data) { item in

            }
        }
        .padding(.all, 20)
    }
}
```

8. Inside the `ForEach` loop body, we present an `Image` component:

```
ForEach(data) { item in
    Image(item.image)
        .resizable()
        .aspectRatio(contentMode: .fill)
        .cornerRadius(10)
        .shadow(radius: 5)
}
```

9. After the `.shadow` modifier, we apply the secret ingredient: `.matchedGeometryEffect`! This will be explained in the *How it works...* section, but for the moment, just apply it to the `Image` component:

```
Image(item.image)
    //...
    .shadow(radius: 5)
    .matchedGeometryEffect(id: item.image,
                           in: animation)
```

10. Finally, a `.onTapGesture` callback will select the item to show and will open the detail page:

```
Image(item.image)
    //...
    .onTapGesture {
        selectedItem = item
        withAnimation {
            showDetail.toggle()
        }
    }
```

11. Let's move on to implementing the details page, where we define the view and its properties:

```
struct DestinationDetailView: View {
    var selectedItem: Item!
    @Binding
    var showDetail: Bool
    let animation: Namespace.ID

    var body: some View {
    }
}
```

12. The body function presents a `ZStack` component, with the details of the holiday destination, and a `Button` component to close the page:

```
var body: some View {
    ZStack(alignment: .topTrailing){
        VStack{
        }
        .ignoresSafeArea(.all)
        Button {
            //...
        }
        .background(Color.white
                      .ignoresSafeArea(.all))
}
```

13. Let's start with the `Button` component, where we simply dismiss the page toggling the `showDetail` flag:

```
Button {
    withAnimation {
        showDetail.toggle()
    }
} label: {
    Image(systemName: "xmark")
        .foregroundColor(.white)
        .padding()
        .background(Color.black.opacity(0.8))
        .clipShape(Circle())
}
.padding(.trailing,10)
```

14. The `VStack` component contains the info of the product, notably the big image at the top:

```
VStack{
    Image(selectedItem.image)
        .resizable()
        .aspectRatio(contentMode: .fit)
    Text(selectedItem.title)
        .font(.title)
    Text(selectedItem.details)
        .font(.callout)
        .padding(.horizontal)
    Spacer()
}
.ignoresSafeArea(.all)
```

15. Finally, we apply `.matchedGeometryEffect` to the `Image` component on the details page:

```
Image(selectedItem.image)
    .resizable()
    .aspectRatio(contentMode: .fit)
    .matchedGeometryEffect(id: selectedItem.image,
                            in: animation)
```

Running the app now, when we select a picture from the list, the image smoothly animates, moving to the top of the screen when the details page is fully visible. When we close the page, the image flies back to the original position in the list:

Figure 7.11 – Hero view transition

How it works...

It has been said that `.matchedGeometryEffect` is a sort of **Keynote Magic Move** for SwiftUI, where you set the start component and the end component, and SwiftUI magically creates an animation for you.

The `.matchedGeometryEffect` modifier sets the relationship between the initial and final component so that SwiftUI can create the animation to transform the initial to the final component. To store this relationship, `.matchedGeometryEffect` needs an identifier – in this case, the name of the image – and a place to save the identifiable relationship. In our code, this is done in the following line:

```
.matchedGeometryEffect(id: item.image, in: animation)
```

In iOS 14, SwiftUI adds a new property wrapper, `@Namespace`, which transforms the property of a view in a global place to save the animations that SwiftUI must render. The animation engine will use this property under the hood to create the various steps of the animation.

We can simplify this to say that to use `.matchedGeometryEffect`, we define a starting component and an ending component in different views, and then we say to SwiftUI that those components are the same, and then SwiftUI will figure out what transformations it has to apply.

In our case, the transformations are as follows:

- The *y* offset position (from *inside the scroll view* to the *top of the screen*)
- The size (from the *thumbail* to the *big picture*)
- Rounded corners (from *with rounded corners* to *without rounded corners*)

When the `showDetail` Boolean flag is `false`, only the list is presented, and the thumbnail images are the initial state of the animation. Toggling the value of `showDetail` makes the details page appear animated. In this case, the big picture on the page is the final state of the animation. Since the identifier is the same in both the components, SwiftUI assumes it is the same component in two different moments in time and renders an animation to transform it from one moment to another.

When `showDetail` is toggled again when showing the details page, the roles of the initial and final state are inverted and the animation is rendered in reverse.

To visually appreciate the transformation of the animation, I invite you to enable **Debug | Slow Animations** from the menu in the simulator, run the app, and see the various steps of the transition, from the thumbnail to the big picture and back.

Creating an animated pressable button

As you probably noticed, when you use a `Button` component, the effect of the *pressed* state is particularly plain; it is just a change of opacity of the whole button. But what if we could have a sort of scale-up when it is pressed?

In this recipe, we'll see how to implement a custom button that scales up when it is pressed, and it returns to normal size when the touch is outside its frame or the button is released.

Getting ready

For this recipe, you don't need any external resources, so creating a SwiftUI project called `AnimatableButtonApp` is enough.

How to do it...

We are going to implement a button that will scale up when pressed and scale down when released. Also, we need to have a callback to be called when the button is released.

If you try to add an animation to a `Button` object using `DragGesture` to simulate the touch, you'll see that the action associated is not called, but we'll discuss this in the *How it works...* section:

1. Let's start by creating an `AnimatableButton` component, which is simply a `Text` component wrapped in `GeometryReader`. The `Text` component can be decorated as you prefer, but I suggest filling the frame of `GeometryReader` – that is, don't clip it with a `Circle` component:

```
struct AnimatableButton: View {
    let text: String
    let action: () -> Void

    var body: some View {
        GeometryReader { geometry in
            Text(self.text)
                .foregroundColor(.white)
                .font(.title)
                .fontWeight(.heavy)
                .frame(width: geometry.size.width,
                       height: geometry.size.height)
                .background(Color.red)
                .shadow(radius: 10)
                .cornerRadius(15)
        }
        .frame(width: 200, height: 100)
    }
}
```

2. Use the button in `ContentView`:

```swift
struct ContentView: View {
    var body: some View {
        AnimatableButton(text: "Press Me") {
            print("Pressed")
        }
    }
}
```

3. Running the app now, we can see that the button looks nice, but nothing happens if we tap on it.

    Let's add a `@State` variable to keep track of the pressing state, and to change the scale of the button:

```swift
struct AnimatableButton: View {
    @State
    private var isPressed: Bool = false
//...
    var body: some View {
        GeometryReader { geometry in
            //...
        }
        .frame(width: 200, height: 100)
        .scaleEffect(self.isPressed ? 1.2 : 1)
        .animation(.easeInOut(duration: 0.5))
    }
}
```

4. Again, when running the app, the button is not responsive, so let's add a gesture to detect touches:

```swift
var body: some View {
    GeometryReader { geometry in
    // ...
        .cornerRadius(15)
        .gesture(DragGesture(minimumDistance: 0,
                             coordinateSpace: .global)
```

```
                    .onChanged { dragGesture in
                        isPressed = dragGesture
                            .location.isContained(in:
                                geometry)
                    }
                    .onEnded { dragGesture in
                        isPressed = false
                        if dragGesture
                            .location.isContained(in:
                                geometry) {
                            action()
                        }
                    }
                )
            }
// ...
```

The last touch is to add the convenience function in `CGPoint` to return if it is inside a `GeometryProxy` frame:

```
extension CGPoint {
    func isContained(in geometry: GeometryProxy) -> Bool
    {
        geometry.frame(in: .global).contains(self)
    }
}
```

5. Running the app, we can see our button increasing in size when we tap on it. Notice that it stays at a bigger size when the touch is down and the finger is in the frame of the button, but it decreases when still touching it, as the finger leaves the frame:

Figure 7.12 – Animatable button on touch

How it works...

In this version of SwiftUI, there is no gesture to detect a simple touch and the movement of the finger, but it can be simulated using DragGesture with a minimum distance of 0, meaning that as soon the finger touches the component to which the gesture is attached, an onChanged event is raised

The other parameter to pass to the gesture is the coordinate space, which can be either .global or .local.

The former returns the coordinate in the space of the whole screen, while the latter in the space of the component itself.

It is important to have it as global to correspond with the space of the GeometryProxy frame so that we can detect whether the point is contained or not.

Lottie animations in SwiftUI

You probably already know about Lottie, https://airbnb.design/lottie/, which is a library for embedding animations made in After Effects in iOS.

Lottie fills the gap between motion designers and developers: the designers can implement their animations using their favorite tool, then export it in JSON format to be used by the developers and reproduced in high quality on the device.

In this recipe, we'll use an animation downloaded from `https://lottiefiles.com/`, where you can find thousands of animations either free or paid for, so it is definitely a website to keep an eye on.

Getting ready

In this recipe, we'll use a resource, `filling-heart.json`, that we can find in the GitHub repo, and we'll import Lottie using Xcode's Swift Package Manager integration.

Let's start by creating a SwiftUI project called `LottieInSwiftUIApp`.

Then, add the `filling-heart.json` file, which you can find in the GitHub repo at `https://github.com/PacktPublishing/SwiftUI-Cookbook/blob/master/Resources/Chapter07/recipe10/filling-heart.json`. Remember to tick the **Copy items if needed** box when dragging the file into the Xcode project.

Now we must include the Lottie framework in the project using the Swift Package Manager Xcode integration:

1.   From the menu, select **Files | Swift Packages | Add Package Dependency...**:

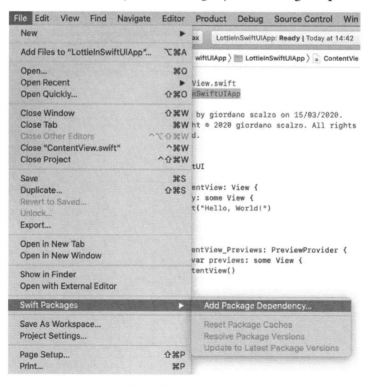

Figure 7.13 – The Add Package Dependency menu

2. Add the `https://github.com/airbnb/lottie-ios` URL to the package repository form:

Figure 7.14 – The package repository form

3. Select the latest version of Lottie:

Figure 7.15 – Selecting Lottie's version

4. After downloading the framework, Lottie should be ready to use:

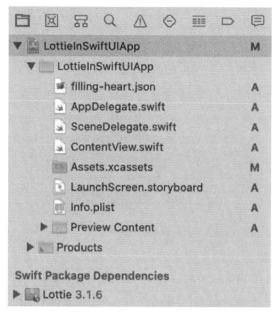

Figure 7.16 – Lottie ready in the project

How to do it...

We are going to implement a simple player of an animation. There will be just two components on the screen: an animation view and a button to trigger it:

1. Firstly, let's add a placeholder component for Lottie:

```swift
struct LottieAnimation: View {
    var animationName: String

    @Binding
    var isToPlay: Bool
    var body: some View {
        Circle()
    }
}
```

2. Add the `LottieAnimation` component in `ContentView`, along with a button to trigger the animation:

```
struct ContentView: View {
    @State
    private var isToPlay = false

    var body: some View {
        ZStack {
            Color.yellow
                .edgesIgnoringSafeArea(.all)
            VStack {
                LottieAnimation(animationName:
                    "filling-heart", isToPlay: $isToPlay)
                    .frame(width: 200, height: 200)
                Button {
                    isToPlay = true
                } label: {
                    Text("Fill me!")
                        .fontWeight(.heavy)
                        .padding(15)
                        .background(Color.white)
                        .cornerRadius(10)
                }
            }
        }
    }
}
```

3. Let's now implement the `LottieAnimation` view, without forgetting to import `Lottie`:

```
import SwiftUI
import Lottie

struct LottieAnimation: UIViewRepresentable {
    private let animationView = AnimationView()
```

```
        var animationName = ""

        @Binding
        var isToPlay: Bool

        func makeUIView(context: Context) -> UIView {
            let view = UIView()

          animationView
            .translatesAutoresizingMaskIntoConstraints = false
            view.addSubview(animationView)
            animationView.widthAnchor
                .constraint(equalTo: view.widthAnchor)
                .isActive = true
            animationView.heightAnchor
                .constraint(equalTo: view.heightAnchor)
                .isActive = true

            animationView.animation = Animation
              .named(animationName)
            animationView.contentMode = .scaleAspectFill
            animationView.scalesLargeContentImage = true
            return view
        }

        func updateUIView(_ uiView: UIView, context: Context)
        {
        }
    }
```

4. Finally, we can implement the updateUIView() function to start the animation when the isToPlay variable changes:

```
    func updateUIView(_ uiView: UIView, context: Context) {
        guard isToPlay else { return }

        animationView.play { _ in
```

```
        isToPlay = false
    }
}
```

Running the app, we can see how, with a few lines of code, we were able to use a nice Lottie animation:

Figure 7.17 – A gorgeous Lottie animation

How it works...

Lottie exposes a `UIView` subclass called `AnimationView`, where we set the animation name and can customize the animation itself – for example, by changing the speed.

Given that it is a `UIView` subclass, we need to wrap it in a `UIViewRepresentable` class to use it in SwiftUI.

The `updateUIView()` function is called every time the view needs to be refreshed – in our case, when the `isToPlay` bound variable changes – so that we can call the `play()` function in `AnimationView`.

Implementing a stretchable header in SwiftUI

A stretchable header is a well-known effect where, on top of a scroll view, there is an image that scales up when the user slides down the entries.

An example can be found on the artist page of the Spotify app, but in general, it is so common that you are expecting it when a page has a big image as a banner on top of a list of items.

In this recipe, we'll implement a skeleton of the artist page on the Spotify app, and we'll see that this effect is easy to implement in SwiftUI too.

Getting ready

There are a couple of images that we will use in this recipe, both of them courtesy of *crommelincklars* on *Flickr* (`https://www.flickr.com/photos/142899511@N03`).

Let's create a SwiftUI app called `StretchableHeaderApp` and add the two images – `avatar.jpg` and `header.jpg` – which you can find in the GitHub repo at `https://github.com/PacktPublishing/SwiftUI-Cookbook/tree/master/Resources/Chapter07/recipe11`:

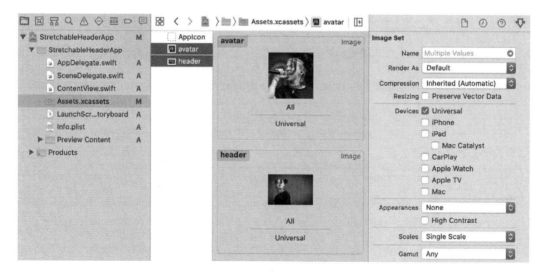

Figure 7.18 – Importing the images

How to do it...

We are going to implement two components, one for each row and the other for the header.

The former is a simple horizontal stack with a few components, while the latter is an `Image` component with some tricks to stick it to the top and scale it up when we drag the list of items:

1. Let's start by adding the `Row` component:

```swift
struct Row: View {
    var body: some View {
        HStack {
            Image("avatar")
                .resizable()
                .frame(width: 60, height: 60)
                .clipShape(Circle())
            Spacer()
            VStack(alignment: .trailing) {
                Text("Billie Eilish")
                    .fontWeight(.heavy)
                Text("Bad guy")
            }
        }
        .padding(.horizontal, 15)
    }
}
```

2. Let's add the rows to `ContentView`:

```swift
struct ContentView: View {
    var body: some View {
        ScrollView(.vertical, showsIndicators: false) {
            VStack {
                ForEach(0..<6) { _ in
                    Row()
                }
            }
        }
        .edgesIgnoringSafeArea(.all)
    }
}
```

3. Let's add `StretchebleHeader` then, which is just a wrapper around an image:

```swift
struct StretchableHeader: View {
    let imageName: String

    var body: some View {
        GeometryReader { geometry in
            Image(self.imageName)
                .resizable()
                .scaledToFill()
                .frame(width: geometry.size.width,
                       height: geometry.height)
                .offset(y: geometry.verticalOffset)
        }
        .frame(height: 300)
    }
}
```

4. To make it work, we need to add a couple of functions in `GeometryProxy`:

```swift
extension GeometryProxy {
    private var offset: CGFloat {
        frame(in: .global).minY
    }

    var height: CGFloat {
        size.height + (offset > 0 ? offset : 0)
    }

    var verticalOffset: CGFloat {
        offset > 0 ? -offset : 0
    }
}
```

5. Finally, we can add the header to `ContentView`:

```
struct ContentView: View {
//...
    VStack {
        StretchableHeader(imageName: "header")
        ForEach(0..<6) { _ in
//...
    }
```

Running the app, you can see that the header moves to the top when you slide up, but sticks to the top and increases in size when you slide down:

Figure 7.19 – Drag to stretch the header

How it works...

As you can see, the trick is in the way we calculate the vertical offset: when we try to slide the image down, the top of the image becomes greater than 0, so we apply a negative offset to compensate for the offset caused by the slide, and the image sticks to the top.

Same for the height: when the image moves up, the height is normal, but when it moves down after being stuck to the top, the height increases following the drag.

Note that the image is modified with `.scaledToFill()` so that when the height increases, the width increases proportionally, and we have an effect of a scale-up.

Creating floating hearts in SwiftUI

When Periscope was introduced in 2015, it was the first app to popularize the live-streaming feature that is now part of other apps, such as Facebook, Instagram, and YouTube.

A way of appreciating the streamer was to send a bunch of floating hearts, a feature that is also now implemented on Instagram and Facebook.

In this recipe, we'll see how to implement this feature in SwiftUI, as an example of a fairly complex real-world animation that can still be done easily in SwiftUI.

Getting ready

Let's start by creating a SwiftUI app called `FloatingHeartsApp`.

For this recipe, we are going to use a third-party framework that provides a function to create an interpolation when given a small set of points.

The library is called `SwiftCubicSpline` and can be found at `https://github.com/gscalzo/SwiftCubicSpline`:

1. From the menu, select **Files | Swift Packages | Add Package Dependency...**:

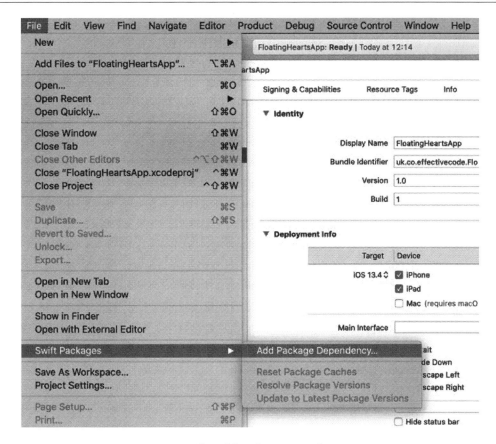

Figure 7.20 – The Add Package Dependency menu

2. Add the `https://github.com/gscalzo/SwiftCubicSpline` URL to the package repository form:

Figure 7.21 – The package repository form

3. Select the last version of `SwiftCubicSpline`:

Figure 7.22 – Select the SwiftCubicSpline version

4. After having downloaded the framework, `SwiftCubicSpline` should be ready to be used:

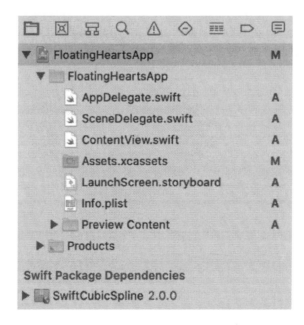

Figure 7.23 – SwiftCubicSpline ready in the project

How to do it...

In our simplified version of the floating hearts animation, we are going to trigger the animation via a bottom-left button.

The general idea is to have a sort of collection of heart components where we add a new heart every time we tap on the button; the heart will be removed from the list after the animation finishes – that is, when the heart reaches the top of the screen.

We are now going to add the code. It's a pretty long and sophisticated recipe, so don't worry if you don't precisely understand every step – everything will be explained in the next section:

1. Let's start with `ContentView`, adding the trigger button and preparing for the hearts:

```
struct ContentView: View {
    var body: some View {
        ZStack {
            VStack {
                Spacer()
                HStack {
                    Button {
                    } label: {
                        Image(systemName: "heart")
                            .font(.title)
                            .frame(width: 80, height: 80)
                            .foregroundColor(Color.white)
                            .background(Color.blue)
                            .clipShape(Circle())
                            .shadow(radius: 10)
                    }
                    Spacer()
                }.padding(.horizontal, 30)
            }
        }
    }
}
```

Running the app, you should see the button, which does nothing when tapped.

2. To keep the app runnable, we will introduce a placeholder for the Heart view, which we will implement properly later.

    However, the view must be marked as Identifiable, to be rendered as a list, and Equatable so that it can found and removed from the list:

```
// Placeholder
struct Heart: View, Identifiable {
    let id = UUID()
    var body: some View {
        Circle()
    }
}


extension Heart: Equatable {
    static func == (lhs: Heart, rhs: Heart) -> Bool {
        lhs.id == rhs.id
    }
}


extension Array where Element: Equatable {
    mutating func remove(object: Element) {
        guard let index = firstIndex(of: object) else
            {return}
        remove(at: index)
    }
}
```

We will now add the container for the animation and a class to model the list of hearts.

The Hearts class is an observable object, so it raises an event when its @ Published properties change.

The Hearts view simply iterates on the list of hearts to render them:

```
class Hearts: ObservableObject {
    @Published
    private(set) var all: [Heart] = []

    func new() {
```

```
        let heart = Heart()
        all.append(heart)
        DispatchQueue.main.asyncAfter(deadline: .now() +
            10.0) {
            self.all.remove(object: heart)
        }
    }
}

struct HeartsView: View {
    @ObservedObject
    var hearts: Hearts

    var body: some View {
        ForEach(hearts.all) { $0 }
    }
}
```

3. Now it's time to add the model and view to `ContentView`:

```
struct ContentView: View {
    var hearts = Hearts()

    var body: some View {
        //...
                Button {
                    hearts.new()
                } label: {
        //...
                }.padding(.horizontal, 30)
            }

        HeartsView(hearts: hearts)
        }
    }
}
```

Running the app, a big black circle appears in the center of the screen. We don't know it yet, but our stream of floating hearts is almost ready to flow!

4. Before implementing the hearts, let's add a convenience function to `Color` to create a random color:

```
extension Color {
    init(r: Double, g: Double, b: Double) {
        self.init(red: r/255, green: g/255, blue: b/255)
    }

    static func random() -> Color {
        Color(r: Double.random(in: 100...144),
              g: Double.random(in: 10...200),
              b: Double.random(in: 200...244))
    }
}
```

5. Let's replace the `Heart` placeholder with the proper implementation:

```
struct Heart: View, Identifiable {
    let id = UUID()

    @State
    private var opacity = 1.0
    @State
    private var scale: CGFloat = 1.0
    @State
    private var toAnimate = false

    var body: some View {
        Image(systemName: "heart.fill")
            .foregroundColor(Color.random())
            .opacity(opacity)
            .modifier(MoveShakeScale(pct: toAnimate ? 1 :
                0))
            .animation(Animation.easeIn(duration: 5.0))
            .onAppear {
                toAnimate.toggle()
                withAnimation(.easeIn(duration: 5)) {
```

```
                opacity = 0
            }
        }
    }
}
```

6. The last thing missing is the `MoveShakeScale` view modifier, which, basically, implements the three animations. Let's start implementing the curves needed for the scale and horizontal movement animations:

```
import SwiftCubicSpline
struct MoveShakeScale: GeometryEffect {
    private(set) var pct: CGFloat
    private let xPosition = UIScreen.main.bounds.width/4 +
        CGFloat.random(in: -20..<20)

    private let scaleSpline = CubicSpline(points: [
        Point(x: 0, y: 0.0),
        Point(x: 0.3, y: 3.5),
        Point(x: 0.4, y: 3.1),
        Point(x: 1.0, y: 2.1),
    ])

    private let xSpline = CubicSpline(points: [
        Point(x: 0.0,  y: 0.0),
        Point(x: 0.15, y: 20.0),
        Point(x: 0.3,  y: 12),
        Point(x: 0.5,  y: 0),
        Point(x: 1.0,  y: 8),
    ])
}
```

7. `GeometryEffect` has only one function, `effectValue()`, which receives a
size and returns the transformation to apply. In our case, we are applying all the
intermediate transformations at the place indicated by the `pct` value, which is also
the animated value that goes from 0 to 1 in the given duration:

```swift
struct MoveShakeScale: GeometryEffect {
    //...
    var animatableData: CGFloat {
        get { pct }
        set { pct = newValue }
    }

    func effectValue(size: CGSize) -> ProjectionTransform
    {
        let scale = scaleSpline[x: Double(pct)]
        let xOffset = xSpline[x: Double(pct)]

        let yOffset = UIScreen.main.bounds.height/2 -
                pct * UIScreen.main.bounds.height/4*3

        let transTrasf = CGAffineTransform(
                translationX: xPosition + CGFloat(xOffset),
                y: yOffset)
        let scaleTrasf = CGAffineTransform(
                                    scaleX: CGFloat(scale),
                                    y: CGFloat(scale))
        return ProjectionTransform(scaleTrasf

.concatenating(transTrasf))
    }
}
```

8. Finally, running the app, we can see our nice stream of floating hearts!

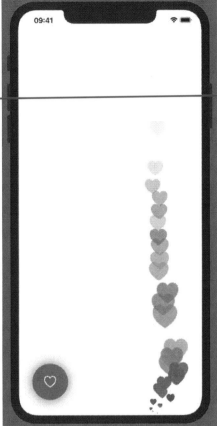

Figure 7.24 – A stream of floating hearts

How it works...

The basic idea of this recipe is to have four animations in parallel:

- Moving from the bottom to the top
- Fading
- Scaling up and down
- Slightly shaking while moving up

Also, we want to have the scaling and the shaking following a curve that we create given a few known points.

The technique to create a curve given a set of points is called interpolation, and for that, we use the `SwiftCubicSpline` library.

For example, the scale curve starts from zero, it grows to a maximum, and then it settles down to an intermediate value.

You can see the curve in the following figure:

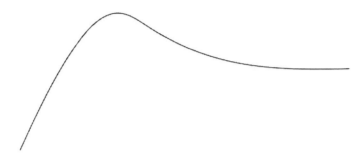

Figure 7.25 – Scaling curve

On the other hand, the curve for the horizontal movement is a sort of zigzag, and you can see it here:

Figure 7.26 – Horizontal movement curve

While it is simple to animate the opacity, because the curve is linear, there isn't a way to use a custom curve.

We circumvent this limitation using `GeometryEffect`.

`GeometryEffect` is a view modifier that returns a transformation to apply.

The trick here is to consider the *time* (called `pct` as a variable) as an animatable entity so that it will be called at every step of the animation.

In the `effectValue()` function, we are then calculating the required transformations – scaling, vertical moving, and horizontal shaking – at a given point in time, and we return it as a single transformation to apply to the component it is attached to.

There is one last thing to note, which is the way we remove the hearts from the list.

As you can see in *step 4*, and noted here in the following code, we use a delayed callback to remove the hearts:

```
func new() {
    let heart = Heart()
    all.append(heart)
    DispatchQueue.main.asyncAfter(deadline: .now() + 10.0) {
        self.all.remove(object: heart)
    }
}
```

The goal is to remove the hearts when the animation has finished, but in this version of SwiftUI, there is no way to attach a callback to be called on animation completion, so we dispatch a delayed callback after some time, making it big enough to be sure that it is removed after the animation has finished.

I'll admit, it is a bit hacky, but it is effective!

See also

You can find more information on the use of `GeometryEffect` in this article at **objc.io**, `https://www.objc.io/blog/2019/09/26/swiftui-animation-timing-curves/`, and in the second part of a series on Advanced SwiftUI animation at **swiftui-lab.com**, `https://swiftui-lab.com/swiftui-animations-part2/`.

How to implement a swipeable stack of cards in SwiftUI

Every now and then, an app solves a common problem in such an elegant and peculiar way that it becomes a sort of de facto way to do it in other apps as well.

I am referring to a pattern such as *pull to refresh*, which started in the Twitter app and then became part of iOS itself.

A few years ago, Tinder introduced the pattern of swipeable cards to solve the problem of indicating in a list of cards which cards we like and which we dislike.

From then on, countless apps have applied the same visual pattern, not just in the dating sector but in every sector that needed a way to make a match between different users, including anything from business purposes, such as coupling mentors and mentees, to indicating which clothes we like for a fashion e-commerce app.

In this recipe, we are going to implement a barebones version of Tinder's swipeable stack of cards.

Getting ready

This recipe doesn't need any external resource, so just create a SwiftUI app called `SwipeableCardsApp`.

How to do it...

For our simple swipeable card recipe, we are not using images but a simple gradient.

In our `User` struct, we are then going to record the gradient for that user. To calculate the width and the offset of a card, we are going to use a trick, where each user has an incremental ID; the greater IDs are at the front, and the lower ones are at the back.

In that way, we can calculate the width and offset of the card using a mathematical formula and give the impression of stacked cards without using a 3D UI that is too complicated:

1. Let's start by adding the `User` struct:

```
struct User: Identifiable {
    var id: Int
    let firstName: String
    let lastName: String
    let start: Color
    let end: Color
}
```

2. Given that struct, add a list of users in `ContentView`:

```
struct ContentView: View {
    @State
    private var users: [User] = [
        User(id: 0, firstName: "Mark",
            lastName: "Bennett",
```

```
                  start: .red, end: .green),
       User(id: 1, firstName: "John",
            lastName: "Lewis",
            start: .green, end: .orange),
       User(id: 2, firstName: "Joan",
            lastName: "Mince",
            start: .blue, end: .green),
       User(id: 3, firstName: "Liz",
            lastName: "Garret",
            start: .orange, end: .purple),
    ]
    var body: some View {
       //...
    }
}
```

3. If you think that three users are not enough, add some more:

```
    private var users: [User] = [
       //...
       User(id: 4, firstName: "Lola",
            lastName: "Pince",
            start: .yellow, end: .gray),
       User(id: 5, firstName: "Jim",
            lastName: "Beam",
            start: .pink, end: .yellow),
       User(id: 6, firstName: "Tom",
            lastName: "Waits",
            start: .purple, end: .blue),
       User(id: 7, firstName: "Mike",
            lastName: "Rooney",
            start: .black, end: .gray),
       User(id: 8, firstName: "Jane",
            lastName: "Doe",
            start: .red, end: .green),
    ]
```

4. Then, in the `ContentView` body, let's add the list of `CardView`:

```swift
var body: some View {
    GeometryReader { geometry in
        ZStack {
            ForEach(self.users) { user in
                if user.id > users.maxId - 4 {
                    CardView(user: user, onRemove: {
                                        removedUser in
                        users.removeAll { $0.id ==
                        removedUser.id }
                    })
                    .animation(.spring())
                    .frame(width:
                        users.cardWidth(in: geometry,
                            userId: user.id), height: 400)
                    .offset(x: 0,
                        y: users.cardOffset(
                            userId: user.id))
                }
            }
        }
    }.padding()
}
```

5. Let's add an extension to the array of users to calculate `maxID`, which is used to limit the number of visible cards to 4, and the width and offset of a card given an ID:

```swift
extension Array where Element == User {
    var maxId: Int { map { $0.id }.max() ?? 0 }

    func cardOffset(userId: Int) -> CGFloat {
        CGFloat(count - 1 - userId) * 8
    }

    func cardWidth(in geometry: GeometryProxy,
                userId: Int) -> CGFloat {
        geometry.size.width - cardOffset(userId: userId)
```

```
        }
    }
```

6. Finally, let's implement `CardView`, starting with the private variables:

```swift
struct CardView: View {
    @State
    private var translation: CGSize = .zero
    private var user: User
    private var onRemove: (_ user: User) -> Void

    private var threshold: CGFloat = 0.5

    init(user: User, onRemove: @escaping (_ user: User)
        -> Void) {
        self.user = user
        self.onRemove = onRemove
    }
    var body: some View {
        //...
    }
}
```

7. Then, let's add `VStack` with the various components in body, wrapping it in `GeometryReader`, which will be used in `DragGesture`:

```swift
var body: some View {
    GeometryReader { geometry in
        VStack(alignment: .leading, spacing: 20) {
            Rectangle()
                .fill(LinearGradient(gradient:
                        Gradient(colors: [user.start, user.
                            end]),
                        startPoint: .topLeading,
                        endPoint: .bottomTrailing))
                .cornerRadius(10)
                .frame(width: geometry.size.width - 40,
```

```
                                    height: geometry.size.height *
                                        0.65)
                        Text("\(user.firstName) \( user.lastName)")
                            .font(.title)
                            .bold()
                    }
                    .padding(20)
                    .background(Color.white)
                    .cornerRadius(8)
                    .shadow(radius: 5)
                    .animation(.spring())
                    .offset(x: translation.width, y: 0)
            }
        }
```

8. After the `.offset()` modifier, we must add a `.rotationEffect()` modifier
    to give the effect of rotating the card when it is dragged toward the border of the
    screen, and `DragGesture` to change the translation and remove the card or release
    it when the finger leaves the touch:

```
    .rotationEffect(.degrees(
            Double(self.translation.width /
                geometry.size.width)
            * 20), anchor: .bottom)
    .gesture(
        DragGesture()
        .onChanged {
            translation = $0.translation
        }.onEnded {
            if $0.percentage(in: geometry) > threshold {
                onRemove(self.user)
            } else {
                translation = .zero
            }
        }
    )
```

9. The last thing that is missing is the percentage convenience function in the
    `DragGesture` value:

```
extension DragGesture.Value {
    func percentage(in geometry: GeometryProxy) ->
        CGFloat {
        abs(translation.width / geometry.size.width)
    }
}
```

Running the app, we can smoothly swipe to the left or right, and when a swipe is
more than 50%, the card disappears from the stack:

Figure 7.27 – Stack of swipeable cards

How it works...

Even though the code looks a bit long, in reality, it is very simple.

Let start from *step 3*, where the `ContentView` body is populated.

Note that we are showing only the last 4 cards, using the following condition:

```
if user.id > self.users.maxId - 4 {
```

If you want to show more cards, change 4 to something else.

Another thing to notice is that in the callback we are passing to `CardView`, we are removing the card from our list.

The `onRemove` parameter is called by `CardView` when it is released, and it is translated from the origin for more than 50% of its size. In that case, the card is well close to the left or right border of the device and so it must be removed.

Finally, note that the vertical offset and the width are calculated depending on the ID of the user.

In *step 4*, we are calculating the width and offset as a simple proportion of the ID of the user, assuming that they are discrete and incremental.

Step 5 is where most of the logic resides.

Let's skip almost all the code, which is basically configuring the layout of the card, and concentrate on the gesture.

`onChange` of `DragGesture` sets the `@State` variable `translation` to the value of the dragged object.

The `translation` variable is then used to move the card horizontally and to rotate it around the *Z* axis slightly.

When the drag terminates, we calculate the current percentage: if it is greater than 50%, we call the `onRemove` callback; otherwise, we set the translation variable back to `0`.

That is pretty much it: if you understand the parts we have just discussed, you'll be able to apply the same concepts to many other animations.

8
Driving SwiftUI with Data

In this chapter, we'll learn how to manage the state of single or multiple Views. In the declarative world of SwiftUI, you should consider Views as functions of their state, whereas in UIKit, in the imperative world, you are telling a view what it has to do depending on the state. In SwiftUI, the Views react to the changes.

SwiftUI has two ways of reaching these goals:

- Using the binding property wrappers that SwiftUI provides
- Using **Combine**, a new reactive framework Apple introduced in iOS 13

Property wrappers are a way to decorate a property introduced in Swift 5.1.

There are three different ways of using them in SwiftUI:

- `@State`, to change state variables that belong to the same view. These variables should not be visible outside the view and should be marked as **private**.

- `@ObservedObject`, to change state variables for multiple, but connected Views, for example, when there is a parent-child relationship. These properties must have reference semantics.

- `@EnvironmentObject`, when the variables are shared between multiple and unrelated Views, and defined somewhere else in the app. For example, you can set the color and font themes as common objects that will be used everywhere in the app.

Under the hood, some of these property wrappers use Combine to implement their functionalities. However, for more complex interactions, you can use Combine directly by exploiting its capabilities, such as chaining streams and filtering.

In this chapter, we'll look at recipes on how to use the **state binding** property wrappers, with some simple, but realistic, recipes. If you have already read the recipes in the previous chapters, you have already encountered these property wrappers, but now is the moment to concentrate on those and understand them better.

Using the previous property wrappers, you should be able to create stateless Views that change when their stateful model changes.

By the end of the chapter, you should be able to decide which property wrappers to use to bind the state to the components, depending on the relationships between the state and multiple or single Views.

In the next chapter, *Driving SwiftUI with Combine*, we'll see how to use Combine to drive changes in SwiftUI Views.

In this chapter, we are going to learn how to use the SwiftUI binding mechanism to populate and change the Views when data changes.

This chapter comprises the following recipes:

- Using `@State` to drive Views behavior
- Using `@Binding` to pass a state variable to child Views
- Implementing a `CoreLocation` wrapper as `@ObservedObject`
- Sharing state objects with multiple Views using `@EnvironmentObject`

Technical requirements

The code in this chapter is based on Xcode 12, with iOS 13 as the minimum iOS target.

You can find the code in the book's GitHub repository at the following link: https://github.com/PacktPublishing/SwiftUI-Cookbook/tree/master/Chapter08%20-%20Driving%20SwiftUI%20with%20data.

Using @State to drive Views behavior

As mentioned in the introduction, when a state variable belongs only to a single view, its changes are bound to the components using the @State property wrapper.

To understand this behavior, we are going to implement a simple To-do List app, where a static set of to-dos are changed to 'done' when we tap on the row.

In the next recipe, *Using @Binding to pass a variable to child Views*, we'll expand on this recipe, adding the possibility of adding new to-dos.

Getting ready

Let's start the recipe by creating a SwiftUI app called StaticTodoApp.

How to do it...

To demonstrate the use of the @State variable, we are going to create an app that holds its state in a list of Todo structs: each Todo can be either undone or done, and we change its state by tapping on the related row.

When the user taps on one row in the UI, they change the done state in the related Todo struct:

1. Let's start by adding the basic Todo struct:

```
struct Todo: Identifiable, Equatable {
    let id = UUID()
    let description: String
    var done: Bool
}
```

2. Then, in `ContentView`, add in the list of to-dos, marking them with `@State`:

```
struct ContentView: View {
    @State
    private var todos: [Todo] = [
        .init(description: "review first chapter",
            done: false),
        .init(description: "buy wine", done: false),
        .init(description: "paint kitchen", done: false),
        .init(description: "cut the grass", done: false),
    ]
    //...
}
```

3. Now, render the to-dos, striking a line through the description if it is done, and
    changing the checkmark accordingly:

```
var body: some View {
    NavigationView {
        List {
            ForEach(todos) { todo in
                HStack {
                    Text(todo.description)
                        .strikethrough(todo.done)
                    Spacer()
                    Image(systemName:
                        todo.done ?
                            "checkmark.square" :
                            "square")
```

```
                    }
                }
            }.navigationBarTitle("TODOs")
        }
    }
```

4. A tap gesture is then added to the `Todo` component to change the state of the doneness:

```
HStack {
    //...
}
.contentShape(Rectangle())
.onTapGesture {
    todos.toggleDone(to: todo)
}
```

5. The `todo` variable passed in the block of `ForEach` is a constant, so we create a function in the array of the `todo` to mutate the corresponding element therein:

```
private extension Array where Element == Todo {
    mutating func toggleDone(to todo: Todo) {
        guard let index = self.firstIndex(
            where: { $0 == todo }
        ) else { return }
        self[index].done.toggle()
    }
}
```

Running the app, you can see that the way the `todo` items look, changes when you tap on a row:

Figure 8.1 – Different to-do renderings depending on their doneness

How it works...

If there is only one recipe to understand and remember from this chapter, I believe this is the one you should read.

Even if it is really simple, it depicts the change of mindset needed to understand the dynamic behavior of SwiftUI. Instead of dictating the changes to the UI, we are changing the state, and this is reflected in the UI.

Another thing to note is that everything in the `body` computed variable is immutable, and we cannot change it in place, but we must change the state that is bound to the `body`. The `todo` variable is an immutable copy of `todo`, and when we want to change its state, we must find the original and mutable element in the array.

Finally, you probably noticed the modifier, `.contentShape()`, that we apply to the row. This is necessary to give the whole row as a hit area to the gesture, otherwise only the text would have been sensitive to the touches.

See also

You can find more information in the Apple tutorial, *State and Data Flow*, at this address: `https://developer.apple.com/documentation/swiftui/state_and_data_flow`.

Also, it is worthwhile watching the *WWDC 2019* video *Data Flow through SwiftUI*, which you can find here: `https://developer.apple.com/videos/play/wwdc2019/226/`.

Using @Binding to pass a state variable to child Views

In the previous recipe, *Using @State to drive Views behavior*, you saw how to use an `@State` variable to change a UI. But what if we want to have another view that changes that `@State` variable?

Given that an array has a value-type semantic, if we pass down the variable, Swift creates a copy whose changes are not reflected in the original.

SwiftUI solves this with the `@Binding` property wrapper, which, in a certain way, creates a reference semantic for specific structs.

To explore this mechanism, we are going to create an extension to the `TodoApp` we created in the previous recipe, *Using @State to drive Views behavior*, where we are going to add a child view that allows the addition of a new to-do to the list.

Getting ready

The starting point for this project is the final code of the previous recipe, so you could use the same `StaticTodoApp` project.

If you want to keep the recipes separate, you can create a new SwiftUI project called `DynamicTodoApp`.

How to do it...

The main difference compared with the previous `StaticTodoApp` project is the addition of an `InputView` that allows the user to add a new task to perform.

The first steps are the same as the previous recipe, so feel free to skip them if you are starting your code from the source of that recipe:

1. Let's start by adding the basic `Todo` struct:

```
struct Todo: Identifiable, Equatable {
    let id = UUID()
    let description: String
    var done: Bool
}
```

2. Then, in the `ContentView` struct, add in the list of to-dos, marking them with `@State`:

```
struct ContentView: View {
    @State
    private var todos: [Todo] = [
        .init(description: "review first chapter",
              done: false),
        .init(description: "buy wine", done: false),
        .init(description: "paint kitchen", done: false),
        .init(description: "cut the grass", done: false),
    ]
    //...
}
```

3. Now, render the to-dos, striking a line through the description if it is done, and changing the checkmark accordingly:

```
var body: some View {
    NavigationView {
        List {
            ForEach(todos) { todo in
                HStack {
                    Text(todo.description)
                        .strikethrough(todo.done)
```

```
                    Spacer()
                  Image(systemName:
                    todo.done ?
                      "checkmark.square" :
                    "square")
              }
            }
          }.navigationBarTitle("TODOs")
      }
    }
```

4. A tap gesture is then added to the `Todo` component to change the state of the doneness:

```
HStack {
  //...
}
.contentShape(Rectangle())
.onTapGesture {
    self.todos.toggleDone(to: todo)
}
```

5. The `todo` variable passed in the block of `ForEach` is a constant, so we create a function in the array of to-dos to mutate the corresponding element therein:

```
private extension Array where Element == Todo {
    mutating func toggleDone(to todo: Todo) {
        guard let index = self.firstIndex(
            where: { $0 == todo }
        ) else { return }
        self[index].done.toggle()
    }
}
```

6. Let's now create a new component that we will use to add a new To-do task:

```swift
struct InputTodoView: View {
    @State
    private var newTodoDescription: String = ""

    @Binding
    var todos: [Todo]

    var body: some View {
        HStack {
            TextField("Todo", text: $newTodoDescription)
                .textFieldStyle(CustomTextFieldStyle())
            Spacer()
            Button(action: {
            }) {
                Text("Add")
                    .padding(.horizontal, 16)
                    .padding(.vertical, 8)
                    .foregroundColor(.white)
                    .background(Color.green)
                    .cornerRadius(5)
            }
        }
        .frame(height: 60)
        .padding(.horizontal, 24)
        .padding(.bottom, 30)
        .background(Color.gray)
    }
}
```

7. To customize the TextField, we introduce a custom TextFieldStyle:

```swift
struct CustomTextFieldStyle: TextFieldStyle {
    func _body(configuration:
        TextField<Self._Label>) -> some View {
        configuration
            .padding(.horizontal, 8)
```

```
        .autocapitalization(.none)
        .frame(height: 40)
        .background(Color.white)
        .cornerRadius(5)
    }
}
```

8. Having finished with the component layout, let's add the action to the button, where we create a new task if the description is not empty:

```
//...
Button {
    guard !newTodoDescription.isEmpty else {
        return
    }
    todos.append(Todo(description: newTodoDescription,
                      done: false))
    newTodoDescription = ""
} label: {
    Text("Add")
    //...
```

9. If you run the app now, you can't see any difference compared with the previous app: can you spot what's wrong?

   Exactly, we haven't added `InputTodoView` to `ContentView` yet!
   Before adding it, let's embed the `List` view in a `ZStack` that ignores the safe area at the bottom:

```
var body: some View {
    NavigationView {
        ZStack(alignment: .bottom) {
            List {...}.navigationBarTitle("TODOs")
        }
        .edgesIgnoringSafeArea(.bottom)
    }
}
```

10. Finally, put `InputTodoView` in the `ZStack` along with the `List` view:

```
ZStack(alignment: .bottom) {
    List {...}.navigationBarTitle("TODOs")
    InputTodoView(todos: $todos)
}
```

Finally, the app is improved: not only can we change the state of the to-dos, but we can also add new to-dos:

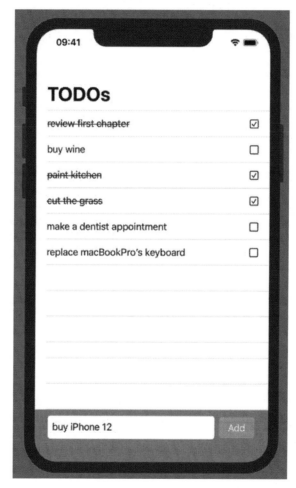

Figure 8.2 – Adding new to-dos to the list

How it works...

As mentioned in the introduction to the recipe, when a child view has to change the state of a parent view, passing the variable directly is not enough. Because of the value type semantic, a copy of the original variable is made.

SwiftUI uses the `@Binding` property wrapper, which basically creates a two-way binding:

- Any changes in the parent's variable are reflected in the child's variable.
- Any changes in the child's variable are reflected in the parent's variable.

This is achieved by using the `@Binding` property wrapper in the child's definition and by using the $ symbol when the parent passes the variable, meaning that it isn't passing the variable itself, but its reference, similar to using & for the `inout` variables in normal Swift code.

TextField styling

Something unrelated to the `@Binding` concept is the way we customize the `TextField` in the recipe. As you can see, `TextFieldStyle` doesn't expose a `makeBody()` function in the same way as `ButtonStyle`, for example, meaning we use the `_body()` function, whose underscore prefix would suggest that it is an Apple internal, meaning this could change in a future version of SwiftUI.

Don't rely on that for your production code and keep an eye on the newer version of SwiftUI.

Implementing a CoreLocation wrapper as @ObservedObject

We mentioned in the introduction to the chapter that `@State` is used when the state variable has value-type semantics. This is because any mutation of the property creates a new copy of the variable, which triggers a rendering of the view's body, but what about a property with reference semantics?

In this case, any mutation of the variable is applied to the variable itself and SwiftUI cannot detect the variation by itself.

In this case, we must use a different property wrapper, `@ObservedObject`, and the observed object must conform to `ObservableObject`. Furthermore, the properties of this object that will be observed in the view must be decorated with `@Published`. In this way, when the properties mutate, the view is notified, and the body is rendered again.

This will also help in case we want to bridge iOS foundation objects to the new SwiftUI model, such as `CoreLocation` functionalities. `CoreLocation` is the iOS framework that determines the device's geographic location. Location determination requires always having the mechanism on, even if in the background, and comes with the associated privacy concerns. For this reason, an explicit permission must be granted by the user.

In this recipe, we'll see how simple it is to wrap `CLLocationManager` in an `ObservableObject` and consume it in a SwiftUI view.

Getting ready

Let's create a SwiftUI project called `SwiftUICoreLocationManagerApp`.

For privacy reasons, every app that needs to access the location of the user must seek permission prior to accessing it. To allow this, a message should be added to the *Privacy – Location When in Use Usage Description* key in `Info.plist`:

1. Open `Info.plist` with Xcode, and right-click to select **Raw Keys & Values**:

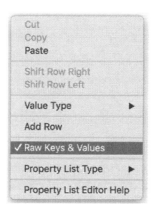

Figure 8.3 – Selecting Raw Keys & Values in Info.plist

2. Add the **NSLocationWhenInUseUsageDescription** key and a value with a message to the user:

▶ UIRequiredDeviceCapabilities	⌃	Array	(1 item)
▶ UISupportedInterfaceOrientations	⌃	Array	(3 items)
NSLocationWhenInUseUsageDescription	⌃ ⊕ ⊖	String	⌃ Enable location services please
▶ UISupportedInterfaceOrientations~ipad	⌃	Array	(4 items)

Figure 8.4 – Message to the user to enable location services

How to do it...

In this recipe, we are simply wrapping `CLLocationManager` in an `ObservableObject`, publishing two properties:

- The location status
- The current location

A SwiftUI view will present the user location and subsequent location update when the user moves more than 10 meters:

1. Let's start with the `ObservableObject` that owns the `CLLocationManager` and exposes the two state variables:

```swift
import CoreLocation
class LocationManager: NSObject, ObservableObject {
    private let locationManager = CLLocationManager()
    @Published
    var status: CLAuthorizationStatus?
    @Published
    var current: CLLocation?
}
```

2. Then, implement `init()`, where we configure `CLLocationManager` to react when the position changes by 10 meters, and we begin updating the location detection:

```swift
class LocationManager: NSObject, ObservableObject {
        // ...
    override init() {
        super.init()
        self.locationManager.delegate = self
        self.locationManager.distanceFilter = 10
        self.locationManager.desiredAccuracy =
                kCLLocationAccuracyBest
        self.locationManager.
            requestWhenInUseAuthorization()
        self.locationManager.startUpdatingLocation()
    }
}
```

3. Now, the app doesn't compile because we are setting `LocationManager` as a delegate to `CLLocationManager` without conforming it to the appropriate protocol.

4. Let's now undertake this conformance:

```
extension LocationManager: CLLocationManagerDelegate {
    func locationManager(_ manager: CLLocationManager,
        didChangeAuthorization status:CLAuthorizationStatus)
        {
        self.status = status
    }
    func locationManager(_ manager: CLLocationManager,
        didUpdateLocations locations: [CLLocation]) {
        guard let location = locations.last else { return
    }
        self.current = location
    }
}
```

5. Before using the class in `ContentView`, we add a convenient extension to `CLAuthorizationStatus` to format the status in a descriptive way:

```
extension Optional where Wrapped == CLAuthorizationStatus
    {
    var description: String {
        guard let self = self else {
            return "unknown"
        }

        switch self {
        case .notDetermined:
            return "notDetermined"
        case .authorizedWhenInUse:
            return "authorizedWhenInUse"
```

```
        case .authorizedAlways:
            return "authorizedAlways"
        case .restricted:
            return "restricted"
        case .denied:
            return "denied"
        @unknown default:
            return "unknown"
        }


    }
}
```

6. We then do the same for the `CLLocation` class:

```
extension Optional where Wrapped == CLLocation {
    var latitudeDescription: String {
        guard let self = self else {
            return "-"
        }
        return "\(self.coordinate.latitude)"
    }

    var longitudeDescription: String {
        guard let self = self else {
            return "-"
        }
        return "\(self.coordinate.longitude)"
    }
}
```

7. Finally, we set `LocationManager` as an observed object in `ContentView`:

```
struct ContentView: View {
    @ObservedObject
    private var locationManager = LocationManager()

    var body: some View {
        VStack {
            Text("Status:
                \(locationManager.status.description)")
            HStack {
                Text("Latitude:
                    \(locationManager.current.
                        latitudeDescription)")
                Text("Longitude:
                    \(locationManager.current.
                        longitudeDescription)")
            }
        }
    }
}
```

When running the app the first time after granting permission for the location services, you should see your coordinate printed in the view. If you move more than 10 meters, you should see the values update:

Figure 8.5 – Showing user locations with SwiftUI

How it works...

Using a class as a state variable for SwiftUI is a matter of making a subclass of `ObservableObject` and deciding what properties will trigger a re-rendering of a view.

You can consider the `@Published` property wrapper as a sort of automatic property observer that triggers a notification when its value changes. The view, with the decoration `@ObservedObject`, registers the changes in the published properties and every time one of these mutates, it renders the body again.

In reality, `@Published` is syntactic sugar for a Combine publisher, and if you are curious to see what you can do with Combine, we'll introduce it further in a later chapter, in a recipe entitled *Introducing Combine in a SwiftUI project*.

Sharing state objects with multiple views using @EnvironmentObject

In many cases, there are dependent collaborators that must be shared between several Views, even without having a tight relationship between them. Think of `ThemeManager`, or `NetworkManager`, or `UserProfileManager`.

Passing them through the chain of Views can be really annoying, without thinking of the coupling we could create. If a view doesn't need `NetworkManager`, for example, it should still have it as a property in case one of its child Views needs it.

SwiftUI solves this with the concept of `Environment`, a place to add common objects, usually `ObservableObject` objects, which will be shared between a chain of Views. An `Environment` is started in the root ancestor of the view graph, and it can be changed further down in the chain, adding new objects.

To present this feature, we are going to implement a basic song player with three Views:

- A list of songs view
- A mini player view, always on top of the Views when a song is played
- A song details view

All three of these Views always have an indication of the song currently playing and a button to play or stop a song.

It's important that the Views are in sync with the actual audio player, and we must also decouple the view logic from the actual song playing.

For that, we use a simple `MusicPlayer` object that simulates the actual song playing and is saved in `Environment`.

By the end of the recipe, you will have a grasp of what to put in `Environment` and how, and also how to separate the view logic from the business logic.

Getting ready

Let's start by creating a new SwiftUI app and calling it `SongPlayerApp`.

To present the songs in the player, we need some covers, `cover0.png` to `cover5.png`, which you can find in the GitHub repository at `https://github.com/PacktPublishing/SwiftUI-Cookbook/tree/master/Resources/Chapter08/recipe4`.

Add them to the **Assets** images and we are ready to go:

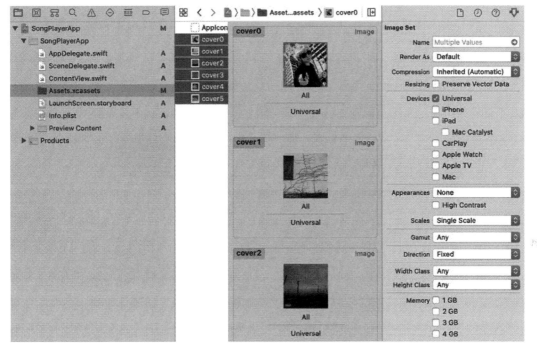

Figure 8.6 – Importing the images

How to do it...

We are going to implement three Views to present a playable song and a `MusicPlayer` class that simulates a real audio player:

1. Let's model the song with a proper `Song` struct:

```swift
struct Song: Identifiable, Equatable {
    let id = UUID()
    let artist: String
    let name: String
    let cover: String
}
```

2. Before moving to the Views implementation, let's make the `MusicPlayer` class, a class that represents the part of the SDK that plays audio, whose state, playing or not playing, is determined by whether or not it has a song playing. You can see this in the `thereIsASong` property:

```swift
class MusicPlayer: ObservableObject {
    @Published
    var currentSong: Song?
    var thereIsASong: Bool {
        currentSong != nil
    }

    func pressButton(song: Song) {
        if currentSong == song {
            currentSong = nil
        } else {
            currentSong = song
        }
    }
    func isPlaying(_ song: Song) -> Bool {
        song == currentSong
    }
}
```

3. Add the list of songs to the `ContentView` struct and present them in a `ScrollView` struct:

```swift
struct ContentView: View {
    private let songs: [Song] = [
        .init(artist: "Luke", name: "99",
                            cover: "cover0"),
        .init(artist: "Foxing", name: "No Trespassing",
                            cover: "cover1"),
        .init(artist: "Breaking Benjamin", name:
            "Phobia", cover: "cover2"),
        .init(artist: "J2", name: "Solenoid",
                            cover: "cover3"),
```

```
                    .init(artist: "Wildflower Clothing",
                        name: "Lightning Bottles", cover: "cover4"),
                    .init(artist: "The Broken Spirits", name:
                        "Rubble", cover: "cover5"),
            ]

        var body: some View {
            NavigationView {
                ScrollView {
                    ForEach(self.songs) { song in
                    }
                }
                .padding(.horizontal, 24)
                .navigationBarTitle("Music Player")
            }
        }
    }
```

4. To present the Play/Stop image button, we add an extension to the `MusicPlayer` class, which returns the correct image depending on the state of the player:

```
extension MusicPlayer {
    func buttonImage(for song: Song) -> some View {
        Image(systemName: isPlaying(song) ? "stop" :
            "play")
        .font(.system(.largeTitle))
        .foregroundColor(.black)
    }
}
```

5. For each song in the list, we must present a proper `SongView`:

```
ScrollView {
    ForEach(self.songs) { song in
        SongView(song: song)
    }
}
.padding(.horizontal, 24)Code
```

6. The layout of each view presents the cover to the left, the author and song title in the center, and the play/stop button to the right. Also, when we tap on the cover image, we navigate to a full-screen player view:

```swift
struct SongView: View {
    @EnvironmentObject
    private var musicPlayer: MusicPlayer
    let song: Song

    var body: some View {
        HStack {
            NavigationLink(destination: PlayerView(song:
                song)) {
                Image(song.cover)
                    .renderingMode(.original)
                    .resizable()
                    .aspectRatio(contentMode: .fill)
                    .frame(width: 100, height: 100)
            }

            VStack(alignment: .leading) {
                Text(song.name)
                Text(song.artist).italic()
            }
            Spacer()
            Button{
                musicPlayer.pressButton(song: song)
            } label: {
                musicPlayer.buttonImage(for: song)
            }
        }
    }
}
```

7. Our full-screen `PlayerView` is a simple bigger cover image and the play/stop button:

```
struct PlayerView: View {
    @EnvironmentObject
    private var musicPlayer: MusicPlayer
    let song: Song

    var body: some View {
        VStack {
            Image(song.cover).renderingMode(.original)
                .resizable()
                .aspectRatio(contentMode: .fill)
                .frame(width: 300, height: 300)
            HStack {
                Text(song.name)
                Text(song.artist).italic()
            }
            Button {
                self.musicPlayer.pressButton(song: song)
            } label: {
                musicPlayer.buttonImage(for: song)
            }
        }
    }
}
```

Now, the app should be compilable, but if we try to run it, we will get a runtime error. The reason is that we are reading from the `Environment`, with @ `EnvironmentObject`, but nowhere are we setting the value of `MusicPlayer`.

8. Let's add the `MusicPlayer` to `SceneDelegate`:

```
// Create the SwiftUI view that provides the window
contents.
let contentView = ContentView()
    .environmentObject(MusicPlayer())
```

9. Now, the app runs properly, but we still have an error when we try to open it in preview. Can you spot the reason?

    Yes, it is because we are not running the app from `SceneDelegate` in the preview, but from `ContentView_Previews`.

    Let's add a similar code to `SceneDelegate`:

    ```swift
    static var previews: some View {
        ContentView()
            .environmentObject(MusicPlayer())
    }
    ```

10. Almost there. The final missing component is `MiniPlayerView`, which is a view that simply wraps a `SongView` component:

    ```swift
    struct MiniPlayerView: View {
        @EnvironmentObject
        private var musicPlayer: MusicPlayer

        var body: some View {
            VStack {
                if musicPlayer.thereIsASong {
                    SongView(song: musicPlayer.currentSong!)
                        .padding(.all, 24)
                } else {
                    EmptyView()
                }
            }
        }
    }
    ```

11. Finally, in `ContentView` struct, embed `ScrollView` in a `ZStack` and add `MiniPlayerView` at the bottom:

```
var body: some View {
    ZStack(alignment: .bottom) {
        NavigationView {... }

        MiniPlayerView()
            .background(Color.gray)
        .offset(y: 44)
    }
}
```

Running the app, we can see that all the Views are in sync, and when selecting different songs to play in different Views, they always present the correct play/stop button:

Figure 8.7 – Playing a song in different Views

How it works...

The `@Environment` feature is a really nice (and official way) of resolving a problem that often has been solved using singletons or global variables: the problem of common dependencies. If you have something that could be needed in multiple unrelated Views, storing it in `Environment` could be a viable solution.

Every view has access to the `Environment` set by their ancestors, and it can retrieve a value from it, marking the property with the `@EnvironmentObject` wrapper.

You can imagine the feature as being a sort of shared `HashMap`, where the keys are the type of object and the values are an instance of the object itself.

We can then deduce that we cannot have two objects of the same type in `Environment`, but this shouldn't usually prove to be a problem.

Moreover, there is a way to have different objects of the same type there, but this goes beyond the scope of this book (hint: define custom keys).

See also

Although not explicitly declared by Apple, this talk by *Stephen Celis* could have been an inspiration for this feature: *How to Control the World* (`https://vimeo.com/291588126`).

9
Driving SwiftUI with Combine

In this chapter, we'll learn how to manage the state of SwiftUI Views using Combine. In the **Worldwide Developers Conference (WWDC)** 2019, Apple not only introduced SwiftUI but also introduced Combine, a perfect companion to SwiftUI for managing the declarative change of state in Swift.

In recent years, given the success of **Functional Reactive Programming (FRP)** in different sectors of the industry, the same concept has started to be used in the iOS ecosystem, firstly with **ReactiveCocoa**, the original framework in Objective-C, then in porting **ReactiveSwift**, and then **RxSwift**, which is the Swift implementation of **ReactiveX**, an umbrella of frameworks in different languages that have the same interfaces and functionalities.

In a typical Apple way, Apple took the best practices matured over years of trial and error from the community, and instead of acquiring either ReactiveSwift or RxSwift, Apple decided to reimplement the concepts, simplify their version, and specialize it for mobile development: Combine was born!

An in-depth examination of Combine is out of the scope of this book, but in this recipe, we'll see a shallow introduction to Combine and how to use it.

Just as SwiftUI is a declarative way of describing a **User Interface** (**UI**) layout, Combine is a declarative way of describing the flow of changes.

The basic foundation of Combine is the concept of *Publisher* and *subscriber*. A *Publisher* emits events, pushed by something else that can be a part of the **Software Development Kit** (**SDK**) or another part of the app you are implementing. One or more *subscribers* can observe that publisher and react when a new event is published. You can consider this mechanism as a sort of *Observable/Observer* pattern on steroids.

The main difference with a plain *Observable/Observer* pattern is that in the case of the Observer, the interface of the object is custom and depends on the particular object, whereas in the Combine case, the interface is standard, and the only difference is on the type of events and errors a publisher emits.

Given that the interface is standard, it is possible to *combine* (hence the name) multiple *Publishers* into one, or apply modifiers such as filters, retry-ers, and so on.

I admit that this may sound confusing and complicated, but if you try a few recipes in this chapter, you should understand the philosophy of reactive programming and, in particular, the way it is implemented in Combine.

At the end of the chapter, you should know when and how to use Combine (or if it is overkill for your needs), and when you need to learn Combine in more depth.

In this chapter, we are going to learn how to use the SwiftUI binding mechanism and **Combine** to populate and change the views when data changes.

We are implementing the following recipes:

- Introducing Combine in a SwiftUI project
- Managing the memory in Combine to build a timer app
- Validating a form using Combine
- Fetching remote data using Combine and visualizing it in SwiftUI
- Debugging an app based on Combine
- Unit testing an app based on Combine

Technical requirements

The code in this chapter is based on Xcode 12 and iOS 14.

You can find the code in the book's GitHub repository under the following path: `https://github.com/PacktPublishing/SwiftUI-Cookbook/tree/master/Chapter09%20-%20Driving%20SwiftUI%20with%20Combine`.

Introducing Combine in a SwiftUI project

In this recipe, we are going to add publish support to `CoreLocation`. `CLLocationManager` will emit status and location updates, which will be observed by a SwiftUI View. It is a different implementation of the problem that is presented in *Chapter 8, Implementing a CoreLocation Wrapper as @ObservedObject*.

Usually, when a reactive framework is used, instead of the common **Model-View-Controller** (**MVC**) architecture, people tend to use **Model-View-ViewModel** (**MVVM**).

In this architecture, the view doesn't have any logic. That is instead encapsulated in the intermediate object, the *ViewModel*, which has the responsibility of being the model for the view and talking to the business logic model, services, and so on to update that model. For example, it will have a property for the current location that the view will use to present it to the user, and at the same time, the *ViewModel* will talk to the *LocationService* hiding that relationship to the View. In this way, the UI is completely decoupled from the business logic, and the *ViewModel* acts as an adapter between the two.

The *ViewModel* is bound to the view with a one-to-one relationship between the basic components and the properties of the *ViewModel*.

If this is the first time you have heard of **MVVM** and you are confused by this description, no worries: the recipe is really simple, and you'll understand it while implementing it. I promise!

Getting ready

Let's create a SwiftUI project called `CombineCoreLocationManagerApp`.

For privacy reasons, every app that needs to access the location of the user must ask permission before accessing it. To allow this, a message should be added for the *Privacy – Location When In Use Usage Description* key in `Info.plist`.

We can do this with the following steps:

1. Open `Info.plist` with Xcode, and right-click to select **Raw Keys & Values**:

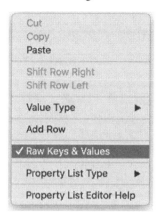

Figure 9.1 – Selecting Raw Keys & Values in Info.plist

2. Add the `NSLocationWhenInUseUsageDescription` key and a value with a message to the user:

Figure 9.2 – Message to the user to enable location services

How to do it...

As I mentioned in the introduction, we are going to implement this recipe following the *MVVM* architecture.

We are going to implement three components:

- The status and location view in `ComponentView`: the **View**

- A `LocationViewModel` class that interacts with the model and updates the view: the **ViewModel**

- A `LocationManager` service that listens to the location changes and sends events when they happen: the **Model**

Let's move to the code, starting from the Model:

1. As a first step, import `CoreLocation` and Combine, and implement a wrapper to `CLLocationManager`:

```
import CoreLocation
import Combine

class LocationManager: NSObject {
    enum LocationError: String, Error {
        case notDetermined
        case restricted
        case denied
        case unknown
    }

    private let locationManager = CLLocationManager()

    override init() {
        super.init()
        self.locationManager.delegate = self
        self.locationManager.desiredAccuracy =
            kCLLocationAccuracyBest
        self.locationManager.
            requestWhenInUseAuthorization()
    }

    func start() {
        locationManager.startUpdatingLocation()
    }
}
```

2. Until now, there is nothing particularly *reactive*. Let's then add two publishers: one for the status and the other for the location updates. As you can see, they are called **Subjects**: we'll explain the meaning in the *How it works...* section. For the time being, just consider them as *Publishers*. Their declaration shows the type of their events and the type of their error:

```
class LocationManager: NSObject, ObservableObject {
    //...
    let statusPublisher =
        PassthroughSubject<CLAuthorizationStatus,
            LocationError>()
    let locationPublisher =
        PassthroughSubject<CLLocation?, Never>()

    private let locationManager = CLLocationManager()
    //...
}
```

3. Let's now send the events to the publishers. This means that in the `delegate` functions, we push events in the publishers:

```
extension LocationManager: CLLocationManagerDelegate {
    func locationManager(_ manager: CLLocationManager,
                         didChangeAuthorization status:
CLAuthorizationStatus) {
        switch status {
        case .notDetermined:
            statusPublisher.send(completion:
                .failure(.notDetermined))
        case .restricted:
            statusPublisher.send(completion:
                .failure(.restricted))
        case .denied:
            statusPublisher.send(completion:
                .failure(.denied))
        case .authorizedAlways, .authorizedWhenInUse:
            statusPublisher.send(status)
        @unknown default:
```

```
                    statusPublisher.send(completion:
                        .failure(.unknown))
            }
        }

        func locationManager(_ manager: CLLocationManager,
                            didUpdateLocations
                            locations: [CLLocation]) {
            guard let location = locations.last else { return
    }
            locationPublisher.send(location)
        }
    }
```

4. Now, let's add the `LocationViewModel` class, starting from its public interface:

```
class LocationViewModel: ObservableObject {
    @Published
    private var status: CLAuthorizationStatus =
        .notDetermined
    @Published
    private var currentLocation: CLLocation?
    @Published
    var isStartable = true
    @Published
    var errorMessage = ""

    private let locationManager = LocationManager()
    func startUpdating() {
        locationManager.start()
        isStartable = false
    }
}
```

5. That interface is not complete, and we have to add a few more computed properties to fulfill all the UI needs:

```swift
class LocationViewModel: ObservableObject {
    //...
    var thereIsAnError: Bool {
        !errorMessage.isEmpty
    }
    var latitude: String {
        currentLocation.latitudeDescription
    }
    var longitude: String {
        currentLocation.longitudeDescription
    }
    var statusDescription: String {
        switch status {
        case .notDetermined:
            return "notDetermined"
        case .authorizedWhenInUse:
            return "authorizedWhenInUse"
        case .authorizedAlways:
            return "authorizedAlways"
        case .restricted:
            return "restricted"
        case .denied:
            return "denied"
        @unknown default:
            return "unknown"
        }
    }
    //...
}
```

6. In order to have a meaningful description for the optional `CLLocation`, we add a convenience extension to `Optional`:

```
extension Optional where Wrapped == CLLocation {
    var latitudeDescription: String {
        guard let self = self else {
            return "-"
        }
        return String(format: "%0.4f",
                      self.coordinate.latitude)
    }

    var longitudeDescription: String {
        guard let self = self else {
            return "-"
        }
        return String(format: "%0.4f",
                      self.coordinate.longitude)
    }
}
```

7. Finally, for this class, let's add the *subscribers* in the `init()` function:

```
class LocationViewModel: ObservableObject {
    //...
    private var cancellableSet: Set<AnyCancellable> = []

    init() {
        locationManager.statusPublisher
            .debounce(for: 0.5, scheduler: RunLoop.main)
            .removeDuplicates()
            .sink { completion in
                switch completion {
                case .finished:
                    break
                case .failure(let error):
                    self.errorMessage = error.rawValue
                }
```

```
        } receiveValue: { self.status = $0}
    .store(in: &cancellableSet)

    locationManager.locationPublisher
        .debounce(for: 0.5, scheduler: RunLoop.main)
        .removeDuplicates(by: lessThanOneMeter)
            .assign(to: \.currentLocation, on: self)
    .store(in: &cancellableSet)
    }
}
```

8. As you can see, we remove all the location event updates where the distance is less than a meter. The following function does the job of removing the locations closest to the previous location:

```
class LocationViewModel: ObservableObject {
    //...
    private func lessThanOneMeter(_ lhs: CLLocation?,
      _ rhs: CLLocation?) -> Bool {
        if lhs == nil && rhs == nil {
            return true
        }
        guard let lhr = lhs,
            let rhr = rhs else {
                return false
        }
        return lhr.distance(from: rhr) < 1
    }
}
```

9. After finishing the reactive *ViewModel*, let's complete the app with the *View*. First, let's add the component for the coordinate:

```
struct ContentView: View {
    @ObservedObject
    var locationViewModel = LocationViewModel()

    var body: some View {
```

```
VStack(spacing: 24) {
    VStack(spacing: 8) {
        if locationViewModel.thereIsAnError {
            Text("Location Service terminated with error:
                \(locationViewModel.errorMessage)")
        } else {
            Text("Status:
                \(locationViewModel.
                    statusDescription)")
            HStack {
                Text("Latitude:
                    \(locationViewModel.latitude)")
                Text("Longitude:
                    \(locationViewModel.longitude)")
            }
        }
    }.padding(.horizontal, 24)
    }
    }
}
```

10. Then, in the external VStack, let's add the code for the initial start button:

```
var body: some View {
    VStack(spacing: 24) {
        //...
        if locationViewModel.isStartable {
            Button{
                locationViewModel.startUpdating()
            } label: {
                Text("Start location updating")
                    .foregroundColor(.white)
                    .padding(.horizontal, 24)
                    .padding(.vertical, 16)
                    .background(Color.green)
                    .cornerRadius(5)
            }
```

```
            } else {
                EmptyView()
            }
        }
    }
```

Running the app, after allowing the location service, you can start the location services and see your current location:

Figure 9.3 – A reactive location manager

Congratulations—you implemented your first Combine app!

How it works...

A thing to notice is that the first time the app starts, you receive a popup asking for the location permission, and when you accept it, the app is stuck in error. The reason is that for Combine, an error situation is a completion situation.

A *Publisher* sends an event until it completes, either successfully or with an error. After it completes, the stream is closed, and if you want to send more events, you need to create a new stream and the client must subscribe to the new one.

Back to our app, what happens is that at the beginning, the location status is .notDetermined and the stream is closed. A quick solution could be to consider this case as a *non-error* case and proceed normally.

Another interesting thing is that we set two @Published variables as private. This must seem counterintuitive because usually, the @Published variables are the variables that the View uses to render something, but in this case the *ViewModel* exposes other variables, latitude, longitude, and statusDescription, which derive from the @Published variables, and the View uses them to render their components.

It should be clear now that the goal of the @Published variables is to trigger a re-render, even though the View won't directly use the variables that are decorated with @Published.

Let's now have a quick look at the two most important parts of the recipe: *Publishers* and *Subscriptions*.

Publishers in Combine

In our example, the *Publishers* are two *Subjects*. In the Combine world, a Publisher can be considered as a function, with one *Input* and one *Output*.

The protocol that manages *Output*, to which a client can subscribe, is the Publisher, whereas the protocol that manages the *Input* is the *Subject*. *Subject* basically provides a send() function to emit events.

There are two already implemented *Subjects*: CurrentValueSubject and PassthroughSubject.

The former has an initial value and maintains the changed value even if it doesn't have any subscriber. The latter doesn't have an initial value and drops changes if nobody is observing it.

To send an event, the client has to call the send() function, as we do for changes of status and location:

```
statusPublisher.send(status)
//...
locationPublisher.send(location)
```

As already mentioned, the error case is a completion case and the
`send(cancellation:)` has either `.finished` or `.failure` as its output:

```
statusPublisher.send(completion: .failure(.restricted))
//...
statusPublisher.send(completion: .failure(.denied))
//...
statusPublisher.send(completion: .failure(.unknown))
```

In a nutshell, we just saw the publishing capabilities of Combine.

Subscribing in Combine

The subscription part of Combine is probably more complex and sophisticated. A full
discussion of subscription is beyond the scope of this book, but let's at least see what we
have done in our recipe.

The whole subscription part is in the `init()` function of the `LocationViewModel`
class where we subscribe to our two subscriptions.

The first thing to notice is that we connect different functions together to create a
combination of effects, in the same way that we are modifying the views in SwiftUI.

Let's dissect the `locationPublisher` subscription:

```
locationManager
    .locationPublisher
    .debounce(for: 0.5, scheduler: RunLoop.main)
    .removeDuplicates(by: lessThanOneMeter)
    .assign(to: \.currentLocation, on: self)
    .store(in: &cancellableSet)
```

First, we subscribe with the `debounce()` function, which basically discards all the events
that happen too quickly and allows the changes to be passed every 0.5 seconds; it also
moves the computation in the `mainThread` that the event can be sent by a background
thread, but the UI must always be updated in the `mainThread`.

The `removeDuplicates()` function receives a subscription and modifies it, removing
all the duplicates according to the predicate we pass, which, in our case, considers
duplicating all the locations with a distance less than one meter.

The `assign()` function is the final modifier that puts the event in a property of an object—
in this case, the `currentLocation` property in the `LocationViewModel` class.

The last step, `.store(in:)`, puts the subscription in a set that has the same life cycle as the container, and it will be *dealloc-ed* when the container is *dealloc-ed* (we'll see more on Combine memory management in the *Managing the memory in Combine to build a timer app* recipe):

```
locationManager.statusPublisher
    .debounce(for: 0.5, scheduler: RunLoop.main)
    .removeDuplicates()
    .sink { completion in
        switch completion {
        case .finished:
            break
        case .failure(let error):
            self.errorMessage = error.rawValue
        }
    } receiveValue: { self.status = $0}
    )
    .store(in: &cancellableSet)
```

We already know that the `debounce()` function and, here, `removeDuplicates()` don't have a parameter because the event type is an equatable enum.

The `sink()` function is a final and extended step similar to the `assign()` function we saw previously; it receives the values but also the completion, so it can apply different logic depending on the received value.

This concludes our Combine 101. If you are feeling confused, don't worry: reactive programming is a big change of mindset, but after trying it in a few sample apps, you should start to see that using it in a proper way, programming a UI is even simpler than doing it in the usual imperative way.

See also

You can find more information regarding ReactiveX at this **Uniform Resource Locator (URL)**: `http://reactivex.io/`.

To have a visual understanding of the Rx operators, and similarly for the Combine operators, the *RxMarbles* website (`https://rxmarbles.com/`) has a nice collection of pictures explaining them.

Managing the memory in Combine to build a timer app

When a client subscribes to a publisher, the result should be held somewhere. Usually, it is stored in a `Set` of `AnyCancellable`. If the client subscribes to multiple publishers, the code is a bit repetitive: it would be better to have a way to wrap all subscriptions and put all the results in the same set.

In this recipe, we'll use a new feature of Swift 5.1, the function builders, to create an extension to the `Set` of `AnyCancellable`, wrap all the subscriptions, and store them in the set.

In this recipe, we are going to create a **StopWatch** app using three publishers: one for the deciseconds, one for the seconds, and one for the minutes. We will also learn how to use timers in Combine.

Getting ready

Let's create a SwiftUI app called `StopWatchApp`.

How to do it...

The goal of the app is to have a stopwatch that can be started and stopped using a button. We are going to implement the counter using three timed publishers that emit events at different intervals: one every decisecond, one every second, and one every minute.

We are going to wrap them in a single closure to store them in the usual `Set` of `AnyCancellable`:

1. We start by importing Combine and creating our reactive timer:

```
import Combine


class StopWatchTimer: ObservableObject {
    @Published
    var deciseconds: Int = 0
    @Published
    var seconds: Int = 0
    @Published
    var minutes: Int = 0
    @Published
    var started = false
```

```
    private var cancellableSet: Set<AnyCancellable> = []

    func start() {

    }

    func stop() {

    }
}
```

2. Before implementing the `start()` function, let's quickly do the `stop()` function:

```
func stop() {
    cancellableSet = []
    started = false
}
```

3. Let's move to the `start()` function, where we reset the counters and create the publishers and subscribe to them:

```
func start() {
    deciseconds = 0
    seconds = 0
    minutes = 0

    cancellableSet.store {
        Timer.publish(every: 0.1, on: RunLoop.main,
                      in: .default)
            .autoconnect()
            .sink { _ in
                self.deciseconds = (self.deciseconds +
                    1)%10
            }
        Timer.publish(every: 1.0, on: RunLoop.main,
                      in: .default)
            .autoconnect()
            .sink { _ in
                self.seconds = (self.seconds + 1)%60
```

```
            }
            Timer.publish(every: 60.0, on: RunLoop.main,
                          in: .default)
                .autoconnect()
                .sink { _ in
                    self.minutes = (self.minutes + 1)%60
                }
        }
        started = true
    }
}
```

4. The code is terse and good-looking, but it doesn't compile because the .store{} function is undefined. Let's define that:

```
typealias CancellableSet = Set<AnyCancellable>
extension CancellableSet {
    mutating func store(@CancellableBuilder _
        cancellables: () -> [AnyCancellable]) {
        formUnion(cancellables())
    }

    @_functionBuilder
    struct CancellableBuilder {
        static func buildBlock(_ cancellables:
            AnyCancellable...) -> [AnyCancellable] {
            return cancellables
        }
    }
}
```

5. Now that we are finished with the timer, let's move to the View, starting with the digits:

```
struct ContentView: View {
    @ObservedObject
    private var timer = StopWatchTimer()

    var body: some View {
        VStack(spacing: 12) {
```

```
HStack(spacing: 0) {
    Text("\(timer.minutes.formatted)")
        .font(.system(size: 80))
        .frame(width: 100)
    Text(":")
        .font(.system(size: 80))
    Text("\(timer.seconds.formatted)")
        .font(.system(size: 80))
        .frame(width: 100)
    Text(":")
        .font(.system(size: 80))
    Text("\(timer.deciseconds.formatted)")
        .font(.system(size: 80))
        .frame(width: 100)
}
            }
        }
    }
```

6. Then, add a button to start/stop the timer:

```
var body: some View {
    VStack(spacing: 12) {
        //...
        Button{
            if timer.started {
                timer.stop()
            } else {
                timer.start()
            }
        } label: {
            Text(timer.started ? "Stop" : "Start")
                .foregroundColor(.white)
                .padding(.horizontal, 24)
                .padding(.vertical, 16)
                .frame(width: 100)
                .background(timer.started ?
```

```
                                    Color.red : Color.green)
                    .cornerRadius(5)
            }
        }
    }
```

7. The only bit missing is an extension to `Int` to format it properly:

```
extension Int {
    var formatted: String {
        String(format: "%02d", self)
    }
}
```

We can now run the app and see that it measures the time in a nice and precise way:

Figure 9.4 – A reactive StopWatch application in action

How it works...

In this recipe, we introduced a couple of new things: a timer publisher and a way to collect all the cancellable chain of subscriptions in one go. Let's remember that a chain of subscriptions means subscribers that connect to a publisher, possibly with a series of modifiers in between. A chain of subscriptions returns a token, of type `AnyCancellable`, which can be used to cancel that chain. If that cancellable token is collected in a `Set`, when the `Set` is cleared, all the tokens are cancelled.

Combine adds a publisher function to the `Timer` foundation class, where you can set the interval and the thread where it will emit the events. The `.autoconnect()` modifier will basically make the publisher start immediately.

Regarding the `.store {}` function extension, it uses the `CancellableBuild` function builder, which in practice produces a closure where all the values created inside are returned as elements of an array. So, for example, we may have to define a builder from `Int`, such as the following:

```
@_functionBuilder
struct IntBuilder {
    static func buildBlock(_ values: Int...) -> [Int] {
        values.map { 2*$0 }
    }
}
```

We would then give it a few functions returning an `Int`:

```
func functionReturningOne() -> Int { 1 }
func functionReturningTwo() -> Int { 2 }
func functionReturningThree() -> Int { 3 }
```

We can define a function that prints the double of the `Int` that is passed as a parameter:

```
func printDoubleInt(@IntBuilder builder: () -> [Int]) {
    print(builder())
}
```

We run the app with the following code:

```
printDoubleInt{
    functionReturningOne()
    functionReturningTwo()
    functionReturningThree()
    4
    5
}
```

We should see the following result:

```
[2, 4, 6, 8, 10]
```

Given that example, it is pretty clear now that in our extension, the builder takes the array of the `AnyCancellable` and adds the content to the original set.

If everything still seems too complicated, don't worry too much since the feature isn't a part of the standard yet, as you can deduct from the underscore in front of the `@_functionBuilder` keyword. But if, on the other hand, you understood that feature, you should have a better understanding of SwiftUI.

Validating a form using Combine

Sometimes, the reactive way of thinking feels academic and not connected to the usual problems a developer has to solve. In reality, most of the programs we usually write would benefit from using reactive programming, but some problems fit better than others.

Let's consider as an example a part of an app where the user has to fill in a form. The form has several fields, each one with a different way of being validated; some can be validated on their own while others have validation depending on different fields, and all together concur to validate the whole form.

In the imperative way, this turns out to usually create a mess of spaghetti code, but switching to the reactive declarative way, the code becomes really natural.

In this recipe, we'll implement a simple signup page with a username text field and two password fields, one for the password and the other for password confirmation.

The username has a minimum number of characters, and the password must be at least eight characters long, comprising mixed numbers and letters, with at least one uppercase letter and a special character such as *!*, *#*, *$*, and so on. Also, the password and the confirmation password must match. When all the fields are valid, the form is valid, and we can proceed to the next page.

Each field will be a publisher, and the validations are subscribers of those publishers.

At the end of the recipe, you'll be able to model each form validation using a reactive architecture and move a step further into understanding this way of building programs.

Getting ready

Let's create a SwiftUI app with Xcode called `FormValidationApp`, and we are ready to go.

How to do it...

To explore the validation pattern for a form, we are going to implement a simple signup page.

As usual, when dealing with the UI and a reactive framework, we will separate the View from the business logic using *MVVM*.

In our case, the business logic is the validation logic, and it will be encapsulated in a class called `SignupViewModel`:

1. Let's start defining the public interface of `SignupViewModel`, indicating the `@Published` properties for the input and for the output:

```
import Combine


class SignupViewModel: ObservableObject {
    // Input
    @Published
    var username = ""
    @Published
    var password = ""
    @Published
    var confirmPassword = ""


    // Input
    @Published
    var isValid = false
    @Published
    var usernameMessage = " "
    @Published
    var passwordMessage = " "


    private var cancellableSet: Set<AnyCancellable> = []
}
```

2. The whole validation logic will be in the `init()` function, separated into three streams: one for the *username*, one for the *password*, and one for the *form*.

    Let's start adding the one for the *username*:

```
init() {

    usernameValidPublisher

        .receive(on: RunLoop.main)

        .map { $0 ? " "

            : "Username must be at least 6 characters
                long" }

        .assign(to: \.usernameMessage, on: self)

        .store(in: &cancellableSet)


}
```

3. In a similar way, let's add the validation for the password, noting that the *Publisher* emits an `enum` and not a simple `Bool`:

```
init() {

    //...

    passwordValidPublisher

        .receive(on: RunLoop.main)

        .map { passwordCheck in

            switch passwordCheck {

            case .invalidLength:

                return "Password must be at least 8
                    characters long"

            case .noMatch:

                return "Passwords don't match"

            case .weakPassword:

                return "Password is too weak"

            default:

                return " "

            }

        }

        .assign(to: \.passwordMessage, on: self)

        .store(in: &cancellableSet)

}
```

4. Finally, let's add the *Publisher* form validation subscription:

```
init() {
    // ...
    formValidPublisher
        .receive(on: RunLoop.main)
        .assign(to: \.isValid, on: self)
        .store(in: &cancellableSet)
}
```

5. For convenience, we add the *Publishers* as computed properties in a private extension of `SignupViewModel`. The first one is the publisher for the username, whose only logic is checking if the length of the `username` is correct:

```
private extension SignupViewModel {
    var usernameValidPublisher: AnyPublisher<Bool, Never>
    {
        $username
            .debounce(for: 0.5, scheduler: RunLoop.main)
            .removeDuplicates()
            .map { $0.count >= 5 }
            .eraseToAnyPublisher()
    }
}
```

6. The password validation is a bit more complex since it needs to check three properties: a valid length, the strength of the password, and if the password and the confirmed password match.

Let's start with the password length validation:

```
private extension SignupViewModel {
    //...
    var validPasswordLengthPublisher: AnyPublisher<Bool,
        Never> {
        $password
            .debounce(for: 0.5, scheduler: RunLoop.main)
            .removeDuplicates()
            .map { $0.count >= 8 }
```

```
                        .eraseToAnyPublisher()
        }
    }
```

7. Then, let's check for the strength:

```
private extension SignupViewModel {
    //...
    var strongPasswordPublisher: AnyPublisher<Bool,
        Never> {
        $password
            .debounce(for: 0.2, scheduler: RunLoop.main)
            .removeDuplicates()
            .map(\.isStrong)
            .eraseToAnyPublisher()
    }
}
```

8. You should notice that here, we are checking if a string is strong using an isStrong function that doesn't exist yet. Let's add it as an extension of String. It basically checks if the string contains letters, digits, uppercase letters, and special characters such as £, $, !, and so on:

```
extension String {
    var isStrong: Bool {
        containsACharacter(from: .lowercaseLetters) &&
        containsACharacter(from: .uppercaseLetters) &&
        containsACharacter(from: .decimalDigits) &&
        containsACharacter(from:
            CharacterSet.alphanumerics.inverted)
    }

    private func containsACharacter(from
                            set: CharacterSet) -> Bool {
        rangeOfCharacter(from: set) != nil
    }
}
```

9. While we are here, let's also add the enum returned by the password validations:

```
enum PasswordCheck {
    case valid
    case invalidLength
    case noMatch
    case weakPassword
}
```

10. Let's go back to the password validation stream, adding the one that checks whether the password and confirmed passwords match:

```
private extension SignupViewModel {
    //...
    var matchingPasswordsPublisher: AnyPublisher<Bool,
      Never> {
        Publishers.CombineLatest($password,
          $confirmPassword)
            .debounce(for: 0.2, scheduler: RunLoop.main)
            .map { password, confirmedPassword in
                return password == confirmedPassword
            }
            .eraseToAnyPublisher()
    }
}
```

11. The final password validation stream combines all the previous together:

```
private extension SignupViewModel {
    //...
    var passwordValidPublisher:
      AnyPublisher<PasswordCheck, Never> {
        Publishers.
          CombineLatest3(validPasswordLengthPublisher,
            strongPasswordPublisher,
              matchingPasswordsPublisher)
            .map { validLength, strong, matching in
                if (!validLength) {
                    return .invalidLength
```

```
                }
        if (!strong) {
            return .weakPassword
        }
        if (!matching) {
            return .noMatch
        }
        return .valid
    }
    .eraseToAnyPublisher()
  }
}
```

12. The last validator is the *form* validator that combines the *username* and *password* validators together:

```
private extension SignupViewModel {
    //...
    var formValidPublisher: AnyPublisher<Bool, Never> {
        Publishers.CombineLatest(usernameValidPublisher,
        passwordValidPublisher)
            .map { usernameIsValid, passwordIsValid in
                return usernameIsValid &&
                    (passwordIsValid == .valid)
            }
        .eraseToAnyPublisher()
    }
}
```

13. Before starting the ContentView, we add a bunch of convenience modifiers for TextField and SecureField:

```
struct CustomStyle: ViewModifier {
    func body(content: Content) -> some View {
        content
            .frame(height: 40)
            .background(Color.white)
```

```
                    .cornerRadius(5)
        }
}
extension TextField {
    func custom() -> some View {
        modifier(CustomStyle())
            .autocapitalization(.none)
    }
}
extension SecureField {
    func custom() -> some View {
        modifier(CustomStyle())
    }
}
```

14. The `ContentView` is a simple vertical stack of `TextFields` and `Texts` that represents the fields to add and the possible error messages. We modify the `ContentView` to have a yellow background and a `VStack` with the fields:

```
struct ContentView: View {
    @ObservedObject
    private var signupViewModel = SignupViewModel()

    var body: some View {
        ZStack {
            Color.yellow.opacity(0.2)
            VStack(spacing: 24) {
                //...
            }
            .padding(.horizontal, 24)
        }
        .edgesIgnoringSafeArea(.all)
    }
}
```

15. Then, we add the field for the username:

```
VStack(spacing: 24) {
    VStack(alignment: .leading) {
        Text(signupViewModel.usernameMessage)
                        .foregroundColor(.red)
        TextField("Username",
                    text: $signupViewModel.username)
            .custom()
    }
}
```

16. Let's move now to the password, where we add two `textfield` parameters, one for the password and another to confirm it, so that the user is sure to have inserted it without misspellings:

```
VStack(spacing: 24) {
    //...
    VStack(alignment: .leading) {
        Text(signupViewModel.passwordMessage)
                            .foregroundColor(.red)
        SecureField("Password",
            text: $signupViewModel.password)
            .custom()
        SecureField("Repeat Password",
            text: $signupViewModel.confirmPassword)
            .custom()
    }
}
```

17. Finally, let's add the **Register** button, which will be enabled only when the form is fully valid:

```
VStack(spacing: 24) {
    //...
    Button {
```

```
            print ("Succesfully registered!")
        } label: {
            Text ("Register")
                .foregroundColor (.white)
                .frame (width: 100, height: 44)
                .background (signupViewModel.isValid ?
                            Color.green : Color.red)
            .cornerRadius (10)
        }.disabled (!signupViewModel.isValid)
}
```

I admit that this looks like a long recipe, but you can observe how nicely the logic flows. Now, it's time to run our app:

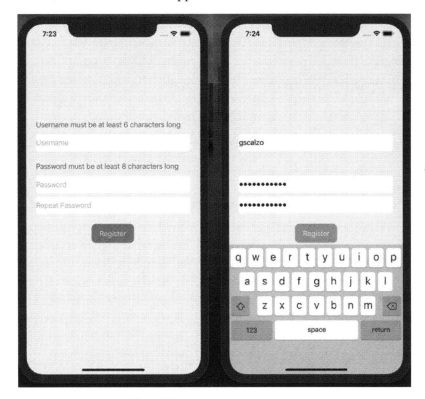

Figure 9.5 – A reactive signup page

How it works...

In this kind of problem, Combine really shines: splitting the flow of the logic in simple substeps and then combining them together.

A few things to notice here would be:

- At the end of each publisher, there is the `eraseToAnyPublisher()` modifier. The reason is that the composition of the modifiers on the publishers creates some complex nested types, where in the end the subscriber needs only an object of type `Publisher`. The function does some `eraseToAnyPublisher()` magic to flatten these types and just return a generic `Publisher`.

- The `.debounce()` function only sends events if they happen in the interval passed as parameters; that way, the subscriber is not bombarded by events. In this case, if the user is a fast typist, we are evaluating password or username only after a few characters have been inserted.

- The `.map(\.isStrong)` function is a nice shortcut added in Swift 5.2 and it is equivalent to this:

```
.map { password in
    return password.isStrong
}
```

- Finally, `Publishers.CombineLatest` and `Publishers.CombineLatest3` create a new publisher that emits a single tuple, or triple, with the latest events of each publisher passed as parameters.

There's more...

Now that have you seen how easy and obvious it is to create validators, why not improve our simple signup page a little?

For example, you may have noticed that at the beginning, both the error messages are present when you should probably be concentrating on adding a valid username.

The improvement I suggest you do is to change the validators in a manner that the password is validated only after the username is correct.

Do you think you'll be able to do it?

Fetching remote data using Combine and visualizing it in SwiftUI

A common characteristic most mobile apps have is that they fetch data from a remote web service.

Given the asynchronous nature of the problem, it is often problematic when this is implemented in the normal imperative world.

However, it suits the reactive world nicely, as we'll see in this recipe.

We are going to implement a simple weather app, fetching the current weather and a 5-day forecast from **OpenWeather**, a famous service that also has a free tier.

After fetching the forecast, we present the result in a list view, with the current weather fixed on the top.

Getting ready

We start by creating a SwiftUI app called `WeatherApp`.

To use the service, we must create an account on **OpenWeather**.

Go to the **OpenWeather** signup page (`https://home.openweathermap.org/users/sign_up`) and fill it with your data:

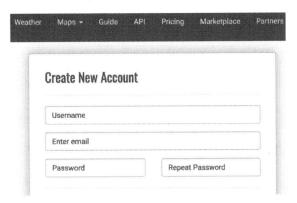

Figure 9.6 – OpenWeather signup page

After confirming the login, let's create a new **application programming interface (API)** key from the **API keys** page (`https://home.openweathermap.org/api_keys`):

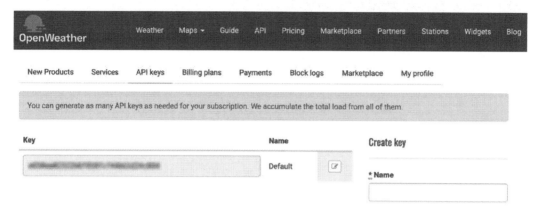

Figure 9.7 – OpenWeather API keys

We'll use the created key when calling the endpoints to fetch the weather and the forecast.

How to do it...

We are going to separate the implementation in two parts: web service and UI.

Because **OpenWeather** is exposing two different endpoints for the current weather and the forecast, the web service will use two streams.

The View will observe the two variables—current weather and forecast—and it will update accordingly:

1. Before starting to implement the objects, let's decide the model we want to have and how to create it from the **JavaScript Object Notation (JSON)** we get from the service. The model we need for the weather is really simple:

```
struct Weather: Decodable, Identifiable {
    var id: TimeInterval { time.timeIntervalSince1970 }
    let time: Date
    let summary: String
    let icon: String
    let temperature: Double
}
```

2. An example returned from the service is shown as follows:

```json
{
    // ...
    "weather": [
        {
            "id": 804,
            "main": "Clouds",
            "description": "overcast clouds",
            "icon": "04d"
        }
    ],
    "main": {
        "temp": 8.04,
        "feels_like": 5.33,
        "temp_min": 6.67,
        "temp_max": 9,
        "pressure": 1017,
        "humidity": 66
    },
    "dt": 1585900538,
    // ...
}
```

3. As you can see from the highlighted lines, it has all the needed values, but we have to extract them in the `init()` function.

    Let's then define the keys and the `init()` function from the `decoder` so that it can be decoded from JSON:

```swift
struct Weather: Decodable, Identifiable {
    //...
    enum CodingKeys: String, CodingKey {
        case time = "dt"
        case weather = "weather"
        case summary = "description"
        case main = "main"
        case icon = "icon"
        case temperature = "temp"
```

```
        }
        init(from decoder: Decoder) throws {
            let container = try decoder
                .container(keyedBy: CodingKeys.self)
            time = try container.decode(Date.self, forKey: .time)
            var weatherContainer = try container
                .nestedUnkeyedContainer(forKey: .weather)
            let weather = try weatherContainer
                .nestedContainer(keyedBy: CodingKeys.self)
            summary = try weather.decode(String.self,
                                            forKey: .summary)
            icon = try weather.decode(String.self, forKey:
                .icon)
            let main = try container
                .nestedContainer(keyedBy: CodingKeys.self,
                                        forKey: .main)
            temperature = try main.decode(Double.self,
                forKey: .temperature)
        }
    }
```

4. The forecast struct is a simple list of the `Weather` records:

```
struct ForecastWeather: Decodable {
    let list: [Weather]
}
```

5. Let's move now to the `WeatherService` class, the `ObservableObject` whose goal it is to connect to the service and fetch the data. We are exposing three variables: the current weather, the forecast, and a message if there is an error. Replace the `<INSERT YOUR KEY>` string (highlighted in the code) with the API key we created in the *Getting ready* section. The API key should be added in double quotes.:

```
class WeatherService: ObservableObject {
    @Published
    var errorMessage: String = ""
    @Published
    var current: Weather?
```

```
    @Published
    var forecast: [Weather] = []


    private let apiKey = <INSERT YOUR KEY>
    private var cancellableSet: Set<AnyCancellable> = []
}
```

6. Given that we have two endpoints, we are going to use them in a `load()` function, starting from the current weather:

```
func load(latitude: Float, longitude: Float) {
    let decoder = JSONDecoder()
    decoder.dateDecodingStrategy = .secondsSince1970

    let currentURL = URL(string:
        "https://api.openweathermap.org/data/2.5/
            weather?lat=\(latitude)&lon=\(longitude)&appid=\
            (apiKey)&units=metric")!

    URLSession.shared
        .dataTaskPublisher(for: URLRequest(url:
            currentURL))
        .map(\.data)
        .decode(type: Weather.self, decoder: decoder)
        .receive(on: RunLoop.main)
        .sink { completion in
            switch completion {
            case .finished:
                break
            case .failure(let error):
                self.errorMessage = error.
                    localizedDescription
            }
        } receiveValue: {
            self.current = $0
        }
        .store(in: &cancellableSet)
}
```

7. The call for the forecast is similar:

```
func load(latitude: Float, longitude: Float) {
    let decoder = JSONDecoder()
    decoder.dateDecodingStrategy = .secondsSince1970
    //...
    let forecastURL = URL(string:
    "https://api.openweathermap.org/data/2.5/
        forecast?lat=\(latitude)&lon=\(longitude)&appid=\
        (apiKey)&units=metric")!
    URLSession.shared
        .dataTaskPublisher(for: URLRequest(url:
            forecastURL))
        .map(\.data)
        .decode(type: ForecastWeather.self, decoder:
            decoder)
        .receive(on: RunLoop.main)
        .sink { completion in
            switch completion {
            case .finished:
                break
            case .failure(let error):
                self.message = error.localizedDescription
            }
        } receiveValue: {
            self.forecast = $0.list
        }
        .store(in: &cancellableSet)
}
```

8. Before implementing the views, let's add a few extensions to format some values of the weather:

```
extension Double {
    var formatted: String {
        String(format: "%.0f", self)
    }
}
```

```
extension Date {
    var formatted: String {
        let formatter = DateFormatter()
        formatter.dateStyle = .long
        formatter.timeStyle = .medium

        return formatter.string(from: self)
    }
}
```

9. If you look at **OpenWeather** in the **Weather icons** page (`https://openweathermap.org/weather-conditions`), you can find the relation between the icon code and a proper image. Using that page, let's create a map to translate from the code to an equivalent **SF Symbols** icon, starting from the icon to use during the day:

```
extension String {
    var weatherIcon: String {
        switch self {
        case "01d":
            return "sun.max"
        case "02d":
            return "cloud.sun"
        case "03d":
            return "cloud"
        case "04d":
            return "cloud.fill"
        case "09d":
            return "cloud.rain"
        case "10d":
            return "cloud.sun.rain"
        case "11d":
            return "cloud.bolt"
        case "13d":
            return "cloud.snow"
        case "50d":
```

```
            return "cloud.fog"
        }
    }
}
```

10. Now, let's add the icons for the forecast during the night:

```
extension String {
    var weatherIcon: String {
        //…
        case "01n":
            return "moon"
        case "02n":
            return "cloud.moon"
        case "03n":
            return "cloud"
        case "04n":
            return "cloud.fill"
        case "09n":
            return "cloud.rain"
        case "10n":
            return "cloud.moon.rain"
        case "11n":
            return "cloud.bolt"
        case "13n":
            return "cloud.snow"
        case "50n":
            return "cloud.fog"
        default:
            return "icloud.slash"
        }
    }
}
```

11. Let's move our attention to the `ContentView`, where we must present different components, depending on the service state. We are always presenting the error message on top, which is empty by default, and then either the **Start** button or the weather information:

```
struct ContentView: View {
    @ObservedObject
    var weatherService = WeatherService()
    var body: some View {
        VStack {
            Text(weatherService.errorMessage)
                .font(.largeTitle)
            //... Button or Weather Information
        }
    }
}
```

12. Finally, we add the button and the weather information:

```
if weatherService.current != nil {
    VStack {
        CurrentWeather(current: weatherService.current!)
        List {
            ForEach(weatherService.forecast) {
                WeatherRow(weather: $0)
            }
        }
    }
} else {
    Button {
        weatherService.load(latitude: 51.5074,
                            longitude: 0.1278)
    } label: {
        Text("Refresh Weather")
            .foregroundColor(.white)
            .padding(.horizontal, 24)
            .padding(.vertical, 16)
            .background(Color.green)
```

```
        .cornerRadius(5)
    }
}
```

It has been a long recipe, but now, you finally have your reward! Launching the app, you can see the precise forecast for 5 days, with a granularity of 3 hours:

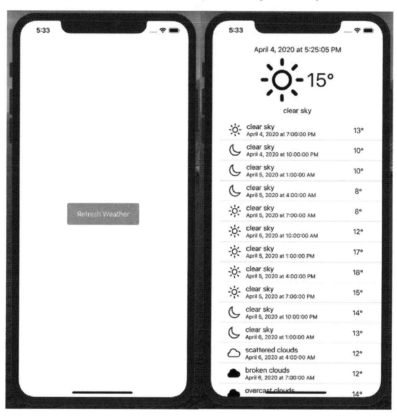

Figure 9.8 – WeatherApp with a 5-day forecast

How it works...

After a long session of coding, let's see the fetching part in detail:

```
URLSession.shared
    .dataTaskPublisher(for: URLRequest(url: currentURL))
    .map(\.data)
    .decode(type: Weather.self, decoder: decoder)
    .receive(on: RunLoop.main)
```

```
    .sink { completion in
        switch completion {
        case .finished:
            break
        case .failure(let error):
            self.errorMessage = error.localizedDescription
        }
    } receiveValue: {
        self.current = $0
    }
    .store(in: &cancellableSet)
```

First of all, we can notice that Combine adds a reactive function to the normal URLSession, sparing us from having to implement an adapter.

.dataTaskPublisher() returns a publisher to which we extract the .data() field with .map(\.data).

Here, we can see the power of Swift 5.2, where we can pass the keypath to extract instead of doing a longer .map { $0.data }; it's not just a matter of sparing a bunch of keystrokes, but the former expresses the intent of the code better.

The data blob is then processed by .decode(type: Weather.self, decoder: decoder), which decodes the Weather object.

After that step, the publisher transmits a Weather object and the .receive(on: RunLoop.main) moves the computation in the MainThread, ready to be used for UI changes.

The final computational step, the .sink() function, extracts the error or the values and puts them in the correct @Published variable.

Finally, the publisher is put in the cancellable set to be removed when the WeatherService is disposed.

As you can see, all the steps of the computation are feeling natural and are obvious.

Just for an exercise, try to implement the same logic using the conventional declarative way without Combine, and try to understand the differences.

Unrelated to Combine and SwiftUI is the decodable process, where the model doesn't match the structure of JSON.

To solve this, we use `.nestedContainer`, which returns a keyed sub-container like a dictionary, and `.nestedUnkeyedContainer`, which returns a sub-container like an array.

The JSON we received was similar to the following:

```
{
  "weather": [
    {
      "description": "overcast clouds",
    }
  ],
  "main": {
    "temp": 8.04,
  },
  "dt": 1585900538,
}
```

Using the following code, we are then able to reach the two sub-containers: `weather` and `main`, from which we can extract the needed values:

```
var weatherContainer = try container
    .nestedUnkeyedContainer(forKey: .weather)
let weather = try weatherContainer
    .nestedContainer(keyedBy: CodingKeys.self)
summary = try weather.decode(String.self, forKey: .summary)
icon = try weather.decode(String.self, forKey: .icon)

let main = try container
    .nestedContainer(keyedBy: CodingKeys.self, forKey: .main)
temperature = try main.decode(Double.self, forKey:
    .temperature)
```

As I said, this is unrelated to Combine, but it is a good refresher on how Decodable works, hence I thought it was worth mentioning it.

There's more...

I believe that what you learned in this recipe will be one of the Combine concepts you'll use more in your apps, so it's worth trying to understand it.

As already mentioned in the previous section, a good exercise would be to implement it in the normal Foundation way using `delegate` functions and so on, to see the differences of this approach.

Given that we have two endpoints, one for the current weather and the other for the forecast, we implemented two asynchronous and separated streams: what about combining them in a third stream that finishes when both of them finish and creates a single object with both the variables?

Finally, we hardcoded the coordinates, but what about using the `CoreLocationManager` implemented in the *Introducing Combine in a SwiftUI project* recipe to get the proper current location of the user?

Debugging an app based on Combine

It's a common idea that debugging reactive code is more difficult than debugging imperative code. Unfortunately, this is not completely wrong: in part, because of the nature of the code; in part, because the development tools are not sophisticated enough to follow this new paradigm.

Combine, however, implements a few convenient ways to help us better understand what happens in our streams.

In this recipe, we'll learn three techniques to debug a Combine stream.

I admit that all three are a bit basic; however, they are a starting point and should be enough to start to understand how to deal with errors in the streams.

Getting ready

Let's create a SwiftUI app called `DebuggingCombineApp` in Xcode.

How to do it...

Given the limited possibilities of debugging Combine, we are not implementing a sophisticated app, but a trivial three-button app that calls the three possible ways of debugging Combine:

- Handling events
- Printing events
- Conditional breakpoint

The Combine publishers we are going to test are plain transmitters that emit a string or an integer:

1. Let's start implementing the simple object with three functions:

```
import Combine
class ReactiveObject {
    private var cancellableSet: Set<AnyCancellable> = []
    func handleEvents() {

    }
    func printDebug() {

    }
    func breakPoint() {

    }
}
```

2. The View just contains three buttons, one for each function, but before adding them, let's prepare the View:

```
struct ContentView: View {
    var reactiveObject = ReactiveObject()
    var body: some View {
        VStack(spacing: 24) {

        }
    }
}
```

3. Let's now add the buttons in the VStack:

```
VStack(spacing: 24) {
    Button {
        reactiveObject.handleEvents()
    } label: {
        Text("HandleEvents")
            .foregroundColor(.white)
            .frame(width: 200, height: 50)
            .background(Color.green)
    }
    Button {
```

```
            reactiveObject.printDebug()
    } label: {
        Text("Print")
            .foregroundColor(.white)
            .frame(width: 200, height: 50)
            .background(Color.orange)
    }

    Button {
        reactiveObject.breakPoint()
    } label: {
        Text("Breakpoint")
            .foregroundColor(.white)
            .frame(width: 200, height: 50)
            .background(Color.red)
    }
}
```

4. Move back the `ReactiveObject` class. We are going to implement the first function, `handleEvents()`:

```
func handleEvents() {
    let subject = PassthroughSubject<String, Never>()
    subject
        .handleEvents(receiveSubscription: {
            print("Receive subscription: \($0)")
        }, receiveOutput: {
            print("Received output: \($0)")
        }, receiveCompletion: {
            print("Receive completion: \($0)")
        }, receiveCancel: {
            print("Receive cancel")
        }, receiveRequest: {
            print("Receive request: \($0)")
        })
        .sink { _ in }
```

```
        .store(in: &cancellableSet)


    subject.send("New Message!")
}
```

5. The `printDebug()` function is even simpler:

```
func printDebug() {
    let subject = PassthroughSubject<String, Never>()
    subject
        .print("Print").sink { _ in }
    .store(in: &cancellableSet)


    subject.send("New Message!")
}
```

6. The final function, `breakpoint()`, adds a conditional breakpoint when the counter is at 7:

```
func breakPoint() {
    (1..<10).publisher
        .breakpoint(receiveOutput: {
            $0 == 7
        }) { $0 == .finished
        }
    .sink { _ in }
    .store(in: &cancellableSet)
}
```

7. You can run the app and see the effects of the different strategies:

Figure 9.9 – Debugging Combine handling and printing events

In the following screenshot, you can see what happens when the breakpoint is enabled:

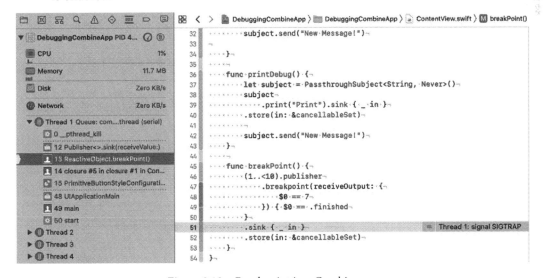

Figure 9.10 – Breakpoint in a Combine app

How it works...

Even if it is quite basic, the debug functionalities that Combine brings to us are quite useful.

The `.handleEvents()` function has a few closures whereby we can do more sophisticated activities instead of simple printing, as in our example.

The `.print()` function is a shortcut for the previous, where every event is printed in the Xcode console with the prefix we pass, which we can use to filter those messages in the Xcode console.

Finally, `.breakpoint()` stops the execution of the code when it is called.

There's more...

It's worth signaling a super-useful tool implemented by *Marin Todorov* called **Timelane** that allows you to follow the streams and present the result in **Instruments**. It is a pretty advanced tool, but it is also sophisticated and flexible, and it's worth giving it a try.

It can be found at `http://timelane.tools/` and is illustrated here:

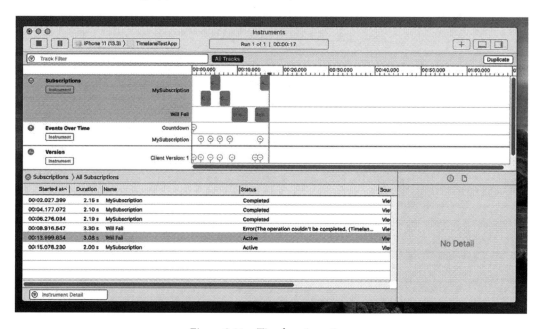

Figure 9.11 – Timelane in action

Unit testing an app based on Combine

I must confess that the topic of this recipe is very close to my heart: unit testing an app based on Combine.

We are going to implement an app that retrieves a list of GitHub users and shows them in a list view.

The code is pretty similar to the one in the *Fetching remote data using Combine and visualizing it in SwiftUI* recipe, but in this case we'll see how to unit test it—something that, even if it is very important, isn't well covered in documentation and tutorials.

Getting ready

Let's open Xcode and create a SwiftUI app called `GithubUsersApp`, paying attention to enabling the **Unit Tests**:

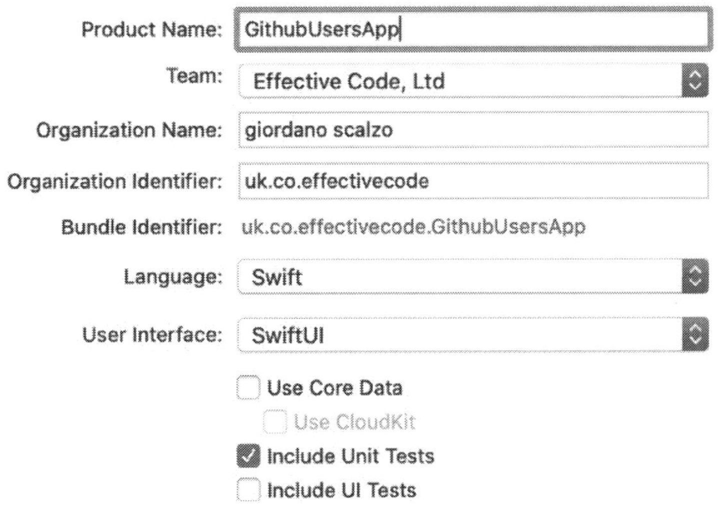

Product Name:	GithubUsersApp
Team:	Effective Code, Ltd
Organization Name:	giordano scalzo
Organization Identifier:	uk.co.effectivecode
Bundle Identifier:	uk.co.effectivecode.GithubUsersApp
Language:	Swift
User Interface:	SwiftUI

☐ Use Core Data
☐ Use CloudKit
☑ Include Unit Tests
☐ Include UI Tests

Figure 9.12 – Creating a SwiftUI app with Unit Tests enabled

Then, add the `githubUsers.json` file to the `GithubUsersAppTests` folder. You can find it in the GitHub repository at `https://github.com/PacktPublishing/SwiftUI-Cookbook/blob/master/Resources/Chapter09/recipe6/githubUsers.json`:

Figure 9.13 Fixture for the tests

How to do it...

We divide the recipe into two logic parts: the first part will implement the app retrieval and show the GitHub users, while the second will add a unit test for the fetching code.

1. Let's start by importing `Combine` and creating a model for the user:

```
import Combine

struct GithubUser: Decodable, Identifiable {
    let id: Int
    let login: String
    let avatarUrl: String
}
```

2. Implementing a `Github` class that fetches the user from `github.com` is matter of creating a publisher from `URLSession`:

```
class Github: ObservableObject {
    @Published
    var message: String = ""
    @Published
    var users: [GithubUser] = []

    private var cancellableSet: Set<AnyCancellable> = []

    func load() {
```

```
        let url = URL(string: "https://api.github.com/
            users")!
        let decoder = JSONDecoder()
        decoder.keyDecodingStrategy =
            .convertFromSnakeCase

        URLSession.shared
            .dataTaskPublisher(for: URLRequest(url: url))
            .map(\.data)
            .decode(type: [GithubUser].self, decoder:
                decoder)
            .receive(on: RunLoop.main)
            .sink { completion in
                switch completion {
                case .finished:
                    break
                case .failure(let error):
                    self.message = error.
                        localizedDescription
                }
            } receiveValue: {
                self.users = $0
            }
            .store(in: &cancellableSet)
        }
    }
```

3. The view will have the previous class as an @ObservedObject and will present a
   button when the list of the users is empty, or otherwise a list view of the users:

```
struct ContentView: View {
    @ObservedObject
    private var github = Github()

    var body: some View {
        if !github.users.isEmpty {
            List {
                ForEach(github.users) { user in
```

```
                        GithubUserView(user: user)
                    }
                }
                .padding(.horizontal)
            } else {
                Button {
                    github.load()
                } label: {
                    Text("Load users")
                        .foregroundColor(.white)
                        .frame(width: 120, height: 50)
                        .background(Color.green)
                }
            }
        }
    }
```

4. Finally, for each user, we show the username and a link to the avatar image:

```
struct GithubUserView: View {
    let user: GithubUser

    var body: some View {
        VStack(alignment: .leading) {
            Text("\(user.login)")
            Text("\(user.avatarUrl)")
                .font(.system(.footnote))
        }
    }
}
```

The app runs correctly and it presents the users after fetching them, as you can see from the following screenshot:

Figure 9.14 – Fetching and presenting GitHub users

How can you be sure it will always work when we add more features and change the code? The answer is: unit test it!

In the next part of this recipe, we'll see how to test a Combine publisher.

5. Let's move to the `GithubUsersAppTests` file, `import Combine`, and add a simple function to `XCTestCase` to read a JSON file we'll use in our mock:

```
import Combine
extension XCTestCase {
    func loadFixture(named name: String) -> Data? {
```

```
        let bundle = Bundle(for: type(of: self))
        let path = bundle.url(forResource: name,
            withExtension: "json")!
        return try? Data(contentsOf: path)
    }
}
```

6. A standard way of mocking a `URLSession` call is to create a custom `URLProtocol`:

```
final class MockURLProtocol: URLProtocol {
    static var requestHandler: ((URLRequest) throws ->
                            (HTTPURLResponse, Data?))?
    override class func canInit(with request: URLRequest)
        -> Bool {
        return true
    }

    override class func canonicalRequest(for
            request: URLRequest) -> URLRequest {
        return request
    }

    override func startLoading() {
        guard let handler = MockURLProtocol.
            requestHandler else {
            fatalError("Handler is unavailable.")
        }
        do {
            let (response, data) = try handler(request)
            client?.urlProtocol(self, didReceive:
                response, cacheStoragePolicy: .notAllowed)
            if let data = data {
                client?.urlProtocol(self, didLoad: data)
            }
            client?.urlProtocolDidFinishLoading(self)
        } catch {
            client?.urlProtocol(self, didFailWithError:
                error)
        }
    }
}
```

```
        override func stopLoading() {
    }
}
```

7. We want to test that the call returns a list of 30 users and the first one has the id of 1.

Let's write our test accordingly:

```
class GithubUsersAppTests: XCTestCase {
    let apiURL = URL(string: "https://api.github.com/
        users")!
    func testUsersCallResult() throws {
        // Arrange
        URLProtocol.registerClass(MockURLProtocol.self)
        MockURLProtocol.requestHandler = { request in
            let response = HTTPURLResponse(url: self.apiURL,
                statusCode: 200, httpVersion: nil,
                    headerFields: nil)!
            return (response, self
                .loadFixture(named: "githubUsers")!)
        }
        let github = Github()
        let exp1 = expectValue(of: github.$users,
            equalsTo: { $0.first?.id ==  1 })
        let exp2 = expectValue(of: github.$users,
            equalsTo: { $0.count == 30})
        // Act
        github.load()
        // Assert
        wait(for: [exp1.expectation, exp2.expectation],
            timeout: 1)
    }
}
```

8. Finally, let's implement the `expectValue()` function to verify the result of `Publisher`:

```swift
extension XCTestCase {
    typealias CompletionResult =
        (expectation: XCTestExpectation,
        cancellable: AnyCancellable)
    func expectValue<T: Publisher>(of publisher: T,
        equalsTo closure: @escaping(T.Output) -> Bool)
        -> CompletionResult {
        let exp = expectation(description:
            "Correct values of " +
                String(describing: publisher))
        let cancellable = publisher
            .sink(receiveCompletion: { _ in },
                receiveValue: {
                    if closure($0) {
                        exp.fulfill()
                    }
                })
        return (exp, cancellable)
    }
}
```

Running the test, we should see that the test we wrote is green.

How it works...

Explaining the benefits of unit testing is beyond the scope of this book, but I think you will agree with me that testing is something that should be part of every professional developer's skill set.

The trick here is to realize that any `@Published` variable is syntactic sugar for a Combine publisher: SwiftUI creates an automatic publisher called `$variable` for any `@Published` variable.

Given that it is a publisher, we can subscribe to it to test its value, and for this we create the `expectValue()` convenience function, to which we pass a closure to verify the expected value.

I believe that this could be a useful tool to have in your test toolbox.

To understand it better, try to play with it—for example, see what happens when you change the first check with the following:

```
let exp1 = expectValue(of: github.$users,
    equalsTo: { $0.first?.id == 2 })
```

When and where do you think it is going to fail?

Also, try to change the code of the `expectValue()` function and make it fail if the closure is false: is it going to be useful?

10

Handling Authentication and Firebase with SwiftUI

Since the creation of the mobile apps market, one of the most important features most apps utilize is authentication.

The normal way app creators ensure authentication is provided is by ensuring the user creates a new profile in the app they are using.

However, this creates some problems regarding the user-friendliness of the app. This is because before the user can use the app, they must do something that could be considered time-consuming, which means they might leave the app without using it.

There are also security concerns here. Because creating a new profile for each app we use is a repetitive process, we could be tempted to reuse a password we've already used somewhere else. For example, if a data breach occurs on any of the apps we've used and we've used the password for that app elsewhere, our other accounts that use that password are vulnerable to being hacked.

To overcome this problem, some big giants of the social app arena, including Facebook, Twitter, and Google, implemented a mechanism to authenticate a user for third-party apps: instead of using a new profile, we can use the one we already have on their respective sites.

This is convenient for the user, as well as the app developer, as the only thing the user needs to do is tap on the **Login with Facebook** button to be redirected to the Facebook app and use it to authenticate the third-party app.

This seems to be a perfect solution, doesn't it? Unfortunately, there are concerns about the privacy of the user. This is because, even though the authenticator service won't know what we are doing in the app we are authenticating in, it still knows that we are using that particular app and when we log into it.

This may not seem like an important issue at first glance, but it wouldn't be appropriate to hand out this kind of information if, for example, the app is related to health or it is about sensitive topics such as a person's religion or sexuality.

There is another point to take into consideration here. When we use an app in iOS, we are already being authenticated via our Apple ID, so it would be convenient to use that information in other apps so that we can be authenticated automatically.

In iOS 13, Apple introduced its *Sign in with Apple* service, which does exactly this.

A third-party developer can use this authentication system in their app easily for other social media login systems.

Since privacy is of paramount importance to Apple's clients, the *Sign in with Apple* service is implemented in such a way that authentication information never leaves your device and everything is considered private.

Furthermore, since the app usually asks for the email of the user, *Sign in with Apple* enforces its own privacy regulations. Here, it creates an anonymous email that you can link to your real one; it then sends the anonymous one to the app.

In the first two recipes of this chapter, you will learn how to use **Sign in with Apple** in a SwiftUI app to exploit this nice new capability of iOS. In the first recipe, we'll use the new `SignInWithApple` SwiftUI view that was introduced in iOS 14, while in the second recipe, we'll wrap the `SignInWithApple` UIKit button so that all the developers that cannot use iOS 14 in their app yet will be able to.

However, social login functionalities aren't going anywhere, so we'll also learn how to integrate the login functions of Google and Facebook into our SwiftUI apps.

To simplify their integration, will use a common platform service called **Firebase**, which allows us to integrate different authentications in a simple and uniform way. One of the most used features of Firebase is its distributed database on the cloud called **Firestore**.

We'll learn how to use it in a SwiftUI app later in this chapter.

As you will see, we'll spend more time configuring and adjusting the compilation of the app than writing code. This could be considered the boring part, but you will use the information you'll learn about in these recipes every time you implement new authentication or a new Firebase-based app. By doing this, you'll see how convenient it is to have all the necessary steps in the same place so that you can return to them for reference.

In this chapter, you'll learn how to handle authentication with *Sign in with Apple* and the Firebase service, a place where we can store a distributed database.

We are going to cover the following recipes:

- Implementing SwiftUI **Sign in with Apple**
- Implementing UIKit **Sign in with Apple** to be used in SwiftUI
- Integrating Firebase into a SwiftUI project
- Using Firebase to sign in using Google
- Implementing a distributed Notes app with Firebase and SwiftUI

Technical requirements

The code in this chapter is based on Xcode 12. The recipes in this chapter are to be implemented with iOS 14, apart from *UIKit Sign in with Apple with SwiftUI*, which is to be implemented with iOS 13.

You can find the code for this chapter in this book's GitHub repository at `https://github.com/PacktPublishing/SwiftUI-Cookbook/tree/master/Chapter10%20-%20Handling%20authentication%20and%20Firebase%20with%20SwiftUI`.

Implementing SwiftUI Sign in with Apple

In this recipe, you'll learn how to use **Sign in with Apple** in a SwiftUI app. Apple enforces the use of this method for authentication, making it mandatory if an app uses a third-party social login such as Facebook or Google, so it's a useful skill to learn.

Sign in with Apple is the official method Apple uses for authentication and SwiftUI supports it natively.

Since the native SwiftUI **Sign In with Apple** button was added in iOS 14, the app deployment target must be iOS 14.

We are going to implement a simple app that permits us to log in using our Apple ID and presents our credentials once we are logged in.

> **Important Note**
> Sign in with Apple doesn't work reliably with a simulator, so for this recipe, I recommend using a real iOS device.

The app we are going to implement is very basic, but it will give you the foundation for building something more sophisticated. However, there are a couple of points that we must take into consideration.

First, the framework will only pass the user's credentials the first time they log in, so if they are of importance to us, we must save them in an appropriate manner.

For simplicity, we'll save them in `UserDefaults` using the iOS 14 `@AppStorage("name")` property wrapper. Please don't do this in your production app since `UserDefaults` is not secure. These credentials should be stored in the keychain.

Second, Apple doesn't provide a `Logout` API, so the user must go into the **Settings** part of iOS 14 and remove the authentication properties, meaning that our app must check, at startup, if the credentials are still valid. We'll cover this as well.

Getting ready

Let's create a SwiftUI app called `SignInWithAppleApp` using Xcode 12 while setting iOS 14 as the target version.

How to do it...

As usual with features that rely on security or privacy, we must configure the capabilities of the app in the Xcode project:

1. First, we must add the capability to the app so that the app has permission to use **Sign in with Apple**. Select the **Signing & Capabilities** tab in the target configuration and search for **Sign in with Apple**:

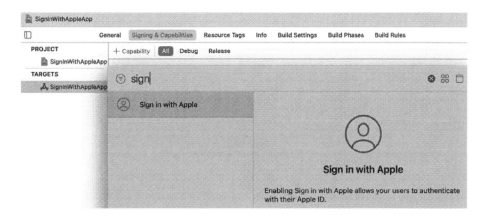

Figure 10.1 – Searching for the Sign in with Apple capability

2. After selecting **Sign in with Apple**, you will see that there is a new entry in the
    Signing & Capabilities section:

Figure 10.2 – Sign in with Apple added to the project

3. Now, let's move on to the code. Here, we'll start creating the main `ContentView`,
    which will show a message when the user is logged in, and prepare it for showing
    the `SignInWithApple` button when we wish to import SwiftUI:

```
Import SwiftUI
import AuthenticationServices


struct ContentView: View {
    @State
    private var userName: String = ""
    @State
    private var userEmail: String = ""


    var body: some View {
        ZStack{
            Color.white
```

```
            if userName.isEmpty{
                //...
            } else {
                Text("Welcome\n\(userName), \
                    (userEmail)")
                    .foregroundColor(.black)
                    .font(.headline)
            }
        }
        .onAppear(perform: onAppear)
    }
}
```

4. Since we imported the `AuthenticationServices` framework, SwiftUI provides us with a native button called `SignInWithAppleButton`. The button needs two callbacks: one for configuring the request and another for receiving the sign-in result. We provide the callbacks as private functions in the `ContentView` struct:

```
struct ContentView: View {
    var body: some View {
        //...
            if userName.isEmpty{
                SignInWithAppleButton(.signIn,
                        onRequest: onRequest,
                        onCompletion: onCompletion)
                    .signInWithAppleButtonStyle(.black)
                    .frame(width: 200, height: 50)
            } else {
        //...
        }

    private func onRequest(_ request:
                    ASAuthorizationAppleIDRequest)
    {
    }
```

```
private func onCompletion(_ result:
            Result<ASAuthorization, Error>) {

}
private func onAppear() {

}
}
```

5. Now, let's implement the `onRequest` function, where we ask the framework to return the full name and email of the user:

```
private func onRequest(_ request:
    ASAuthorizationAppleIDRequest) {
    request.requestedScopes = [.fullName, .email]
}
```

6. The `SignInWithApple` API only returns the credentials the first time we call it, so we must save them somewhere. Use the `@Appstorage` property wrapper to save them locally:

```
@AppStorage("storedName")
private var storedName : String = "" {
    didSet {
        userName = storedName
    }
}
@AppStorage("storedEmail")
private var storedEmail : String = "" {
    didSet {
        userEmail = storedEmail
    }
}
@AppStorage("userID")
private var userID : String = ""
```

7. The `OnCompletion` function simply saves the result of the `login` class in local storage:

```
private func onCompletion(_ result:
                            Result<ASAuthorization,
Error>) {
    switch result {
    case .success (let authResults):
        guard let credential = authResults.credential
                as? ASAuthorizationAppleIDCredential
        else { return }
        storedName = credential.fullName?.givenName ?? ""
        storedEmail = credential.email ?? ""
        userID = credential.user
    case .failure (let error):
        print("Authorization failed: " +
                error.localizedDescription)
    }
}
```

8. Finally, every time the app starts, we must verify whether the user is logged in. For this, implement an `onAppear` function:

```
private func onAppear() {
    guard !userID.isEmpty else {
        userName = ""
        userEmail = ""
        return
    }

    ASAuthorizationAppleIDProvider()
    .getCredentialState(forUserID: userID) { state, _ in
            DispatchQueue.main.async {
                if case .authorized = state {
                    userName = storedName
                    userEmail = storedEmail
                } else {
                    userID = ""
```

```
                         }
                    }
                }
            }
```

Now, we can run the app and use our **Apple ID** to sign in:

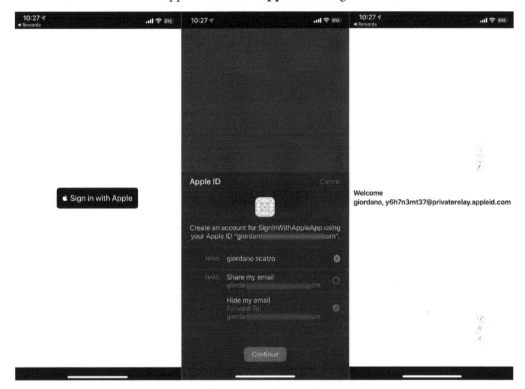

Figure 10.3 – Sign in with Apple in action

How it works...

The native SwiftUI `Sign In With Apple` implementation is an awaited iOS 14 feature that enforces the Apple policy of using this mechanism for app authentication.

The `SignInWithAppleButton` component works is a SwiftUI way where we pass two callbacks.

In the first one, we configure the type of request we are going to make, what scope of credentials we require, and more.

The second is called when the request is completed and its result is shown. If it is a success, we can save the credentials somewhere so that we can reuse them in the future and show them in the UI. By doing this, we can check if the credentials are still valid.

Being a view, `SignInWithAppleButton` doesn't check whether the credentials are still valid when the app starts, so in our recipe, we used the `.getCredentialState()` function of `ASAuthorizationAppleIDProvider()` to check whether the saved credentials are still valid.

Sign in with Apple doesn't provide a *Sign-Out* API, so the logout process cannot be done inside the app. To log out from our app, the user must disable the credentials provided in the **Settings** section of iOS, in the **Password & Security** section of their profile, as shown in the following screenshot:

Figure 10.4 – Removing credentials for Apple ID login

Implementing UIKit Sign in with Apple to be used in SwiftUI

In this recipe, you'll learn how to use **Sign in with Apple** in a SwiftUI app by wrapping the UIKit component.

In iOS 14, SwiftUI provides a native `SignInWithApple` button, but if you don't have support for it yet and are still using iOS 13, then don't worry – in this recipe, we are going to implement a wrapper around the UIKit class that works very well with SwiftUI.

Here, we are going to implement a simple app that permits us to log in using our Apple ID and presents our credentials when we are logged in.

> **Important Note**
> **Sign in with Apple** is still a bit flaky when it's run in a simulator, so it is safer to run this recipe on an iOS device.

The app that we'll be implementing in this recipe is simple, but it can be a good foundation to implement a proper app with Apple's authentication.

As you may recall, the `AuthenticationServices` framework only passes the user's credentials the first time they log in, so if they are of importance to us, we must store them in the app.

For simplicity, in this recipe, we are going to save these credentials in `UserDefaults`. Due to this, we should store this in `Keychain` since `UserDefaults` is not secure. However, the code for securely storing the credentials isn't trivial and would distract us from our main goal, which is using **Sign in with Apple**.

Getting ready

Let's create a SwiftUI app called `SignInWithAppleApp`. Please set the target to iOS 13 for this recipe.

How to do it...

As usual with features that rely on security or privacy, we must configure the capabilities of the app in the Xcode project:

1. First, we must add the capability to the app so that the app has permission to use **Sign in with Apple**. Select the **Capabilities** tab in the target configuration and search for **Sign in with Apple**:

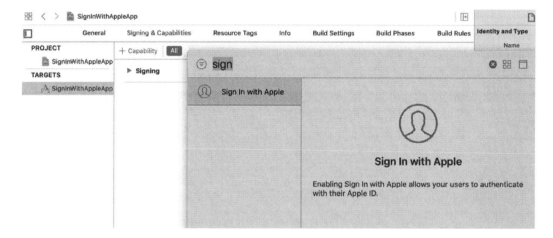

Figure 10.5 – Searching for the Sign in with Apple capability

2. After selecting **Sign in with Apple**, you'll see that there is a new entry in the **Signing & Capabilities** section:

Figure 10.6 – Sign in with Apple added to the project

3. Now, let's move on to the code. Here, we'll start creating the main `ContentView`, where we'll add a button for the logged-out state and two `Text` views for the user's full name and email:

```
struct ContentView: View {
    @State
    private var name : String = ""
    @State
```

```
        private var email : String = ""


    var body: some View {
        ZStack{
            Color.white
            if name.isEmpty{
                SignInWithApple(name: $name, email:
                    $email)
                    .frame(width: 200, height: 50)
            } else {
                Text("Welcome\n\(name), \(email)")
                    .foregroundColor(.black)
                    .font(.headline)
            }
        }
    }
}
```

4. You may have noticed that we introduced the `SignInWithApple` component here, which doesn't compile. Let's implement it by wrapping the **Sign In** button:

```
import AuthenticationServices
struct SignInWithApple: UIViewRepresentable {
    @Binding
    var name: String
    @Binding
    var email: String

    func makeUIView(context: Context) ->
    ASAuthorizationAppleIDButton {
        let button = ASAuthorizationAppleIDButton(
            authorizationButtonType: .signIn,
            authorizationButtonStyle: .black)
        return button
    }
```

```
func updateUIView(_ uiView:
    ASAuthorizationAppleIDButton, context: Context) {

    }
}
```

5. The **Sign in with Apple** button is presented in the middle of the screen, but it doesn't do anything. Let's implement a `Coordinator` class so that we can manage the button delegate:

```
struct SignInWithApple: UIViewRepresentable {
    //...
    func makeCoordinator() -> Coordinator {
        Coordinator(self)
    }

    func makeUIView(context: Context) ->
            ASAuthorizationAppleIDButton {
        //...
        button.addTarget(context.coordinator,
        action: #selector(Coordinator.didTapButton),
        for: .touchUpInside)
        return button
    }
    //...
    class Coordinator: NSObject,
    ASAuthorizationControllerDelegate,
    ASAuthorizationControllerPresentationContextProviding
    {
        let parent: SignInWithApple?
        init(_ parent: SignInWithApple) {
            self.parent = parent
        }
    }
}
```

6. Now, let's implement the signing-in action when the button is clicked:

```
class Coordinator: NSObject,
  ASAuthorizationControllerDelegate,
    ASAuthorizationControllerPresentationContextProviding {
        //...
    @objc
    func didTapButton() {
        let appleIDProvider =
            ASAuthorizationAppleIDProvider()
        let request = appleIDProvider.createRequest()
        request.requestedScopes = [.fullName, .email]

        let authorizationController =
          ASAuthorizationController(authorizationRequests:
            [request])
        authorizationController
                .presentationContextProvider = self
        authorizationController.delegate = self
        authorizationController.performRequests()
    }
}
```

7. Now, we must implement the first of the two protocols. We'll start with the one that provides a `viewController` instance, which presents the `ActionSheet` class:

```
class Coordinator: NSObject,
  ASAuthorizationControllerDelegate,
    ASAuthorizationControllerPresentationContextProviding {
        //...
    func presentationAnchor(for controller:
      ASAuthorizationController) -> ASPresentationAnchor {
        let vc = UIApplication.shared.windows.last?.
                rootViewController
        return (vc?.view.window!)!
    }
}
```

8. Next, we'll implement the protocol that will receive the user's credentials – or return an error – after we've completed the authentication:

```
class Coordinator: NSObject
  ASAuthorizationControllerDelegate,
  ASAuthorizationControllerPresentationContextProviding {
    //...
    func authorizationController(controller:
      ASAuthorizationController,
        didCompleteWithAuthorization authorization:
        ASAuthorization) {
      guard let credentials = authorization.credential
        as? ASAuthorizationAppleIDCredential else {
          print("credentials not found....")
          return
        }
      // Usually, Keychain is used for saving
      // the credentials, but for simplicity of
      // this article, we use the UserDefaults.
      // Please don't do this in your production app!
      UserDefaults.standard.set(credentials.user,
                                forKey: "userId")
      UserDefaults.standard.set(
        credentials.fullName?.givenName,
          forKey: "username")
      UserDefaults.standard.set(
        credentials.email, forKey: "email")
      parent?.name = credentials.fullName?.givenName ?? ""
      parent?.email = credentials.email ?? ""
    }

    func authorizationController(controller:
      ASAuthorizationController,
        didCompleteWithError error: Error) {
    }
}
```

9. Finally, in the `init()` function, check if the user credentials are still valid. If they are, present the logged in state; otherwise, clear the credentials in your storage and present the **Sign in with Apple** button:

```
class Coordinator: NSObject,
  ASAuthorizationControllerDelegate,
    ASAuthorizationControllerPresentationContextProviding {
      init(_ parent: SignInWithApple) {
        self.parent = parent
        super.init()

        guard let user = UserDefaults.standard
            .object(forKey: "userId") as? String,
          let name = UserDefaults.standard
            .object(forKey: "username") as? String,
          let email = UserDefaults.standard
            .object(forKey: "email") as? String else {
              return
        }
        let appleIDProvider =
            ASAuthorizationAppleIDProvider()
        appleIDProvider.getCredentialState(
          forUserID: user) { (state, error) in
            DispatchQueue.main.async {
              if case .authorized = state {
                self.parent?.name = name
                self.parent?.email = email
              } else {
                UserDefaults.standard
                    .set(nil, forKey: "userId")
              }
            }
        }
      }
      //...
}
```

Now, we can run the app and use our **Apple ID** to sign in:

Figure 10.7 – Sign in with Apple in action

How it works...

As we mentioned in the introduction, **Sign in with Apple** is UIKit-based, so we wrapped it in a `UIViewRepresentable` component.

The `Coordinator` in the wrapper takes care of calls from the framework. It stores the received credentials in `UserDefaults` and populates the variables to be presented in the `ContentView` component.

With this simple component, you can conform to the Apple guidelines for authentication with your SwiftUI code without the need to target iOS 14 devices.

Integrating Firebase into a SwiftUI project

Firebase is a mobile development platform that has several products that simplify the implementation of mobile apps. These apps need a backend for persistence, authentication, notifications, and more. A mobile developer can concentrate on implementing only the mobile app without worrying about implementing the services on the cloud that they need to power their app.

Firebase provides a framework so that their services can be used in Swift. Unfortunately, not all of them work smoothly in SwiftUI, so you need to apply some workarounds. Hopefully, Firebase will release a version for SwiftUI soon. We'll start our exploration of Firebase in SwiftUI by integrating their **RemoteConfig** product.

RemoteConfig is a service that lets the developer change the behavior or appearance of the app without requiring the users to download an update of the app. In this recipe, we are going to implement two sample main screens so that the developer can select which one to present.

Firebase is a pretty sophisticated service, and although it's definitely much easier to use than implementing a backend from scratch, there are a few steps to follow to configure it properly.

We'll follow them step by step and use this recipe as a base for the recipes we will look at later in this chapter.

Getting ready

One of the limitations of Swift Package Manager is that Firebase cannot be distributed as a package yet (at the time of writing).

This recipe imports the Firebase framework using **Cocoapods**, a standard dependency manager for iOS. You can find out more about it by going to the official website: `https://cocoapods.org/`.

If you don't have it installed already, you can do so with the following command:

```
$ sudo gem install cocoapods
```

Now that you've installed `Cocoapods`, let's create a new SwiftUI app called `FirebaseRemoteConfigApp`.

How to do it...

In this recipe, we'll encounter more configuration than code. Even though this may appear to be overkill, consider that this is the same amount of configuration for a Hello World application, as well as for a full-fledged social messenger app.

We'll use this recipe as a reference for creating a Firebase-based app. Follow these steps to get started:

1. Let's start by going to the main Firebase website, `https://firebase.google.com/`. After logging into the website with a valid Google account, click on **Get started** to be sent to the main console:

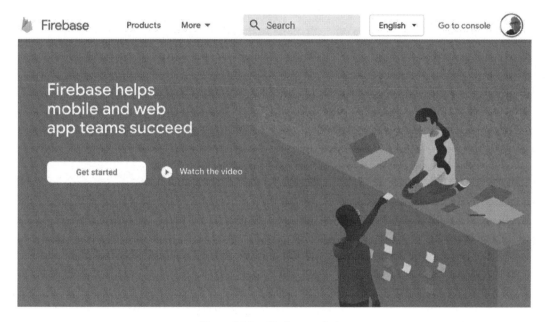

Figure 10.8 – Firebase website

2. From the console, create a new project by selecting **Add project**:

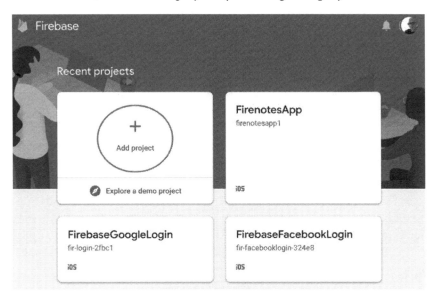

Figure 10.9 – Firebase console

3. Use a mnemonic name for the project:

Figure 10.10 – Creating a new Firebase project

4. On the next screen, disable **Google Analytics** since we don't need it for this recipe:

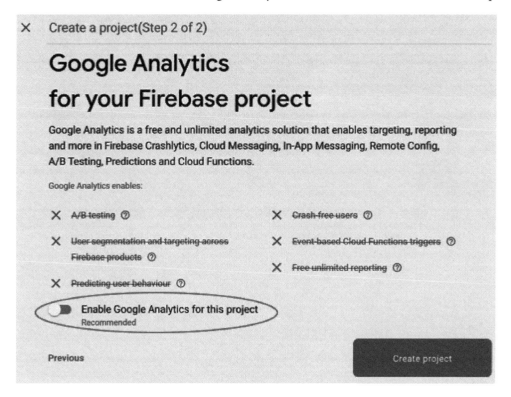

Figure 10.11 – Disabling Google Analytics

5. Once you have created the project, it is time to configure **Remote Config.** Expand the **Grow** section and select the **Remote Config** option. Then, add a parameter called screenType, whose default value is screenA:

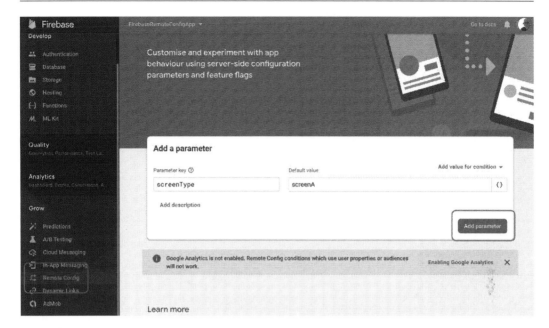

Figure 10.12 – Adding a Remote Config parameter

6.   Once you're happy with the parameter, publish it by clicking on **Publish changes**:

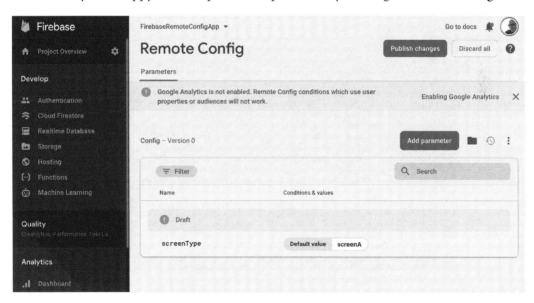

Figure 10.13 – Remote Config parameter added

7. Publishing these changes makes them immediately available to our customers:

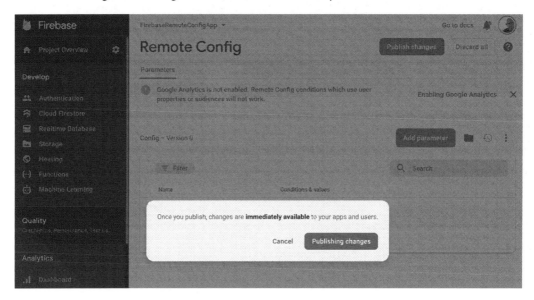

Figure 10.14 – Publishing our parameters

8. Once you have finished the **Remote Config** configuration, move back to the **Project Overview** page and select the **iOS** button, as shown in the following screenshot:

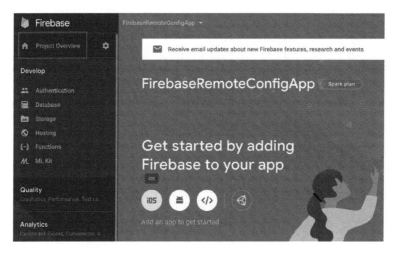

Figure 10.15 – Configuring iOS for Firebase

9. To prepare the Firebase configuration file, we must register the app with our **iOS bundle ID**:

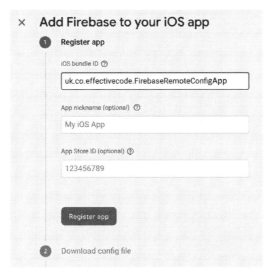

Figure 10.16 – Registering the iOS Bundle ID

10. This Bundle ID generates a `.plist` file, which must be imported into the app. To do this, first, download the file:

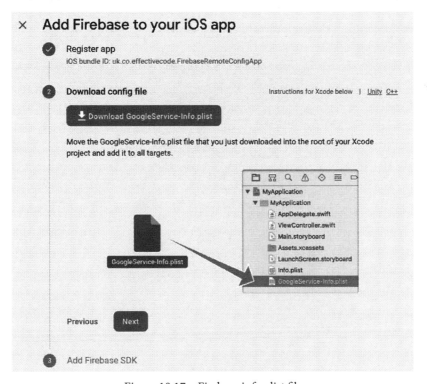

Figure 10.17 – Firebase info.plist file

11. Once you've downloaded the file, drag it into the project, taking care to select **Copy items if needed**:

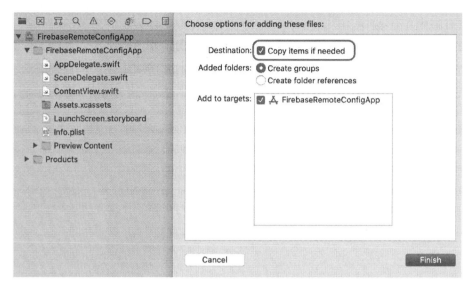

Figure 10.18 – Importing the GoogleService-Info.plist file

12. This is how our project should appear in Xcode:

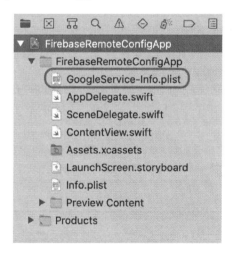

Figure 10.19 – Imported GoogleService-Info.plist file

13. Now, let's move on to configuring the app. Start by creating the Cocoapods configuration by running the following command in your project folder:

```
$ pod init
```

14. Cocoapods creates a `Podfile` file, where we can add the required dependencies. Open that file with an editor and add the dependency to the `FirebaseRemoteConfigApp` framework:

```
target 'FirebaseRemoteConfigApp' do
    use_frameworks!
    pod 'Firebase/RemoteConfig'
end
```

15. Now, install the pods with the following command:

```
$ pod install
```

16. Cocoapods will install the dependencies and create a workspace that contains our project and the other frameworks we just installed. Being a workspace, from now on, you must open the `FirebaseRemoteConfig.xcworkspace` file instead of `FirebaseRemoteConfig.xcodeproj`:

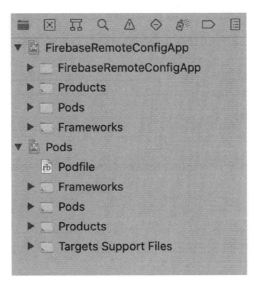

Figure 10.20 – The project and its dependencies

17. Finally, let's move on to the code. The first thing we must do is configure Firebase in the `AppDelegate` class:

```
import Firebase
@main
class AppDelegate: UIResponder, UIApplicationDelegate {
    func application(_ application: UIApplication,
        didFinishLaunchingWithOptionslaunchOptions:
    [UIApplication.LaunchOptionsKey: Any]?) -> Bool {
        FirebaseApp.configure()
        return true
    }
    //...
}
```

18. The next step is to implement a `View` that depends on a `RemoteConfig` parameter:

```
struct ContentView: View {
    @ObservedObject
    private var remoteConfig = RemoteConfig()
    var body: some View {
        VStack {
            Text("This is the Screen")
                .font(.system(size: 50))
            if remoteConfig.activeScreen == "screenA" {
                Text("A").font(.system(size: 100))
            } else {
                Text("B").font(.system(size: 100))
            }
        }
    }
}
```

19. The `RemoteConfig` class is a simple wrapper around Firebase's `RemoteConfig` class:

```
import Firebase
class RemoteConfig: ObservableObject {
    @Published
```

```
    var activeScreen = "screenA"
    private var remoteConfig: Firebase.RemoteConfig {
        Firebase.RemoteConfig.remoteConfig()
    }
}
```

Now, we can run the app. **Screen A** will appear.

20. Now, let's enable Developer Mode in `RemoteConfig` and fetch the required parameters from the cloud:

```
class RemoteConfig: ObservableObject {
    //...
    init() {
        // Configure in developer mode
        let settings = RemoteConfigSettings()
        settings.minimumFetchInterval = 0
        remoteConfig.configSettings = settings
        refreshConfig()
    }
}
```

21. The `refreshConfig()` function calls Firebase and then actives the result in the local configuration of the app:

```
class RemoteConfig: ObservableObject {
    //...
    private func refreshConfig() {
        let expirationDuration = 1
        remoteConfig.fetch(withExpirationDuration:
            TimeInterval(expirationDuration)) { [weak
                self] (status, error) -> Void in
                guard status == .success else { return }
                self?.remoteConfig.fetchAndActivate { _,
                    _ in
                    DispatchQueue.main.async {
                        self?.setProperties() }
                }
        }
    }
}
```

```
private func setProperties() {
    activeScreen = remoteConfig["screenType"]
                    .stringValue ?? "screenA"
}
}
```

Now, if you go to the Firebase console to change the value of the parameter and publish these changes, this will be reflected the next time you open the app:

Figure 10.21 – Selecting the View from Remote Config

How it works...

Firebase is a really powerful service that, after doing a bit of tedious configuration, gives your app real superpowers.

In this recipe, you learned how to drive the appearance of our SwiftUI app from a remote configuration, without asking our users to download an update.

We've only just scratched the surface of Remote Config, though. You can also define conditions regarding when a particular parameter should be applied, such as applying a rule to only a particular version of iOS or to a percentage of our customer base. Usually, the changes are not immediate, and you can give a longer duration to your parameters – 1 day, for example – so that the APIs are not hit too much.

Despite the long configuration phase, we have seen that the required code is very short and concise. Nonetheless, it gives us a really nice feature.

There's more...

In our implementation, we only check the parameters while the app is being started up, but what about extending this and doing this more often during the life cycle of the app? Using a timer should do the trick – try it out!

Also, I encourage you to explore the conditional rules in Firebase's `RemoteConfig` in order to learn how and when to apply them to your real app.

Using Firebase to sign in using Google

A social login is a method of authentication where the authentication is delegated to a trustworthy social networking service outside our app. A common social networking service that offers this kind of opportunity is Google.

In this recipe, you'll learn how to integrate a social login with Google using Firebase.

Getting ready

First, we need to create a SwiftUI app called `FirebaseGoogleLoginApp` with Xcode.

If it's not already installed on your computer, install Cocoapods. See the previous recipe to learn how to do this.

In the Firebase console, create a project called `FirebaseGoogleLoginApp`, remembering to disable Google Analytics.

Then, add the Bundle ID of the iOS app to the Firebase project, generate the `GoogleService-Info.plist` file, and add it to the Xcode project.

> **Firebase Configuration**
>
> In this recipe, we will assume you are already familiar with the **Firebase** console and how to install **Cocoapods**.
>
> If this is your first time using Firebase, please refer to the *Integrating Firebase into a SwiftUI project* recipe, which contains all the steps you need to follow to create a project in Firebase.

How to do it...

Firebase provides a library for using Google Login. However, it is based on UIKit and sometimes, there are some hiccups since it expects a view controller to present the Google login action sheet.

However, wrapping the provided component in a `UIViewRepresentable` allows us to implement it in a SwiftUI project.

Before you start coding, you must go to Firebase to configure the authentication providers for this app. Follow these steps to do so:

1. The first step is to select the **Authentication** section of the app in Firebase:

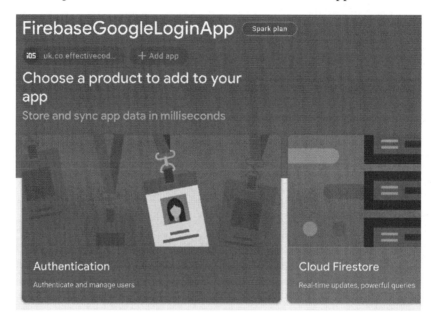

Figure 10.22 – Firebase authentication section

2. In the **Authentication** section, click on the **Set up sign-in method** option:

Figure 10.23 – Firebase project authentication page

3. From the list of the providers, enable Google as the authentication provider and save this change:

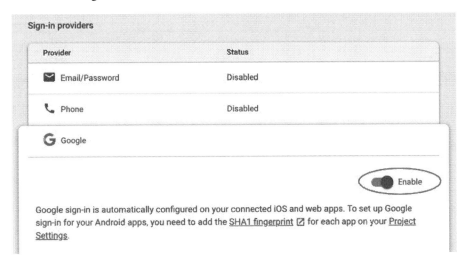

Figure 10.24 – Google sign-in provider

4. After adding the Google provider, you must go to the iOS configuration, where you must add the bundle ID of your app to create the `GoogleService-Info.plist` configuration file:

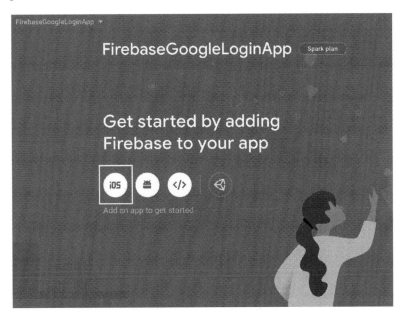

Figure 10.25 – Firebase project's iOS configuration

5. From there, a new `GoogleService-Info.plist` file is generated. Download it and add it to Xcode:

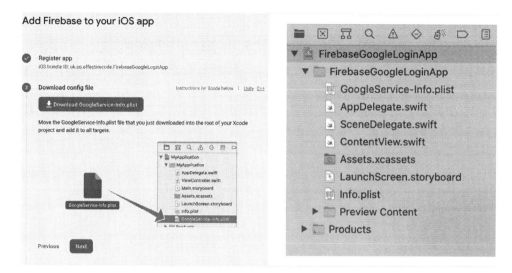

Figure 10.26 – Downloading the latest GoogleService-Info.plist file

6. In the `GoogleService-Info.plist` file there is a value for the `REVERSED_CLIENT_ID` field that must be added to the project's configuration. Open `GoogleService-Info.plist` and copy the value to the clipboard.

Select the app from the **TARGETS** section, select the **Info** tab, and expand the **URL Types** section. Paste the copied value into the **URL Schemes** box:

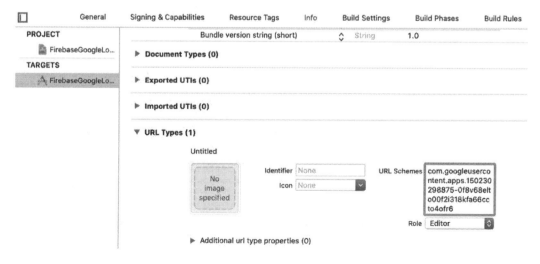

Figure 10.27 – Configuring URL Schemes

7. Now, go back to our app. After initializing Cocoapods with the `pod init` command, add the needed pods to `Podfile`:

```
target 'FirebaseGoogleLoginApp' do
  use_frameworks!
  pod 'Firebase/Auth'
  pod 'GoogleSignIn'
end
```

After doing this, run `pod install` to download the dependencies and create the Xcode workspace.

8. As usual, the first thing a Firebase app must do is configure the Firebase framework. In the `AppDelegate` class, add the `configure()` function to the `FirebaseApp` class:

```
import Firebase
@main
class AppDelegate: UIResponder, UIApplicationDelegate {
    func application(_ application: UIApplication,
didFinishLaunchingWithOptionslaunchOptions:
            [UIApplication.LaunchOptionsKey: Any]?) ->
            Bool {
        FirebaseApp.configure()
        return true
    }
}
```

9. Now, go to `ContentView` and create a wrapper around the Google **Sign In** button:

```
import Firebase
import GoogleSignIn

struct GoogleLogin: UIViewRepresentable {
    func makeUIView(context: Context) ->UIView {
        GIDSignIn.sharedInstance().clientID =
            FirebaseApp.app()?.options.clientID
        GIDSignIn.sharedInstance()?
            .presentingViewController = UIApplication.
shared
```

```
                              .windows.last?.
rootViewController
            GIDSignIn.sharedInstance()?.
restorePreviousSignIn()
            return GIDSignInButton()
    }


    func updateUIView(_ uiView: UIView, context: Context)
{

    }
}
```

10. Now, incorporate the button in `ContentView`:

```
struct ContentView: View {
    var body: some View {
        GoogleLogin(signedIn: $signedIn, username:
            $username, email: $email)
            .frame(width: 200, height: 30, alignment:
                .center)
    }
}
```

11. Now, the app works, and we can select the login. However, after logging in, nothing changes. Let's fix this. First, add some `@State` variables to `ContentView` to show when the user is logged in:

```
struct ContentView: View {
    @State
    private var signedIn = false
    @State
    private var username: String = ""
    @State
    private var email: String = ""
    //...
}
```

12. The body must be conditional to show either the **Google Login** button or the username and email of the logged-in user:

```
var body: some View {
    ZStack {
        Color.white
        if signedIn {
            VStack(spacing: 4) {
                Text("Username: \(username)")
                    .foregroundColor(.black)
                Text("Email: \(email)")
                    .foregroundColor(.black)
            }
        } else {
            GoogleLogin(signedIn: $signedIn, username:
                $username, email: $email)
            .frame(width: 200, height: 30, alignment:
                .center)
        }
    }.edgesIgnoringSafeArea(.all)
}
```

13. The component to change these `@State` variables is `GoogleLogin`, so we are going to add them as `@Binding` variables:

```
struct GoogleLogin: UIViewRepresentable {
    @Binding
    var signedIn: Bool
    @Binding
    var username: String
    @Binding
    var email: String
    //...
}
```

14. We must also change the instantiation in `ContentView`:

```
if signedIn {
    //...
} else {
    GoogleLogin(signedIn: $signedIn, username:
                $username, email: $email)
    .frame(width: 200, height: 30, alignment: .center)
}
```

15. The sign-in mechanism works via a delegate, so let's create a `Coordinator` in `GoogleLogin`:

```
struct GoogleLogin: UIViewRepresentable {
    //...
    func makeCoordinator() -> Coordinator {
        Coordinator(self)
    }

    class Coordinator: NSObject, GIDSignInDelegate {
        private let parent: GoogleLogin

        init(_ parent: GoogleLogin) {
            self.parent = parent
        }
    }
}
```

16. `Coordinator` conforms to the `GIDSignInDelegate` protocol, and there are two functions to be implemented: one for `signIn` and one for `signOut`. The former receives the credentials from Google and sends them to the `authentication` endpoint in Firebase. When we get a successful response from Firebase, we update the properties:

```
struct GoogleLogin: UIViewRepresentable {
    //...
    class Coordinator: NSObject, GIDSignInDelegate {
        //...
        func sign(_ signIn: GIDSignIn!,
                  didSignInFor user: GIDGoogleUser?,
```

```
                    withError error: Error?) {
        guard let authentication =
            user?.authentication else {
                return
        }
        let credential = GoogleAuthProvider.
            credential(withIDToken: authentication.
            idToken,accessToken: authentication.
            accessToken)


        Auth.auth().signIn(with: credential) {
            (authResult, error) in
            self.parent.signedIn = true
            if let username = authResult?.user.
                displayName {
                self.parent.username = username
            }
            if let email = authResult?.user.email {
                self.parent.email = email
            }
        }
    }
}
```

17. The `signout` callback in this `Coordinator` will be empty because it will be implemented by another component. The `signout` callback is notified of this with the `disconnect` parameter:

```
class Coordinator: NSObject, GIDSignInDelegate {
    //...
    func sign(_ signIn: GIDSignIn!,
        didDisconnectWith user: GIDGoogleUser!,
        withError error: Error!) {
    }
}
```

18. The last thing we need to do here is set `Coordinator` as the delegate of the `GIDSignIn` instance:

```
struct GoogleLogin: UIViewRepresentable {
    //...
    func makeUIView(context: Context) ->UIView {
        GIDSignIn.sharedInstance().clientID =
            FirebaseApp.app()?.options.clientID
        GIDSignIn.sharedInstance()?.
            presentingViewController =
            UIApplication.shared.windows.last?.
            rootViewController

        GIDSignIn.sharedInstance().delegate = context.
            coordinator
        //...
    }
}
```

19. If you run the app now, you will see that the sign-in procedure works fine but that there is no way to sign. Let's implement a `GoogleLogout` component so that we can log out:

```
struct GoogleLogout: UIViewRepresentable {
    @Binding
    var signedIn: Bool

    func makeUIView(context: Context) -> UIView {
        GIDSignIn.sharedInstance().delegate =
                                context.coordinator

        let button = UIButton(frame: .zero)
        button.setTitle("Logout", for: .normal)
        button.backgroundColor = UIColor.red
        button.addTarget(context.coordinator,
            action: #selector(Coordinator.onLogout),
            for: .touchUpInside)
        return button
```

```
        }

    func updateUIView(_ uiView: UIView, context: Context)
{

    }
}
```

20. `Coordinator` will just call the `disconnect` function in the Google shared instance and reset the `Boolean` flag to notify `View` to render the logged-out state:

```
struct GoogleLogout: UIViewRepresentable {
    //...
    func makeCoordinator() -> Coordinator {
        Coordinator(self)
    }

    class Coordinator: NSObject, GIDSignInDelegate {
        private let parent: GoogleLogout

        init(_ parent: GoogleLogout) {
            self.parent = parent
        }

        @objc
        func onLogout(button: UIButton) {
            GIDSignIn.sharedInstance()?.disconnect()
        }

        func sign(_ signIn: GIDSignIn!,
            didSignInFor user: GIDGoogleUser?,
            withError error: Error?) {
        }

        func sign(_ signIn: GIDSignIn!,
            didDisconnectWith user: GIDGoogleUser!,
            withError error: Error!) {
                self.parent.signedIn = false
```

```
            }
        }
    }
```

After defining the **GoogleLogout** button we must add it in the **body** of the
ContentView component, when the user is logged in:

```
var body: some View {
    ZStack {
    //...
        Text("Email: \(email)")
            .foregroundColor(.black)
        GoogleLogout(signedIn: $signedIn)
            .frame(width: 200, height: 30, alignment:
            .center)
    //...
    }
}
```

Finally, we can view the full scenario in the app:

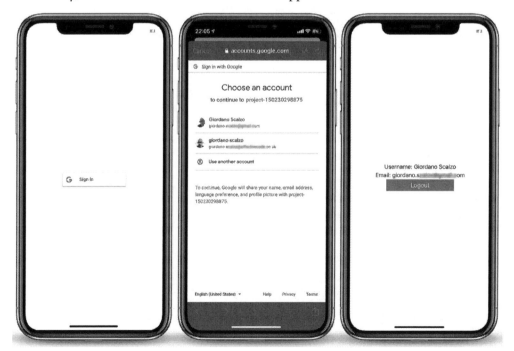

Figure 10.28 – Signing in with Google

How it works...

As you can see, all the interaction that's created between the Firebase components is done via singletons or static functions, making the code more difficult to test. However, it looks like the integration with SwiftUI wasn't so difficult.

As always, when wrapping a UIKit component, it is important to have a `Coordinator` that handles the logic beside the UI part. The only tricky part is that `GDSignIn` requires a `UIViewController` to present the `WebView` so that it can log in with Google, and in a SwiftUI project, you don't have one explicitly.

In this recipe, we found a workaround to retrieving `rootViewController` from the `MainWindow` hierarchy. However, this isn't a reliable and future-proof way of providing a `viewController` to present the Google Login since Apple can change how the View hierarchy of an iOS app is created.

Until Firebase and Google release a pure SwiftUI solution, the safest implementation would be to have a `UIViewController` that encapsulates that login part so that we are sure the `UIViewController` hierarchy is in place.

Implementing a distributed Notes app with Firebase and SwiftUI

One of the strongest features of Firebase is its distributed database capabilities. Since its first release, the possibility of having a distributed database in the cloud gave mobile developers a simple way of handling secure persistent storage in the cloud.

Firebase offers two type of databases:

Realtime Database, which is the original one, and **Cloud Firestore**, which is a new and more powerful implementation.

For this recipe we are going to use **Cloud Firestore**.

It not only allows apps to save data in the repository, but it also sends events when it is updated by another client, permitting your app to react to these changes in a seamless way. This asynchronous feature works very well with SwiftUI.

In this recipe, we are going to implement a simplified version of the default Notes app where we can save our notes in a Firestore collection, without being concerned of explicitly saving the notes or handling offline mode, since this is managed automatically by the Firebase SDK.

Getting ready

First, we need to create a SwiftUI app called `FirebaseNotesApp` with Xcode, setting iOS 14 as the deployment target.

If it's not already installed on your computer, install Cocoapods. See the *Integrating Firebase into a SwiftUI project* recipe, earlier in this chapter, to learn how to do this.

In the Firebase console, create a project called `FirebaseNotesApp`, remembering to disable Google Analytics.

Then, add the bundle ID of the iOS app to the Firebase project, generate the `GoogleService-Info.plist` file, and add it to the Xcode project.

> **Firebase Configuration**
>
> In this recipe, we're assuming you are already familiar with the **Firebase** console and how to install **Cocoapods**.
>
> If this is your first time, please refer to the *Integrating Firebase into a SwiftUI project* recipe, which contains all the steps you need to follow to create a project in Firebase.

How to do it...

The app we are going to implement will have two main parts: the UI and the repository manager.

The repository manager will be implemented around the Firestore SDK so that it can be managed by SwiftUI.

As usual, we must configure the project in Firebase based on our needs. Follow these steps to get started:

1. Go to the `FirebaseNotesApp` project in Firebase to create a database, selecting the entry. Select **Cloud Firestore** from the left menu and click on **Create database**:

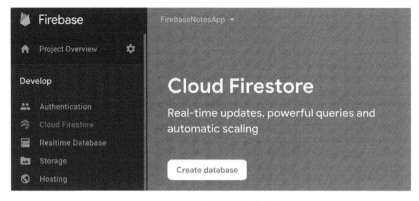

Figure 10.29 – Creating a database

2. Once you've created a new database, select the level of security you require.
    Exploring Firebase's security rules is beyond the scope of this book, so select the
    Start in test mode option, which is good enough for our goals:

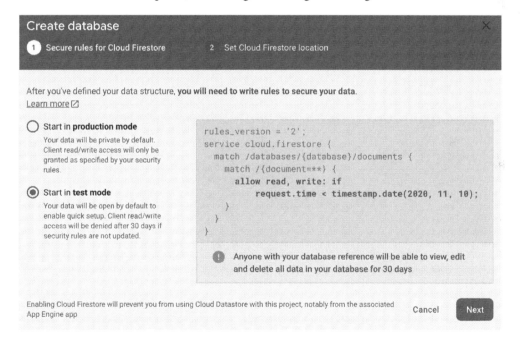

Figure 10.30 – Database security rules

3. Now, we must select the region where we're creating the database. Select the one closest to your area:

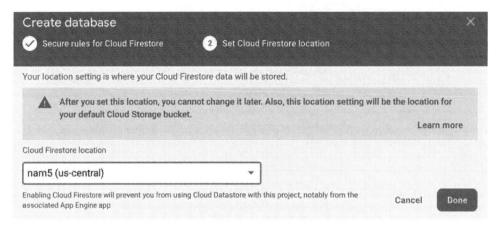

Figure 10.31 – Cloud Firestore location

4. By doing this, we have created the database:

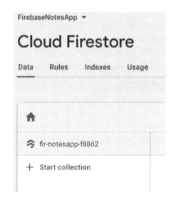

Figure 10.32 – Database overview on Firebase

5. Now, go back to the app. After creating `Podfile` with `pod init`, we need to add the necessary frameworks:

```
target 'FirebaseNotesApp' do
use_frameworks!
  pod 'Firebase/Firestore'
  pod 'FirebaseFirestoreSwift'
end
```

Install it by running the `pod install` command.

6. Now, open the app in Xcode using the `.xcworkspace` file. In the `AppDelegate` file, initialize `Firebase`:

```
import Firebase


@main
class AppDelegate: UIResponder, UIApplicationDelegate {
    func application(_ application: UIApplication,
        didFinishLaunchingWithOptionslaunchOptions:
        [UIApplication.LaunchOptionsKey: Any]?) -> Bool {
            FirebaseApp.configure()
            return true
    }
}
```

7. The `Note` we are going to implement is a simple struct with a title, a body, and its creation date visible. Since we'll show a list of notes in a List View, make it `Identifiable`:

```
struct Note: Identifiable {
    let id: String
    let title: String
    let date: Date
    let body: String
}
```

8. A note can be created and deleted. We also have a list of notes. Model these features in a class called `NotesRepository`:

```
class NotesRepository: ObservableObject {
    @Published
    var notes: [Note] = []
    func newNote(title: String, date: Date, body: String)
    {

    }
    func remove(at index: Int) {

    }
}
```

9. This repository uses `Firestore`, so let's have an instance as a property:

```
import Firebase
class NotesRepository: ObservableObject {
    private let db = Firestore.firestore()
    //...
}
```

10. For every change that's made in the repository, we must load all the notes again. For this, we need to implement a `loadAll()` function. In this function, we access the `"notes"` collection, fetch all the children, and convert them into a `Note` struct:

```
class NotesRepository: ObservableObject {
    //...
    private func loadAll() {
        db.collection("notes")
            .getDocuments { (snapshot, error) in
                if let error = error {
                    print(error) // manage errors
                    return
                }
                guard let documents = snapshot?.documents
                    else {
                    return
                }
                self.notes = documents.compactMap {
                    document in
                    let data = document.data()
                    guard let title = data["title"]
                        as? String,
                        let timestamp = data["date"]
                            as? Timestamp,
                        let body = data["body"]
                            as? String else {
                        return nil
                    }
                    return Note(id: document.documentID,
                                title: title,
                                date: timestamp.dateValue(),
```

```
                        body: body)
            }
        }
    }
}
```

11. We are going to load the notes when the app starts, as well as when we create or delete a note:

```
class NotesRepository: ObservableObject {
    //...
    init() {
        loadAll()
    }
    func newNote(title: String, date: Date, body: String)
    {
        loadAll()
    }
    func remove(at index: Int) {
        loadAll()
    }
    //...
}
```

12. To create a new Note in Firestore, the framework provides the addDocument() function, where a document is modeled using a dictionary:

```
class NotesRepository: ObservableObject {
    //...
    func newNote(title: String, date: Date, body:
        String) {
        db.collection("notes").addDocument(data: [
            "title": title,
            "date": date,
            "body": body,
        ])
        loadAll()
    }
}
```

13. To delete a document in Firestore, we must access it via its `documentId`:

```
class NotesRepository: ObservableObject {
    //...
    func remove(at index: Int) {
        let noteToDelete = notes[index]
        db.collection("notes").document(noteToDelete.id)
            .delete()
        loadAll()
    }
    //...
}
```

14. Now that we have finished the repository, let's concentrate our efforts on visualizing the notes. We are going to implement three views: `ContentView` to show the notes, `NewNote` to create a new one, and `ShowNote` to visualize it. Let's start with `ContentView`, where we'll add the properties to watch and a convenient `DateFormatter` instance:

```
struct ContentView: View {
    static let taskDateFormat: DateFormatter = {
        let formatter = DateFormatter()
        formatter.dateStyle = .long
        return formatter
    }()
    @ObservedObject
    var repository: NotesRepository = NotesRepository()
    @State
    var isNewNotePresented = false
    //...
}
```

15. In the body, add a `List` to present the notes. If the user clicks on the row, they will be redirected to a new view that shows the selected note:

```
var body: some View {
    NavigationView {
        List {
            ForEach(repository.notes) { note in
```

```
NavigationLink(destination:
    ShowNote(note: note)) {
        VStack(alignment: .leading) {
            Text(note.title)
                .font(.headline)
                .fontWeight(.bold)
            Text("\(note.date,
                formatter: Self.
                    taskDateFormat)")
                .font(.subheadline)
        }
    }
```

16. To create a new note, add a `"plus"` button to the navigation bar that toggles the `isNewNotePresented@State` variable:

```
var body: some View {
    NavigationView {
        List {
            //...
        }
        .navigationBarTitle("FireNotes",
            displayMode: .inline)
        .navigationBarItems(trailing:
            Button {
                isNewNotePresented.toggle()
            } label: {
                Image(systemName: "plus")
                    .font(.headline)
            })
    }
}
```

17. The `NewNote` view is presented using the `.sheet()` modifier:

```
var body: some View {
    NavigationView {
        //...
        .navigationBarItems(trailing:
        //...
        })
        .sheet(isPresented: $isNewNotePresented) {
            NewNote(isNewNotePresented:
                $isNewNotePresented,
                repository: repository)
        }
    }
}
```

With this modifier, we can slide to the left of the note's row to delete it.

18. Before implementing the two ancillary views, add the `.onDelete()` modifier to remove a note:

```
var body: some View {
    NavigationView {
        List {
            ForEach(repository.notes) { note in
                //...
            }
            .onDelete{ indexSet in
                if let index = indexSet.first {
                    repository.remove(at: index)
                }
            }
        }
        //...
    }
}
```

19. Now, let's implement a view for adding a new note. It must be possible to add a title, a body, and save it. Follow the same pattern we followed for `ContentView`, presenting the components in a `NavigationView` with a checkmark bar button item to indicate we are happy with our changes. We only make the title mandatory, so the `"done"` button will only be enabled after we fill in the `title` component. For the body of the note, we are going the use the `TextEditor` component, which supports multi-line text, just like the `UITextView` class does in UIKit. Start by defining the interface of the `NewNote` view:

```
struct NewNote: View {
    @State
    private var title: String = ""
    @State
    private var bodyText: String = ""
    @Binding
    var isNewNotePresented: Bool
    var repository: NotesRepository
    //...
}
```

20. In `body`, present a `VStack` with a title and body that's encapsulated in a `NavigationView`:

```
var body: some View {
    NavigationView {
        VStack(spacing: 12) {
            TextField("Title", text: $title)
                .padding(4)
                .border(Color.gray)
            TextEditor(text: $bodyText)
                .border(Color.gray)
        }
    }
}
```

21. Now, add some padding and a title to the View:

```swift
var body: some View {
    NavigationView {
        VStack(spacing: 12) {
            //...
        }
        .padding(32)
        .navigationBarTitle("New Note", displayMode:
            .inline)
    }
}
```

22. Finally, add the *done* button in the form of a `checkmark`:

```swift
var body: some View {
    NavigationView {
        //...
        .navigationBarTitle("New Note", displayMode:
            .inline)
        .navigationBarItems(trailing:
        Button {
            repository.newNote(title: title,
                               date: Date(),
                               body: self.bodyText)
            isNewNotePresented.toggle()
        } label: {
            Image(systemName: "checkmark")
                .font(.headline)
        }
        .disabled(title.isEmpty)
        )
    }
}
```

Note that the enabled/disabled state is determined by the state of the title's `TextField` component.

23. Finally, the `ShowNote` view is a simplified version of the `NewNote` view:

```
struct ShowNote: View {
    let note: Note
    var body: some View {
        VStack(spacing: 12) {
            Text(note.title)
                .font(.headline)
                .fontWeight(.bold)
            ReadonlyTextEditor(text: note.body)
                .border(Color.gray)
        }
        .padding(32)
    }
}
```

24. When viewing a note, its content shouldn't be editable. Since the `TextEditor` component doesn't support read-only mode, we must implement a simple `UIViewRepresentable` around a read-only `UITextView`:

```
struct ReadonlyTextEditor: UIViewRepresentable {
    var text: String
    func makeUIView(context: Context) -> UITextView {
        let view = UITextView()
        view.isScrollEnabled = true
        view.isEditable = false
        view.isUserInteractionEnabled = true
        return view
    }
    func updateUIView(_ uiView: UITextView,
                      context: Context) {
        uiView.text = text
    }
}
```

Done! The app is now complete. We can try it out by adding recipes to it, as shown in the following screenshot:

Figure 10.33 – Notes app in the cloud

How it works...

The first thing to notice is the unbalanced amount of code needed to implement this recipe; the code we needed to manage the database is probably about one third of the code needed for the UI!

Also, note that the bridging between the Firebase library and SwiftUI is pretty natural and that it works the way it should. Firestore is a so-called document store, where the data is saved in an informal way in the form of a collection of dictionaries.

If you have minimal experience with relational databases, then you should know that the first thing you should do is model the data and define a schema for the database. If, in the future, our data needs an extension, we need to define a new schema, provide a migration script, and so on. In the case of Firestore, after creating a project in Firebase, you are ready to start creating documents, updating them, and so on.

We didn't add it here, but the Firestore instance also provides sophisticated functions for performing queries, such as for returning all the documents that contain a particular word, or those that have been created on a particular day.

Another interesting feature is the notification mechanism, where the app is notified when the repository changes – maybe because another device has changed it or because the repository has been changed directly from the Firebase console.

Firebase provides a web console for viewing and editing a database, providing a simple but powerful tool we can use to administer our databases.

The following screenshot shows what the database we created in this recipe looks like:

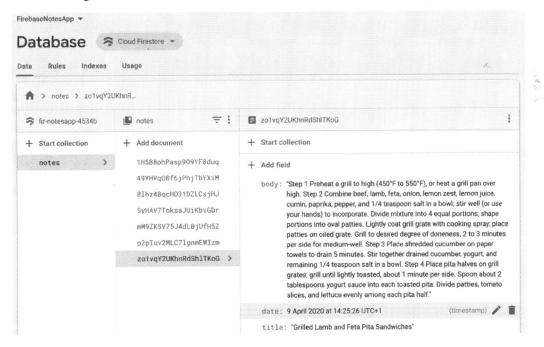

Figure 10.34 – Firestore's web console

There's more...

As we have seen, using Firestore is really easy and fits well with the SwiftUI model. From here, we can add more features.

The first obvious one would be to add the possibility of editing a note.

Firestore has a powerful mechanism that notifies the code that uses it when the repository has changed. At the moment, we are only refreshing the notes at startup or when we add or delete a new note.

I encourage you to explore the notification capabilities of Firestore and add a reload when someone else changes the repository. You can test this by launching the app in two different simulators.

I'm pretty sure you'll be amazed by the simplicity of adding these features, thus making our basic notes app really close to Apple's official Notes App.

11
Handling Core Data in SwiftUI

Core Data is definitely one of the most essential Apple frameworks in the iOS and macOS ecosystem. Core Data provides persistence, meaning it can save data outside the app's memory, and the data you saved can be retrieved after you restart your app.

Given its importance, it's not a surprise that Apple has implemented some extensions for Core Data to make it work nicely with SwiftUI.

In Core Data language, a stored object is an instance of `NSManagedObject`, and from iOS 13, `NSManagedObject` conforms to the `ObservableObject` protocol so that it can be observed directly by a SwiftUI's view.

Also, `NSManagedObjectContext` is injected into the environment of the View's hierarchy so that the SwiftUI's View can access it to read and change its managed objects.

A very common feature of Core Data is that you can fetch the objects from the repository. F or this purpose, SwiftUI provides the `@FetchRequest` property wrapper, which can be used in a view to load the data.

You can check the **Use Core Data** checkbox to make Xcode generate the code needed to inject the Core Data stack into your code when you create a new project in Xcode. In the first recipe of this chapter, we'll learn how to do this manually in order to understand where Core Data fits into an iOS app architecture.

In the remaining recipes, we'll learn how to perform the basic persistence operations; that is, creating, reading, and deleting persistent objects in Core Data and SwiftUI.

In this chapter, we are going to learn how to integrate the default Apple way of performing persistence with Core Data in SwiftUI.

We'll explore the basics of Core Data in SwiftUI by covering the following recipes:

- Integrating Core Data with SwiftUI
- Showing Core Data objects with `@FetchRequest`
- Adding Core Data objects to a SwiftUI view
- Filtering Core Data requests using a predicate
- Deleting Core Data objects from a SwiftUI view

Technical requirements

The code in this chapter is based on Xcode 12. The minimum iOS version required is iOS 13.

You can find the code for this chapter in this book's GitHub repository at `https://github.com/PacktPublishing/SwiftUI-Cookbook/tree/master/Chapter11%20-%20Handling%20Core%20Data%20and%20SwiftUI/01%20-%20Integrating%20Core%20Data%20with%20SwiftUI`.

Integrating Core Data with SwiftUI

Over the years, you may have found different ways of using Core Data in your apps from an architectural point of view; for example, using Apple with the Xcode templates proposed to create containers in `AppDelegate` so that you can use them when needed, other templates wrapped with Core Data inside manager classes, and so on. However, others prefer abstracting Core Data entirely so that it's easy to move to another solution, such as **Realm**, if needed.

SwiftUI's integration, however, points firmly in one direction: create the container when the app starts, inject it into our `Environment`, and then use it to fetch data or make changes.

When building a new app with Xcode, you can check the **Use Core Data** checkbox so that Xcode creates a template that injects the Core Data stack in the most efficient way possible.

Even though this is the way we usually do this, in this recipe, we'll introduce Core Data manually in a SwiftUI project so that you understand all the steps that Xcode does for you.

Getting ready

Let's create a SwiftUI app called `SwiftUICoreDataStackApp`, ensuring that we leave the **Use Core Data** option unchecked:

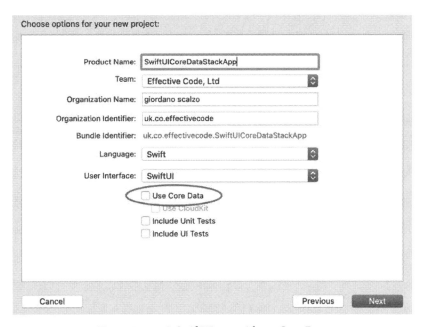

Figure 11.1 – A SwiftUI app without Core Data

How to do it...

In this recipe, we are going to wrap the Core Data stack into a class called `CoreDataStack` (what a surprise) and instantiate it in the `SceneDelegate` class, which will handle its life cycle. Let's get started:

1. First, let's add a Core Data model called `ContactsModel`. We should add some entities to the model, but for the moment, let's leave it as it is:

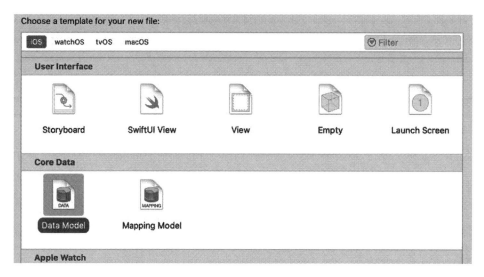

Figure 11.2 – Core Data model

2. Now, let's implement a class that will wrap the Core Data framework. This class will be called `CoreDataStack`. We are going to pass the name of the model as a parameter. This class will then create and hold the container:

```
import Foundation
import CoreData


class CoreDataStack {
    private let persistentContainer:
        NSPersistentContainer
    var managedObjectContext: NSManagedObjectContext {
        persistentContainer.viewContext
    }
    init(modelName: String) {
        persistentContainer = {
```

```
        let container = NSPersistentContainer(name:
            modelName)
        container.loadPersistentStores { description,
            error in
            if let error = error {
                print(error)
            }
        }
        return container
    }()
    }
}
```

3. Another function we need in this class is one that saves the changed objects:

```
class CoreDataStack {
    //...
    func save () {
        guard managedObjectContext.hasChanges else {
            return }
        do {
            try managedObjectContext.save()
        } catch {
            print(error)
        }
    }
}
```

4. After implementing the stack, we must use it. Let's add it as a property to the
    SceneDelegate class:

```
class SceneDelegate: UIResponder, UIWindowSceneDelegate {
    private let coreDataStack =
        CoreDataStack(modelName: "ContactsModel")
    //...
}
```

5. `NSManagedObjectContext` must then be injected into the View environment:

```
class SceneDelegate: UIResponder, UIWindowSceneDelegate {
    func scene(_ scene: UIScene, willConnectTo
      session: UISceneSession, options connectionOptions:
        UIScene.ConnectionOptions) {
        let contentView = ContentView()
            .environment(\.managedObjectContext,
                coreDataStack.managedObjectContext)
        //...
    }
}
```

6. Something else we need to do is save all the changes before the app goes into the background. For this, we'll call the `save()` function of the `coreDataStack` object, which can be found in the `sceneDidEnterBackground()` function of the `SceneDelegate` class:

```
class SceneDelegate: UIResponder, UIWindowSceneDelegate {
    func sceneDidEnterBackground(_ scene: UIScene) {
        coreDataStack.save()
    }
}
```

7. Finally, we can access `managedObjectContext` from the `ContentView` class:

```
struct ContentView: View {
    @Environment(\.managedObjectContext)
    var managedObjectContext

    var body: some View {
        Text("\(managedObjectContext)")
    }
}
```

By running the app, we can see that `ManagedObjectContext` is valid:

Figure 11.3 – NSManagedObjectContext in SwiftUI

How it works...

In this recipe, we learned how to create a container for a Core Data database. In a SwiftUI architecture, Apple gives us a strong indication of how to use a Core Data stack in the app; that is, is passing `NSManagedObjectContext` into `Environment`.

This context is not needed if the view just reads data, as shown in the *Showing Core Data objects with @FetchRequest* recipe next, but it is necessary if any other operations are performed on the store, such as adding or deleting objects.

To better understand the code shown in this recipe, I encourage you to create another SwiftUI Core Data project. In this new project, add some support for Core Data during the creation of the project so that Xcode will use its template. By doing this, you can compare that code with our `CoreDataStack` implementation to see their similarities and differences.

Showing Core Data objects with @FetchRequest

Probably the most critical feature of persistent storage is its fetching capability. Indeed, we could prebuild a Core Data database and bundle it with our app, which would just read and present the data. An example of this kind of app could be a catalogue for a clothes shop, which contains the clothes for the current season. When the new fashion season arrives, a new app with a new database is created and released.

Given the importance of having this skill, Apple have added a powerful property wrapper to make fetching data from a repository almost trivial. In this recipe, we'll create a simple contact list visualizer in SwiftUI. The objects in the repository will be added the first time we run the app, and ContentView will present the contacts in a list view.

Getting ready

Let's create a SwiftUI app called FetchContactsApp. Ensure that you check the **Use Core Data** checkbox, as shown in the following screenshot:

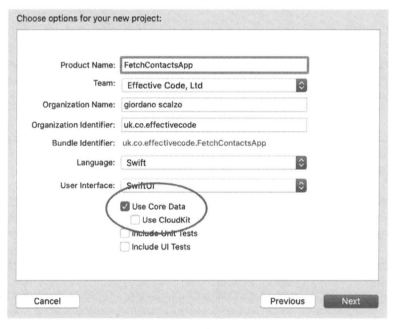

Figure 11.4 – Creating a SwiftUI app with Core Data

How to do it...

In this recipe, we will add a bunch of hardcoded contacts at app startup, ensuring that we only do this the first time the app launches.

In ContentView, we are going to use the @FetchRequest property wrapper to automatically populate a reactive list of contacts to be presented. Let's get started:

1. The first thing we must do is create the Core Data model. To do this, select the FetchContactsApp.xcdatamodeld file and do the following:

   a. Add a new entity called Contact (1)

   b. Add three string attributes called firstName, lastName, and phoneNumber (2)

   c. Check that **Codegen** is set to **Class Definition** (3)

   The following screenshot shows the steps you must follow to update the model:

Figure 11.5 – Creating the Core Data model

2. Setting **Codegen** to **Class Definition** means that Xcode creates a convenience class that will manage the entities; in our case, it creates a `Contact` class. To simplify this interaction, let's add a static function that will create a full `Contact` object:

```
import CoreData

extension Contact {
    static func insert(in context:
NSManagedObjectContext,
                       firstName: String,
                       lastName: String,
                       phoneNumber: String) {
        let contact = Contact(context: context)
        contact.firstName = firstName
        contact.lastName = lastName
        contact.phoneNumber = phoneNumber
    }
}
```

3. Now, let's create a function that will insert a bunch of contacts, but only if this is the first time we're running the app; otherwise, the repository will be filled with duplicates. To check that this is the first time we're running the app, we need to set a flag in `UserDefaults`.

    For this purpose, I've created a `Contacts.swift` file that you can find in this book's GitHub repository at `https://github.com/PacktPublishing/SwiftUI-Cookbook/blob/master/Chapter11%20-%20Handling%20Core%20Data%20and%20SwiftUI/02%20-%20Showing%20Core%20Data%20objects%20with%20%40FetchRequest/FetchContactsApp/FetchContactsApp/Contacts.swift`. It contains the following contents:

```
func addContacts(to managedObjectContext:
NSManagedObjectContext) {
    guard UserDefaults
        .standard.bool(forKey: "alreadyRun") == false else {
        return
    }
    UserDefaults.standard.set(true, forKey: "alreadyRun")

    [("Daenerys", lastName: "Targaryen", "02079460803"),
```

```
        ("Bran", lastName: "Stark", "02079460071"),
        ("Jon", lastName: "Snow", "02079460874"),
        //… the rest is in the GitHub repo
        ("Cersei", lastName: "Lannister", "02890180492"),
        ("Davos", lastName: "Seaworth", "02079460848"),
        ("Sansa", lastName: "Stark", "02890180764")]
            .forEach { (firstName, lastName, phoneNumber) in
            Contact.insert(in: managedObjectContext,
                            firstName: firstName,
                            lastName: lastName,
                            phoneNumber: phoneNumber)
            try? managedObjectContext.save()
        }
    }
```

4. In the `SceneDelegate` class, we are going to call the `addContacts()` function
    before injecting `managedObjectContext` into our `Environment`:

```
class SceneDelegate: UIResponder, UIWindowSceneDelegate {
    func scene(_ scene: UIScene, willConnectTo
    session: UISceneSession, options connectionOptions:
        UIScene.ConnectionOptions) {
        let context = (UIApplication.shared.delegate
            as! AppDelegate).persistentContainer.
            viewContext
        addContacts(to: context)
        //...
    }
}
```

5. Now, let's move on to the `ContentView` class, where we'll add the list of contacts via the `@FetchRequest` property wrapper:

```swift
struct ContentView: View {
    @FetchRequest(
        sortDescriptors: [
            NSSortDescriptor(keyPath: \Contact.lastName,
                             ascending: true),
            NSSortDescriptor(keyPath: \Contact.firstName,
                             ascending: true),
        ]
    )
    var contacts: FetchedResults<Contact>
}
```

6. Finally, the body will simply render the list of contacts:

```swift
var body: some View {
    List(contacts, id: \.self) { contact in
        Text(contact.firstName ?? "-")
        Text(contact.lastName ?? "-")
        Spacer()
        Text(contact.phoneNumber ?? "-")
    }
}
```

Upon running the app, we'll see our list of contacts:

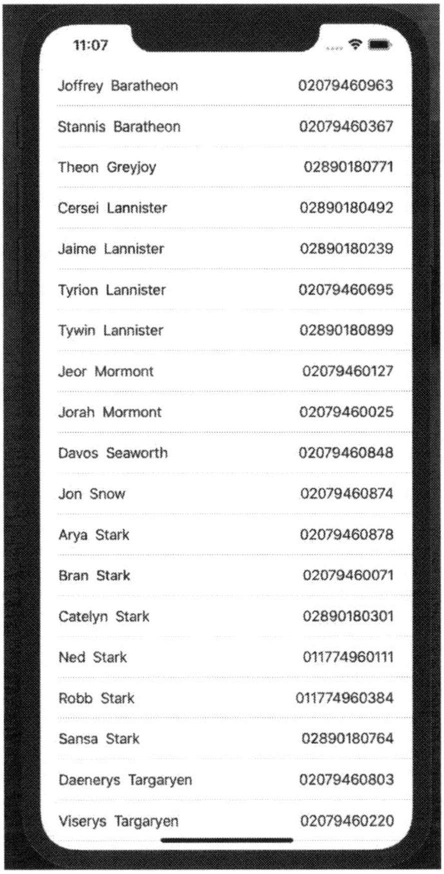

Figure 11.6 – List of contacts from Core Data

How it works...

All the magic of our SwiftUI Core Data integration resides in the `@FetchRequest` property wrapper, where we set our SortDescriptors and they magically populate the `contacts` property.

`@FetchRequest` infers the type of the entity from the type of the property so that we don't need to provide the type of the object to fetch.

`@FetchRequest` also accepts an optional `Predicate` as a parameter so that we can filter the fetched data before it's extracted from the repository.

@FetchRequest retrieves an object from managedObjectContext and expects it in @Environment(\.managedObjectContext). As you may recall, in SceneDelegate, we are injecting managedObjectContext into @Environment(\.managedObjectContext) so that our code will work without any further configuration needing to be made.

Adding Core Data objects to a SwiftUI view

A store without any data is useless. In this recipe, we will learn how easy it is to implement a function that will add data to Core Data in SwiftUI.

In this recipe, we are going to implement a simple Contact app where we can add storable contact profiles in a Core Data database.

Getting ready

Let's create a SwiftUI app called AddContactsApp, ensuring that the **Use Core Data** checkbox is checked, as shown in the following screenshot:

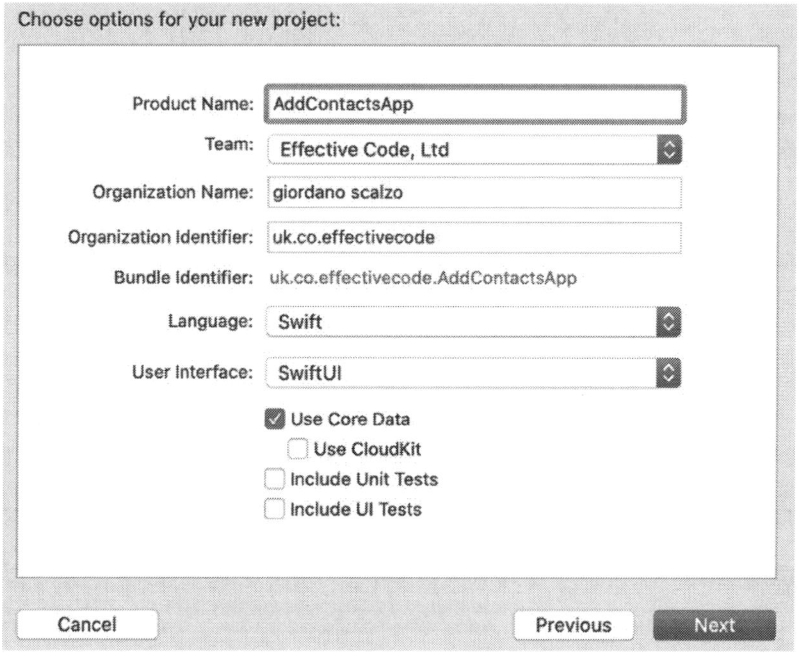

Figure 11.7 – Creating a SwiftUI app with Core Data

How to do it...

Besides adding profiles, we must present our list of already saved contacts. For this, we are going to reuse some of the code from the *Showing Core Data objects with @FetchRequest* recipe.

To add a profile, we are going to implement a simple modal view with three text fields: two for the full name and one for the phone number. Let's get started:

1. The first thing we must do is create the Core Data model. To do this, select the `AddContactsApp.xcdatamodeld` file and do the following:

    a. Add a new entity called `Contact` (1)

    b. Add three string attributes called `firstName`, `lastName`, and `phoneNumber` (2)

    c. Check that **Codegen** is set to **Class Definition** (3)

    The following screenshot shows the steps for updating the model:

Figure 11.8 – Creating the Core Data model

2. Now, let's add a convenience extension to the generated `Contact` class to simplify the creation of a new persistent object:

```
import CoreData
extension Contact {
    static func insert(in context:
      NSManagedObjectContext,
                        firstName: String,
                        lastName: String,
                        phoneNumber: String) {
        let contact = Contact(context: context)
        contact.firstName = firstName
        contact.lastName = lastName
        contact.phoneNumber = phoneNumber
    }
}
```

3. Let's continue inside the `ContentView` struct. This is where we'll add the contact list:

```
struct ContentView: View {
    @FetchRequest(
        sortDescriptors: [
            NSSortDescriptor(keyPath: \Contact.lastName,
                             ascending: true),
            NSSortDescriptor(keyPath: \Contact.firstName,
                             ascending: true),
        ]
    )
    var contacts: FetchedResults<Contact>
}
```

4. The `body` function simply iterates on this `contacts` list and presents each profile. The list is embedded in a `NavigationView`:

```
var body: some View {
    NavigationView {
        List(contacts, id: \.self) { contact in
            Text(contact.firstName ?? "-")
```

```
                    Text(contact.lastName ?? "-")
                    Spacer()
                    Text(contact.phoneNumber ?? "-")
                }
                .navigationBarTitle("Contacts", displayMode:
                    .inline)
            }
        }
```

5. To present a modal so that we can add a contact, we'll add a button to the navigation bar that toggles an @State flag:

```
    struct ContentView: View {
        //...
        @State
        Private var isAddContactPresented = false
        var body: some View {
            NavigationView {
                //...
            }
            .navigationBarTitle("Contacts", displayMode:
                .inline)
            .navigationBarItems(trailing:
                Button {
                    isAddContactPresented.toggle()
                } label: {
                    Image(systemName: "plus")
                        .font(.headline)
                })
            }
        }
    }
```

6. If the flag is true, we present our View so that we can add the necessary contact details:

```
    struct ContentView: View {
        //...
        @Environment(\.managedObjectContext)
```

```
        private var managedObjectContext
    var body: some View {
            //...
            .navigationBarItems(trailing:
                //...
        })
            .sheet(isPresented:
                $isAddContactPresented) {
                AddNewContact(isAddContactPresented:
                    $isAddContactPresented)
                .environment(\.managedObjectContext,
                        managedObjectContext)
            }
        }
    }
}
```

7. The `AddNewContactView` struct has three text fields for the profile details. These are for the first name, last name, and phone number:

```
struct AddNewContact: View {
    @Environment(\.managedObjectContext)
    private var managedObjectContext

    @Binding
    var isAddContactPresented: Bool
    @State
    var firstName = ""
    @State
    var lastName = ""
    @State
    var phoneNumber = ""
}
```

8. The body function renders the text fields in a vertical stack, embedded in a `NavigationView`:

```
var body: some View {
    NavigationView {
        VStack(spacing: 16) {
            TextField("First Name", text: $firstName)
            TextField("Last Name", text: $lastName)
            TextField("Phone Number", text: $phoneNumber)
                .keyboardType(.phonePad)
            Spacer()
        }
        .padding(16)
        .navigationBarTitle(Text("Add A New Contact"),
            displayMode: .inline)
    }
}
```

9. Inside our NavigationView, we need to add a button for when we have finished filling in the contact details:

```
var body: some View {
    //...
        .navigationBarTitle(Text("Add A New Contact"),
                                displayMode: .inline)
        .navigationBarItems(trailing:
            Button(action: saveContact) {
                Image(systemName: "checkmark")
                    .font(.headline)
            }
            .disabled(isDisabled))
    }
}
```

10. This button is only enabled if all the fields have been filled in:

```
private var isDisabled: Bool {
    firstName.isEmpty || lastName.isEmpty ||
        phoneNumber.isEmpty
}
```

11. When the button is clicked, we insert a new `Contact` into the database and we save it:

```
private func saveContact() {
    Contact.insert(in: managedObjectContext,
                   firstName: firstName,
                   lastName: lastName,
                   phoneNumber: phoneNumber)
    do {
        try managedObjectContext.save()
    } catch {
        print(error)
    }
    isAddContactPresented.toggle()
}
```

Now, we can run the app, add contacts, and see them visualized in the list:

Figure 11.9 – Adding a contact to the list

How it works...

As we have seen, the code for adding a new object to the Core Data database creates a new `Contact` in `managedObjectContext` and saves it. In this case, it is pretty obvious that the context has some changes that must be saved. Still, in general, since saving is a costly operation, it is better to check if any changes have been made before saving the context. For this, we could use something similar to the following:

```
guard managedObjectContext.hasChanges else { return }
do {
    try managedObjectContext.save()
} catch {
    print(error)
}
```

Again, for simplicity, we didn't add any error recovery functions, so if there is an error while saving the contact, the app prints an error in the console. I strongly recommend enriching this app, such as by adding something to warn the user that the contact wasn't saved in case of an error, and maybe try again.

Filtering Core Data requests using a predicate

An essential characteristic of Core Data is the possibility of filtering the results of a `FetchRequest`, so that only the objects that match a filter are retrieved from the repository and transformed into actual objects.

A predicate is a condition the Core Data objects must satisfy to be fetched; for example, the name must be shorter than 5 characters, or the age of a person should be greater than 18. The conditions in a predicate can also be composite, such as in *fetch all the data where the name is equal to "Lewis" and the age is greater than 18*.

Even though the property wrapper accepts `NSPredicate`, which is a filter for Core Data, the problem is that this cannot be dynamic, meaning that it must be created at the beginning. It cannot change during the life cycle of the view as a result of a search text field, for example.

In this recipe, we'll learn how to create a dynamic filter for a contact list, where the user can restrict the list of the visualized contacts with a search text field. When we set something in that search field, we are filtering the contacts whose surname starts with the value of the search field.

Getting ready

Let's create a SwiftUI app called `FilterContactsApp`, ensuring that the **Use Core Data** checkbox is checked, as shown in the following screenshot:

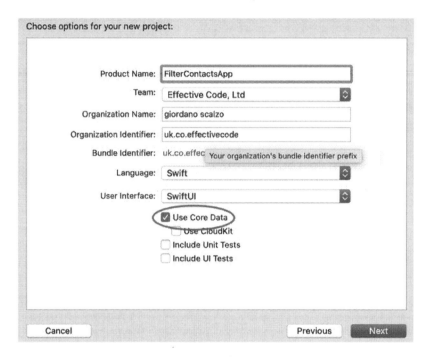

Figure 11.10 – Creating a SwiftUI app with Core Data

How to do it...

To show our contacts, we are going to reuse part of the code provided in the *Showing Core Data objects with @FetchRequest* recipe. I suggest that you go back to it if you want to gain a better insight.

Now, we are going to add a `SearchBar` view so that we can filter the results from the database. Follow these steps:

1. The first step is to create the Core Data model. To do this, select the `FilterContactsApp.xcdatamodeld` file and do the following:

    a. Add a new entity called `Contact` (1)

    b. Add three string attributes called `firstName`, `lastName`, and `phoneNumber` (2)

    c. Check that **Codegen** is set to **Class Definition** (3)

The following screenshot shows the steps that need to be followed to update the model:

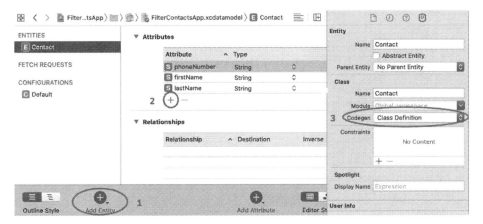

Figure 11.11 – Creating the Core Data model

2. Setting **Codegen** to **Class Definition** means that Xcode creates a convenience class that will manage our entities. In our case, it creates a `Contact` class. To simplify this interaction, let's add a static function that will create a full `Contact` object:

```
import CoreData


extension Contact {
    static func insert(in context:
        NSManagedObjectContext,
                           firstName: String,
                           lastName: String,
                           phoneNumber: String) {
        let contact = Contact(context: context)
        contact.firstName = firstName
        contact.lastName = lastName
        contact.phoneNumber = phoneNumber
    }
}
```

3. Now, let's create a function that will insert a bunch of contacts, but only if this is the first time we've run the app; otherwise, the repository will be filled with duplicates. To check that this is the first time we've run the app, we need to set a flag in `UserDefaults`.

    You can find the remainder of the following file, which contains the `addContacts()` function, in this book's GitHub repository at `https://github.com/PacktPublishing/SwiftUI-Cookbook/blob/master/Chapter11%20-%20Handling%20Core%20Data%20and%20SwiftUI/04%20-%20Filter%20Core%20Data%20requests%20using%20a%20predicate/FilterContactsApp/FilterContactsApp/Contacts.swift`:

```swift
func addContacts(to managedObjectContext:
NSManagedObjectContext) {
    guard UserDefaults
        .standard.bool(forKey: "alreadyRun") == false else {
        return
    }

    UserDefaults.standard.set(true, forKey: "alreadyRun")

    [("Daenerys", lastName: "Targaryen", "02079460803"),
    ("Bran", lastName: "Stark", "02079460071"),
    ("Jon", lastName: "Snow", "02079460874"),
    //… the rest is in the github repo
    ("Cersei", lastName: "Lannister", "02890180492"),
    ("Davos", lastName: "Seaworth", "02079460848"),
    ("Sansa", lastName: "Stark", "02890180764")]
        .forEach { (firstName, lastName, phoneNumber) in
        Contact.insert(in: managedObjectContext,
                            firstName: firstName,
                            lastName: lastName,
                            phoneNumber: phoneNumber)
        try? managedObjectContext.save()
    }
}
```

4. In `SceneDelegate`, we are going to call this function before injecting `managedObjectContext` into our `Environment`:

```
class SceneDelegate: UIResponder, UIWindowSceneDelegate {
    func scene(_ scene: UIScene, willConnectTo
                                session: UISceneSession,
    options connectionOptions: UIScene.ConnectionOptions) {
        let context = (UIApplication.shared.delegate
                        as! AppDelegate)
                            .persistentContainer.viewContext
        addContacts(to: context)
        //...
    }
}
```

5. Now, let's move on to the `ContentView` class. Here, we want to have a search bar field and a list of our filtered contacts. Since we cannot have a dynamic predicate in the `@FetchRequest` property wrapper, we'll implement a dedicated view component to show the filtered contacts where we inject the search text written by the user.

However, SwiftUI doesn't have a component for `SearchBar`, so we are going to implement it by wrapping the UIKit `UISearchBar` inside a `UIViewRepresentable` component, like so:

```
struct SearchBar: UIViewRepresentable {
    @Binding var text: String

    func makeUIView(context:
        UIViewRepresentableContext<SearchBar>)
        -> UISearchBar {
        let searchBar = UISearchBar(frame: .zero)
        searchBar.searchBarStyle = .minimal
        return searchBar
    }

    func updateUIView(_ uiView: UISearchBar,
```

```
        context: UIViewRepresentableContext<SearchBar>) {
     uiView.text = text
   }
 }
```

6. Now, we must add a delegate to `UISearchBar`. We do this by adding a
    `Coordinator` to the component:

```
struct SearchBar: UIViewRepresentable {
    class Coordinator: NSObject, UISearchBarDelegate {
        @Binding
        var text: String
        init(text: Binding<String>) {
            _text = text
        }
        func searchBar(_ searchBar: UISearchBar,
                textDidChange searchText: String) {
            text = searchText
        }
    }

    func makeCoordinator() -> SearchBar.Coordinator {
        Coordinator(text: $text)
    }

    func makeUIView(context:

UIViewRepresentableContext<SearchBar>)
                                -> UISearchBar {
        let searchBar = UISearchBar(frame: .zero)
        searchBar.delegate = context.coordinator
        //...
    }
}
```

7. Our `SearchBar` can now be added to the body of our `ContentView`:

```
struct ContentView: View {
    @State
    private var searchText : String = ""

    var body: some View {
        NavigationView {
            VStack {
                SearchBar(text: $searchText)
                FilteredContacts(filter: searchText)
            }
            .navigationBarTitle("Contacts",
                                displayMode: .inline)
        }
    }
}
```

8. In the `FilteredContacts` view, we must implement a `FetchRequest` with an `NSPredicate`, with the passed parameter as a condition:

```
struct FilteredContacts: View {
    var fetchRequest: FetchRequest<Contact>

    init(filter: String) {
        let predicate: NSPredicate? = filter.isEmpty ?
            nil :
            NSPredicate(format: "lastName BEGINSWITH %@",
                filter)
        fetchRequest = FetchRequest<Contact>(
            sortDescriptors: [
                NSSortDescriptor(keyPath: \Contact.
                    lastName, ascending: true),
                NSSortDescriptor(keyPath: \Contact.
                    firstName, ascending: true)],
            predicate: predicate)
    }
}
```

9. The body of the `FilteredContacts` view simply presents the contacts in a
    `List` view:

```
var body: some View {
    List(fetchRequest.wrappedValue, id: \.self) { contact
      in
        Text(contact.firstName ?? "-")
        Text(contact.lastName ?? "-")
        Spacer()
        Text(contact.phoneNumber ?? "-")
    }
}
```

Upon running the app, we can see that changing the text in our `SearchBar`
changes the list of visualized contacts accordingly:

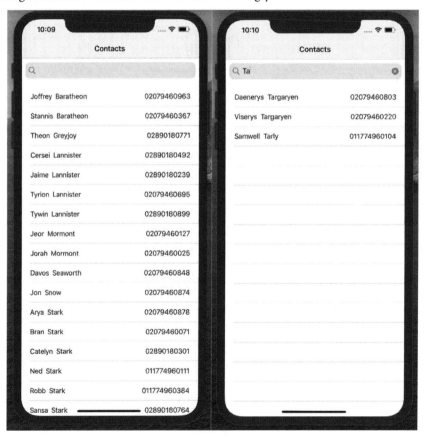

Figure 11.12 – Core Data dynamic filtering

How it works...

Taking inspiration from the *Showing Core Data objects with @FetchRequest* recipe, it would have been nice to write a definition such as the following:

```
@FetchRequest(
    sortDescriptors: [
        NSSortDescriptor(keyPath: \Contact.lastName,
                         ascending: true),
        NSSortDescriptor(keyPath: \Contact.firstName,
                         ascending: true),
    ],
    predicate: NSPredicate(format: "lastName BEGINSWITH %@",
        filter))
```

Unfortunately, this is not possible (at least yet), since the filter is an `@State` variable that can change during the life cycle of the view.

To overcome this limitation, we created a dedicated component, `FilteredContacts`, to present the filtered contacts, injecting the text that acts as a filter.

In the `FilteredContacts` component, we create a `FetchRequest` with the text we passed as a parameter into `.init()` as a filter for the `FetcRequest` class.

The `FetchRequest` component, via `managedObjectContext`, retrieves the objects and stores them internally. We can reach them via the `.wrapped()` function. Since these objects are returned as a collection, we can iterate them as follows:

```
List(fetchRequest.wrappedValue, id: \.self) { contact in
    //...
}
```

This is a solution that follows the SwiftUI philosophy: split the logic into smaller components that can be represented as a `View`.

Beside the actual problem this solves, I think that, in this recipe, we learned how to solve this problem in the SwiftUI way. This is a process that can be used every time we face a similar problem in SwiftUI code.

Deleting Core Data objects from a SwiftUI view

How can you delete objects from a Core Data repository? Removing objects is almost as important as adding them. In this recipe, we'll learn how to integrate the Core Data delete options into a SwiftUI app.

Getting ready

Let's create a SwiftUI app called `DeleteContactsApp`, ensuring that we check the **Use Core Data** checkbox, as shown in the following screenshot:

Figure 11.13 – Creating a SwiftUI app with Core Data

How to do it...

We are going to reuse part of the code provided in the *Showing Core Data objects with @ FetchRequest* recipe. Please refer to that recipe if you want to find out more.

Let's get started:

1. The first step is to create the Core Data model. To do this, select the
    `DeleteContactsApp.xcdatamodeld` file and do the following:

    a. Add a new entity called `Contact` (1)

    b. Add three string attributes called `firstName`, `lastName`, and `phoneNumber`
    (2)

    c. Check that **Codegen** is set to **Class Definition** (3)

    The following screenshot shows the steps that need to be followed to update
    the model:

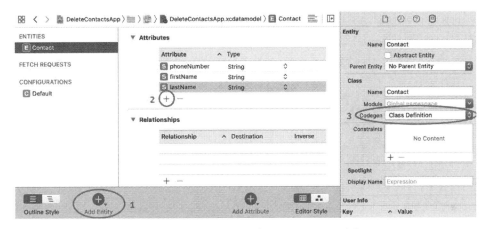

Figure 11.14 – Creating the Core Data model

2. Setting **Codegen** to **Class Definition** means that Xcode creates a convenience class
    that will manage our entities. In our case, it creates a `Contact` class. To simplify
    this interaction, let's add a static function that will create a full `Contact` object:

```
import CoreData


extension Contact {
    static func insert(in context:
        NSManagedObjectContext,
                       firstName: String,
                       lastName: String,
                       phoneNumber: String) {
        let contact = Contact(context: context)
        contact.firstName = firstName
```

```
            contact.lastName = lastName
            contact.phoneNumber = phoneNumber
        }
    }
```

3. Now, let's create a function that will insert a bunch of contacts, but only if it is the first time we've run the app; otherwise, the repository will be filled with duplicates. To check if this is the first time we've run the app, we will set a flag in UserDefaults.

   You can find the remainder of the following file, which contains the addContacts() function, in this book's GitHub repository at https://github.com/PacktPublishing/SwiftUI-Cookbook/blob/master/Chapter11%20-%20Handling%20Core%20Data%20and%20SwiftUI/05%20-%20Deleting%20Core%20Data%20objects%20from%20a%20SwiftUI%20view/DeleteContactsApp/DeleteContactsApp/Contacts.swift:

```
func addContacts(to managedObjectContext:
NSManagedObjectContext) {
    guard UserDefaults
    .standard.bool(forKey: "alreadyRun") == false else {
        return
    }
    UserDefaults.standard.set(true, forKey: "alreadyRun")

    [("Daenerys", lastName: "Targaryen", "02079460803"),
    ("Bran", lastName: "Stark", "02079460071"),
    ("Jon", lastName: "Snow", "02079460874"),
    //… the rest is in the github repo
    ("Cersei", lastName: "Lannister", "02890180492"),
    ("Davos", lastName: "Seaworth", "02079460848"),
    ("Sansa", lastName: "Stark", "02890180764")]
        .forEach { (firstName, lastName, phoneNumber) in
            Contact.insert(in: managedObjectContext,
                           firstName: firstName,
                           lastName: lastName,
```

```
                    phoneNumber: phoneNumber)
        try? managedObjectContext.save()
    }
}
```

4. In `SceneDelegate`, we are going to call this function before injecting `managedObjectContext` into our `Environment`:

```
class SceneDelegate: UIResponder, UIWindowSceneDelegate {
    func scene(_ scene: UIScene, willConnectTo
        session: UISceneSession, options connectionOptions:
            UIScene.ConnectionOptions) {
        let context = (UIApplication.shared.delegate
            as! AppDelegate).persistentContainer.viewContext
        addContacts(to: context)
        //...
    }
}
```

5. Now, let's move on to the `ContentView` struct. This is where we'll add the @ `FetchRequest` property wrapper so that we can list our contacts:

```
struct ContentView: View {
    @Environment(\.managedObjectContext)
    var managedObjectContext

    @FetchRequest(
        sortDescriptors: [
            NSSortDescriptor(keyPath: \Contact.lastName,
                ascending: true),
            NSSortDescriptor(keyPath: \Contact.firstName,
                ascending: true),
        ]
    )
    var contacts: FetchedResults<Contact>
}
```

6. In the body, we iterate over the contacts, rendering each one in a horizontal stack:

```
var body: some View {
    List {
        ForEach(contacts, id: \.self) { contact in
            HStack {
                Text(contact.firstName ?? "-")
                Text(contact.lastName ?? "-")
                Spacer()
                Text(contact.phoneNumber ?? "-")
            }
        }
    }
}
```

7. So far, this is the code we've been using to render a list of objects from Core Data. Now, let's add the `.onDelete()` modifier, which will call the `deleteContact()` function:

```
var body: some View {
    List {
        ForEach(contacts, id: \.self) { contact in
            //...
        }.onDelete(perform: deleteContact)
    }
}
```

8. The `deleteContact()` function simply fetches the `Contact` object from the list and removes it from the `managedObjectContext` instance:

```
private func deleteContact(at offsets: IndexSet) {
    guard let index = offsets.first else {
        return
    }

    managedObjectContext.delete(contacts[index])
    try? managedObjectContext.save()
}
```

When you run the app, the cells can now be swiped. Upon swiping a cell to the left, the standard red **Delete** button will be shown so that you can remove that cell:

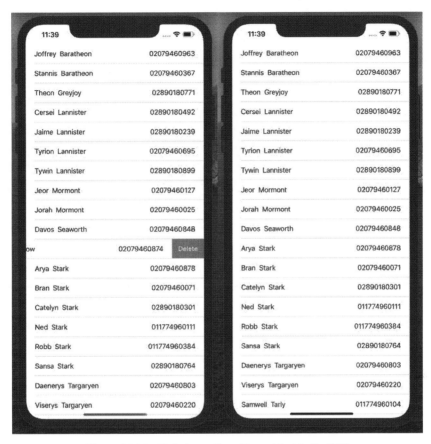

Figure 11.15 – Deleting a Core Data object in SwiftUI

How it works...

If you want more information regarding how to create objects and how to render them in the View, please read the *Showing Core Data objects with @FetchRequest* recipe in this chapter. Here, we are only looking at the *delete* feature.

As you have seen, the way you can integrate a `delete()` function into Core Data from SwiftUI is just a matter of calling the function with the right object.

Here, we added a `.onDelete()` modifier to the `ForEach` component inside the `List` view. From there, we called a function to delete the selected object.

The `.onDelete()` modifier is called with the index of the row to remove as a parameter. However, to delete an object in Core Data, we must have the exact `ManagedObject`.

Luckily, we have the list of this `ManagedObject` in the `contacts` property, which means we can refer to the object to delete using that property and its index.

12
Cross-Platform SwiftUI

SwiftUI makes it easy to take some or all of the code written for one Apple platform, and use it to create an app for another platform in the Apple ecosystem. For example, in this chapter, we start by creating an iOS app and then reusing some of the components to create a macOS and a watchOS app.

When using Cross-Platform development in SwiftUI, we share common resources between each platform, while creating other resources that are platform-specific. For example, models may be shared across platforms, but certain images and SwiftUI views would be made platform-specific. Creating platform-specific views allows us to follow platform-specific best-practice design guidelines and improve the user experience provided by our apps.

This chapter covers some of the Cross-Platform functionalities of SwiftUI with the following recipes:

- Creating an iOS app in SwiftUI
- Creating the macOS version of the iOS app
- Creating the watchOS version of the iOS app

Technical requirements

The code in this chapter is based on Xcode 12.

You can find the code in the book's GitHub repo under the path `https://github.com/PacktPublishing/SwiftUI-Cookbook/tree/master/Chapter12%20-%20Cross-Platform%20SwiftUI`.

Creating an iOS app in SwiftUI

Before going Cross-Platform with your development, we will first create an iOS app. This app will be similar to the app created during our work on the *Using mock data for previews* recipe in *Chapter 3, Viewing while Building with SwiftUI Preview*. The version created for this recipe will be made more modular to allow for code reuse across platforms and the resources will not be stored in the preview section of the app.

The app will display a list of insects where you can click on any insect in the list to see more details about it. The data regarding the insects will be read from a JSON file and made available to our views through the use of an `@Environment` variable.

Getting ready

Let's create a new single-view iOS app in SwiftUI named `Cross-Platform`.

How to do it

We will set up the model and data source used in this recipe and then proceed to create the views and subviews needed to display the list of insects and the details of each one. The steps are as follows:

1. To stay organized, let's create a group to store our models:

    a. Right-click on the `Cross-Platform` folder in the navigation pane.

    b. Select **New Group**.

    c. Name the new folder `Models`.

2. Create a folder for the resource files used in the project:

    a. Right-click on the `Cross-Platform` folder in the navigation pane.

    b. Select **New Group**.

    c. Name the new folder `Resources`.

3. Drag and drop the `insectData.json` file from the book's `Resources` folder from GitHub into this project's `Resources` folder (`https://github.com/PacktPublishing/SwiftUI-Cookbook/tree/master/Resources/Chapter12/Recipe%2001`).

4. Click on `insectData.json` to view its content. From the data, we notice every insect has an ID, an image name, a habitat, and a description. Let's create a model to match the JSON content.

5. Select the `Models` folder from the project navigation pane:

    a. Press ⌘ + *N*.

    b. Select **Swift File**.

    c. Click **Next**.

    d. Click on the **Save As** field and enter the text `Insect`.

    e. Click **Finish**.

6. Create the `Insect struct`:

    ```swift
    struct Insect : Decodable, Identifiable{
        var id: Int
        var imageName:String
        var name:String
        var habitat:String
        var description:String
    }
    ```

7. Below the `struct` declaration, create an instance of the struct that will be used for previews:

    ```swift
    let testInsect = Insect(id: 1, imageName: "grasshopper",
        name: "grass", habitat: "pond", description: "long
            description here")
    ```

8. With the `Models` folder still selected, create the `insectData` model. We'll use the model to read the JSON file and make it available to the app:

    a. Press ⌘ + *N*.

    b. Select **Swift File**.

    c. Click **Next**.

    d. Click on the **Save As** field and enter the text `InsectData`.

    e. Click **Finish**.

9. Create an `Observable` object to store the data from the `insectData.json` file as an array of insects:

```
final class InsectData: ObservableObject {
    @Published var insects = testInsects
}
```

10. The code does not build yet because we have not yet defined the value of the `testInsects` variable. Let's read the file and decode its contents into `Insect` structs. Place this code below the class definition in the previous step:

```
var testInsects : [Insect]{
    guard let url = Bundle.main.url(forResource:
        "insectData", withExtension: "json"),

        let data = try? Data(contentsOf: url)
        else{
            return[]
    }
    let decoder   = JSONDecoder()
    let array = try?decoder.decode([Insect].self,
        from: data)
    return array ??  [testInsect]
}
```

11. The rest of the files we'll create should be placed within the `Cross-Platform` folder. Let's create a SwiftUI view named `InsectCellView`:

    a. Press ⌘+ *N*.

    b. Select **SwiftUI View**.

    c. Click **Next**.

    d. Click on the **Save As** field and enter the text `InsectCellView`.

    e. Click **Finish**.

12. The `InsectCellView` will contain the design for a row in our insect list:

```
struct InsectCellView: View {
    var insect:Insect
    var body: some View {
        HStack{
            Image(insect.imageName)
                .resizable()
                .aspectRatio(contentMode: .fit)
                .clipShape(Rectangle())
                .frame(width:100, height: 80)

            VStack(alignment: .leading){
                Text(insect.name).font(.title)
                Text(insect.habitat)
            }.padding(.vertical)
        }
    }
}
```

13. To preview the design, pass the `testInsect` variable to the `InsectCellView` function call in `InsectCellView_Previews`:

```
InsectCellView(insect: testInsect)
```

14. The `InsectCellView` preview should look as follows:

Figure 12.1 – InsectCellView preview

15. We will also show the details regarding a particular insect in its own view. Let's create a SwiftUI view called `InsectDetailView` (the steps are similar to *steps 21 to 25* of this recipe). The `InsectDetailView` should display the attributes of the insect passed to it using a `VStack`:

```
struct InsectDetailView: View {
    var insect:Insect
    var body: some View {
        VStack{
            Text(insect.name)
                .font(.largeTitle)
            Image(insect.imageName)
                .resizable()
                .aspectRatio(contentMode: .fit)
```

```
                Text("Habitat")
                    .font(.title)
                Text(insect.habitat)
                Text("Description")
                    .font(.title)
                    .padding()
                Text(insect.description)
            }
        }
    }
```

16. Preview the design by passing the `testInsect` variable to the
    `InsectDetailView()` function call in the `previews` section:

```
static var previews: some View {
        InsectDetailView(insect: testInsect)
    }
```

17. The `InsectDetailView` preview should look as follows:

Figure 12.2 – InsectDetailView preview

18. Now create a SwiftUI view called `InsectListView` (the steps are similar to *steps 21* to *25* in this recipe).

19. Above the body variable of our `InsectListView` SwiftUI view, declare and initialize our `@EnvironmentObject` that contains the insect data as an array of `Insect` structs:

```
@EnvironmentObject var insectData: InsectData
```

20. Within the `InsectListView` body, implement a `List` view that iterates over the data and displays it using the `InsectCellView` SwiftUI views:

```
List{
        ForEach(insectData.insects){insect in
            NavigationLink(
            destination: InsectDetailView(insect:
                insect)){
                InsectCellView(insect: insect)
            }
        }
    }.navigationBarTitle("Insects",displayMode:
        .inline)
```

21. To preview the design, add the `.environmentObject()` modifier to the `InsectListView()` function call in our canvas preview code:

```
static var previews: some View {
        InsectListView().environmentObject(InsectData())
    }
```

22. The `InsectListView` preview should look as follows:

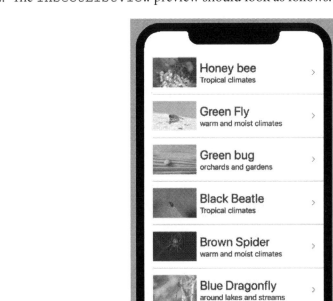

Figure 12.3 – InsectListView preview

23. So far, we have not provided a path for the user to view our list when running the app. The `ContentView.swift` file is the entry point for the app. Let's set it up. Add the `@Enviroment` variable above the `body` variable:

```
@EnvironmentObject var insectData: InsectData
```

24. Add a `NavigationView` and `InsectListView` to the body variable:

```
var body: some View {
        NavigationView{
            InsectListView()
        }
    }
```

25. Add the `.enviromentObject()` modifier to the `ContentView_Previews` to fetch our data:

```
static var previews: some View {
        ContentView().environmentObject(InsectData())
    }
```

26. The `ContentView` preview should look as follows:

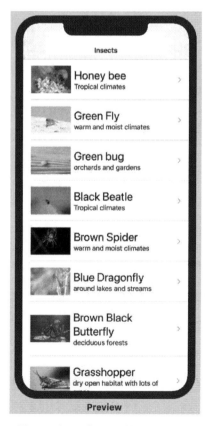

Figure 12.4 – ContentView preview

27. Now you should be able to run the preview in the Xcode canvas to view the list of insects and insect details. However, running the program in an iPhone simulator presents a blank screen. Let's solve this by passing our `.environmentObject()` modifier to our `scene` function in the `SceneDelegate.swift` file:

```
func scene(_ scene: UIScene, willConnectTo session:
    UISceneSession, options connectionOptions: UIScene.
    ConnectionOptions) {

    ...

    // Create the SwiftUI view that provides the
    // window contents.
    let contentView = ContentView().
        environmentObject(InsectData())

    ...

    }

}
```

Congrats! You can now view the list of insects from the device previews or within a simulated device.

How it works

Our goal in this recipe was to read insect data from a JSON file and display the content in our SwiftUI app. To get started, we observed the raw JSON data and created a struct that holds the data – that is, the `Insect` struct.

The `Insect` struct implements the `Decodable` and `Identifiable` protocols. The `Decodable` protocol allows us to decode data from our `insectData.json` file and store it in our `Insect` struct. The `Identifiable` protocol allows us to *uniquely* identify each insect in an array and use the `ForEach` loop without an `id` parameter.

The `InsectData.swift` file is the most important component of this recipe. It is used to read data from the `insectData.json` file and store it in an `ObservableObject` called `InsectData`. The `Observable` object contains the `@Published` variable called `insects`. The `Observable` objects allow us to share data between multiple views.

We used a modular app design since our goal is to create a Cross-Platform application. Each view handles a single task. The `InsectCellView` SwiftUI view takes an insect parameter and displays its content horizontally in an `HStack`.

The `InsectListView` SwiftUI view iterates through our insect data and displays the content in a list where each row is an `InsectCellView` SwiftUI view.

When a cell in the `InsectListView` is clicked, the app opens an `InsectDetailView` that contains the full information we have regarding the selected insect.

Creating the macOS version of the iOS app

Our app's iOS version showed a list of insects in one view, and details regarding the selected insect in a separate view because of the limited amount of space available on a phone. However, a laptop screen has a larger amount of screen space. We can display the list of insects on the left side of the screen, and the details regarding the selected insect on the right side.

Getting ready

Download the chapter materials from GitHub:

```
https://github.com/PacktPublishing/SwiftUI-Cookbook/tree/
master/Chapter12%20-%20Cross-Platform%20SwiftUI/02%20-%20
Create%20the%20MacOS%20version
```

Open the `StartingPoint` folder and double-click on `Cross-Platform.xcodeproj` to open the app built in the *Creating an iOS app in SwiftUI* recipe of this chapter. We will be continuing from where we left off in the first recipe.

How to do it

We'll create the macOS version of the app by reusing some components from the iOS version and creating custom components for the macOS version. The steps are as follows:

1. Create a macOS **Target...** in Xcode:

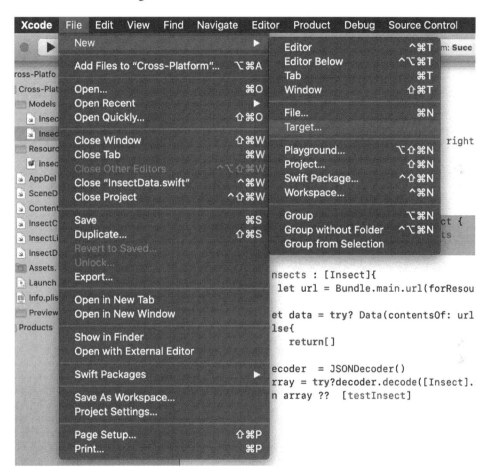

Figure 12.5 – Creating a new target

2. Choose the macOS template, scroll down, select **App**, then click **Next**:

Figure 12.6 – Selecting macOS App

3. In the next screen, enter the product name, `macOS-Cross-Platform`.

4. To preview and run macOS applications, set the Xcode active scheme to **macOS-Cross-Platform**:

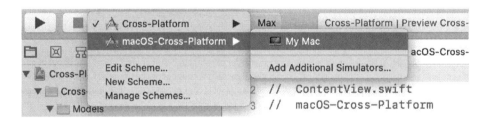

Figure 12.7 – Changing Xcode scheme to macOS-Cross-Platform

5. The preview should look as follows:

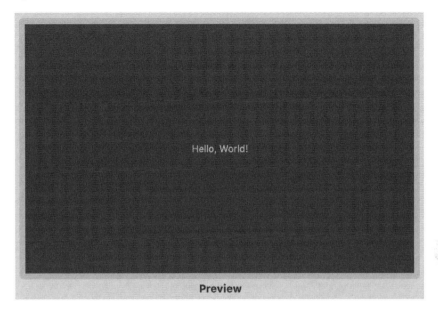

Figure 12.8 – macOS empty ContentView preview

6. For the next step, make sure the Navigator and Inspector panes are open. We will be using both panes to make certain files and resources available across targets:

Figure 12.9 – Navigator and Inspector panes in Xcode

7. Let's share files between multiple platforms. Select the `Insect.swift`, `InsectData.swift`, `insectData.json`, `InsectCellView.swift`, `InsectDetailView.swift`, and `Assets.xcassets` files located in the `Models` folder in our Cross-Platform app. To select multiple files, hold the *Command* key and click on the files listed:

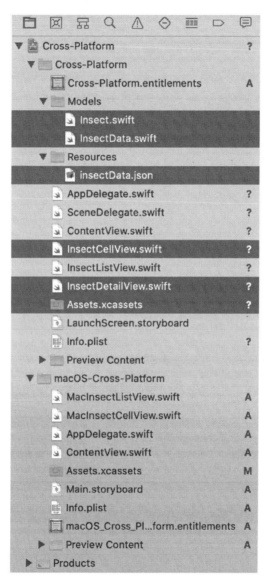

Figure 12.10 – Selecting multiple files in Xcode Navigator

8.   In the Inspector pane, check the **macOS-Cross-Platform** checkbox:

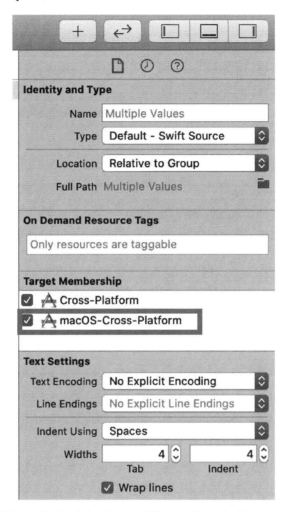

Figure 12.11 – Selecting macOS target from the Inspector

9. Create a new `MacInsectCellView` SwiftUI view in the **macOS-Cross-Platform** folder. Make sure the right platform target is selected (**macOS-Cross-Platform**):

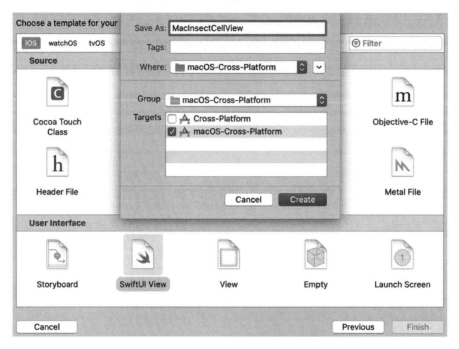

Figure 12.12 – Creating a new macOS view and selecting the right target

10. The content of `MacInsectCellView` is similar to that of `InsectCellView` in the iOS Cross-Platform app. The only difference is the size of the frame. The file content should look as follows:

```
struct MacInsectCellView: View {
    var insect:Insect
    var body: some View {
        HStack{
            Image(insect.imageName)
                .resizable()
                .aspectRatio(contentMode: .fit)
                .clipShape(Rectangle())
```

```
                    .frame(width:160, height: 100)

            VStack(alignment: .leading){
                Text(insect.name).font(.subheadline)
                Text(insect.habitat)
            }.padding(.vertical)
        }
    }
}
```

11. Pass the testInsect variable in the preview to view the design within the Xcode canvas:

```
static var previews: some View {
    MacInsectCellView(insect: testInsect)
}
```

12. The preview should look as follows:

Figure 12.13 – MacInsectCellView preview

13. Create MacInsectListView to show a list of items. Make sure the **macOS-Cross-Platform** target is selected.

14. Add the @EnvironmentObject and @Binding variables above the MacInsectListView struct's body variable:

```
@EnvironmentObject var insectData: InsectData
@Binding var selectedInsect: Insect?
```

15. Add a List view to the body. The List view should display the contents of our insectData array obtained from our environment variable. Add a .tag() modifier toMacInsectCellView so that we can use it to identify the selected cell. Also add the .listStyle() modifier that presents the list using SideBarListStyle():

```
List(selection: $selectedInsect){
            ForEach(insectData.insects){ insect in
                MacInsectCellView(insect: insect).
                tag(insect)
        }
    }.listStyle(SidebarListStyle())
```

16. Let's preview the design by passing in a constant binding and adding the .environmentObject() modifier to our MacInsectListView() function call in the preview:

```
static var previews: some View {
        MacInsectListView(selectedInsect:
        .constant(testInsect)).
            environmentObject(InsectData())
    }
```

17. The preview should look as follows:

Figure 12.14 – MacInsectListView preview

18. At this point, the code doesn't build because the selection parameter of the List view requires the item being selected to be hashable. Let's make our Insect struct implement the Hashable protocol. Open the Insect.swift file in the Cross-Platform folder and add the Hashable protocol:

```
struct Insect : Decodable, Identifiable, Hashable{

    ...

}
```

19. Open the ContentView.swift file. Add a @State variable to hold the selected insect from our insect list, and an @EnvironmentObject variable to hold the insectData we'll be displaying:

```
@State  var selectedInsect: Insect?
@EnvironmentObject var userData: InsectData
```

20. Within the body, add a NavigationView and VStack that display the list of insects. Also set the size of the view by adding a .frame() modifier at the end of the VStack:

```
NavigationView{
        VStack{
                MacInsectListView(selectedInsect:
                    $selectedInsect)
            }.frame(minWidth: 250, maxWidth: 400)
    }
```

21. Below the VStack code, let's add an if statement to display the insect details within a ScrollView view. A ScrollView view is used because the content may be larger than the amount of screen space available since window sizes are controlled by users:

```
if selectedInsect != nil  {
        ScrollView{
                InsectDetailView(insect:
                    selectedInsect!)
            }
        }
```

22. Add the `.environmentObject` modifier to the preview in order to view the design in the canvas preview:

```
static var previews: some View {
        ContentView().environmentObject(InsectData())
    }
```

23. The resulting `ContentView` preview should look as follows:

Figure 12.15 – ContentView preview at the end of the recipe

24. Finally, let's add a `.environmentObject()` modifier to the `contentView()` call located in the `AppDelegate.swift` file of our `macOS-Cross-Platform` folder:

```
func applicationDidFinishLaunching(_ aNotification:
    Notification) {

    ...

    let contentView = ContentView().
        environmentObject(InsectData())

    ...

    }
```

Adding the `.environmentObject()` modifier to `AppDelegate.swift` makes our data globally available to our app.

How it works

When using SwiftUI code written for one platform across iOS platforms, we need to add targets for the new platforms in question. In this recipe, we were building a macOS app from an existing iOS app, so we added the macOS app target to our Xcode project.

To run apps for a particular platform, we first have to change Xcode's active scheme. For example, if we try running the code from the **macOS-Cross-Platform** section without changing the scheme first, we'll get an error. The error occurs because Xcode requires the scheme to match the type of code being run.

To reuse certain iOS files in macOS, we selected those files from the **Navigator** pane and checked the macOS target within the **Inspector** pane. Taking such steps allows us to reuse the code without copying it over. Any changes and updates to the code can thus be done in a single place.

To implement selection within our `MacInsectListView`, we had to make the `Insect` struct `Hashable` and add a `.tag()` modifier to our `MacInsectCellView`. Without the `.tag()` modifier, the app would still build and run, but we would be unable to select an item from the list to view its details.

Lastly, the `.listStyle(SidebarListStyle())` modifier in `MacInsectListView` is only available in macOS and causes a list to be displayed on the side so that content can be displayed to the right of the list.

Creating the watchOS version of the iOS app

So far we've created an iOS app and a macOS version of that app, so finally, we'll create the watchOS version. When creating apps for watchOS, we need to keep in mind that the screen space available on watches is small, and make appropriate design choices based on that constraint.

In this recipe, we will create the watchOS version of our insect app.

Getting ready

Download the chapter materials from GitHub:

```
https://github.com/PacktPublishing/SwiftUI-Cookbook/tree/
master/Chapter12%20-%20Cross-Platform%20SwiftUI/03%20-%20
Create%20the%20watchOS%20version
```

Open the `StartingPoint` folder and double-click on `Cross-Platform.xcodeproj` to open the app that we built in the preceding *Creating the macOS version of the iOS app* recipe of this chapter. We will be continuing from where we left off in the first recipe.

The complete project can be found in the `Complete` folder to use as a reference.

How to do it

We will create a watchOS app based on our initial iOS app by sharing some views and creating custom views where the original iOS views would not be appropriate. The steps are as follows:

1. Create a new **Target...** in Xcode:

Figure 12.16 – Creating a new target

2. Choose the watchOS template, scroll down, and select **Watch App for iOS App**, then click **Next**:

Figure 12.17 – Selecting watchOS app

3. In the next screen, enter the product name, `watchOS-Cross-Platform`.

4. Click **Activate** in the pop-up window that appears:

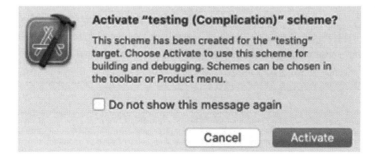

Figure 12.18 – watchOS Activate popup

5. The watchOS folders should appear in the navigation pane. Select the
    `ContentView.swift` file in the `watchOS-Cross-Platform Extension`
    folder. Run it in the Xcode canvas. The preview should look as follows:

Figure 12.19 – Initial watchOS preview

6. For the next step, make sure the **Navigator** and **Inspector** panes are open. We will
    be using both panes to make certain files and resources available across targets:

Figure 12.20 – Navigator and Inspector panes in Xcode

7. Let's share some files between the iOS and watchOS platforms. In the navigation pane, select the following files from our `Cross-Platform` folder: `Insect.swift`, `InsectData.swift`, `insectData.json`, `InsectCellView.swift`, `InsectListView.swift`, and `Assets.xcassets`:

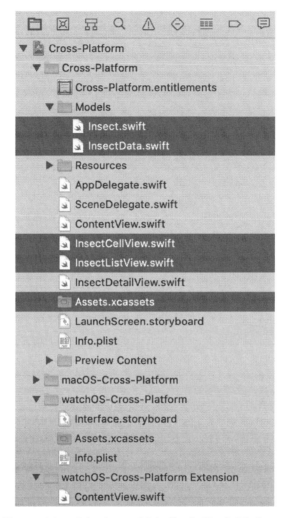

Figure 12.21 – Selecting multiple files in Xcode Navigator

8. In the **Inspector** pane, check the **watchOS-Cross-Platform** checkbox:

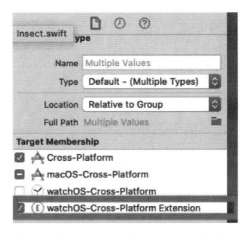

Figure 12.22 – Selecting macOS target from the Inspector

9. Open the `Resources` folder, and select `insectData.json` and `watchOS-Cross-Platform`.

10. In the Inspector pane, under **Target Membership**, check the `watchOS-Cross-Platform Extension` checkbox to make the previous files reachable from our watchOS code.

11. Create a new `WatchInsectDetailView` SwiftUI view in the `watchOS-Cross-Platform Extension` folder. Make sure the right platform target is selected (`watchOS-Cross-Platform Extension`):

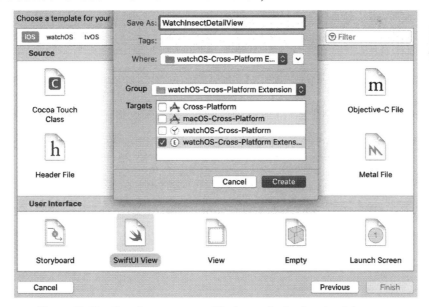

Figure 12.23 – Creating a new macOS view and selecting the right target

12. The `WatchInsectDetailView.swift` and `InsectCellView.swift` files have similar designs, but the former should use smaller font sizes to accommodate for the small display size of the Apple Watch. Replace the content of `WatchInsectDetailView` with the following:

```
var insect:Insect
var body: some View {
    VStack{
        Text(insect.name)
        Image(insect.imageName)
            .resizable()
            .aspectRatio(contentMode: .fit)
            .clipShape(Circle())
        HStack {
            Text("Habitat")
            Text(insect.habitat)
        }
    }
}
```

13. To preview the design in the Xcode canvas, add a sample insect to the preview function call:

```
static var previews: some View {
    WatchInsectDetailView(insect: testInsect)
}
```

14. Trying to build the project at this point fails. We get an **Unresolved identifier** error from `InsectListView.swift`. The error happens because `InsectDetailView.swift` is not available to our watchOS app. The `InsectListView.swift` file will need some tweaking.

15. Change the `InsectListView` type declaration to make it generic:

```
struct InsectListView<DetailView: View>: View
```

16. Below the `@EnvironmentObject` declaration, add a property closure that creates the detail view:

```
let detailViewProducer: (Insect) -> DetailView
```

17. Use the `detailViewProducer` property to create detail views for insects. In the `NavigationLink` struct, change the destination to the following:

```
self.detailViewProducer(insect).environmentObject(self.
    insectData)
```

18. Now that we are using the same file across platforms, create a `typealias` that captures the platform being used:

```
#if os(watchOS)
typealias PreviewDetailView = WatchInsectDetailView
#else
typealias PreviewDetailView = InsectDetailView
#endif
```

19. Modify the `InsectListView_Previews` to use the `typealias` for previews:

```
static var previews: some View {
        InsectListView{PreviewDetailView(insect:$0)}.
        environmentObject(InsectData())
    }
```

20. The `.navigationBarTitle()` modifier does not work on watchOS, so let's delete it.

21. Select `ContentView.swift` (from the `Cross-Platform` folder) and replace the body variable's content with a closure to create a detail view:

```
var body: some View {
        InsectListView{InsectDetailView(insect: $0) }
            .environmentObject(InsectData())
    }
```

22. Select the `InsectListView.swift` file and run the preview. It should look as follows:

Figure 12.24 – InsectListView preview

23. With all errors resolved, the `WatchInsectDetailView` from earlier can now be previewed. Click on `WatchInsectDetailView` and open the canvas preview. The preview should look as follows:

Figure 12.25 – WatchInsectDetailView preview

24. You can reduce the font size of the insect name in `InsectCellView.swift` so that it works better with the small screen size. Just remember that the change will be reflected in all other platforms where the `InsectCellView.swift` file is used.

25. Now, let's open the `ContentView.swift` file located in `watchOS-Cross-Platform Extension` and replace the `Text` view with our `InsectListView`:

```
InsectListView{WatchInsectDetailView(insect: $0) }
        .environmentObject(InsectData())
    }
```

26. Add the `.environmentObject()` modifier to the preview:

```
ContentView().environmentObject(InsectData())
```

Build and run the app or run the app live on the canvas. You should see a list of insects, and clicking on an insect should present the detail view for that insect.

How it works

When building Cross-Platform iOS applications, it is important to first spend some time figuring out how to make the app modular. Making the app modular by building smaller components greatly improves reusability. We were able to use the `InsectCellView.swift` and `InsectListView.swift` files from the iOS app we built in our watchOS app. Selecting the files and then selecting **watchOS-Cross-Platform Extension** from the Xcode file inspector pane made the code from both files reachable from our watchOS code. Adding `InsectListView.swift` to our watchOS target, however, caused a compiling problem because even though they share the same list view, a click on a list item in iOS will lead to the iOS-specific details view, `InsectDetailView`, while a click on the list in watchOS should open up the `watchInsectDetailView` struct. The issue was solved by changing the `InsectListView` type declaration to a generic type and adding a property closure that creates the detail view we need.

We also had to make some changes for the `InsectListView.swift` struct to enable the canvas preview. We added a conditional compilation to check the current debug operating system and set the `typealias` to the appropriate detail view.

When reusing the `InsectCellView` we ran into a problem where some of the text was too big for the watchOS screen. Changing the text in `InsectCellView` would change the design of the iOS version too. If we decide to create a separate version of `InsectCellView` we'll need to also create a different version of `InsectListView`, thereby repeating code in multiple locations.

> **Important note**
>
> Xcode sometimes gets bogged down and will fail to build your code after you fix an error. When this happens, click on **Product** in the menu bar, and then on **Clean Build Folder** (⇧+⌘+K). Remember to clean your builds when it seems like code updates no longer fix existing issues.

13
SwiftUI Tips and Tricks

In the previous chapters, we tried to collect different problems, and therefore different recipes, grouping them for a common theme.

In this chapter, instead, the recipes are not connected, apart from the fact that they are solutions for real-world problems.

We'll start viewing two ways of testing SwiftUI's views, and then we'll see how to localize the strings to create an international app.

Sometimes we must show some kind of documentation in the app, so we'll see how to present PDF documents.

One of the coolest features of an iPhone is the possibility of viewing and navigating the real world using its GPS and its map view; you can do this in your app using the `MapKit framework`, which, though it's not entirely integrated with SwiftUI, we'll see a recipe on how to wrap it and make it work nicely with SwiftUI.

With Swift 1.0, Xcode introduced the possibility of creating coding with **Playground**, decreasing the feedback time from writing code to seeing its results and improving the productivity of mobile developers. We'll see a recipe on how to use SwiftUI in a Playground.

The default fonts provided by SwiftUI are pretty cool, but sometimes we need more flexibility. So we'll see how to use custom fonts in SwiftUI.

Finally, we'll implement something that almost every app needs: a way of handling images when they aren't local but are served from a network service.

In this chapter, we will cover different topics in SwiftUI and real-world problems that you are likely to encounter during the development of your SwiftUI apps.

We will cover them in the following recipes:

- Snapshot testing SwiftUI views
- Unit testing SwiftUI with `ViewInspector`
- Implementing a multilanguage app with localized strings in SwiftUI
- Showing a PDF in SwiftUI
- Embedding a `MapView` in SwiftUI
- Embedding a UIKit `MapView` in SwiftUI
- Implementing SwiftUI views using Playground
- Using custom fonts in SwiftUI
- Implementing asynchronous images in SwiftUI

Technical requirements

The code in this chapter is based on Xcode 12 and iOS 14.

The first recipe, *Snapshot testing SwiftUI views*, has the optional requirement of using **Kaleidoscope** (`https://www.kaleidoscopeapp.com`) to compare two images. Kaleidoscope is not free, but it offers a 14-day trial.

You can find the code in the book's GitHub repo under the path `https://github.com/PacktPublishing/SwiftUI-Cookbook/tree/master/Chapter13%20-%20SwiftUI%20Tips%20and%20Tricks`.

Snapshot testing SwiftUI views

While **snapshot testing** is more common in other technologies, for example, JavaScript and the Jest testing library, (see `https://jestjs.io/docs/en/snapshot-testing.html`), in the iOS world it is not so common.

Snapshot testing is another name for characterization testing. Here's the definition by Michael Feathers, the guru of improving legacy code: `https://michaelfeathers.` `silvrback.com/characterization-testing`. In the SwiftUI implementation, we are taking a snapshot of the current component we want to preserve, and we run a test against that component so that if in the future someone mistakenly changes its appearance, the test will fail.

In the case of iOS, usually a component we want to preserve is `UIViewController` or a `UIView`.

Depending on the library we are going to use, we can take the snapshot in different ways: as a textual description or an actual screenshot. For this recipe, we'll use the **Swift Snapshot Testing** library that you can find here: `https://github.com/` `pointfreeco/swift-snapshot-testing`.

Even though it still doesn't support SwiftUI natively, it's composable architecture allows us to adapt it to SwiftUI without too much effort.

Getting ready

Let's start creating an Xcode SwiftUI project called `SnapshotTestingApp`, remembering to enable the **Unit Tests** as shown in the following screenshot:

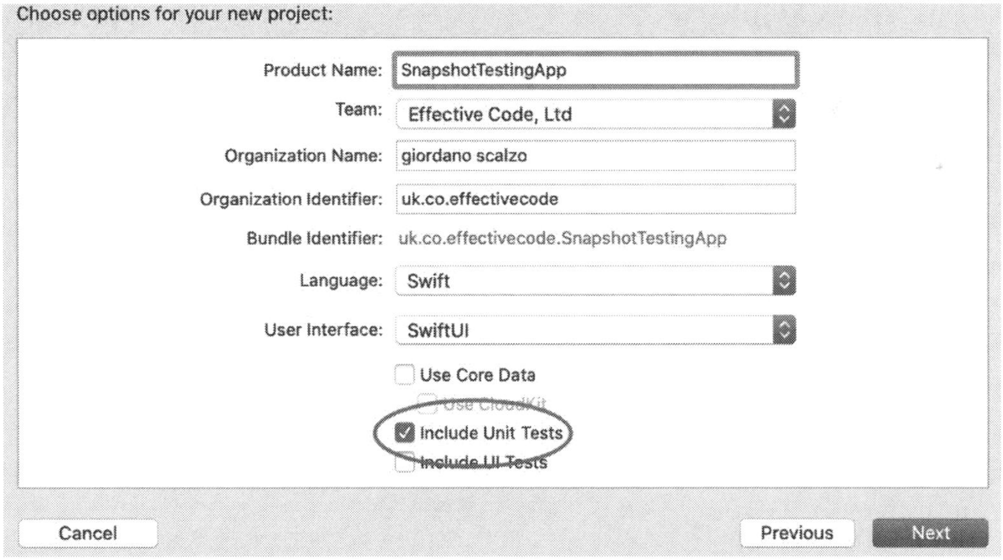

Fig. 13.1 – SnapshotTestingApp with unit tests enabled

After creating the project, let's add the Swift Snapshot Testing package by selecting **Add Package Dependency...** from the **Swift Packages** option in the **File** menu entry:

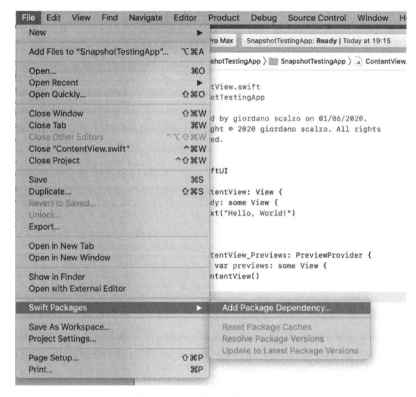

Fig. 13.2 – Add a Swift package

On the next screen, let's add the package URL:

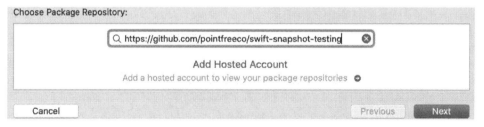

Fig. 13.3 – Add the package URL

Then select the latest version:

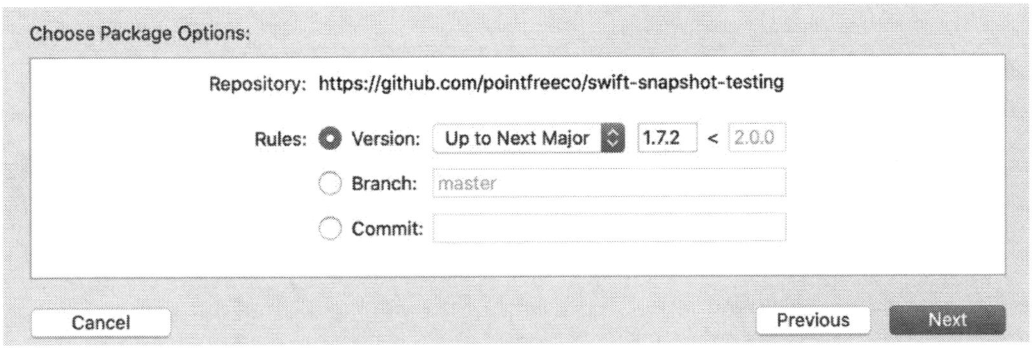

Fig. 13.4 – Selecting the package version

On the final screen, pay attention to adding the package to the test target and not to the app target:

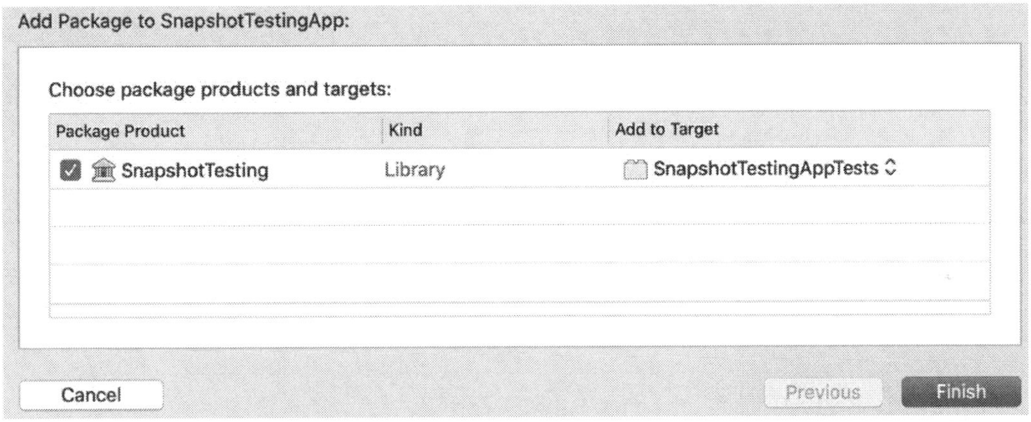

Fig. 13.5 – Add the package to the test target

We are now ready to prepare some tests.

How to do it...

We are going to implement a simple view with three cards, mimicking three different credit cards.

We then run a snapshot test to take the golden plate, an image file that we expected to be correct, to protect us from accidentally changing that view.

Finally, we are going to change the order of the cards and see what happens when we run the test:

1. Let's start defining a list of cards:

```
struct ContentView: View {
    let cards: [(title: String, color: Color)] = [
        ("Visa Card", .yellow),
        ("Mastercard Credit Card", .red),
        ("Apple Credit Card", .black),
    ]
}
```

2. Then, for each card, we create a rounded rectangle of the color defined in the list:

```
struct ContentView: View {
    //...
    var body: some View {
        VStack(spacing: 16) {
            ForEach(0..<cards.count) { index in
                Text(cards[index].title)
                    .font(.system(.title))
                    .frame(maxWidth: .infinity,
                           maxHeight: .infinity)
                    .foregroundColor(.white)
                    .background(cards[index].color)
                    .cornerRadius(16)
            }
        }.padding(.horizontal, 16)
    }
}
```

3. We can run the app now to see the view with the three cards:

Fig. 13.6 – Three-card app

4. Let's move now to the test where we create an extension to use SwiftUI in Swift
    Snapshot Testing:

```
import SnapshotTesting
import SwiftUI
@testable import SnapshotTestingApp


extension Snapshotting where Value:View, Format ==
  UIImage {
    public static func image(
    on config: ViewImageConfig) -> Snapshotting {
        Snapshotting<UIViewController, UIImage>.image(on:
          config).pullback(UIHostingController.
            init(rootView:))
    }
}
```

5. Finally, we write our simple test:

```
class PointFreeAppTests: XCTestCase {
    override class func setUp() {
        diffTool = "ksdiff"
    }
    func testContentView() throws {
        assertSnapshot(matching: ContentView(),
                as: .image(on: .iPhoneX))
    }
}
```

6. The first time we run the test, it fails since it doesn't find the reference image and it does record one:

```
21
   class PointFreeAppTests: XCTestCase {
23     override class func setUp() {
24         diffTool = "ksdiff"
25     }
   func testContentView() throws {
27         assertSnapshot(matching: ContentView(), as:
               .image(on: .iPhoneX))
28 
29 
30 
31 
```

failed - No reference was found on disk. Automatically recorded snapshot: ...

open "/Users/giordanoscalzo/Dropbox/B15845_SwiftUI_Cookbook/Repo/
SwiftUI-Cookbook/Chapter13 - SwiftUI Tips and Tricks/01 - Snapshot
testing SwiftUI views/SnapshotTestingApp/SnapshotTestingAppTests/
__Snapshots__/SnapshotTestingAppTests/testContentView.1.png"

Re-run "testContentView" to test against the newly-recorded snapshot.

Fig. 13.7 – Recording a reference image

7. After that, the test runs fine. What would happen if we changed the order of the cards by mistake?

```
struct ContentView: View {
    let cards: [(title: String, color: Color)] = [
        ("Apple Credit Card", .black),
        ("Visa Card", .yellow),
        ("Mastercard Credit Card", .red),
    ]
    //...
}
```

8. We run the test and it fails with the following message:

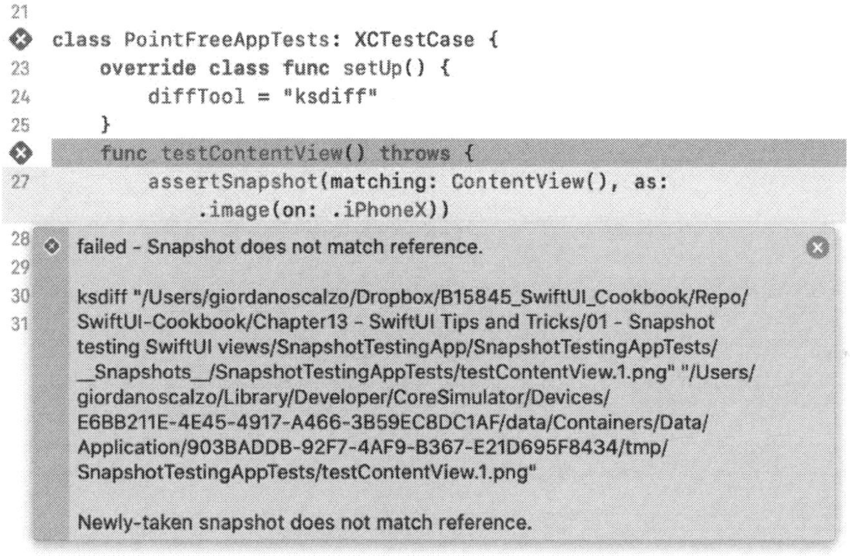

```
21
⊗   class PointFreeAppTests: XCTestCase {
23       override class func setUp() {
24           diffTool = "ksdiff"
25       }
⊗       func testContentView() throws {
27           assertSnapshot(matching: ContentView(), as:
                 .image(on: .iPhoneX))
28
29
30
31
```

failed – Snapshot does not match reference.

ksdiff "/Users/giordanoscalzo/Dropbox/B15845_SwiftUI_Cookbook/Repo/
SwiftUI-Cookbook/Chapter13 – SwiftUI Tips and Tricks/01 – Snapshot
testing SwiftUI views/SnapshotTestingApp/SnapshotTestingAppTests/
Snapshots/SnapshotTestingAppTests/testContentView.1.png" "/Users/
giordanoscalzo/Library/Developer/CoreSimulator/Devices/
E6BB211E-4E45-4917-A466-3B59EC8DC1AF/data/Containers/Data/
Application/903BADDB-92F7-4AF9-B367-E21D695F8434/tmp/
SnapshotTestingAppTests/testContentView.1.png"

Newly-taken snapshot does not match reference.

Fig. 13.8 – Failing snapshot test

9. This is optional, but if we have Kaleidoscope (`https://www.kaleidoscopeapp.com`) installed, we can run the command in the Terminal to compare the two images:

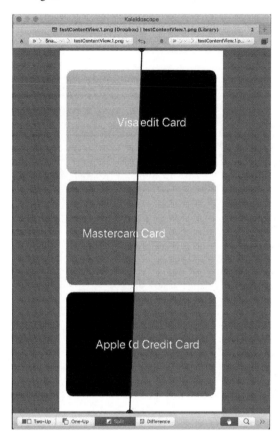

Fig. 13.9 – Comparing test images

How it works...

Swift Snapshot Testing has a mechanism, called `pullback`, to adapt the component we want to test to something that the library already supports.

In our case, the component already supported is `UIVIewController`, so the pullback bridges the `View` to `UIViewController`, embedding it in `UIHostingController`.

This pattern is also useful for non-SwiftUI views if, for example, you want to test a modal `UIViewController` when it is presented from another `UIViewController` – you can create another extension and then prepare the scenario to show the `UIVIewController`.

Regardless of the extension that you can copy in your code and use when you need it, it is essential to understand the process:

1. First, you must decide which device you will use for testing since the screenshot density depends on the density of the device screen, and screenshots taken with an iPhone 11 Pro Max cannot be compared with those taken with an SE 2, for example.

2. Then you must run the tests once to create the reference snapshots.

3. You must check that the snapshots are what you expect. The human visual confirmation is essential because if a snapshot is wrong, we are going to release an app with an incorrect rendering and, because our tests will be green, we will think that our app is correct, whereas it will have some rendering errors.

4. Immediately check and fix any new failing test.

I think it is essential to have a way of comparing images to spot the difference. I'm pretty happy with Kaleidoscope (`https://www.kaleidoscopeapp.com`) but you can use whatever you want.

If you set the global variable `diffTool`, the content will be presented in the message of the failing test, as shown in the following screenshot:

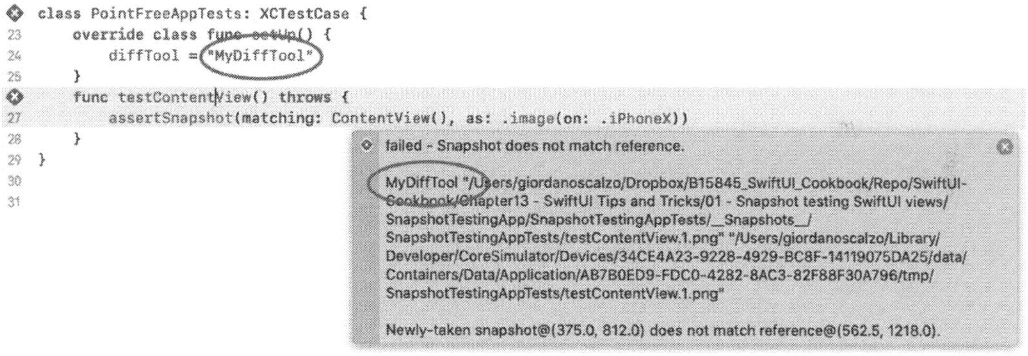

```
class PointFreeAppTests: XCTestCase {
23    override class func setUp() {
24        diffTool = "MyDiffTool"
25    }
26    func testContentView() throws {
27        assertSnapshot(matching: ContentView(), as: .image(on: .iPhoneX))
28    }
29 }
30
31
```

failed - Snapshot does not match reference.

MyDiffTool "/Users/giordanoscalzo/Dropbox/B15845_SwiftUI_Cookbook/Repo/SwiftUI-Cookbook/Chapter13 - SwiftUI Tips and Tricks/01 - Snapshot testing SwiftUI views/ SnapshotTestingApp/SnapshotTestingAppTests/__Snapshots__/ SnapshotTestingAppTests/testContentView.1.png" "/Users/giordanoscalzo/Library/ Developer/CoreSimulator/Devices/34CE4A23-9228-4929-BC8F-14119075DA25/data/ Containers/Data/Application/AB7B0ED9-FDC0-4282-8AC3-82F88F30A796/tmp/ SnapshotTestingAppTests/testContentView.1.png"

Newly-taken snapshot@(375.0, 812.0) does not match reference@(562.5, 1218.0).

Fig. 13.10 – Custom diff image app

In general, snapshot testing not only gives you a safety net when you want to refactor some views, but it also has the effect of making you think of how to separate the presentation logic from the business logic, making the app more modular and thereby more flexible and adaptable to changes.

Unit testing SwiftUI with ViewInspector

Unit testing or test-driven-development are not buzzwords anymore, and in the iOS ecosystem, they are taken almost for granted. Any iOS developer should know the test tools and how to apply them.

XCTest and **XCUITest** are mature frameworks, and so you'd expect to have something similar for SwiftUI.

Unfortunately, SwiftUI doesn't come with any test capabilities from Apple. To test a SwiftUI view, you could rely on either UI Testing, which is flaky by nature, or use snapshot testing, as you can see in the recipe *Snapshot testing SwiftUI views*.

However, the beauty of open source is that given a problem, somehow, the community finds a solution.

This is the case with the unit testing SwiftUI and `ViewInspector`, a framework for the inspection and testing of SwiftUI views.

In this recipe, we'll implement a simple SwiftUI view with some interaction, and we'll see how to test its structure and activity.

Getting ready

1. Let's start creating an Xcode SwiftUI project called `TestingSwiftUIApp`, remembering to enable the unit test as shown in the following screenshot:

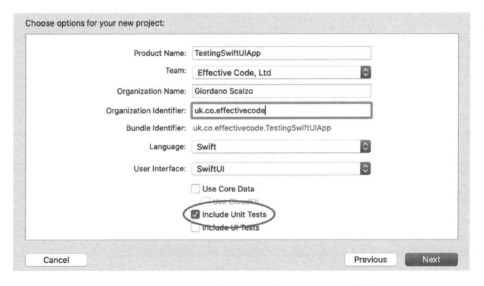

Fig. 13.11 – TestingSwiftUIApp with unit tests enabled

2. After creating the project, let's add the `ViewInspector` package, selecting **Add Package Dependency...** from the **Swift Packages** option in the **File** menu entry:

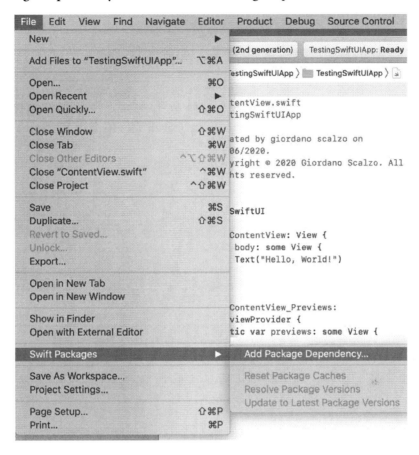

Fig. 13.12 – Add a Swift package

3. On the next screen, let's add the package URL:

Fig. 13.13 – Add a package URL

4. Then select the latest version, which, at the time of the writing, is 0.3.11:

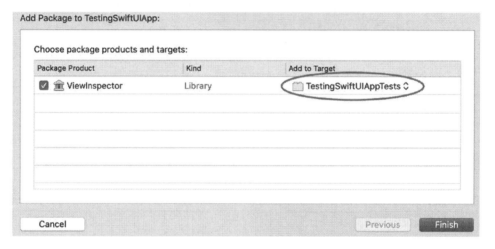

Fig. 13.14 – Selecting the package version

5. On the final screen, pay attention to adding the package to the test target and not to the app target:

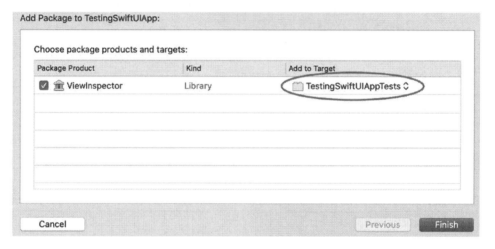

Fig. 13.15 – Add the package to the test target

We are now ready to prepare some tests.

How to do it

We are going to implement an app that asks you your country of origin – imagine that in an airport before entering a new country.

It presents a list of buttons with a few countries, and after selecting one, it changes the text at the center of the screen:

1. Let's start by defining the list of possible countries we can select from, and a `Text` view in the middle of the page where we put the selected country:

```
struct ContentView: View {
    private let countries = [
        "USA",
        "France",
        "Germany",
        "Italy"
    ]
    @State
    var originCountry: Int = 0

    var body: some View {
        VStack(spacing: 12) {
            Text("What is your country of origin?")
            Spacer()
            Text(countries[originCountry])
                .font(.system(size: 40))
            Spacer()
        }
    }
}
```

2. Now let's add the list of buttons to select the countries – one for each country:

```
VStack(spacing: 12) {
    Text("What is your country of origin?")
    HStack(spacing: 12) {
        ForEach(0..<countries.count) { idx in
            Button {
                originCountry = idx
            } label: {
            }
        }
    }
    Spacer()
    //...
}
```

3. Inside each button, we configure the Text object, changing the background color if it is the button currently selected:

```
Button {
    originCountry = idx
} label: {
    Text(countries[idx])
        .frame(width: 80, height: 40)
        .background((originCountry == idx ?
            Color.red :
            Color.blue)
            .opacity(0.6))
        .cornerRadius(5)
        .foregroundColor(.white)
}
```

4. The app is now finished, and after starting with USA as the selected country, tapping on different buttons makes the central text change:

Fig. 13.16 – Select the country of origin

5. Now let's move to the tests, where we prepare importing the frameworks and extend the ContentView struct with the Inspectable protocol:

```
import XCTest
import SwiftUI
import ViewInspector
@testable import TestingSwiftUIApp

extension ContentView: Inspectable { }
```

6. For the first test, we are going to check that the buttons contain the expected labels, and that the central text is set to **"USA"**:

```
class TestingSwiftUIAppTests: XCTestCase {
    func testStartWithUSASelected() throws {
        let view = ContentView()

        let buttons = try
            view.inspect().vStack().hStack(1).forEach(0)

        XCTAssertEqual(try buttons.button(0)
            .text().string(), "USA")
        XCTAssertEqual(try buttons.button(1)
            .text().string(), "France")
        XCTAssertEqual(try buttons.button(2)
            .text().string(), "Germany")
        XCTAssertEqual(try buttons.button(3)
            .text().string(), "Italy")

        let country = try view.inspect().vStack().text(3)
        XCTAssertEqual(try country.string(), "USA")
    }
}
```

7. The next feature we want to test is that after selecting a country, the Text view at the center of the screen changes its label to the name of the selected country.

This feature relies on a @State variable. Unfortunately, currently, @State variables aren't supported by ViewInspector out of the box, and we must slightly change the ContentView code to overcome this limitation.

In particular, we must create a function that *captures* the body when it is created to be inspected in the test:

```
struct ContentView: View {
    //...
    var didAppear: ((Self) -> Void)?

    var body: some View {
        VStack(spacing: 12) {
```

```
                    //...
                }
            .onAppear { didAppear?(self) }
        }
    }
```

8. With this closure in place, we can write the test that assures that the central text is in sync with the selected button:

```
func testSelectItaly() throws {
    var view = ContentView()

    let exp = view.on(\.didAppear) { view in
        XCTAssertEqual(try view.actualView().
            originCountry, 0)
        try view.actualView().inspect().vStack().hStack(1)
            .forEach(0).button(3).tap()
        XCTAssertEqual(try view.actualView().
            originCountry, 3)
    }

    ViewHosting.host(view: view)
    wait(for: [exp], timeout: 0.1)
}
```

We can run the tests now, and they will both be green.

How it works

The important thing here is to extend the View we want to test with the Inspectable protocol, which adds a few functions to inspect the content of the view.

The added `inspect()` function returns a struct that mimics the actual view structure and that we can use to extract the sub-views. In our case, `VStack` contains `Text`, `Hstack`, `Spacer`, and another `Text` struct. They can be reached using the proper function and the related index, like this:

```
try view.inspect().vStack().text(0)
try view.inspect().vStack().hStack(1)
try view.inspect().vStack().spacer(2)
try view.inspect().vStack().text(3)
```

Regarding testing the interactive behavior, it's not so easy to do, therefore we added a closure to capture the actual view that can be used in a block testing function:

```
let exp = view.on(\.didAppear) { view in
    XCTAssertEqual(try view.actualView().originCountry, 0)
    try view.actualView().inspect().vStack().hStack(1)
            .forEach(0).button(3).tap()
    XCTAssertEqual(try view.actualView().originCountry, 3)
}
```

The `.actualView()` function returns the view that was captured in the callback we added to our code.

I admit that the tests look a bit convoluted; however, `ViewInspector` is a helpful tool to have in your toolbox, ready to be used when you want to inspect and test your SwiftUI view layout structure.

Implementing a multilanguage app with localized strings in SwiftUI

One of the beauties of iOS and the Apple App Store is that you can sell your app to the whole world, just by configuring the markets in **App Store Connect**.

Given that, you must consider that only one language is not enough, and you should customize the app to be presented in the language of your customers. The localization mechanism in iOS is sophisticated, and luckily it works very well in SwiftUI too.

In this recipe, we'll create a sample app that presents a cooking recipe detail page, and we are going to localize it in English, French, and Italian.

Getting ready

Let's start by creating a SwiftUI app called `RecipeApp` in Xcode.

We are going to use an image for the recipe, and you can find it in the GitHub repo here: `https://github.com/PacktPublishing/SwiftUI-Cookbook/blob/master/Resources/Chapter13/recipe3/recipe.jpg`.

The image was taken by the user *FotoDanilo* on *Flickr* (`https://www.flickr.com/photos/fotodanilo/3629344256`). Add the picture to the `Assets` folder in the project.

Before moving to the code, we must configure the project for localization:

1. Add a new `Strings` file called `Localizable`:

Fig. 13.17 – Add a Localizable Strings file

2. Select the newly created `Localizable.strings` file and enable the localization:

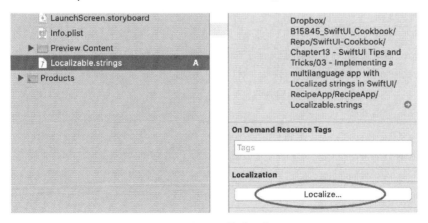

Fig. 13.18 – Strings file localization

3. Select the `RecipeApp` project and add localization for **French and Italian**:

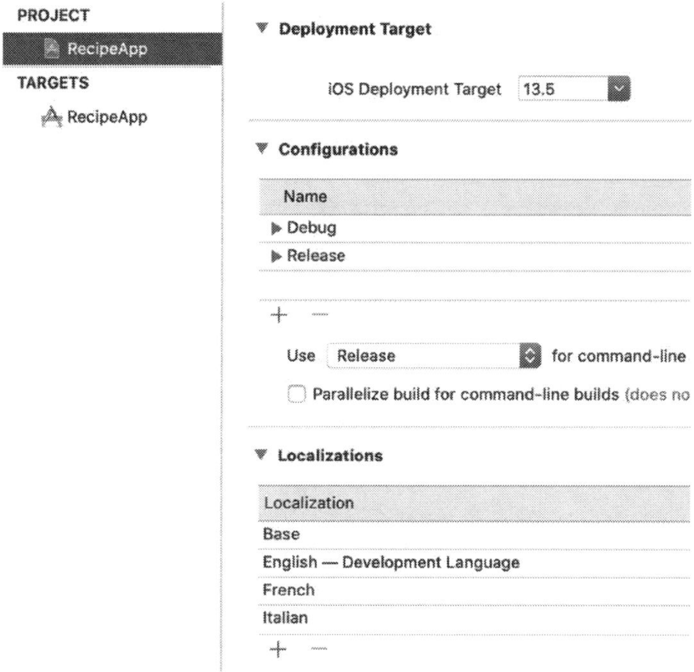

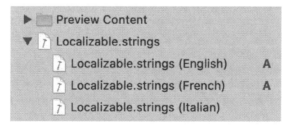

Fig. 13.19 – Localizing the project

4. After that, the `Localizable.strings` file in your project should appear as in the following screenshot:

Fig. 13.20 – Localized Strings file

5. In the GitHub repo, you can find the content of the three files, here: `https:// github.com/PacktPublishing/SwiftUI-Cookbook/tree/master/ Resources/Chapter13/recipe3`

6. Copy the content of each file in the `Localizable.strings` file in the project, and we are ready to go.

How to do it

We are going to implement a simple Details page for a cooking recipe.

The page is split into three parts: cover, timing, and ingredients.

For the labels in the `Text` components, we are going to use the same identifiers we put in the `Localizable.strings` files, and automatically SwiftUI will pick up the correct name:

1. Let's start by creating a convenience struct to save the timings:

```swift
struct Timings {
    let cooking: Int
    let baking: Int
    let resting: Int
}
```

2. The `ContentView` struct's body component simply has the three components we described earlier – cover, timings, and ingredients:

```swift
struct ContentView: View {
    private let timings = Timings(cooking: 20,
                                  baking: 5,
                                  resting: 10)

    var body: some View {
        VStack {
            CoverView()
            Divider()
            TimingsView(timings: timings)
            Divider()
            IngredientsView()
            Spacer()
        }
    }
}
```

3. The `CoverView` component shows a picture of the food, the name of the recipe, and its difficulty:

```swift
struct CoverView: View {
    var body: some View {
        VStack {
            Text("recipe.cover.name")
                .font(.largeTitle)
            Image("recipe")
                .resizable()
                .aspectRatio(contentMode: .fit)
            HStack {
                Text("recipe.cover.difficulty.title")
                    .font(.system(size: 28))
                    .fontWeight(.bold)
                Text("recipe.cover.difficulty.value")
                    .font(.system(size: 28))
            }
        }
    }
}
```

4. The `TimingsView` component is a horizontal stack with three timings: cooking, baking, and resting. Pay attention to the fact that we are using the `String` interpolation to add the actual timing to the localized `String`:

```swift
struct TimingsView: View {
    let timings: Timings

    var body: some View {
        HStack(spacing: 64) {
            VStack {
                Text("recipe.timings.cooking.title")
                    .fontWeight(.bold)
                Text("recipe.timings.cooking.value
                    \(timings.cooking)")
            }
            VStack {
```

```
                    Text("recipe.timings.baking.title")
                        .fontWeight(.bold)
                    Text("recipe.timings.baking.value
                        \(timings.baking)")
                }
            VStack {
                    Text("recipe.timings.resting.title")
                        .fontWeight(.bold)
                    Text("recipe.timings.resting.value \
                    (timings.resting)")
                }
            }
        }
    }
```

5. Finally, the `IngredientsView` component is a simple list of ingredients:

```
struct IngredientsView: View {
    var body: some View {
        VStack(alignment: .leading, spacing: 8) {
            Text("recipe.ingredients.title")
                .font(.system(size: 28))
                .fontWeight(.bold)
            Text("recipe.ingredients.servings")
                .fontWeight(.bold)
            Text("recipe.ingredients.ingredient1")
            Text("recipe.ingredients.ingredient2")
            Text("recipe.ingredients.ingredient3")
            Text("recipe.ingredients.ingredient4")
            Text("recipe.ingredients.ingredient5")


        }
    }
}
```

6. The nice thing about the preview is that we can create three different views, one for each language:

```
struct ContentView_Previews: PreviewProvider {
    static var previews: some View {
        ForEach(["en", "it", "fr"], id: \.self) { l in
            ContentView()
                .environment(\.locale, .init(identifier:
1))
        }
    }
}
```

7. On the **Preview** screen, you can then see the three localized versions. The following screenshot shows the app in English, the default language:

Fig. 13.21 – English localized version in preview

The same app, when the device is configured to the Italian language, looks as follows:

Fig. 13.22 – Italian localized version in preview

Finally, when the device is in French, the app translates itself as you can see in the following screenshot:

Fig. 13.23 – French localized version in preview

8.   However, you may have noticed that the interpolated strings for the timings don't work. But don't worry – it's just a limitation of the `Preview` view, and if you run it in a simulator or an actual device, the timings will work:

Fig. 13.24 – Localized app in a simulator

How it works

The configuration we did in the introduction of the recipe is the usual configuration you have to do in an iOS app and isn't specific to SwiftUI.

In a SwiftUI app, the operating system puts in the `Environment` the current language of the device. Hence, setting different values as we did in `ContentView_Previews` allowed us to generate different language scenarios.

The label in a `Text` component defines what has to be presented, and if SwiftUI finds that label in a `Localizable` strings file as a key, it shows the value in the language set in the `Environment`.

If there is a match with a key, but the language is not one of the supported languages, SwiftUI falls back to the default one, which is English in our recipe.

Finally, you can use string interpolation to add dynamic content to the string, as we have done in the various timing values.

In that example, a localizable string was written as follows:

```
"recipe.timings.baking.value %lld" = "%lld min.";
```

As you can see, there is a formatting symbol, %lld, in both the key and the value. The symbol will be replaced with a proper value when referenced in the code.

In particular, the string %lld can then be replaced with an Int value. For example, we may have a localizable string like the one here:

```
"recipe.timings.resting.value %lld" = "Resting %lld min.";
```

We can use it in the code as follows:

```
Text("recipe.timings.resting.value \(11)")
```

We end up with a message on the screen that says: **Resting 11 min.**.

This allows you to have great flexibility when putting a value in a translated string without having to compose strings like this:

```
Text("recipe.timings.resting.part1" + "\(11)" + "recipe.
timings.resting.part2")
```

Showing a PDF in SwiftUI

Since iOS 11, Apple has provided **PDFKit**, a robust framework to display and manipulate PDF documents in your applications.

As you can imagine, PDFKit is based on UIKit; however, in this recipe, we'll see how easy it is to integrate it with SwiftUI.

Getting ready

Let's create a new SwiftUI app in Xcode called PDFReaderApp.

We then need a PDF document to present. We are providing an example in the repo https://github.com/PacktPublishing/SwiftUI-Cookbook/blob/master/Resources/Chapter13/recipe4/PDFBook.pdf, but feel free to use a PDF document of your choice.

Copy the document in the project:

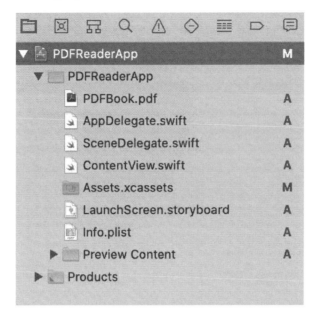

Fig. 13.25 – PDF document in the Xcode project

With the PDF document in the project, we are ready to implement our PDF viewer in SwiftUI.

How to do it

PDFKit provides a class called PDFView to render a PDF document.

Because the PDFView class is a subclass of UIView, it must be encapsulated in a UIViewRepresentable class to be used in SwiftUI.

We are going to implement a PDFKitView view to represent a viewer for a PDF document. That view will be then used in other SwiftUI views to present a PDF document:

1. Let's define a struct called PDFKitView to bridge PDFView to SwiftUI:

```
import PDFKit

struct PDFKitView: UIViewRepresentable {
    let url: URL
```

```
func makeUIView(context:
UIViewRepresentableContext<PDFKitView>)
    -> PDFView {
        let pdfView = PDFView()
        pdfView.document = PDFDocument(url: self.url)
        return pdfView
    }


func updateUIView(_ uiView: PDFView,
    context: UIViewRepresentableContext<PDFKitView>) {
    }
}
```

2. The newly created component can then be used anywhere in our SwiftUI code:

```
struct ContentView: View {
    let documentURL = Bundle.main.url(forResource:
        "PDFBook", withExtension: "pdf")!
    var body: some View {
        VStack(alignment: .leading) {
            Text("The Waking Lights")
                .font(.largeTitle)
            Text("By Urna Semper")
                .font(.title)
            PDFKitView(url: documentURL)
        }
    }
}
```

As you can see on running the app, the PDF document is accurately rendered in our `PDFKitView` component:

Fig. 13.26 – PDF document rendered in SwiftUI

How it works

This recipe is straightforward, thanks to the encapsulated nature of it.

We firstly define a `PDFKitView` struct extending `UIViewRepresentable`, which creates and holds an instance of the UIKit class `PDFView`.

After creating it, we set the URL of the document to present in the `View`.

This `PDFKitView` view is then used in the `ContentView` as a normal SwiftUI view.

Even though the sample PDF document we are using is local, the UIKit `PDFView` class renders a document from a URL so we must provide the local document using a URL.

However, this gives the possibility to have a remote document: why not try to present the document from a remote location? Would you make any code changes?

There's more

The use we make of the UIKit `PDFView` class is elementary, but it can do more, such as zooming, navigating through pages, highlighting sections, and so on.

As an exercise, I suggest you start from this recipe and implement a custom fullscreen PDF reader, where we present a page in fullscreen, and we can navigate each page using custom buttons. It should be a matter of exposing the `PDFView` class functions in `PDFKitView` and connecting them to normal SwiftUI buttons.

Embedding a MapView in SwiftUI

A handy feature of a smartphone, and iOS in particular, is its capacity to replace a car satellite navigation system, showing where you are and the best route to reach your destination.

Since the introduction of the first iPhone, more than 10 years ago, iOS provides a sophisticated map view.

It was initially provided by Google, but since iOS 6, Apple replaced it with its own version. In iOS 14, SwiftUI supports it natively with a `Map` component.

In this recipe, we'll implement a simple app based on the **MapKit** framework, where we can set several favorite places. A viewfinder image in the center of the view allows us to add a favorite when we tap on the add favorite (+) button.

Getting ready

Let's implement a SwiftUI app called `MapInSwiftUIApp` in Xcode. Since this recipe is only for iOS 14, set the deployment target to iOS 14.

How to do it

In a few steps, we are going to create a map centered on the UK with a viewfinder in the center. A button on the navigation bar will add the location indicated by the viewfinder to the list of favorite places.

We can do this with the following steps:

1. Let's import the `MapKit` framework and define the structure of the view:

```swift
import SwiftUI
import MapKit
struct ContentView: View {
    var body: some View {
        NavigationView {
            ZStack {
                Image(systemName: "viewfinder")
                    .font(.system(size: 32, weight:
                    .regular))
                    .foregroundColor(.blue)
            }
            .navigationBarTitle("My Favorite Places",
                displayMode: .inline)
        }
    }
}
```

2. To be rendered, a `Map` component needs a `Region` that defines its center and its size, and a list of `Location` objects. The `Location` is a struct that must be identifiable and that contains the coordinates of the place. Let's define the struct:

```swift
struct Location: Identifiable {
    let id = UUID()
    let coordinate: CLLocationCoordinate2D
}
```

3. With this defined struct, let's add an `@State` array of `locations` in the `ContentView` struct:

```swift
struct ContentView: View {
    @State private var locations: [Location] = []
    //...
}
```

4. The Map view is driven by a MKCoordinateRegion instance that we are adding as an @State variable:

```
struct ContentView: View {
    @State
    private var region = MKCoordinateRegion(
        center: CLLocationCoordinate2D(latitude: 54.4609,
            longitude: -3.0886),
        span: MKCoordinateSpan(latitudeDelta: 10,
                                longitudeDelta: 10))
    //...
}
```

5. We can finally add the Map component to the body of the ContentView struct:

```
var body: some View {
    NavigationView {
        ZStack {
            Map(coordinateRegion: $region,
                annotationItems: locations) {
                MapPin(coordinate: $0.coordinate,
                    tint: .blue)
            }
            .edgesIgnoringSafeArea(.all)
            Image(systemName: "viewfinder")
                .font(.system(size: 32, weight:
                    .regular))
                .foregroundColor(.blue)
        }
    }
}
```

6. The last thing missing is the button to add the current location to the list
    of favorites:

```
struct ContentView: View {
    //...
    private func addFavorite() {
        locations.append(Location(coordinate: region.
            center))
    }


    var body: some View {
        //...
            .navigationBarTitle("My Favorite Places",
                displayMode: .inline)
            .navigationBarItems(trailing:
                Button(action: addFavorite) {
                Image(systemName: "plus")
                    .font(.headline)
                })
        }
    }
}
```

We can now run the app and add favorites to our map:

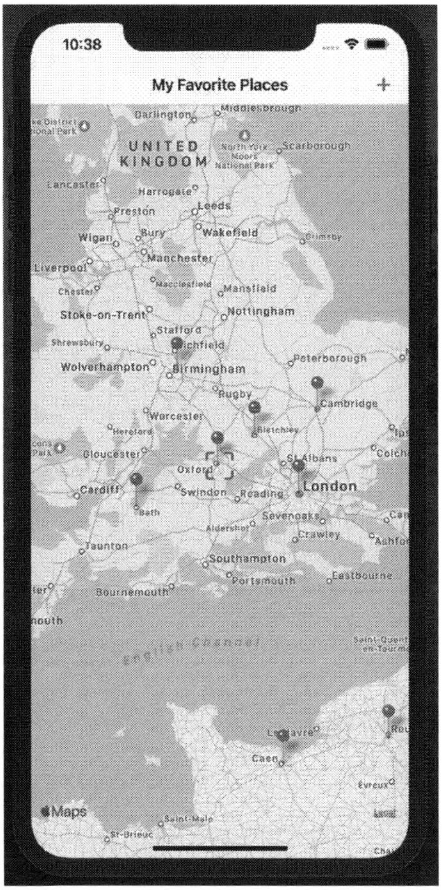

Fig. 13.27 – Favorite places in a Map view

How it works

The native `Map` component follows the philosophy of SwiftUI very well.

In this recipe, we saw two important features of the `Map` component. The first is that via an `MKCoordinateRegion` instance, we can set the center and the zoom level of the map. Passing it as an `@State` variable, we can create a bidirectional connection with the `Map` component: on moving and zooming the map, the value region changes and it stays aligned with what is shown on the map.

Because the center of the `region` variable always matches the center of the map, we can easily add it to the list of favorites when we tap on the plus button.

The other functionality we used in this recipe is adding a pin to each location of a list we passed in the constructor.

The `Map` component accepts a list of `Identifiable` structs as parameters when it is created. The last callback in the `.init()` transforms a single struct in an instance of the type `MapPin` that can be rendered in the `Map` view.

Creating an `@State` variable for the list of favorites, we can add a set of pins to be represented on the map.

Every time we add a new object in the list, the `Map` view is rendered again and a new pin is added to the view.

Embedding a UIKit MapView in SwiftUI

One of the reasons for the success of smartphones is the possibility of showing the current position on a map in real time, preventing users from getting lost in an unknown part of a city.

Since the its release, the iPhone has provided a fantastic map experience thanks to **MapKit**, the framework implemented by Apple that, from iOS 6, replaces the Google Maps SDK.

In the preceding recipe, *Embedding a MapView in SwiftUI*, we saw how simple it is to show a `Map` SwiftUI component.

However, the SwiftUI native `Map` component is available from iOS 14 only. Since not all iOS apps can be updated to support only the latest version of iOS, because most customers are still on iOS 13, in this recipe, we'll see how to wrap the UIKit `MKMapView` component in `UIViewRepresentable` and use it in a SwiftUI app.

We'll implement the same app as we did in *Embedding a MapView in SwiftUI*, where we create a list of favorite places.

Getting ready

Let's implement a SwiftUI app called `MapInSwiftUIApp` in Xcode. You can set iOS 13 as the deployment target for this project, even though it works fine in iOS 14 as well.

How to do it

We'll start by implementing a `UIViewRepresentable` class to render an `MKMapView`; then, we'll add a button to add the place in the center of the map to the list of favorites, which will then be rendered as map annotations in the `MapView` component. We can do this with the following steps:

1. Being UIKit-based, we wrap an `MKMapView` class in `UIViewRepresentable`:

```
import MapKit
struct MapView: UIViewRepresentable {
    func makeUIView(context: Context) -> MKMapView {
        let mapView = MKMapView()
        return mapView
    }

    func updateUIView(_ view: MKMapView,
            context: Context) {
    }
}
```

2. The `MapView` component can now be simply used in the body of `ContentView`:

```
struct ContentView: View {
    var body: some View {
        MapView()
            .edgesIgnoringSafeArea(.all)
    }
}
```

The goal of this app is to save favorites by selecting them when they are in the center of the map. Let's indicate the center overlapping a `viewfinder` image:

```
var body: some View {
    ZStack {
        MapView()
            .edgesIgnoringSafeArea(.all)
        Image(systemName: "viewfinder")
            .font(.system(size: 32, weight: .regular))
            .foregroundColor(.blue)
    }
}
```

3. The new favorite is triggered by a "plus" button in the navigation view, so let's add a `NavigationView` component to the body:

```
var body: some View {
    NavigationView {
        ZStack {
            //...
        }
        .navigationBarTitle("My Favorite Places",
                displayMode: .inline)
    }
}
```

4. The right bar button item will be a "plus" that will activate an `addFavorite()` function:

```
        .navigationBarTitle("My Favorite Places",
                displayMode: .inline)
        .navigationBarItems(trailing:
            Button(action: addFavorite) {
                Image(systemName: "plus")
                    .font(.headline)
        })
```

5. To add the favorite in the center of the map, we must add two `@State` variables to hold the center coordinates and the list of favorites, and an `addFavorite()` function to populate it:

```
struct ContentView: View {
    @State
    private var center = CLLocationCoordinate2D()
    @State
    private var favorites = [MKPointAnnotation]()

    private func addFavorite() {
        let place = MKPointAnnotation()
        place.coordinate = center
        favorites.append(place)
    }
    //...
}
```

6. The variables must then be implemented in the `MapView` struct too:

```
struct MapView: UIViewRepresentable {
    @Binding
    var center: CLLocationCoordinate2D
    var favorites: [MKPointAnnotation]
    //...
}
```

7. The variables must be passed during the building of the `MapView` struct:

```
ZStack {
    MapView(center: $center, favorites: favorites)
    //...
}
```

8. Now we must pass the coordinate of the center to the ContentView and to do
    that we need to create a Coordinator class to connect the MKMapView to
    the MapView:

```
struct MapView: UIViewRepresentable {
    func makeUIView(context: Context) -> MKMapView {
        let mapView = MKMapView()
        mapView.delegate = context.coordinator
        return mapView
    }

    func makeCoordinator() -> Coordinator {
        Coordinator(mapView: self)
    }

    class Coordinator: NSObject, MKMapViewDelegate {
        var mapView: MapView

        init(mapView: MapView) {
            self.mapView = mapView
        }

        func mapViewDidChangeVisibleRegion(_ mapView:
            MKMapView) {
            self.mapView.center = mapView.
                centerCoordinate
        }
    }
}
```

9. Finally, when the MapView is updated, we are going to replace the annotations with
    the new favorites, but only if the favorites have changed:

```
struct MapView: UIViewRepresentable {
    //...
    func updateUIView(_ view: MKMapView, context:
        Context) {
        if favorites.count != view.annotations.count {
```

```
                view.removeAnnotations(view.annotations)
                view.addAnnotations(favorites)
        }
    }
}
```

We can now run the app and add favorites to our map:

Fig. 13.28 – Favorite places in a MapView

How it works

`MKMapView` is a UIKit-based component, and to make it work, we have to wrap it in a `UIViewRepresentable` struct.

In this example, we have two different contexts: the context of the geographic world where there are the coordinates of the center of the map and the list of the annotations, and the context of the device screen where we are moving the `MapView`, and we add the center to the list of favorites.

To create a link of communication between those two environments, we are using two variables: `center` and the list of favorites.

When the map moves, it saves the coordinate of the center, which is then bubbled up to the content view, ready to be added to the list of favorites when the user taps on the "plus" button.

When the favorites variable changes, its content is pushed down to the `MapView` via the `updateUIView()` function to update the annotations.

In this way, we are merely creating a unidirectional flow of information between the `MapView` and the `ContentView` components.

Implementing SwiftUI views using Playground

One of the most surprising and useful innovations brought by Swift is the **Playground**, a simple file that contains Swift code and that can be seen and modified in real time without waiting for a full cycle of a rebuild.

Again, Playground supports UIKit, but since SwiftUI can be quickly embedded in a UIKit component, we can use Playground for rapidly prototyping SwiftUI views too.

Getting ready

Create a Playground file (**File | New | Playground**) in Xcode called `SwiftUIPlayground`.

How to do it

The power of Playground is that you can make a change and immediately see the result. Importing the `PlaygroundSupport` framework, you can also render a `UIViewController` class to be shown during the Playground session.

We are going to define a simple SwiftUI view to be rendered in Playground:

1. Let's start by importing the needed frameworks:

```
import PlaygroundSupport
import SwiftUI
```

2. Then we create an extension to the Text component to customize its appearance:

```
extension Text {
    func customize(_ color: Color) -> some View {
        self
            .font(.system(.title))
            .frame(width: 300, height: 150)
            .foregroundColor(.white)
            .background(color)
            .cornerRadius(10)
    }
}
```

3. With this handy extension ready, we are going to create a simple View in the ContentView struct:

```
struct ContentView: View {
    var body: some View {
        VStack(spacing: 12) {
            Text("SwiftUI")
                .customize(.yellow)
            Text("in a")
                .customize(.green)
            Text("Playground!")
                .customize(.red)
        }

    }
}
```

4. The `ContentView` struct we created can be shown in Playground as follows:

```
let viewController = UIHostingController(
                     rootView: ContentView())


PlaygroundPage.current.liveView = viewController
```

Running Playground by tapping on the arrow at the bottom left, we can run the code and see the SwiftUI view we implemented:

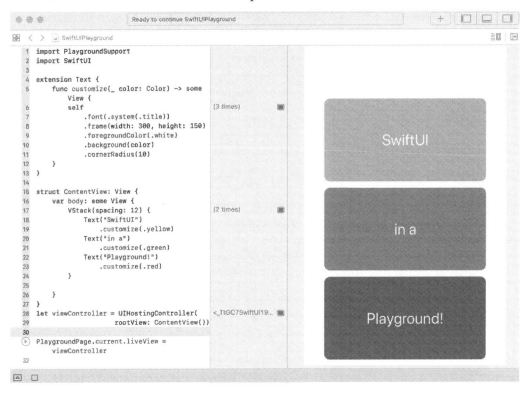

Fig. 13.29 A SwiftUI view in a Playground

How it works

Playground supports rendering a `UIViewController` class via the `liveView` property of the `PlaygroundPage` class.

With the `UIHostingController` class, we can embed a SwiftUI view in a `UIViewController` class. Using these two functionalities, we can then use Playground and SwiftUI together.

Now that you have the necessary code, you could change the colors, or the label and see the changes in real time.

Using custom fonts in SwiftUI

iOS comes with many preinstalled fonts that can be safely used in SwiftUI.

However, sometimes the design needs some custom fonts because they might be a part of the brand of the app maker, for example.

In this recipe, we'll see how to import a couple of custom fonts to use for building a menu page of an Italian restaurant.

Getting ready

Create a SwiftUI app called `MenuApp`.

Copy the customs fonts Sacramento, Oleo Script Regular, and Oleo Script Bold, which you can find in the repo: `https://github.com/PacktPublishing/SwiftUI-Cookbook/tree/master/Resources/Chapter13/recipe8`.

To use the fonts, they must be declared in the `Info.plist` file. Add the font names to the entry **Fonts provided by application** in `Info.plist`. The value of each of them must be its complete font name:

▼ Fonts provided by application	⬍	Array	(3 items)
Item 0		String	OleoScriptSwashCaps-Bold.ttf
Item 1		String	OleoScriptSwashCaps-Regular.ttf
Item 2		String	Sacramento-Regular.ttf
▶ Supported interface orientations (i...	⬍	Array	(4 items)

Fig. 13.30 – Custom fonts in Info.plist

Finally, the fonts must be copied during the installation, so add them in the **Copy Bundle Resources** phase:

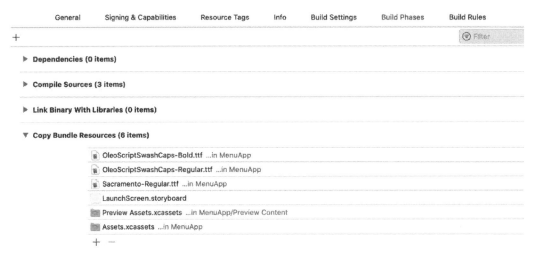

Fig. 13.31 – Copy fonts during the installation

How to do it

Besides the *semantic* fonts, such as *title*, *caption*, *footnote*, and so on, SwiftUI allows us to define other fonts using the static `.custom()` function. We'll use it to use our custom fonts:

1. Let's implement the static functions to return the custom fonts:

```
extension Font {
    static func oleoBold(size: CGFloat) -> Font {
        .custom("OleoScriptSwashCaps-Bold", size: size)
    }

    static func oleoRegular(size: CGFloat) -> Font {
        .custom("OleoScriptSwashCaps-Regular", size:
          size)
    }

    static func sacramento(size: CGFloat) -> Font {
        .custom("Sacramento-Regular", size: size)
    }
}
```

2. With these functions, we can simply customize the `Text` components:

```
struct ContentView: View {
    var body: some View {
        VStack {
            Text("Casa Mia")
                .font(.oleoBold(size: 60))
                Text("Restaurant")
                    .font(.oleoRegular(size: 60))
                Text("Pizza Margherita")
                    .font(.sacramento(size: 40))
                Text("Fettuccine Alfredo")
                    .font(.sacramento(size: 40))
                Text("Pollo Arrosto")
                    .font(.sacramento(size: 40))
                Text("Insalata di Riso")
                    .font(.sacramento(size: 40))
                Text("Gelato")
                    .font(.sacramento(size: 40))
                Spacer()
        }
    }
}
```

Running the app, we can see the sleek interface created by the custom fonts:

Fig. 13.32 – A restaurant menu page

How it works

SwiftUI provides a list of semantic fonts, such as *body*, *callout*, and so on, that allows styling the different parts of a page with a lot of text.

It also has a static function called `custom()`, whose parameters are the name of the font and its size, that returns a font read from the custom font built with the app, which is either a `.ttf`, *TrueType Font*, or `.otf`, *OpenType Font*.

Passing the name of the font every time we have to use it can be error-prone so it is better to create a static function in an extension of the `Font` class so that it can be statically checked during the compilation, reducing the possibility of error.

Implementing asynchronous images in SwiftUI

Most of the app you are going to implement depends on a remote service that provides data.

Imagine an e-commerce app or a hotel booking app.

All the content is on the server, and the app must download it and present it smoothly, taking care of the possible delay, lag, error, and so on. An essential part of this content is images. We could download and synchronously present images, but that would mean blocking the UI waiting for the download, making the app clunky and unpleasant to use.

That said, implementing images that asynchronously download and present themselves is a valuable tool to have in our toolbox.

In this recipe, we are going to implement an `AsyncImage` component that you can reuse in your apps whenever you need this feature.

Getting ready

No external resources are needed in this recipe, so just create a SwiftUI project in Xcode called `AsyncImageApp`.

How to do it

Two ingredients make the recipe: an `ImageFetcher` class to retrieve the image from the network, and an `AsyncImage` view to present it in SwiftUI.

To make it more appealing, we also want to present a spinner to show activity when the image is being downloaded:

1. Let's start by defining the `ImageFetcher` class. It is an `ObservableObject` and it has a single published variable, the optional downloaded image:

    ```
    import Combine
    class ImageFetcher: ObservableObject {
        @Published
        private(set) var image: UIImage?
        private let url: URL
        private var cancellable: AnyCancellable?

        init(url: URL) {
            self.url = url
    ```

```
    }

    func start() {

    }

    func stop() {
        cancellable?.cancel()
    }

    deinit {
        cancellable?.cancel()
    }
}
```

2. Having defined the public interface, we implement the `start()` function that does all the work, in a Combine fashion:

```
func start() {
    cancellable = URLSession(configuration: .default)
        .dataTaskPublisher(for: url)
        .map { UIImage(data: $0.data) }
        .replaceError(with: nil)
        .receive(on: DispatchQueue.main)
        .assign(to: \.image, on: self)
}
```

3. Let's move to the `AsyncImage` view, where we have an `ImageFetcher` instance that we start when the `AsyncImage` view appears:

```
struct AsyncImage: View {
    @ObservedObject
    private var fetcher: ImageFetcher
    init(url: URL) {
        fetcher = ImageFetcher(url: url)
    }
    var body: some View {
        image
            .onAppear(perform: fetcher.start)
```

```
                    .onDisappear(perform: fetcher.stop)
        }
}
```

4. Inside `AsyncImage`, the `body` function returns a spinner while the image is downloading, and the image after it has been downloaded:

```
private var image: some View {
    Group {
        if fetcher.image != nil {
            Image(uiImage: fetcher.image!)
                .resizable()
        } else {
            ProgressView()
        }
    }
    .frame(minWidth: 0, maxWidth: .infinity,
           minHeight: 0, maxHeight: .infinity,
           alignment: .center)
}
```

5. Let's finally move the `ContentView` struct where we define a list of `urls` where the images are hosted:

```
struct ContentView: View {
    let urls = [
        "Ace-Frehley",
        "Paul-Stanley",
        "Gene-Simmons",
        "Peter-Criss"]
            .map {
                URL(string: "https://www.marshallofrock.
                    com/wp-content/uploads/2011/09/KISS-\
                    ($0)-solo-album-cover.jpg")!
        }

    var body: some View {
    }
}
```

6. The body finally contains a grid with the four images:

```
var body: some View {
    VStack {
        HStack {
            AsyncImage(url: urls[0])
                .aspectRatio(contentMode: .fit)
            AsyncImage(url: urls[1])
                .aspectRatio(contentMode: .fit)
        }
        HStack {
            AsyncImage(url: urls[2])
                .aspectRatio(contentMode: .fit)
            AsyncImage(url: urls[3])
                .aspectRatio(contentMode: .fit)
        }
    }
}
```

Running the app now, we can see the spinners while the images are downloading, and the pictures appear:

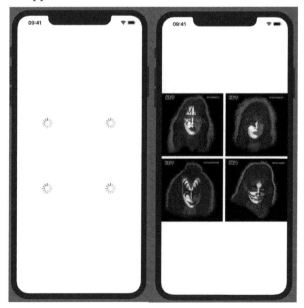

Fig. 13.33 – Asynchronously downloading images

How it works

The `ImageFetcher` class has the responsibility of downloading the image given its URL.

It does it in a Combine way, which chains the signals together:

```
URLSession(configuration: .default)
    .dataTaskPublisher(for: url)
    .map { UIImage(data: $0.data) }
    .replaceError(with: nil)
    .receive(on: DispatchQueue.main)
    .assign(to: \.image, on: self)
```

Firstly, we create a task to download the image. The result is converted to a `UIImage` object.

In the event of an error, the result is `nil` instead of propagating the `Error` object.

Since the image will be manipulated by the UI and the task can be done in a background thread, we must ensure that, eventually, we are running in the `MainThread`, and this is done with the `.receive(on: DispatchQueue.main)` modifier.

Finally, the result is assigned to the published variable `image`.

The `AsyncImage` view simply observes this object and returns either a spinner or an `Image` view; this depends on the state of the variable image in the `ImageFetcher` class.

Do note that `AsyncImage` tries to occupy all the available space with the following:

```
.frame(minWidth: 0, maxWidth: .infinity,
       minHeight: 0, maxHeight: .infinity,
       alignment: .center)
```

Otherwise, the spinners, smaller than the image itself , would be compressed in the center, as in the following image:

Fig. 13.34 – Spinners compressed in the center of the page

There's more

While it's working correctly, you can see that the images appear abruptly, and also, if there is an error downloading, the spinner will stay there forever.

Why not improve it a bit? Given this skeleton you could, for example, implement a fade-in transition when the image is downloaded, or add a broken network symbol when there is an error.

Unleash your fantasy and add these little details to your app to make it more pleasant to use.

Other Books You May Enjoy

If you enjoyed this book, you may be interested in these other books by Packt:

iOS 14 Programming for Beginners - Fifth Edition
Ahmad Sahar

ISBN: 978-1-80020-974-9

- Get to grips with the fundamentals of Xcode 12 and Swift 5, the building blocks of iOS development
- Understand how to prototype an app using storyboards
- Discover the Model-View-Controller design pattern and how to implement the desired functionality within the app
- Implement the latest iOS features such as widgets and app clips
- Convert an existing iPad app into an Apple Silicon Mac app
- Design, deploy, and test your iOS applications with design patterns and best practices

Learn SwiftUI

Chris Barker

ISBN: 978-1-83921-542-1

- Explore the fundamentals of SwiftUI and compare it with existing UI frameworks
- Write SwiftUI syntax and understand what should and shouldn't be included in SwiftUI's layer
- Add text and images to a SwiftUI view and decorate them using SwiftUI's modifiers
- Create basic forms, and use camera and photo library functions to add images to them
- Understand the core concepts of Maps in iOS apps and add a MapView in SwiftUI
- Design extensions within your existing apps to run them on watchOS
- Handle networking calls in SwiftUI to retrieve data from external sources

Leave a review - let other readers know what you think

Please share your thoughts on this book with others by leaving a review on the site that you bought it from. If you purchased the book from Amazon, please leave us an honest review on this book's Amazon page. This is vital so that other potential readers can see and use your unbiased opinion to make purchasing decisions, we can understand what our customers think about our products, and our authors can see your feedback on the title that they have worked with Packt to create. It will only take a few minutes of your time, but is valuable to other potential customers, our authors, and Packt. Thank you!

Index

Symbols

@Binding to pass state variable
    to child views
  using 331-335
  working 337
@EnvironmentObject
  used, for sharing state objects with
    multiple views 344,-352
  working 352
@FetchRequest
  Core Data objects displaying 478-483
@ObservedObject
  used, for implementing CoreLocation
    wrapper 337-340, 342
  working 343
@State to drive Views behavior
  using 327, 328, 330
  working 330

A

actions
  adding, to alert buttons 173
ActionSheet views
  implementing 182, 184, 185
  presenting 182
  working 185, 186
alert buttons
  actions, adding 173
  implementing 174-176
  reference link 177
  working 176, 177
alerts
  displaying 170-173
  presenting 170
  reference link 173
  working 173
animated pressable button
  creating 291
  implementing 292-294
  working 295
animations
  creating 254, 260
  selecting 255-258
  working 259
application programming
    interface (API) 386
asynchronous images
  implementing, in SwiftUI 591-596

B

banner
  creating, with spring animation 264-266
  working 267
bar chart
  building 236-238, 240
border
  filling, with image 234, 235
  rendering, with gradient 229-233
buttons
  adding 34-39
  navigating 34, 36-39

C

Cocoapods
  about 431
  URL 431
Combine
  app, unit testing 403-410
  memory, managing to build
    timer app 368-370, 372
  publishers 365
  reactive code, debugging 397-402
  subscribing 366, 367
  unit test, working 411
  used, for fetching remote data 385-397
  used, for validating form 374,-384
  using, in SwiftUI project 355-364
  working 364
components
  layout 18-22
context menu
  creating 190
  light bulb, displaying 191, 192
  reference link 192
  working 192

Core Data
  integrating, with SwiftUI 472-477
Core Data objects
  adding, to SwiftUI view 484-491
  deleting, from SwiftUI view 500-506
  displaying with @FetchRequest 478-483
Core Data requests
  filtering with predicate 491-499
CoreLocation wrapper
  implementing, as @
    ObservedObject 337-342
curved custom shape
  drawing 207-210
custom fonts
  using, in SwiftUI 587-590
custom rows
  using, in list 75
  working, in list 79
custom shape
  drawing 204-207
custom view transitions
  creating 277
  implementing 278-282
  working 282

D

dark mode
  layout, previewing in 118-120
Data Flow through SwiftUI
  reference link 331
disclosure groups
  implementing 113-115
  using, to display content 113
  using, to hide content 113
  working 116

distributed Notes app
  implementing, with Firebase
    and SwiftUI 455- 470

E

easing functions
  reference link 260
expanding lists
  implementing 109-111
  using 108, 112, 113
  working 111, 112

F

Firebase
  integrating, into SwiftUI project 431-442
  used, for implementing distributed
    Notes app 455-465, 469, 470
  used, for integrating social login
    with Google 443-453, 455
floating hearts
  animation, triggering 309-315
  animation, working 315-317
  creating, in SwiftUI 306, 307
form
  items, disabling 152-154, 156
  items, enabling 152-156
  sections, displaying 148-151
  sections, hiding 148-151
  validating, with Combine 374-384
  working 384
FormValidationApp 374

G

gestures
  using, with TabView 164-167

Google
  social login integration, Firebase
    used 443, 445-453, 455
gradient
  border, rendering with 229-233
gradient view
  rendering, in SwiftUI 224-228

H

hero view transition
  creating, with .matchedGeometryEffect
    282, 284, 286-289
  working 290, 291

I

images
  using 27-34
iOS 14+
  views and controls 59-65
iOS app
  creating, in SwiftUI 508
  macOS version, creating
    518, 520-527, 529
  model and data source,
    setting up 508-517
  watchOS version, creating 530-539
  working 517
items
  disabling, in forms 152-156
  enabling, in forms 152-156

J

JavaScript Object Notation (JSON) 386

K

Kaleidoscope
  reference link 550

L

layout
  previewing, at different dynamic
    type sizes 121-127
  previewing, in dark mode 118-120
  previewing, in navigation view 127-131
  previewing, on different devices 131-134
LazyHGrid
  implementing 100-102
  using 99
  working 103
LazyHStack
  implementing 99
  using 95-98
  working 98, 99
LazyVGrid
  implementing 100-102
  using 99
  working 103
LazyVStack
  implementing 99
  using 95-98
  working 98, 99
list
  creating, of static items 72
  custom rows, implementing 75, 77-79
  custom rows, using 75
  custom rows, working 79
  editing 86-88
  rows, adding 80
  rows, deleting 83, 86
  rows deletion, implementing 83, 84
  rows deletion, working 85
  rows, implementing 80-82
  rows, moving 88, 90, 91
  rows, working 82
  sections, adding 92, 94
  sections, working 94, 95
  struct, creating 72, 73
  struct, working 74
  working 87
Lottie
  URL 295
Lottie animation
  implementing 298-301
  in SwiftUI 295, 296, 298
  reference link 296
  working 301

M

macOS version
  creating, of iOS app 518, 520,-527, 529
  working 529
MapKit framework 573
MapView
  embedding, in SwiftUI 573- 578
mock data
  using, for previews 140-145
Model-View-Controller (MVC) 355
Model-View-ViewModel (MVVM) 355
multilanguage app
  implementing, with localized strings
    in SwiftUI 560, 562-568
multiple alerts
  presenting 177
  VStack, creating 178-180
  working 181
multiple animations
  applying 275, 276
  working 277

N

navigation view
  layout, previewing in 127-131

P

PDF documents
  displaying, in SwiftUI 569-572
pickers
  implementing 39-43
pie chart
  building 241-251
Playground
  used, for implementing
    SwiftUI views 584-587
popover
  implementing 193
  reference link 196
  @State variable, creating 193-195
  working 195, 196
predicate
  Core Data requests filtering 491-499
progress ring
  implementing 213-217

R

reactive code
  debugging, on Combine 397-402
  working 402
ReactiveX
  URL 367
Realtime Database. *See* Firestore
RemoteConfig product 431
remote data
  fetching, with Combine 385-396
  visualizing, in SwiftUI 385-394, 397
  working 394-396

rows
  adding, to list 80
  deleting, from list 83, 86
  moving, in list 88, 90, 91
  working, in list 82
RxMarbles
  URL 367

S

San Francisco Symbols (SFSymbols)
  about 49
  reference link 51
  using, for simple graphics 49, 50
ScrollViewReader
  implementing 104-107
  using 103
  working 107, 108
scroll views
  adding 69, 70
  reference link 72
  using 68
  working 71
sections
  adding, to list 92, 94
  displaying, in forms 148-152
  hiding, in forms 148-152
  working, in list 94, 95
sequence of animations
  creating 268, 269
  creating, with delay to view
    modifier animation 268
  creating, with delay to
    withAnimation function 271
  working 270
shapes
  implementing 261-263
  transforming 260

working 263, 264
sheet modally
   displaying 186-188
   reference link 190
   working 189, 190
snapshot testing
   of SwiftUI views 542-551
spring animation
   used, for creating banner 264-266
State and Data Flow
   reference link 331
state objects
   sharing, with multiple views using @
      EnvironmentObject 344-352
static items
   list, creating 72
StopWatch app 368
stretchable header
   implementing, in SwiftUI 302-304
   working 306
Subjects 358
Swift Snapshot Testing library
   URL 543
SwiftUI
   adding, to existing app 54-58
   asynchronous images,
      implementing 591-596
   Core Data, integrating 472-477
   custom fonts, using 587-590
   dashed border, creating in 201-203
   floating hearts, creating 306, 308
   gradient view, rendering in 224-228
   Lottie animation, using 295, 296, 298
   MapView, embedding 573-578
   multilanguage app, implementing
      with localized strings 560-568
   PDFKit, integrating with 569, 570, 572
   remote data, visualizing 385-394, 397

Sign in with Apple,
   implementing 415-422
stretchable header,
   implementing 302-305
swipeable stack, implementing 317-323
Tic-Tac-Toe game, implementing
   in 218-224
UIBezierPath, using with 210-213
UIKit, integrating into 51-54
UIKit MapView, embedding
   578-582, 584
unit testing, with
   ViewInspector 552-560
used, for implementing distributed
   Notes app 455-470
SwiftUI app
   creating 397
SwiftUI project
   Combine, using 355-364
   Firebase, integrating with 431-443
SwiftUI's built-in shapes
   using 198-201
SwiftUI view
   Core Data objects, adding to 484-491
   Core Data objects, deleting
      from 500-506
   implementing, with Playground 584-587
   snapshot testing 543-551
swipeable stack
   implementing, in SwiftUI 317-323
   working 324

T

TabView
   gestures, using with 164-167
   multiple views, navigating 157-164

text
  dealing with 23-27
Tic-Tac-Toe game
  implementing, in SwiftUI 218-224
Timelane 402
timer app
  building, to manage memory in
    Combine 368-370, 372
  working 372, 374

U

UIBezierPath
  using, with SwiftUI 210-213
UIKit
  integrating, into SwiftUI 51-54
  previews, using in 134-140
UIKit MapView
  embedding, in SwiftUI 578-582, 584
UIKit Sign in with Apple
  implementation, for using
    in SwiftUI 423-430
Uniform Resource Locator (URL) 367

V

ViewBuilder
  reference link 48
  used, for separating presentation
    from content 46-48

ViewInspector
  used, for unit testing SwiftUI 552-560
view modifier animation
  delay, applying to create sequence
    of animations 268
ViewModifiers
  used, for applying groups of styles 44-46

W

watchOS version
  creating, of iOS app 530-539
  working 539, 540
withAnimation function
  delay, applying to create sequence
    of animations 271
  implementing 271-273
  working 274

X

XCTest 552
XCUITest 552

Made in the USA
Columbia, SC
26 November 2020